Innovation, Technology, and Knowledge Management

Series Editor

Elias G. Carayannis
George Washington University, Washington, DC, USA

For further volumes:
http://www.springer.com/series/8124

Tugrul U. Daim • Ramin Neshati
Russell Watt • James Eastham
Editors

Technology Development

Multidimensional Review for Engineering and Technology Managers

Editors
Tugrul U. Daim
Engineering and Technology Management
Portland State University
Portland, OR, USA

Ramin Neshati
Intel Corporation
Hillsboro, OR, USA

Russell Watt
Nike, Inc.
Beaverton, OR, USA

James Eastham
Tri Quint Semiconductos
Hillsboro, OR, USA

ISSN 2197-5698 ISSN 2197-5701 (electronic)
ISBN 978-3-319-05650-0 ISBN 978-3-319-05651-7 (eBook)
DOI 10.1007/978-3-319-05651-7
Springer Cham Heidelberg New York Dordrecht London

Library of Congress Control Number: 2014939935

© Springer International Publishing Switzerland 2014
This work is subject to copyright. All rights are reserved by the Publisher, whether the whole or part of the material is concerned, specifically the rights of translation, reprinting, reuse of illustrations, recitation, broadcasting, reproduction on microfilms or in any other physical way, and transmission or information storage and retrieval, electronic adaptation, computer software, or by similar or dissimilar methodology now known or hereafter developed. Exempted from this legal reservation are brief excerpts in connection with reviews or scholarly analysis or material supplied specifically for the purpose of being entered and executed on a computer system, for exclusive use by the purchaser of the work. Duplication of this publication or parts thereof is permitted only under the provisions of the Copyright Law of the Publisher's location, in its current version, and permission for use must always be obtained from Springer. Permissions for use may be obtained through RightsLink at the Copyright Clearance Center. Violations are liable to prosecution under the respective Copyright Law.
The use of general descriptive names, registered names, trademarks, service marks, etc. in this publication does not imply, even in the absence of a specific statement, that such names are exempt from the relevant protective laws and regulations and therefore free for general use.
While the advice and information in this book are believed to be true and accurate at the date of publication, neither the authors nor the editors nor the publisher can accept any legal responsibility for any errors or omissions that may be made. The publisher makes no warranty, express or implied, with respect to the material contained herein.

Printed on acid-free paper

Springer is part of Springer Science+Business Media (www.springer.com)

Series Foreword

The Springer book series *Innovation, Technology, and Knowledge Management* was launched in March 2008 as a forum and intellectual, scholarly"podium" for global/local, transdisciplinary, transsectoral, public–private, and leading/"bleeding"edge ideas, theories, and perspectives on these topics.

The book series is accompanied by the Springer *Journal of the Knowledge Economy*, which was launched in 2009 with the same editorial leadership.

The series showcases provocative views that diverge from the current "conventional wisdom" that are properly grounded in theory and practice, and that consider the concepts of ***robust competitiveness***,[1] ***sustainable entrepreneurship***,[2] and ***democratic capitalism***,[3] central to its philosophy and objectives. More specifically, the aim of this series is to highlight emerging research and practice at the dynamic intersection of these fields, where individuals, organizations, industries, regions, and nations are harnessing creativity and invention to achieve and sustain growth.

---

[1] We define *sustainable entrepreneurship* as the creation of viable, profitable, and scalable firms. Such firms engender the formation of self-replicating and mutually enhancing innovation networks and knowledge clusters (innovation ecosystems), leading toward robust competitiveness (E. G. Carayannis, *International Journal of Innovation and Regional Development* 1(3), 235–254, 2009).

[2] We understand *robust competitiveness* to be a state of economic being and becoming that avails systematic and defensible "unfair advantages" to the entities that are part of the economy. Such competitiveness is built on mutually complementary and reinforcing low-, medium-, and high-technology and public and private sector entities (government agencies, private firms, universities, and nongovernmental organizations) (E. G. Carayannis, *International Journal of Innovation and Regional Development* 1(3), 235–254, 2009).

[3] The concepts of *robust competitiveness and sustainable entrepreneurship* are pillars of a regime that we call *"democratic capitalism"* (as opposed to "popular or casino capitalism"), in which real opportunities for education and economic prosperity are available to all, especially—but not only—younger people. These are the direct derivatives of a collection of topdown policies as well as bottom-up initiatives (including strong research and development policies and funding, but going beyond these to include the development of innovation networks and knowledge clusters across regions and sectors) (E. G. Carayannis and A. Kaloudis, *Japan Economic Currents*, p. 6–10 January 2009).

Books that are part of the series explore the impact of innovation at the "macro" (economies, markets), "meso" (industries, firms), and "micro" levels (teams, individuals), drawing from such related disciplines as finance, organizational psychology, research and development, science policy, information systems, and strategy, with the underlying theme that for innovation to be useful it must involve the sharing and application of knowledge.

Some of the key anchoring concepts of the series are outlined in the figure below and the definitions that follow (all definitions are from E. G. Carayannis and D. F. J. Campbell, *International Journal of Technology Management*, 46, 3–4, 2009).

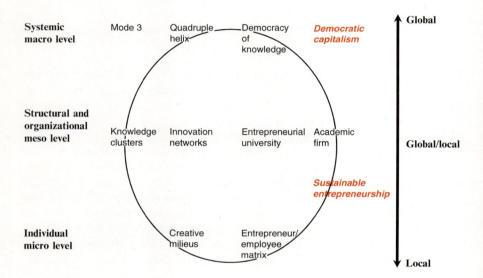

Conceptual profile of the series *Innovation, Technology*, and *Knowledge Management*

- The "Mode 3" Systems Approach for Knowledge Creation, Diffusion, and Use: "Mode 3" is a multilateral, multinodal, multimodal, and multilevel systems approach to the conceptualization, design, and management of real and virtual, "knowledge-stock" and "knowledge-flow," modalities that catalyze, accelerate, and support the creation, diffusion, sharing, absorption, and use of cospecialized knowledge assets. "Mode 3" is based on a system-theoretic perspective of socio-economic, political, technological, and cultural trends and conditions that shape the coevolution of knowledge with the "knowledge-based and knowledge-driven, global/local economy and society."
- Quadruple Helix: Quadruple helix, in this context, means to add to the triple helix of government, university, and industry a "fourth helix" that we identify as the "media-based and culture-based public." This fourth helix associates with "media," "creative industries," "culture," "values," "life styles," "art," and perhaps also the notion of the "creative class."

- Innovation Networks: Innovation networks are real and virtual infrastructures and infratechnologies that serve to nurture creativity, trigger invention, and catalyze innovation in a public and/or private domain context (for instance, government-university-industry public-private research and technology development coopetitive partnerships).
- Knowledge Clusters: Knowledge clusters are agglomerations of cospecialized, mutually complementary, and reinforcing knowledge assets in the form of "knowledge stocks" and "knowledge flows" that exhibit self-organizing, learning-driven, dynamically adaptive competences, and trends in the context of an open systems perspective.
- Twenty-First Century Innovation Ecosystem: A twenty-first century innovation ecosystem is a multilevel, multimodal, multinodal, and multiagent system of systems. The constituent systems consist of innovation metanetworks (networks of innovation networks and knowledge clusters) and knowledge metaclusters (clusters of innovation networks and knowledge clusters) as building blocks and organized in a self-referential or chaotic fractal knowledge and innovation architecture,[4] which in turn constitute agglomerations of human, social, intellectual, and financial capital stocks and flows as well as cultural and technological artifacts and modalities, continually coevolving, cospecializing, and cooperating. These innovation networks and knowledge clusters also form, reform, and dissolve within diverse institutional, political, technological, and socioeconomic domains, including government, university, industry, and nongovernmental organizations and involving information and communication technologies, biotechnologies, advanced materials, nanotechnologies, and next-Generation energy technologies.

Who is this book series published for? The book series addresses a diversity of audiences in different settings:

1. *Academic communities*: Academic communities worldwide represent a core group of readers. This follows from the theoretical/conceptual interest of the book series to influence academic discourses in the fields of knowledge, also carried by the claim of a certain saturation of academia with the current concepts and the postulate of a window of opportunity for new or at least additional concepts. Thus, it represents a key challenge for the series to exercise a certain impact on discourses in academia. In principle, all academic communities that are interested in knowledge (knowledge and innovation) could be tackled by the book series. The interdisciplinary (transdisciplinary) nature of the book series underscores that the scope of the book series is not limited a priori to a specific basket of disciplines. From a radical viewpoint, one could create the hypothesis that there is no discipline where knowledge is of no importance.
2. *Decision makers—private/academic entrepreneurs and public (governmental, subgovernmental) actors*: Two different groups of decision makers are being

---

[4] E. G. Carayannis, *Strategic Management of Technological Learning,* CRC Press, 2000.

addressed simultaneously: (1) private entrepreneurs (firms, commercial firms, academic firms) and academic entrepreneurs (universities), interested in optimizing knowledge management and in developing heterogeneously composed knowledge-based research networks; and (2) public (governmental, subgovernmental) actors that are interested in optimizing and further developing their policies and policy strategies that target knowledge and innovation. One purpose of public *knowledge and innovation policy* is to enhance the performance and competitiveness of advanced economies.
3. *Decision makers in general*: Decision makers are systematically being supplied with crucial information, for how to optimize knowledge-referring and knowledge-enhancing decision-making. The nature of this "crucial information" is conceptual as well as empirical (case-study-based). Empirical information highlights practical examples and points toward practical solutions (perhaps remedies), conceptual information offers the advantage of further driving and further-carrying tools of understanding. Different groups of addressed decision makers could be decision makers in private firms and multinational corporations, responsible for the knowledge portfolio of companies; knowledge and knowledge management consultants; globalization experts, focusing on the internationalization of research and development, science and technology, and innovation; experts in university/business research networks; and political scientists, economists, and business professionals.
4. *Interested global readership*: Finally, the Springer book series addresses a whole global readership, composed of members who are generally interested in knowledge and innovation. The global readership could partially coincide with the communities as described above ("academic communities," "decision makers"), but could also refer to other constituencies and groups.

Elias G. Carayannis
Series Editor

Preface

Bringing technologies to the market place requires attention to the processes used for technology development. This book provides tools for managing the technology development more effectively and demonstrates the use of them through many cases from the sectors where technologies have been playing a key role in the recent decade.

The book is divided into five parts.

Decision Making

Chapters 1–3 demonstrate the use of hierarchical decision modeling. This tool was developed by Dundar F. Kocaoglu of Portland State University. It is an honor for all of us to be his students through the past two decades. The chapters provide examples from industries ranging from semiconductor manufacturing to information technology.

Technology Evaluation

Chapters 4–6 demonstrate the use of multiple tools for technology evaluation. These tools are demonstrated for technologies ranging from energy to material.

Research and Development

Chapters 7–9 provide research and development cases. Each chapter explores a different aspect ranging from exploring product specifications to industry standardization.

International Aspects

Chapters 10 and 11 explore issues regarding the international aspects ranging from outsourcing to international product development.

Social and Political Aspects

Finally, Chaps. 12–14 provide insight into the social and political aspects by providing cases on the social capital of the organizations and regional innovation capacity.

As a whole this book provides insights into tools which will be useful to address issues emerging from different fronts while developing technologies.

We would like to thank all the contributors. They were extremely effective in collecting data for the analyses and cases presented. We also would like to thank Kelly Cowan and Liliya Hogaboam who helped us to edit the book.

Portland, OR, USA	Tugrul U. Daim
Hillsboro, OR, USA	Ramin Neshati
Beaverton, OR, USA	Russell Watt
Hillsboro, OR, USA	James Eastham

Contents

Part I Decision Making

1 **Quality Culture Selection for New Product Development (NPD) Organizations Using Hierarchical Decision Modeling (HDM)** 3
   James Eastham, David Tucker, Joe Smith, Sumir Varma, and Tugrul U. Daim

2 **Call Tracking Technology Selection Model** 23
   Wilson Zehr, Abdussalam Alawini, Mousa Alharbi, and Mohamed Borgan

3 **Location Selection for Fabless Firms** 43
   Niharika Jeena, Meles Hagos, Charles sai, Yuan Xu, and Zack Khalifa

Part II Technology Evaluation

4 **FCC Regulation of the Video Navigation Device Industry: A Benefit-Cost Analysis Using a Dynamic Kano Concept** 73
   Jay Justice

5 **Technology Assessment: Energy Storage Technologies for Wind Power Generation** 91
   Yulianto Suharto and Tugrul U. Daim

6 **Hexavalent Chromium Substitution** 115
   David Tucker, James Eastham, Joe Smith, and Sumir Varma

Part III Research and Development

7 **Exploring Adoption of Services Delivered Through Information Technology: Case of Mobile Services** 139
   Nuri Basoglu, Tugrul U. Daim, and Banu Kargin

8	**Risk Management in Research and Development: A Case Study from the Semiconductor Industry** .... Ramin Neshati and Tugrul U. Daim	163
9	**Technology Standards Development: A Framework** .... Ramin Neshati and Tugrul U. Daim	173

Part IV International Aspects

10	**Managing Issues of IT Service Offshore Outsourcing Projects**.......... Rosine Hanna, David Raffo, and Tugrul U. Daim	197
11	**Global New Product Development** .... Russell Watt	209

Part V Social and Political Aspects

12	**A Comparative Analysis of Career Growth Models in R&D Organizations** .... Sowmini Sengupta, Jorge Garcia, Nayem Rahman, and Daria Spatar	233
13	**Researching Social Capital in R&D Management: A Case Study in High-Tech Industry** .... Songphon Munkongsujarit, Antonie Jetter, and Tugrul U. Daim	251
14	**Researching Innovative Capacity of Local Subsidiaries in Selected CEE Countries** .... Tugrul U. Daim, Zoran Aralica, Marina Dabić, Dilek Özdemir, and A. Elvan Bayraktaroglu	277

Part I
Decision Making

Chapter 1
Quality Culture Selection for New Product Development (NPD) Organizations Using Hierarchical Decision Modeling (HDM)

James Eastham, David Tucker, Joe Smith, Sumir Varma, and Tugrul U. Daim

Abstract Many companies implement quality systems and subsequently the corresponding cultures in an effort to improve product or system quality and increase profits. Selecting which quality culture to employ is often difficult as the differences between the cultures are not always clear. Companies often commit to a quality culture without fully understanding the benefits and drawbacks a certain system might have to different parts of the business, including New Product Development (NPD). In this paper we present a Hierarchical Decision Model (HDM) aimed at assisting senior managers in the selection of the right quality culture that specifically improves NPD factors. We apply the HDM to three different companies, each from different business sectors and with distinct goals. Three quality cultures are compared: Lean, Six Sigma, and Theory of Constraints (ToC). Recommendations are formulated based on the model output. We discuss the results and which quality culture might be best for each company to endorse.

J. Eastham (✉) · S. Varma
TriQuint Semiconductor, Portland, OR, USA
e-mail: jeastham@pdx.edu; Sumir.Varma@tqs.com

D. Tucker
New Kinpo Group, Portland, OR, USA
e-mail: david.tucker@pdx.edu

J. Smith
Blount International, Portland, OR, USA
e-mail: Joe.Smith@Blount.com

T.U. Daim
Engineering and Technology Management Department,
Portland State University, Portland, OR, USA
e-mail: tugrul@etm.pdx.edu

1.1 Introduction

Total Quality Management (TQM) first emerged in the late 1980s, as a general term for quality improvement. Many sources suggest the decision to implement TQM may be the "most critical and difficult" decision a CEO will ever make [1]. TQM is a very broad term and includes many quality improvement systems, methodologies, and tools. Just understanding the difference between all the available systems and tools is challenging enough, let alone selecting a methodology and system for an entire organization. Many sources exist in the body of knowledge regarding implementing a quality culture once one is selected. Authors discuss how best to lead an organization through quality transformations and initiatives. Titles such as "The Executive Guide to Implementing Quality Systems" and "Fast Track to Quality: A 12-Month Program for Small to Mid-Sized Businesses" discuss the organizational challenges related to quality culture adoption. Very few resources exist which provide even subjective guidance regarding quality culture selection. Susan M. Hinkle's book [2] dedicates an entire chapter to selecting a quality system, focusing on the requirements of the different standard bodies and specific tools required by these bodies. However, a selection outline is lacking from this work as well as most existing literature. The issue facing most firms is the confusion surrounding the potpourri of tools, systems, acronyms, etc. As Ron Basu put it in his book entitled Fit Sigma, "business managers can be forgiven [if a quality initiative is not successful], and they are often confused by the grey areas of distinction between quality initiatives [3]." Another problem, as Management Consultant Dave Nave states, is that "many process improvement methodologies appear to conflict with each other or at least down-play the contribution of other methodologies. This montage of tools and philosophies creates the illusion of conflicting strategies [4]."

In Scott Leavengood's (PSU, PhD) dissertation [23] he discusses "widely varying approaches to TQM", and how these approaches impact innovation. The focus of his dissertation is identification of specific quality management practices leading to quality and innovation performance. He presents a framework for quality system implementation which can enable innovation. This work added to the impetus of this paper, as the team wanted to augment such research with a quantitative model.

In this paper, we focus on quality culture selection using more quantitative methods, specifically for New Product Development (NPD). We define "quality culture" as the entire set of tools and methodologies embodied in a given quality management philosophy. Business managers must have a cognitive understanding of the cultures that exist within an organization. That is to say, managers are aware of tangible, "hard" cultures that exist often due to policies, hierarchies, and well-established protocol. Equally as important are the more nuanced, more tacit, "soft" cultures that exist individually from company, to department, to group. These "soft" cultures are malleable and evolve with changes in such things as group members, power dynamics, and stress levels. It is increasingly important for managers to not only recognize the culture within which they work but to also possess the tools necessary to mold the culture to be the healthiest and most efficient for the sake of the employees and productivity. The literature on quality suggests the connection between the quality systems and the organizational cultural must be strong in order for the system to operate successfully [5]. Therefore in this analysis the quality systems will be referred to as quality cultures since it is the output the organization must adopt in order for it to be utilized effectively. In the analysis we compare three state of the art quality cultures including: Lean, Six Sigma, and Theory of Constraints. A Hierarchical Decision Model (HDM) is presented which takes inputs from surveys conducted at specific companies in an effort to help senior managers decide which quality culture to adopt based on their specific New Product Development (NPD) challenges and needs.

1.2 Model Overview and Goal

The HDM is shown graphically in Fig. 1.1. An expanded larger view of this model is shown in Appendix.

The model is structured top down, and follows the Mission, Objectives, Goals, Strategies, and Actions (MOGSA) architecture [6]. Based on pair wise comparison matrix (PCM) weighting of the Goals, Benefits, and Alternatives, an overall score is calculated for each of the quality cultures. This overall score for each culture reflects how that specific culture contributes to the overall mission or goal, "Choose a Quality Culture that is best for New Product Development".

1.3 Criteria Level I: Business Goal for NPD

The Level I criterion was selected by applying the triple constraint found in the Project Management Body of Knowledge Guide (PMBOK) to capture the business goals of a quality focused NPD organization. As defined in the text, the triple constraint consists of Scope, Time and Cost [7]. These three initial criteria where then modified to represent the directional goal of the criteria and organization. The Level I criterion then includes the following three criteria: Reduction in Product Cost, Increase in Customer Satisfaction, and Decrease in Time to Market.

Reduction in Product Cost is a measure of the overall cost of the product including all required raw materials, manufacturing or fabrication, assembly, testing, labor, R&D spending, non-recurring engineering, and all other fixed and variable costs comprehended in the total product cost.

Increase in Customer Satisfaction is a measure of the ability of a product to specifically meet the expectations of the customer(s). Customer satisfaction is generally measured through target customer surveys and typically contains scores related to roadmap alignment, product availability, product cost, quality levels, on-time delivery, customer service responsiveness, etc.

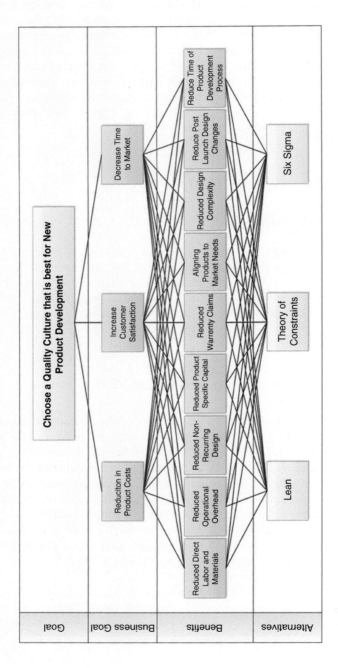

Fig. 1.1 HDM model for selecting a quality culture

Table 1.1 Survey participant totals by sector

Business sector	Number of participants
Hard Goods	5
Semiconductor	4
Automotive Plastics	2
Total level I participants	11

Table 1.2 Tier II: strategic goals

Strategy
1. Reduce labor and material costs
2. Reduce business overhead
3. Reduce non-recurring design expenses
4. Reduce product specific capital investment
5. Reduce customer warranty claims
6. Align product capabilities with customer needs
7. Reduce product complexity
8. Reduce post-launch design changes
9. Reduce the NPD cycle duration

Decrease in Time to Market is a measure of how long the NPD process takes from product concept to market availability. Different industries have different products and therefore have different lifecycles Historically products that are developed as business to consumer (B2C) have a shorter NPD implementation times than products that are business to business (B2B) [8].

The team conducted surveys with select experts from industry for the Level I criteria scoring and pair wise analysis. Senior managers were primarily selected for this level including such titles as: Director of Product Development, Director of Program Management, Sr. Program Manager, and Manager of Product Development Engineering. In total, eleven (11) experts were surveyed for Level I from three (3) industries including Hard Goods, Semiconductor, and Automotive Plastics. Table 1.1 shows the number of survey participants for each company.

1.4 Criteria Level II: Strategic Goals

The model's second tier contains strategic goals aimed at accomplishing subsequent objectives. The team compiled a list of strategies that would contribute to each of the business objectives, and then condensed the list to those strategies that would have the greatest impact on achieving the identified objectives. This list of strategies is shown in Table 1.2. Each strategy impacts one or more of the business objectives.

With respect to product design, reduction of *labor and material costs* requires forethought into manufacturing and assembly processes, and selection of appropriate materials of construction. Often, design features or attributes drive material selection and cost as well as required equipment and manufacturing processes. Consideration of these during the NPD process can significantly impact the cost of labor to manufacture products and the material costs of products; both of which are significant contributors to overall product cost [9].

Business overhead refers to the cost of operating and maintaining a business. These costs are ongoing and are generally consistent over time. They include expenses related to building and facilities, maintenance, utilities, insurance, and administrative functions such as executive management, sales, customer service, finance, payroll, etc. These costs contribute to the overall cost of all products and services sold by the company [9].

Non-recurring design expenses refer to any one-time cost associated with designing or validating a new product. This may include prototyping, lab and field testing, third party certification or approval, etc. These expenses are product or design specific and are not expected to occur again after design completion. Typically, this type of design expense also coincides with increased time of the product development process, and as a result, often impacts time-to-market (TTM) [9].

Product specific capital investment includes all investment in equipment, machinery, and specialized systems for manufacture of a product. Similar to the analysis of design with respect to requirements of production labor and material costs, consideration of product specific capital equipment can have a major impact in overall product costs and TTM. A prime example is the building of a new semiconductor fab which may cost upwards of $10 billion USD and take years to complete [9].

Customer warranty claims reduce product line profits through replacement/repair costs of products that fail to perform as specified as well as administration and processing of these claims by customer service and warranty personnel. Non-conforming products also have a significant effect on customer satisfaction and repeat business. Therefore, the impact may be felt beyond a specific product line. Often times, product designers may be involved in trouble-shooting customer returns when defects are a result of faults in product design. Cases such as these can effectively increase the TTM of products that are currently in development because of resource constraints [10].

Aligning product capabilities with customer needs, or alternatively, including unneeded product features or failing to include customer desired features into products can affect all three of our Tier II criteria. Building features into products that aren't needed or wanted by customers can increase product complexity, cost, and TTM. In addition, inclusion of undesired features or failure to include necessary or desired features negatively impacts customer satisfaction [10, 11].

Product complexity can be viewed from multiple perspectives. From a customer's perspective, features or components that make the product difficult to use will decrease customer satisfaction. From a design and manufacturing perspective, complexity increases as the number of new or unique parts and arrangements rises. Cost to design, manufacture and/or assemble products escalates as the intricacy and number of product-specific components goes up. When possible, pre-existing designs, components, sub-assemblies, and arrangements should be used to make the design and manufacturing processes more efficient with respect to time and cost. This will also reduce the effect of complexity on TTM as well [10, 11].

Post-launch design changes have a ripple effect across an organization which affects resources from product design, testing and certification, manufacturing, sales, distribution, and more. Resources needed due to design changes increase TTM for updated products, and can drive costs significantly due to modification of components, processes, tooling, equipment, etc. These changes also impact customers as products already sold will need to be updated, or worse, the customer is stuck with an older version of the product that they may not be satisfied with. It is evident that changes to products after initial release can negatively impact all three of the Tier I business objectives [10].

The *duration of the new product development* (NPD) cycle contributes to the overall TTM for new products; although, TTM is also influenced by other things such as specification, design, build, and qualification of manufacturing equipment and processes. Since time usually infers the use of resources, there is also a cost associated with NPD duration which will impact overall product cost to some extent [10, 12].

Our team surveyed a total of nine practitioners of quality systems from the same three industries as polled for the Tier I objectives to develop relative weighting for the aforementioned strategies. Those participating in the survey included people from process and manufacturing engineering, quality engineering and management, continuous improvement management, product development management, and applications engineering.

Relative weights for Tier II strategies were derived through pair wise comparison using Kocaoglu's Hierarchy Decision Modeling Process [13]. Consistency indices were calculated for each set of pairwise comparisons. Consistency values greater than 10 % were removed as per Saaty's recommendations to improve reliability or significance of the criteria weighting [14].

1.5 Criteria Level III: Modern Quality Cultures Alternatives

The three quality methods that are viewed as the primary and leading methods in industry are Lean, Six Sigma, and Theory of Constraints. These methods have distinct tools and purposes that vary from each other in their goal, approach, and implementation methods.

Six Sigma is a quality management methodology that was introduced by Motorola in the 1980s [15]. The goal of this methodology is to systematically reduce product variation through the identification and improvement of a product through the systematic improvement of processes. The steps of Six Sigma implementation are as follows [4]:

1. *Define*—The definition of the problem that needs improvement
2. *Measure*—Collection of data related
3. *Analyze*—conversion of the data into information that can and discussed to determine the best course of action
4. *Improve*—the implementation of the corrective action to the process or procedure
5. *Control*—the monitoring of the process after the change to guarantee that the problem has been resolved

The second approach is for designing new processes/products and is called DFSS (Design for Six Sigma) and is more widely used for companies with a six sigma quality culture [16].

1. *Define Goals*—The definition of the problem that needs improvement
2. *Measure*—Collection of data related
3. *Analyze*—designs to select the best design
4. *Design optimization*—this is the main difference wherein the existing design is optimized based on the Analysis section of the process.
5. *Verify*—the chosen design with pilot-testing.

Lean is a quality management methodology that is focused in the creation and implementation process that creates value for the system. The current configuration of this methodology was borrowed from the Toyota Production System and is an evolution of the original work created by the Fredrick Taylor and Henry Ford era [17]. The goal of this methodology is to eliminate non value added process steps and movement that do not add value to the end product. The steps of Lean implementation are as follows [4] [18]:

1. *Identify Value*—the specific identification of elements that create value for the customer
2. *Map the Value Stream*—identification of all of the steps that are required to create the product or service
3. *Create Flow*—establish a flow that will consolidate the value steps closer together so that the product moves smoothly toward customer
4. *Establish Pull*—implement a system that let customers pull value from the upstream activities
5. *Seek Perfection*—continue with the process until all waste has been removed from the process and the customer reaches satisfaction goals

Theory of Constraints (ToC) is a quality management methodology that was developed by Eliyahu Goldratt and introduced in the book titled The Goal [24]. The output of this methodology is to identify constraints or bottlenecks in a system or process and to systemically improve the process to eliminate the identified constraints. The steps of ToC implementation are as follows [19, 20]:

1. *Identify Constraints*—locate the constraints of a system or process, can be identified by visual backlogs
2. *Exploit the Constraint*—determine the utmost capacity that the constraint can handle without implementing expensive improvements to the process
3. *Subordinate other processes to the Constraint*—pace all previous operations to the constraint to the constraint identified
4. *Elevate the constraint*—if the output of the system is not sufficient to meet product demand, implement improvements to the process essentially taking all steps necessary to eliminate the constraint
5. *Repeat the cycle*—After the first constraint is broken other elements of the system or process will become new bottlenecks to the system

1.6 Survey and Pairwise Calculations

A detailed survey was created and distributed to experts in a paper/hard copy format. The paper survey contained all the necessary pairwise comparisons. Figure 1.2 shows an example of the survey. The participant was asked to compare each pair, assigning ratios between the relative contributions (MOGSA approach) of each element of the pair to the above level such that the total for each pair equaled 100. For example, in Fig. 1.2 Reduction in Product Cost was assigned a 28 as compared to Decrease Time to Market for a total of 100.

PCM Software [21] version 1.3 (developed by Bruce J. Bailey) was used to calculate the pair wise comparisons for all the model levels. A screen shot from the PCM software output is shown in Fig. 1.3 for criteria level I.

Reduction in Product Cost	Decrease Time to Market
28	72
Score Each Criteria – Must Sum to 100%	

Reduction in Product Cost	Increase Customer Satisfaction
40	60
Score Each Criteria – Must Sum to 100%	

Decrease Time to Market	Increase Customer Satisfaction
70	30
Score Each Criteria – Must Sum to 100%	

Fig. 1.2 Survey pair wise example

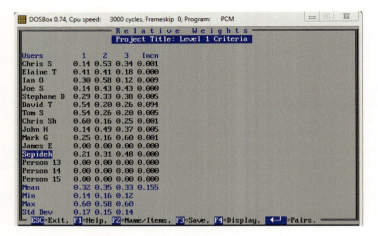

Fig. 1.3 PCM software output for Level I criteria

1.7 Model Results and Validation: Level I Business Goals

Once the pair wise comparisons were made for each level, relative values were calculated for each benefit (Level II) and alternative (Level III). The relative value is a measure of how much each element contributes to the overall objective (above level). For example, *Reduced Design Complexity* has three relative values for each of the business goals: Reduction in Product Cost, Increase Customer Satisfaction, and Decrease Time to Market. For the alternatives, Level III, each alternative has a relative value feeding through to the mission through the Level II benefit. For example, *Lean* has an overall relative value as it relates to the business goals.

Survey results were compared for the business goals (Level I). Table 1.3 shows the pair wise priority given to each of the goals as they relate to the overall mission. The Hard Goods Company which participated in the survey has NPD cycles which can be 3 years or longer. Additionally, their product life cycles are very long, in some cases 20+ years. This company also sells directly to customers through retail and distribution. The pair wise priority made sense to the team given the company's business model. Customer satisfaction scored the highest (46 %), followed by Decrease Time to Market (29 %) and Reduction in Product Costs (26 %). Figure 1.4 shows the results graphically.

The Automotive Plastics Company assigned a priority of 54 %, 23 %, and 23 % for Reduction in Product Costs, Increase Customer Satisfaction, and Decrease Time to Market respectively. This company's typical NPD cycle would be considered "medium" by subjective scoring, typically 2–3 years with product life cycles of 3–10 years. This company's business model is direct sales to OEMs (Business to Business). The automotive industry is cost competitive, so the team was not surprised to see Reduction in Product Costs as the leading priority in support of the mission. Figure 1.5 shows the results graphically.

1 Quality Culture Selection for New Product Development (NPD)...

Table 1.3 Survey responses: quality culture goals by sector

Business sector and goals		Pair wise priority
Hard Goods	Reduction in product costs	0.26
	Increase customer satisfaction	0.46
	Decrease time to market	0.29
Automotive	Reduction in product costs	0.54
	Increase customer satisfaction	0.23
	Decrease time to market	0.23
Semiconductor	Reduction in product costs	0.28
	Increase customer satisfaction	0.33
	Decrease time to market	0.39

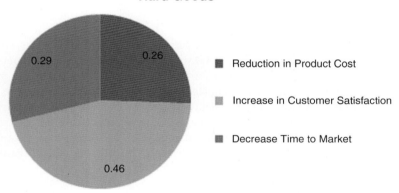

Fig. 1.4 Hard goods level I result

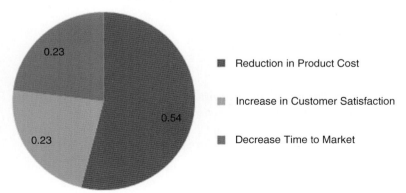

Fig. 1.5 Plastic automotive level I results

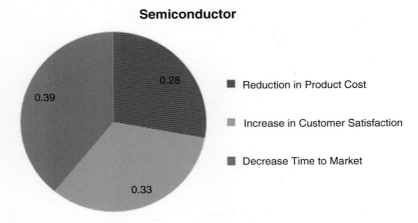

Fig. 1.6 Semiconductor level I results

Semiconductors and electronics typically have very short NPD cycles as well as product life times. The company surveyed supplies Semiconductors for the mobile (cell phone) market. Their NPD cycles are considered "short" as they are 9–12 months from product definition to manufacturing release. Product lifetimes are 2–5 years as consumers tend to get new mobile phones every 2 years due to contract renewals and a desire to have the latest model features and capabilities. Decrease Time to Market scored the highest priority, 39 %, with Increase in Customer Satisfaction scoring 33 % and Reduction in Product Cost scoring 28 %. Figure 1.6 shows the results graphically.

Pair wise inconsistency is a measure of how consistent, or reliable, the survey participant was in their pair wise priority assignments. It is common practice to omit (remove) survey results from participants which are deemed inconsistent based on inconsistency calculations [25].

Inconsistencies were calculated for the Level I survey results based on the following algorithm:

$$Inconsistency = \sqrt{\frac{1}{3}\left[\left(\sigma_{cA}\right)^2 + \left(\sigma_{cB}\right)^2 + \left(\sigma_{cC}\right)^2\right]}$$

Where:
cA: Criteria A, Reduction in Product Cost
cB: Criteria B, Increase in Customer Satisfaction
cC: Criteria C, Decrease Time to Market
σ: Standard Deviation of the Pair Wise Normalized Values

The team used the 10 % inconsistency cut-off rule as proposed by Saaty's Analytic Hierarchy Process methodology [14] requirement for a survey to be considered valid for model validation. No surveys were omitted from the Level I calculations based on the calculations. Table 1.4 shows inconsistency calculations for each of the eleven participants.

Table 1.4 Level I: inconsistency

Participant #	Inconsistency
1	0.000
2	0.009
3	0.000
4	0.005
5	0.094
6	0.005
7	0.001
8	0.005
9	0.001
10	0.000
11	0.000

1.8 Model Results and Validation: Level II Benefits

Participants were asked to pair wise compare how each benefit would help accomplish each of the business goals and ultimately the overall mission. The level II benefits were pair wise compared against each other for each business goal category. A relative value, as it feeds through to the overall mission, was calculated for each of the benefits. The Level II survey focused on practitioners, employees closely coupled to the NPD process (e.g. Program Managers, Development Engineers). Nine (9) experts were selected; four from Hard Goods, three from Semiconductor, and two from Automotive Plastics. Relative Values were calculated as shown below:

$$v_k = \sum_{i=1}^{3} P_i \cdot V_i \; \forall k$$

Where:
v: Overall Relative value to Mission for Level II Benefit
P: Priority for Level I business Goal (Table 1.2)
V: Pairwise value for Level II Benefit
k: Level II Benefit (9 total)

For the Semiconductor company, relative value priority is shown in Table 1.5, sorted from highest (most relevant) to lowest (least relevant). Results showed five most significant benefits: Reduced in Post Launch Design Changes, Decrease Time of Product Development Process, Reduced Product Complexity, and Aligning Products to Market Needs. Given the nature of this company's business and fast development/short product life cycles and the corresponding Level I scoring, the perceived benefits made sense.

Hard Goods relative value scoring showed more priority given to product cost related benefits as shown in Table 1.6. Reduced Warranty Claims had the highest relative value followed by Reduced Direct Labor and Materials. Aligning Products to Market needs ranked third with Reduce Post Launch Design Changes and Decrease Time of Product Development Process fourth and fifth position, respectively.

Table 1.5 Level II: relative value for Semiconductor

Level II benefit	Relative value
Reduce in post launch design changes	0.225
Decrease time of product development process	0.191
Reduced product complexity	0.168
Aligning products to market needs	0.144
Reduced warranty claims	0.113
Reduced investment in product specific capital	0.060
Reduce non-recurring design expenses	0.044
Reduce direct labor and materials	0.037
Reduce operational overhead	0.028

Table 1.6 Level II: relative value for hard goods

Level II benefit	Relative value
Reduced warranty claims	0.174
Reduce direct labor and materials	0.130
Aligning products to market needs	0.122
Reduce post launch design changes	0.122
Decrease time of product development process	0.116
Reduced product complexity	0.112
Reduce investment in product specific capital	0.091
Reduce operational overhead	0.085
Reduce non-recurring design expenses	0.053

Given their high volumes, direct sales to customers, and the fact that the Hard Goods management scored Customer Satisfaction the highest business goal, it seemed fitting that Reduced Warranty Claims would score high. Warranty claims cost companies a lot in terms of required field service to correct problems and perceptions regarding the quality of a product. According to Philip B. Crosby, in his book [22] entitled Quality Without Tears, Crosby states "prices of nonconformance are all the expenses involved in doing things wrong. This includes the efforts to correct salesperson' orders when they come in, to correct the procedures that are drawn up to implement orders and to correct he product or the serve as it goes along, to do work over, and to pay for warranty and other nonconformance claims. When you add all these items together it is an enormous amount expense, representing 20 percent or more of sales in manufacturing companies and 35 percent of operating costs in service companies."

Automotive Plastics, which assigned Product Cost the highest priority in Level I, provided the relative values shown in Table 1.7. Reduce Post Launch Design Changes scored the highest which made sense given the high cost of changing designs after launch in the automotive business.

Table 1.7 Level II: relative value for automotive plastics

Level II benefit	Relative value
Reduce post launch design changes	0.143
Decrease time of product development process	0.127
Aligning products to market needs	0.127
Reduced product complexity	0.127
Reduce direct labor and materials	0.119
Reduce investment in product specific capital	0.113
Reduce operational overhead	0.090
Reduce non-recurring design expenses	0.083
Reduced warranty claims	0.076

1.9 Model Results and Validation: Level III Alternatives

Lean, Six Sigma, and Theory of Constraints were each compared to each of the benefit, again using a pair wise methodology. The team targeted survey participants who were familiar with the different quality methodologies. In most organizations, quality managers/engineers, and manufacturing focused managers/engineers are most familiar with quality methods. Twelve experts were selected for comparing the Level III Alternatives. Six experts were surveyed from Hard Goods, four from Semiconductor, and two from Automotive Plastics.

Relative values were calculated for the feed through contribution to the overall mission for each alternative. These relative values were used to make recommendations to each of the participating companies.

For the Semiconductor company, relative values and corresponding alternative scoring is shown in Table 1.8. For example, Reduce Post Launch Design Changes, which has the highest relative feed through value to the mission, Six Sigma would provide the greatest benefit.

Figure 1.7 shows the model output graphically in a pie chart format. Each of the alternatives, a sum was calculated for their overall relative value (e.g. Six Sigma sum = 0.39). Figure 1.7 shows the percentage contribution of each quality methodology to the overall mission. As can be seen, Six Sigma contributes 38 % to the overall mission, followed by Theory of Constraints at 34 %, and then followed by Lean at 28 %.

The team would recommend Six Sigma methodologies be considered for New Product Development for the Semiconductor company surveyed.

The same approach as described was followed for the Hard Goods company as well as Automotive Plastics. Table 1.9 shows the results for the Hard Goods company.

Figure 1.8 shows model output for the Hard Goods company. As can be seen, Six Sigma would provide the greatest benefit to the mission (39 %), followed closely by Lean (37 %).

Table 1.8 Level III: relative value for semiconductors

Level II benefit	Relative value	Six Sigma	Lean	ToC
Reduce post…	0.225	0.13	0.04	0.06
Decrease time…	0.191	0.04	0.05	0.10
Reduced compl…	0.168	0.03	0.09	0.05
Aligning prod…	0.144	0.06	0.03	0.05
Warranty…	0.113	0.08	0.02	0.02
Investment…	0.060	0.01	0.01	0.03
Non-recurring…	0.044	0.02	0.01	0.01
Direct labor…	0.037	0.01	0.01	0.01
Overhead…	0.028	0.01	0.01	0.01
Sum		0.39	0.28	0.34

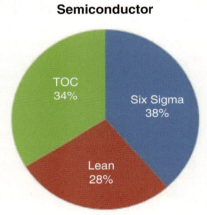

Fig. 1.7 Model output for Semiconductor

Table 1.9 Level III: relative value for hard goods

Level II benefit	Relative value	Six Sigma	Lean	ToC
Warranty…	0.174	0.09	0.06	0.03
Direct labor…	0.130	0.03	0.07	0.03
Aligning prod…	0.122	0.06	0.03	0.03
Reduce post…	0.122	0.06	0.03	0.03
Decrease time…	0.116	0.03	0.04	0.04
Reduced compl…	0.112	0.04	0.05	0.03
Investment	0.091	0.03	0.03	0.03
Overhead…	0.085	0.02	0.04	0.02
Non-recurring…	0.053	0.02	0.02	0.01
Sum		0.39	0.37	0.24

Fig. 1.8 Model output for Hard Goods

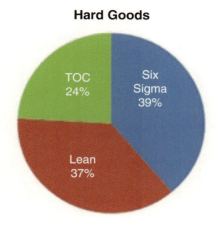

Fig. 1.9 Model output for Automotive Plastics

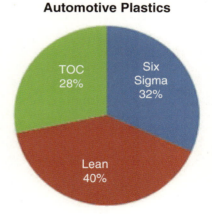

Finally, model output was analyzed for the Automotive Plastics company (Fig. 1.9). Table 1.10 shows the level III alternative relative values for Level III.

As highlighted in the Level I business goals survey reduction in product cost dominated the business goals. Lean is very effective at reducing product cost and the model output confirms this, showing the benefit of Lean at 40 % as compared to Six Sigma at 32 % with ToC at 28 %. The team would recommend Lean in this case as supported by the relative values in Table 1.9.

Table 1.10 Level III: relative value for automotive plastics

Level II benefit	Relative value	Six Sigma	Lean	ToC
Reduce post…	0.143	0.04	0.06	0.04
Decrease time…	0.127	0.04	0.05	0.05
Aligning prod…	0.127	0.04	0.05	0.04
Reduce compl…	0.127	0.04	0.06	0.03
Direct labor…	0.119	0.02	0.06	0.04
Investment…	0.113	0.03	0.05	0.04
Overhead…	0.090	0.02	0.04	0.03
Non-recurring	0.083	0.05	0.02	0.02
Warranty	0.076	0.04	0.02	0.01
Sum		0.32	0.40	0.28

1.10 Conclusion

Selecting which quality culture to implement for NPD is an important decision. In this paper the team presented a model which aids in this selection by focusing on the current challenges within a specific organization. A HDM model was developed which takes inputs from various levels of management and expertise within an organization. Three different quality cultures were considered in the model: Six Sigma, Lean, and Theory of Constrains. Each of these systems has relative advantages when applied to NPD. There is also overlap between the different systems. The model takes input from quality culture experts and recommends which of these systems (or a combination) to implement for NPD. This quantitative approach may be desired by organizations that might otherwise be forced to implement a quality culture based on more subjective input from perceived internal or external experts.

1.11 Future Work

Establishing potential correlations between different industries/business sectors would add to the existing body of knowledge related to quality methodologies and cultures. More companies from different sectors would need to be surveyed and results compiled. Scoring the Level III alternatives proved to be difficult as finding knowledgeable experts on all the alternatives were difficult. In reality, the Level III alternatives could be combined from all companies as the benefits of each system should not be company specific. Providing guidance to firms concerning a set of specific quality tools as opposed to an entire system would also be beneficial, especially for companies who might not have a strong correlation to one specific system. The model output currently recommends which entire system(s) to implement for NPD. However, a better approach might be to recommend specific tools for each of the given Level II relative priority scoring.

The paper survey which was distributed was very time consuming both for the participants and for the team when compiling the results. Compiling the results for the respondents presented in this paper took over 24 working hours, which included data entry, PCM calculations, and analysis. The survey process would need to be streamlined if the model is to be used on a larger scale.

Acknowledgment The team would like to thank Dr. Daim for his supervision and advice during this project.

Appendix: HDM Model (Large View)

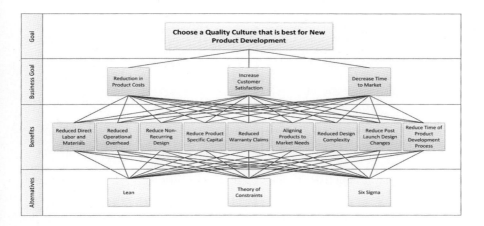

References

1. Tunks R (1992) Understanding the quality initiative. Fast track to quality: a 12-month program for small to mid-sized companies, 1st ed. McGraw-Hill, New York City. ch. 2, pp. 9
2. Hinkle S (2006) The make or buy decision. Take a quality ride: the realities of implementing a quality management system, 1st ed. iUniverse, Lincoln, NE. ch.3
3. Basu R (2011) The evolution of Six Sigma, Lean Sigma, and FIT SIGMA. Fit Sigma: a lean approach to building sustainable quality beyond Six Sigma, 1st ed. Wiley, West Sussex. ch. 1, pp. 1
4. Nave D (2002) How to compare Six Sigma, lean and theory of constraints. Quality Progress (March)
5. Dahlgaard J, Dahlgaard-Park SM (2006) Lean production, six sigma quality, TQM and company culture. TQM Mag 18:263–281
6. Daim T (2012) ETM530. Class lecture. Topic: "MOGSA hierarchy HDM: mission objectives goals strategies and actions", WC309, Faculty of Engineering & Technology Management, Portland State University, Portland, OR, USA, 5 April 2012

7. (2008) A guide to the project management body of knowledge (PMBOK Guide). Project Management Institute, Newtown Square, PA (print)
8. Griffin A (2002) Product development cycle time for business-to-business products. Ind Market Manage 31(4):291
9. Lean 3P (2010) Slash manufacturing costs. Technology Perspectives. http://www.design-for-lean.com/lean%20design.html. Accessed 17 June 2012
10. (2006) "Role of Design for Six Sigma for Total Product Development." MIT LGO. Six Sigma Academy. http://lgosdm.mit.edu/VCSS/web_seminars/docs/eskandari_052606.pdf. Accessed 17 June 2012
11. Mahesh C (2008) Theory of constraints: a theory for operations management. Int J Oper Prod Manage 28(10):991
12. Dalton M (2009) What's constraining your innovation? Res Technol Manage 52(5):52
13. Kocaoglu DF (1976) A systems approach to the resource allocation process in police patrol. PhD dissertation, University of Pittsburgh, Pittsburgh
14. Saaty TL (1977) A scaling methods for priorities in hierarchical structure. J Math Psychol 15:234–281
15. Pearson—Quality Management (n.d.) Pearson—Quality Management. N.p. http://www.pearson-highered.com/educator/course/Quality-Management/91055512.page. . Accessed 17 June 2012
16. Johnson JA, Gitlow H, Widener S, Popovich E (2006) Designing new housing at the University of Miami: a "Six Sigma" DMADV/DFSS case study. Qual Eng 18:299–323
17. Holweg M (2007) The genealogy of lean production. J Oper Manage 25(2):420
18. Principles of Lean (n.d.) What is lean. Lean Enterprise Institute. http://www.lean.org/WhatsLean/Principles.cfm. Accessed 17 June 2012
19. V. Workman, "Applying Theory of Constraints to Product Management", www.rymatech.com/en/applying-the-theory
20. The theory of constraints and its thinking processes (n.d.) Goldratt Institute. AGI. http://www.goldratt.com/pdfs/toctpwp.pdf Accessed 17 June 2012.
21. Bailey, Bruce J (n.d.) PCM software. Computer software. Vers. 1.3, N.p.
22. Crosby P (1995) The fourth absolute: the measurement of quality is the price of nonconformance. Quality without tears: the art of hassle-free management, 1st ed. McGraw-Hill, New York. ch.9, pp. 85
23. Leavengood S (2011) Identifying best quality management practices for achieving quality and innovation performance in the forest product industry. M.S. thesis, University of Portland, USA
24. Goldratt EM, Cox J (1992) The goal: a process of ongoing improvement. North River, Great Barrington, MA
25. Triantaphyllou E (1999) Reductions of pairwise comparisons in decision making via a duality approach. J Multi Criteria Decis Anal 8:299–310

Chapter 2
Call Tracking Technology Selection Model

Wilson Zehr, Abdussalam Alawini, Mousa Alharbi, and Mohamed Borgan

Abstract In this chapter we evaluate the selection of a call tracking feature for an existing marketing automation solution. This type of selection process has become much more complex over time based on the sheer volume of offerings available, different technical approaches to implementation, and service plans (features plus costs). In order to manage this complexity for decision making, we gathered a set of core requirements from the client, assembled a panel of experts to rank the importance of requirements, and then evaluated the potential solutions based on those criteria. The actual decision making methodology used in this study is the hierarchical decision model (HDM) testing two alternative methods for evaluating the expert criteria ranking. In this case, by focusing on client requirements, rather than specific technologies or implementation approaches, allows us to greatly simplify this complex decision making process in the absence of a more detailed technical analysis of every possible solution.

2.1 Introduction

This project was undertaken on behalf of Cendix (www.cendix.com) a company located in Lake Oswego, Oregon, that provides innovative web-to-print solutions. The primary focus of Cendix is to deliver "custom branded" online applications that

W. Zehr (✉)
Oregon State University, Corvallis, OR, USA
e-mail: wilson@cendix.com

A. Alawini • M. Borgan
Portland State University, Portland, OR, USA
e-mail: alawini@gmail.com; mohamedborgan@gmail.com

M. Alharbi
AramCo, Portland, OR, USA
e-mail: alharbmousa@gmail.com

automate the ordering, production, and tracking of direct mail campaigns and marketing materials. The target customers of Cendix are enterprise marketing organizations and commercial printers that offer solutions to enterprise marketing organizations.

The flag-ship product of Cendix is called the Channel Marketing Portal (CMP). The CMP is designed for organizations that sell through "channels" (e.g. distributors, dealers, franchisees …). The marketing organization posts all of their corporate approved templates for direct mail, collateral, advertising, logo items, and other marketing materials in their own branded portal. Then channel members can visit the portal, select corporate approved materials, personalize and approve them, and then route them for automated production and delivery. The system automatically tracks and reports production status (processed, printed, shipped/mailed), delivery details, and response rates giving a complete 360° view of any campaign/order at any point in time.

One important client of Cendix is a large national bank that has been in business for over 75 years. They focus primarily on mortgage loans originated through mortgage brokers located at 200+ branch offices across the United States. The bank requires that all direct mail campaigns are delivered through their CMP. In this case, the portal also serves an important role from a government compliance standpoint by making sure that all the marketing materials comply with government regulations. Non-compliant marketing materials/campaigns can result in fines, branch closure, or even loss of HUD certification.

The bank has instituted a standard process where every direct mail campaign (or marketing material) must be approved by the compliance department. Once approved, the piece is uploaded to the CMP where it is available for branches to use. As campaigns are launched the CMP keeps a complete audit trail of what is produced and delivered; as well as responses to campaigns.

In the current solution, when a direct mail campaign is sent out, the client has the option of including a PIN number on the direct mail piece. This unique PIN number is automatically generated by the system. When a client responds by telephone the Loan Officer enters the PIN number into an online screen (called Lead Tracker) that pulls up the customer record. The information captured by the Loan Officer is added to that record and the response is captured allowing the system to capture responses and report real-time response rates. A version of this offering that uses a PURL (self-service web page for clients) as the response vehicle along with the toll-free number is also available. The end result is an inexpensive and complete end-to-end lead tracking and compliance system that gives the bank a competitive edge (Fig. 2.1).

One additional need the bank has identified is the ability to track and record incoming calls for branches. This is important for at least two reasons. First, if a customer calls outside of normal business hours the branch still wants to capture that lead even if the customer does not leave a message—every lead costs the bank money to generate. Second, some of the branches would like call recordings for training and coaching purposes. In addition, capturing calls provides even richer level of detail for the compliance process. Cendix was asked to add this feature to the CMP (Fig. 2.2).

2 Call Tracking Technology Selection Model

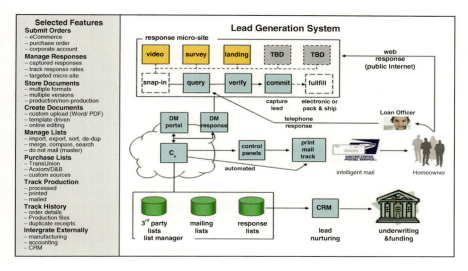

Fig. 2.1 Lead generation system schematic

Fig. 2.2 Call tracking system requirements

The solution from a functional standpoint requires that calls are routed through a telephone switch which can capture call detail records (CDR) and (optionally) record calls. The call detail record will contain information such as the caller ID (name, number, and location), time of call, length of call, and disposition. With a connection to a demographic database a great deal of additional information can be generated about each caller as well. The information that is captured at this level can be displayed to users in a graphical form using pre-defined reports, graphs, or other standard reporting features. This information can either be displayed real-time with direct access to the switch or on a delayed basis if CDR's are batched and moved to other systems.

There are a couple of different ways to approach this problem from a technical standpoint. First, the client could elect to build a solution from scratch. There are telecommunications companies that own switches and provide API's so that vendors can write applications that pull CDR's directly from the switch. In this case the system would need to capture/store CDR's, create the software required to process and display call data, and manage user accounts/access. This type of solution would provide the greatest flexibility from a functionality and integration standpoint; however, it would require additional time to implement, generate additional engineering expense, and introduce delivery risk.

Second, it is possible to find solutions that already have the switch interface and data processing functions implemented. The basic platform could be used as a foundation to create an online application that would display call data and manage user accounts. This second option could be delivered sooner and provide complete flexibility with the features actually delivered to end-users. On the other hand, this solution would also require the expense associated with application development and take time to deliver to the market (although less on both fronts then the first approach).

Third, there are a number of existing solutions in the market that can be private-labeled—the switch integration and application development has already been done. The application just needs to be "private labeled" (e.g. customize the look and feel). The advantage of this solution is that very little, if any, additional engineering work/expense is required on the part of the client, the application can be live almost immediately, and there is no delivery risk. At the same time, this type of solution may include higher operating costs (to compensate the application provider), there is limited flexibility in the features and capabilities offered, and it becomes much easier for a competitor to imitate this solution.

The focus of this investigation is to select the right solution based on the capabilities of the offerings in the marketplace and the requirements dictated by the end-user client.

2.2 Methodology/Model Selection

The methodology selected for this analysis is the Hierarchical Decision Model (HDM). This tool initiates a decision process where both qualitative and quantitative judgments can be measured. It is based on the concept that humans are often less capable of making absolute judgments, and more capable of making relative judgments. This version of the model mitigates the difficulty of dealing with multiple criteria at the same time by using two different approaches: pair wise comparison and a simple scaled ranking based on expert judgment [10, 12, 13].

This model divides the different elements of the problem into smaller elements (sub-problems), so that the decision model is represented as a hierarchy. The simplest units start from the lowest level of the hierarchy, then the level of complexity elevates towards the final objective at the top of the model. A tree diagram can be

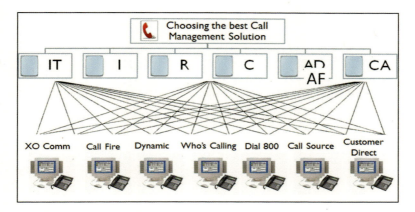

Fig. 2.3 Call tracking hierarchical decision model

used to represent the decision hierarchy; which is for this project is the goal, key criteria, and alternatives as illustrated in Fig. 2.3.

In the pair wise comparison analysis a set of experts use their knowledge and relative judgment to rank the importance of the decision criteria, using pairs of elements, and ranking those two elements in importance by splitting the value of 100 between them. So, in the case where two elements were equally important each element wars get a value of 50. On the other hand, if one element was extremely important, and the other was insignificant, then they might be ranked 90/10. The measurement results are captured as a collection of ratio judgments and used to generate a priority matrix. This process creates a set of weights for each individual element for each expert. We can then use the mean of these collective values to come up with an overall expert-based priority ranking for each criterion.

This mechanism creates a level of redundancy which can help reduce measurement error and bring a higher level of consistency to the results. The "implementation" of this process does not guarantee a high level of consistency, because it is very hard for an individual to be perfectly consistent across a wide array of comparisons by examining only two at a time, but it does provide an expected minimum level of consistency. When the results are outside those bounds then it allows us to explore the reasons for that behavior in more detail. High levels of inconsistency can be due to lack of adequate information, a low level of concentration, inappropriate model structure, or even errors in data values.

The other approach used in this analysis was to display all the values in a single list and allow the expert to assign a point value of 1–10 for each item. The total score for each expert is summed and then normalized scores are created by dividing the score for each element by the total. Since all the elements are on the same sheet, and evaluated at the same time, the expert can see and assign the relative value in the context of ALL the competing criteria. This visual analysis and reporting process can assure that there is no inconsistency on the part of evaluators and elements are ranked with a complete view of the "big picture" as well as the relationship between them.

2.3 Defining HDM Levels

2.3.1 First Level

Choose the best possible call tracking and management system based on the criteria provided by the client and the expert judgment of our panel.

2.3.2 Second Level

We performed a literature review and talked with industry experts to come up with an initial list of the most common criteria that would be used when selecting a call tracking system in this context. The result of this initial analysis was a list of eight criteria (not in priority order):

- Cost

This element includes the cost of development and implementation; as well as the cost of operation and maintenance. There is often a trade-off between up-front cost and ongoing operating cost.

- Reliability

This element considered the overall availability of the system and unplanned down-time. This can have a huge impact for mission critical systems; although unplanned downtime creates frustration on the part of users even when system failure is not catastrophic.

- Implementation Time

On this vector we are considering time to market. We often have a market window to hit and the failure to meet our target can result in lost revenue, lost opportunity, and competitive risk.

- Contract Term

Technology changes at a very rapid rate these days. Long-term contracts can lead to predictability and stability, but they can also expose us to market risk if technology or the state of the industry changes long before our agreement expires. Short-term contracts maximize our flexibility; at the same time, they can also leave us vulnerable when it comes time to renegotiate an extension if the solution is still optimal.

- Additional Features

The customer provided an initial "minimum" list of features. These included the ability to allocate toll free numbers to accounts, track incoming calls for each number, capture and display the details for each call (including a name, geographic location, and callback number), provide a standard set of reports on volume and trends, and (optionally) capture phone calls as WAV (audio) files. The system also has to provide a login for each account so that users can see only their own calls.

There are plenty of additional features beyond this in the market today. This element determines the importance of additional features above and beyond the customers' core requirements.

- Integration Potential

In general, the ability of tools to integrate and work well together improves the end-user experience and the overall utility of the solution. In addition, this element allows us to customize the tool and the features to create an optimal experience for each user or group of users.

- Compatibility

Compatibility allows us to work with existing and future applications. This can be especially important in environments where a great deal of investment has been made in legacy systems.

- Technology Flexibility

Flexibility on this front allows us to solve a wide range of problems based on a single investment in technology [7].

We proposed these eight criteria in our initial discussion with the client (Cendix). The client chose five of these features and insisted on another—Competitive Advantage. The idea with competitive advantage is that if an off-the-shelf system is used then competitors can easily duplicate the solution (e.g. there is a lack of competitive barriers). This was an important "strategic" concern in the mind of the client. Here are the final six criteria (not in priority order) selected by the client:

- Implementation Time (IT)
- Integration Potential (I)
- Reliability (R)
- Cost (C)
- Additional Features (AF)
- Competitive Advantage (CA)

2.3.3 Third Level

Vender Selection (alternatives): Once the decision criteria were established then the team considered service providers and solutions. The mandatory selection criteria were vendor reputation and financial stability [1]. The client also had an existing relationship with two vendors XO Communications and Integra Telecom so they requested that they be included in the evaluation. Plus, there is one industry veteran, Who's Calling that originally invented this market space/solution—no evaluation would be complete without including this latter offering.

Through an initial screen the team identified at least 32 vendors (Appendix) that fit the basic criteria—given more time we undoubtedly would have found even more

Table 2.1 Service provider/solution summary

Provider	Category	First-level screen
XO Communications	Switch provider/telecom	Yes
Call Fire	Switch provider	Yes
Dynamicic	Application provider	Yes
Who's Calling	Application provider	Yes
Dial 800	Application provider	Yes
Call Source	Application provider	Yes
Customer Direct	Application provider	Yes
Integra Telecom	Switch provider/telecom	No
Answer Connect	Call center	No
Call Experts	Call center	No
We Answer	Call center	No
ansafone.com	Call center	No

potential solutions. In consultation with the client the team decided to limit the number of solutions evaluated to 12 in order to have time to explore each in more detail. The team then created an RFI that was submitted to the three mandatory participants, several on the research list, and posted on BuyerZone.com online.

We created a short-list of 12 from the responses received. Then we screened these responses against the mandatory customer requirements which eliminated another five from consideration. This left us with a list of seven vendors/solutions for inclusion in the selection process. A summary of these providers can be found in Table 2.1 below.

When combined with the HDM this resulted in the following model for analysis.

2.4 Criteria Weights Assignment

The expert panel will be used to assign the weights to each of the vendor criteria that will be evaluated. In this section, we will be first discussing the data gathering methods we've used to get expert inputs as well as discussing the application of the constant-sum method in assigning weights to the second level of our HDM model.

2.5 Pairwise and Scaled Ranking

We first considered using a simple scaled ranking methodology (described earlier) to capture the relative importance of each criterion and assign weights. However, we also appreciate the rigor and redundancy associated with the pair wise comparison method; as well as the ability to measure and assesses internal consistency. Thus, we chose to use and evaluate both methods for this project.

2 Call Tracking Technology Selection Model

Pair-wise comparison, utilized in constant-sum method, is characterized by providing an accurate approach of measuring the internal inconsistency of each expert as well as the overall consistency of the HDM model [2]. One of the major limitations of pair-wise method is that when the number of criterion to be evaluated is large then the number of comparison will also be large and experts will face difficulties in maintaining a high degree of consistency. In addition, the process of conducting the pair-wise comparisons can also be time consuming [8].

The number of the criteria we have in our model is considered to be acceptable number for pair-wise comparison method. For the six criteria of our HDM model, each expert needs to conduct 15 comparisons which is still a manageable number for our experts.

Sample Pair Wise Survey   Sample Scaled Ranking Survey

2.6 Pairwise Combined Experts Results

Reliability has the highest weight with 23 %. Cost comes in the second place with 22 % which is very close to reliability criterion. Competitive advantage, integration and implementation time are 18 %, 15 % and 14 % respectively. The lowest weight was for additional features at 9 %. Internal inconsistencies for all experts were below 0.016 which is considered to be an acceptable rate.

2.7 Scaled Ranking Combined Result

The scaled ranking evaluation was a much less time consuming process. The survey shown earlier was given to each of the experts on a web page. They were asked to rate each criteria on scale from 1 to 10 ranking the entire list at the same time.

Table 2.2 Scaled ranking survey results

Expert	Normalized IT	I	R	C	AF	CA	Total
Wilson Zehr	0.20	0.13	0.18	0.25	0.08	0.18	1.00
Rajiv Agarwal	0.14	0.19	0.19	0.16	0.14	0.19	1.00
Jeff Belding	0.10	0.14	0.21	0.19	0.14	0.21	1.00
Ashok Bhatla	0.20	0.18	0.13	0.20	0.15	0.15	1.00
Abdussalam Alawini	0.16	0.16	0.20	0.20	0.11	0.18	1.00
Mark Walker	0.13	0.18	0.23	0.13	0.15	0.20	1.00
	0.15	0.16	0.19	0.19	0.13	0.18	1.00

Table 2.3 Comparison of pairwise and scaled results

Weighting approach	Implementation time	Integration	Reliability	Cost	Additional features	Competitive advantage
Pairwise—original	0.14	0.15	0.23	0.23	0.08	0.18
Pairwise—adjusted	0.14	0.15	0.23	0.22	0.09	0.18
Scaled	0.15	0.16	0.19	0.19	0.13	0.18
Scaled—Internal	0.17	0.16	0.18	0.21	0.11	0.18
Scaled—External	0.14	0.16	0.19	0.18	0.14	0.19
Scaled—Wilson	0.20	0.13	0.18	0.25	0.08	0.18

These results were then normalized by the expert score for each criterion by the sum of their scores. Using this technique there is no internal inconsistency because the experts rank all of the criteria at the same time. The experts can actually see the macro level relationship between the criteria before submitting them. These results are summarized in Table 2.2.

These results indicate that the consensus among our experts, using this scaled ranking technique, tells us that cost and reliability are the two most important facts at 19 % each; this is followed closely by competitive advantage at 18 %; and integration at 16 %. The last two criteria, implementation time and additional features trail the pack with 15 % and 13 % respectively.

These results can be compared with the Pairwise results generated earlier (Table 2.3). We can see that the weights and ranks are consistent with the earlier analysis, with reliability and cost coming out on top with just about equal weights; although the weights are higher in the pairwise analysis then in the scaled analysis, and reliability pulls slightly ahead in the adjusted (consistent) pairwise model. The other difference is that additional features are given a lower weight in the pairwise analysis than in the scaled analysis, yet the ranking as least important among the criteria does not change.

We were also curious about the impact that internal and external experts might have on the results. W5 break out the scaled ranking based on internal vs. external we find the results are consistent; however, the internal results do show a greater emphasis on cost and implementation time (time to market). This is even more pronounced when considering the evaluation of the CEO alone—even greater emphasis cost and time to market with even less weight to additional features. These results seem consistent with the viewpoint of an operating executive responsible for meeting revenue targets and external experts who may be more concerned with the overall goodness of fit of the solution.

2.8 Alternatives Evaluation

2.8.1 Data Gathering and Evaluation

After receiving the responses, all the vendors/proposals were put through a first level screen based on the core requirements. Those vendors that could not meet the minimum core requirements were not evaluated further—this eliminated five vendors from further consideration—leaving with seven to explore further for the final analysis (as detailed earlier).

2.8.2 Criteria Measurement Index (CMI)

Before analyzing the data of the remaining seven vendors, it was vital to first develop a tool for measuring the values with respect to the corresponding criteria.

2.8.2.1 Cost

Cost consists of several elements in this case. There is the cost of the initial system. In the case where we build the solution this might include software development costs. In the case where we build on a solution that already exists there may be a software license or hosting fee. Regardless on which solution is chosen, there will be recurring telecom fees based on usage; although the rates will vary by provider.

It was essential to create a cost metric that could capture all of these elements. We decided to select a minimum configuration based on the customer's requirements (5 toll-free numbers + 200 min; overage at $0.05/min) and then configured this solution for each vendor. In some cases a vendor's minimum configuration is greater than that—in those cases we used the minimum configuration.

We then assumed a 12 month usage period, totaled up all the costs associated with that period (including development and deployment) and then amortized it back out over 12 months to produce an amortized monthly cost for the first year. Given how frequently technology changes in this space we did not feel comfortable using a time period greater than 12 months. If this had been a longer time period, say 3–5 years, especially if borrowing funds, we would also incorporate the time value of money.

2.8.2.2 Implementation Time

When considering implementation time the old saying "time is money" hits home. In general, a shorter implementation time means a faster time to market. The faster we can get to market the faster we can generate revenue, grow market share, and establish a lead with respect to competitors. Thus, there is a inverse relationship between time and ranking—the smaller the value the better. If the client had given us an absolute deadline (e.g. it can't take any longer than 4 months) then we would have included that in the initial screening criteria to eliminate infeasible solutions in advance [3].

2.8.2.3 Integration

The experts expressed that a range from 0 to 5 can be assigned to the vendors by measuring the ability to connect to external systems or applications; with a value of 0 being a "closed system" with no ability to connect, and 5 being an "open" or "custom designed" solution with complete flexibility to connect.

2.8.2.4 Reliability

We considered a measure such as meantime between failure (MTBF) but decided against it because this is mostly a hardware rather than service measure. In addition, most vendors, as service providers, do not track this measure. It was also not feasible to consider just downtime (or uptime) because most systems require periodic maintenance. If this is scheduled maintenance it is routine to manage. Thus, we decided to focus on unscheduled downtime—the smaller the amount of unscheduled downtime that occurs the better for the client and the service provider [4]. This implies an inverse relationship.

2.8.2.5 Additional Feature

Additional features can be quantified by estimating the number of additional features beyond the core feature set required by the client. The ranking is a value from 0 to 5, with 0 being a system that exactly meets the requirements of the client, and 5 representing a solution that has almost unlimited additional features (e.g. custom development)—everything else will lie somewhere in between [5].

2.8.2.6 Competitive Advantage

The experts indicated that competitive advantage can be measured evaluating the solution provided and how easy it is to be duplicated by the competitors. A ratio from 0 to 5 can be assigned depending on how unique the solution is. For instance,

2 Call Tracking Technology Selection Model

Table 2.4 Summary of cost elements

Provider	Cost (index)	Cost: setup (one-time)	Cost: operation (monthly)	Cost (monthly)	Minutes	Numbers	Average
XO Communications	0.32	$13,000.00	$24,000.00	$3,083.00	40,000	As needed	0.050
Call Fire	0.98	$12,000.00	$240.00	$1,020.00	As used	5	0.050
Dynamicic	10.20	$588.00	$588.00	$98.00	750	5	0.069
Who's Calling	1.85	$500.00	$6,000.00	$541.67	2,000	20	0.150
Dial 800	18.10	$75.00	$588.00	$55.25	200	5	0.050
Call Source	3.78	$600.00	$2,572.00	$264.35	50	12	0.069
Customer Direct	1.48	$2,000.00	$6,108.00	$675.67	As used	1	0.050

Who's Calling is assigned a value of 0 since it can be purchased "off the shelf" by any provider; on the other hand a completely custom solution would rank very highly on this scale because no other vendor would have access without the same level of investment.

2.8.3 Proposals Data Analysis

Proposals were collected and all data was gathered from the responses to match the identified criteria of the second level of the model.

The first step in this analysis was to compile and adjust all the cost data. Table 2.4 summarizes all the offers cost information from the proposals.

2.8.3.1 The Cost of Setup

There was a one-time setup cost associated with all the proposals except for Call Fire. In the case of Call Fire and XO Communications considerable custom development will also be required. These costs, are estimated to be ~$12,000 in either case. This estimate is based on 3 months of development time using offshore resources— If developed domestically we would increase these costs by a factor of 3.

Also for Customer Direct, the initial system personalization costs $1,500 (normal $250 waived). Plus the service only comes with a single DID. It costs $100 to setup each DID, so there is another $500 to get us to the same level as the other packages.

The Cost of Operation

The monthly fees were provided in the proposals. Using that information the total annual costs were calculated as the monthly fees times 12 months. Therefore, for the companies that provide less than 200 min, the remaining minutes were also included with the overage charges. For instance, Call Fire charges for the minutes as needed, so their operation cost was calculated as (5*2*12)+(200*0.05*12). This represents $2/toll free number per month for 12 months, plus 200 min/month at the overage rate of $0.05/min for 12 months. Another example of this can be found with Customer Direct, the operation cost was calculated as $499/month for unlimited calls, plus $0.05/min for call tracking and recording for 200 min to be consistent with client requirements.

Total Monthly Cost

As previously outlined, setup and operating costs were rolled up into a single number and then amortized over 12 months to create a single monthly cost estimate. This is the number that was ultimately used in our evaluation.

For the other criteria the raw data are presented in Table 2.5 below.

2.8.3.2 Implementation Time

The offers included the installation times, except for XO Communications and Call Fire as they would require custom application development, which was estimated by the client to be approximately 3 months (12 weeks) worth of work. Of course, software development schedules are often notoriously unreliable. We did not add any additional cushion for software over-runs.

2.8.3.3 Integration

The experts assigned values for the integration (from 0 to 5). As described earlier, custom developed (open) solutions earn a 5, while totally closed solutions earn a 0, others are somewhere between.

2.8.3.4 Reliability

The experts were also to evaluate the reliability values, and they had to contact the service providers to provide some technical assessment, which in return allowed them to estimate total annual unplanned downtime. As we would expect, telecom carriers such as XO should score well on this metric.

2.8.3.5 Additional Features

The additional features that come with the package were quantified and the "package" was assigned a value (from 0 to 5). In the For example, XO owns the switch and thus there are additional capabilities that would allow the customer to squeeze out a richer solution built on this platform.

2 Call Tracking Technology Selection Model

Table 2.5 Summary of additional criteria elements

Provider	Implementation time (weeks)	Implementation time (index)	Integration (0–5)	Reliability (h/year)	Reliability (index)	Additional features (0–5)	Competitive advantage (0–5)
XO Communications	12	0.83	5	2	5.00	5	5
Call Fire	12	0.83	5	4	2.50	3	4
Dynamicic	2	5.00	1	8	1.25	0	1
Who's Calling	3	3.33	2	4	2.50	2	0
Dial 800	1	10.00	1	8	1.25	0	1
Call Source	2	5.00	2	4	2.50	2	1
Customer Direct	2	5.00	2	12	0.83	1	2

Table 2.6 Summary of normalized and adjusted criteria

Provider	Implementation time (index)	Integration (0–5)	Reliability (index)	Additional features (0–5)	Competitive advantage (0–5)	Cost (index)
XO Communications	0.83	5	5.00	5	5	0.32
Call Fire	0.83	5	2.50	3	4	0.98
Dynamicic	5.00	1	1.25	0	1	10.20
Who's Calling	3.33	2	2.50	2	0	1.85
Dial 800	10.00	1	1.25	0	1	18.10
Call Source	5.00	2	2.50	2	1	3.78
Customer Direct	5.00	2	0.83	1	2	1.48

2.8.3.6 Competitive Advantage

This represents the ease of duplication by competitors. As indicated by the experts a value from 0 to 5 can be assigned.

For example, XO Communication was assigned with a value of 5 since it is completely a custom solution based on XO API. Any competitor who wants this solution would need to buy it from the client (unlikely) or commit to the same level of investment (time, capital, and risk). On the other hand, Who's Calling was assigned a zero value since they have an off the shelf offering available to anyone.

2.8.4 *Data Compilation*

After pulling all the data together, the values need to be adjusted so that they all have the same priority orientation—in this case, a larger number being more favorable then a small number. The reciprocals of implementation time (IT), reliability (R), and cost (C) were calculated to make this adjustment. These adjusted values can all be found in Table 2.6.

Once these numbers were compiled then we applied the prioritization from the expert ranking to evaluate the relative attractiveness of the solutions. The results of this analysis, using both pairwise and scaled analysis results, are summarized in Table 2.7.

When exploring these results, we find that regardless of the approach that is taken, pairwise or scaled, the outcome is very similar. The top ranked solution is XO Communications, followed by Dial 800, Call Fire, Call Source, Dynamicic, Customer Direct, and Who's Calling, respectively. It is interesting to note that Who's Calling pioneered this class of solution and was the industry leader for many years. They now rank last at least when considered in the context of our requirements.

Although the outcome is consistent between approaches, and pairwise comparison is a much more rigorous technique, the panel of experts all agreed that the scaled evaluation was far more intuitive and allowed them to see how all the elements related before submission —a characteristic that they really appreciated as a group.

2 Call Tracking Technology Selection Model

Table 2.7 Comparison of pairwise and scaled rankings

Pairwise vs. Scaled Evaluation

Provider	Pairwise score	Rank	Pairwise adj score	Diff	Rank
XO Communications	0.215	1	0.219	−0.004	1
Call Fire	0.158	3	0.160	−0.002	3
Dynamicic	0.127	4	0.124	0.003	5
Who's Calling	0.092	7	0.093	−0.001	7
Dial 800	0.199	2	0.194	0.005	2
Call Source	0.125	5	0.126	−0.001	4
Customer Direct	0.193	6	0.094	0.000	6

Decisions Match

Provider	Scaled score	Rank	Internal	Rank	External	Rank	Wilson	Rank
XO Communications	0.224	1	0.212	1	0.230	1	0.189	2
Call Fire	0.165	3	0.158	3	0.169	3	0.142	3
Dynamicic	0.115	5	0.121	5	0.111	5	0.136	4
Who's Calling	0.093	7	0.092	7	0.094	7	0.088	7
Dial 800	0.180	2	0.194	2	0.173	2	0.223	1
Call Source	0.125	4	0.125	4	0.125	4	0.125	5
Customer Direct	0.097	6	0.097	6	0.096	6	0.097	6

In the case of XO Communications they got top marks for integration, reliability, additional features, and competitive advantage. These scores were able to overcome the lowest ranks in the group for cost and implementation time. The high weights given to reliability really worked in their favor in this analysis.

The other interesting thing to note is that if we re-visit the scaled analysis and break-out the results for internal vs. external weights the ranking remains the same; suggesting a consistent view of the optimal solution from both sides of the fence. On the other hand, when comparing the results using the weights from the CEO alone we find that Dial 800 rises to the top of the list. This is consistent with the high weights he gave to implementation time and cost—the two criteria where Dial 800 leads the pack.

2.9 Other Considerations

One other thought to consider is that the evaluation of these solutions is based on a specific set of client requirements (e.g. 5 toll-free numbers, 200 min, and a specific set of features). If this basket of "required" features were to change then the outcome might change as well. Say, for example, the use of this solution grew to the point that it required 2,000 min a month, then that would tend to favor those solutions that a higher base level of minutes.

Since these solutions are independent, and we considered solutions with no more than a 12 month commitment, it may be possible that there is a chain of optimal solutions. In other words, this is the optimal solution for months 1–12; another

Table 2.8 Software project outcomes 1994–2009

	Standish Group findings by year updated for 2009						
	1994	1996	1998	2000	2002	2004	2009
Succeeded (%)	16	27	26	28	34	19	32
Failed (%)	31	40	28	23	15	18	24
Challenged (%)	53	33	46	49	51	53	44

Source: http://www.galorath.com/wp/software-project-failure-costs-billions-better-estimation-planning- can-help.php

solution might rule for months 13–24; and another might be superior beyond that. Of course, the rapidly changing landscape of technology makes this a little hard to predict, but we may want to explore a "chain" of optimal solutions in future research.

The final factor to take into account is that we did not make an adjustment for implementation risk in the solutions that required custom development. As noted earlier, software development schedules have a nasty habit of stretching out and consuming more time than anyone forecast—and that only considers the case where the project is actually delivered (Table 2.8).

In fact, the Standish Group, in its 2009 Chaos report concludes that only 32 % of software projects are successful (on time, on budget, and include all the required features/functionality); 44 % were challenged (delinquent along one of these vectors); and 24 % failed all together (canceled or never used) [6]. In further research work we would suggest adding an additional factor to compensate for the higher risk associated with custom develop—we know there is almost no implementation risk associated with turning on a private label version of Who's Calling.

Finally, given the extremely large number of solutions in the market, this analysis could be expanded to cover an even large group of vendors and offers. With that said, we did evaluate a representative sample of the different types of solutions available, these solutions meet the customer requirements, and the customer could still feel comfortable moving forward with this analysis; although the larger the investment, the longer the time commitment, the more essential it becomes that we include as many feasible solutions as we can.

2.10 Conclusion

Based on the current set of requirements, and the solutions available at the time of this analysis, XO Communications provides the best overall solution available. In this particular case, we reach this same conclusion whether we use the pairwise comparison method or the scaled ranking method; although our experts appeared to prefer the intuitiveness of the scaled ranking; and the project team appreciates the rigor associated with pairwise comparison. Additional research is still required, but it may be that in some cases where the number of criteria gets very large, an area where pairwise gets more challenging, that the scaled ranking provides a viable alternative.

In this case reliability has the highest weighting which really played to the strength of the solution from XO Communications (along with others). This really helped offset the cost disadvantage of this solution. In the case where a company (client) is more cost sensitive, and is willing to trade reliability, competitive advantage, integration, and additional features for cost and time to market, a solution such as Dial 800 that leads on these fronts might be another alternative to consider.

Regardless of which solution the company chooses today, they should continue to scan the market to be aware of changes to their requirements that might affect this choice, or emerging new technologies that would provide an even more effective solution.

Appendix

No.	Company name	Website address
1	XO Communications	www.xo.com
2	Call Fire	www.callfire.com
3	Dynamicic	www.dynamicic.com
4	Who's Calling	www.whoscalling.com
5	Dial 800	www.dial800.com
6	Call Source	www.callsource.com
7	Customer Direct	www.customerdirect.com
8	Integra Telecom	www.integratelecom
9	Answer Connect	www.answerconnect.com
10	Call Experts	www.callexpert.com
11	We Answer	www.weanswer.com
12	ansafone.com	www.ansafone.com
13	3COM	www.3com.com
14	Aastra Telecom	www.aastra.com
15	ADTRAN Inc.	www.aastra.com
16	Dialexia Communications Inc.	www.dialexia.com
17	Cisco Systems Inc.	www.cisco.com
18	Ring Central	www.ringcentral.com
19	E Voice	www.evoice.com/
20	My 1 Voice	www.my1voice.com
21	Free Voice	www.freevoicepbx.com
22	Fonality	www.fonality.com
23	freelineusa	www.freelineusa.com
24	Intelecom Solutions Inc.	www.intele-com.com
25	Talk Switch	www.talkswitch.com
26	All Worx Corp	www.allworx.com
27	MiTel	www.mitel.com
28	Vertical Communications	www.vertical.com
29	AVAYA Inc.	www.avaya.com
30	SOHOware	www.sohoware.com
31	Shoretel	www.shoretel.com
32	NEC Corp. of America	www.necwave.com

References

1. Kalpana Ettenson (2010) Enterprise Phone Systems Buyer's Guide. Technology Evaluation Centers [Online]. http://whitepapers.technologyevaluation.com/html/20732/enterprise-phone-systems-buyers-guide.html
2. Kocaoglu DF (2011) Hierarchical decision modeling. PSU ETM EMGT 530 Class Notes Spring
3. CrumDD (2011) Introduction to VoIP Business Communications, http://www.positivearticles.com/Article/Criteria-for-Selecting-Your-VOIP-Solution/41687. Accessed 21 May 2011
4. AVAD Hosted VoIP PBX Business (Ed.) (2010) https://sites.google.com/a/avadtechnologies.com/business-voip/business-voip-articles/small-business-voip-articles/critieria-for-selecting-a-voip-service-provider. Accessed 14 Jan 2010
5. PROGNOSIS (2007) Multi-vendor IP telephony management: challenges & solution
6. The Standish Group (2009) CHAOS summary 2009. http://www.standishgroup.com/newsroom/chaos_2009.php
7. Dan Galorath (2008) (updated Sep. 2009) Software project failures cost billions. Better estimating can help. http://www.galorath.com/wp/software-project-failure-costs-billions-better-estimation-planning-can-help.php
8. Daim T et al (2009) Technology assessment for clean energy technologies: the case of the Pacific Northwest. Technol Soc 31:232–243
9. Mantra Solutions. http://www.mantra-solutions.com/about%20us.html
10. Ajgaonkar A, Jefferis S (2003) Use of HDM for site selection of MLB stadium in Portland, PICMET Paper
11. Kocaoglu DF (1983) A participative approach to program evaluation. IEEE Trans Eng Manage EM-30(3)
12. Ajgaonkar, Priya. et. al. " Use of Hierarchical Decision Modeling for Site Selection of a Major League Baseball Stadium in Portland". PICMET 2003.

Chapter 3
Location Selection for Fabless Firms

Niharika Jeena, Meles Hagos, Charles sai, Yuan Xu, and Zack Khalifa

Abstract Site selection for a fabless firm is a key problem for global semiconductor companies. The process of site selection for firms that are involved in research and development is influenced by many criteria. The model developed in this study highlights the most significant criteria that have an impact on the fabless site selection. Some important criteria include: Engineering Talent, Market Development, Policy, Cost, and Communications. In this study, these criteria used in an Hierarchical Decision Model (HDM), along with their associated sub-criteria to select the most attractive site from several potential sites. Candidate sites considered for a fabless semiconductor company were: San Jose, Portland, Hsinchu, Tokyo, Haifa, and Stockholm. A brief background on fabless firms worldwide with all the criteria and sub criteria is discussed. The pairwise comparison method was utilized to quantify expert opinions from the semiconductor industry on fabless site selection. Some data from the literature, such as data regarding engineering talent and market development, was extracted from various sources, normalized, and incorporated into the HDM model. The findings indicated that San Jose, Portland and Hsinchu are the most attractive locations for fabless firms.

N. Jeena (✉)
Portland State University, Hillsboro, OR, USA
e-mail: niha1234@gmail.com

M. Hagos
Intel Corporation, Hillsboro, OR, USA
e-mail: mthagos2002@hotmail.com

C. sai
Fiserv, Portland, OR, USA
e-mail: charles.shengte.tsai@gmail.com

X. Yuan
Chinaunicom, Changchun, Jilin, China
e-mail: xuyuanxiv@gmail.com

Z. Khalifa
Schlumberger, Denver, Colorado, USA
e-mail: zack.kh@gmail.com

3.1 Introduction

Research and development activities provide an important input for any industry. A fabless firm provides design to a semiconductor manufacturing firm. In the early 1980s, all semiconductor firms were vertically integrated with design firms [1]. In 1987, TSMC created its own fab, which became the world's first dedicated semiconductor foundry. This created a new opportunity for a "fabless industry," in which alliances could be formed between foundries supplying chip design and manufacturing semiconductor that did not own foundries. Fabless firms gained momentum and spread across North America, Asia, Europe, and Israel. From 1991 to 1996, fabless firms' revenue grew significantly: From one billion dollar to six billion dollars per year. In the year 2000, fabless firms had 76 % of worldwide market share, with 20 billion dollars in total revenue. There were 700 fabless firms, which soon grew to 1,500. Of these firms, 650 were in North America and 500 were in Asia.

Table 3.10 in Appendix 1 shows that the fabless integrated circuit (IC) design sector grew only 27 % in 2010, while the overall semiconductor industry grew by 31 % [2]. Fabless firms had a 4 % higher growth in 2011 than in 2010 [3]. There are many firms which have announced they will open new branches worldwide. Qualcomm opened a new branch in Cairo, Egypt in 2012 [4]. In 2011, MediaTek, Taiwan's biggest chip design firm, acquired Ralink, which then moved its headquarters from Cupertino California to Hsinchu, Taiwan [5]. This research assesses the decision making process in order to select the location for fabless firms using an HDM model that evaluates alternatives based on critical criteria and sub-criteria.

3.1.1 Research Questions

- Which location would be the best for fabless firms?
- What criteria would be most appropriate for selecting a location for a fabless firm?
- How will each criterion impact the decision making process?

3.2 Methodology

This paper uses an Hierarchical Decision Model for selecting a location for fabless firms. In order to have a quality decision process, a multi-criteria model has been developed. The model development process began with a literature review. A four-level HDM model was then developed to evaluate the alternatives for selecting a location for fabless firms. The nature of the model allows complex decisions to be built from a hierarchy that starts with the overall objective, and then examines criteria, sub-criteria and alternatives. As described in the introduction, there are many criteria and sub criteria that affect the site selection process of fabless for global

3 Location Selection for Fabless Firms

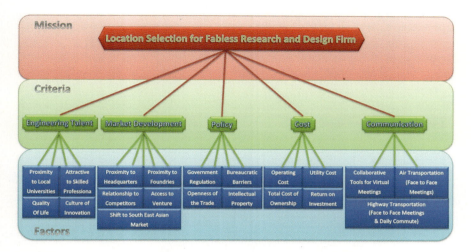

Fig. 3.1 Initial HDM based on literature

fabless semiconductor companies. However, five key criteria were identified and used in the second level of the model. On the third level, each criterion, sub criteria have been defined, and on the fourth level, seven cities were considered as the location alternatives. This approach was assumed for the sake of simplicity and minimizing the number of pairwise comparisons—i.e. the complexity of the model is proportional to the number of elements in each level of the model, which also affects the length of the pairwise comparison survey. At the top level of the model, the main objective of this study is deciding on a site for the location of a hypothetical fabless firm. All of the subsequent levels in the model support the main objective, starting with the criteria and sub criteria, all the way down to the lowest level—the alternatives (Fig. 3.1).

3.2.1 Content Validation

Feedback was received from the experts, providing comments on the criteria and sub-criteria developed from the literature. Interdependency patterns were recognized by the experts in the survey as well as some redundancy in the sub-criteria. For example, human resources cost was part of operating cost; thus, comparison between human resources costs and operating costs is redundant. Cost is a complex criterion and there could be unnecessary inconsistency in the final result due to cost sub-criteria. It is also difficult to get assessments for return of investment for fabless firms. For example, costs in fabless processes are considered to be sunk costs if the project is unsuccessful. It takes 2–3 years to find out if there is a product to sell. Therefore, the experts suggested having cost as a standalone criterion without any sub-criteria.

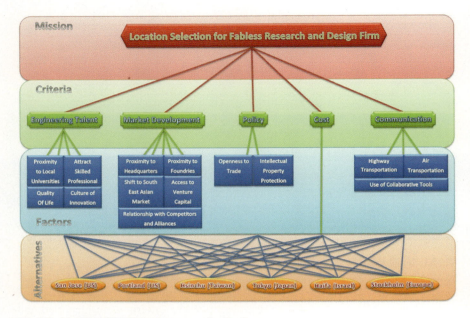

Fig. 3.2 Modified HDM based on expert feedback

Cost can be compared with other criteria and with respect to the objectives. Additionally, alternatives can be evaluated with respect to each other and to cost without passing through any sub-criteria under the cost element of the model. Experts also commented on the policy sub-criteria. They noticed that some sub-criteria under policy seem to be redundant and not significant to the process of pairwise comparison regarding the policy influence of site selection. For instance, government regulation and bureaucratic barriers are interrelated. Thus, the sub-criteria under policy have been reduced to only two: openness to trade and intellectual property protection. Those were deemed to be the most significant criteria for policy aspects of global site selection. The following model is an optimized and modified version of the model after feedback of the experts (Fig. 3.2).

3.2.2 Model Organization

A variety of literature was reviewed in order to define criteria and sub-criteria for the location of fabless firms.

3.2.2.1 First Level: Objective

The first level represents the objective of this study: Site selection of fabless firms.

3.2.2.2 Second Level: Criteria

The second level consists of five criteria: Engineering Talent, Market Development, Policy, Cost, and Communications. The sub-criteria were grouped under these criteria defined from the literature review.

Engineering talent is an important criterion. Fabless firms need highly qualified, educated personnel who can perform research using the latest tool and technologies to develop state of the art designs in semiconductors. Market Development is another criterion that is very important, due to globalization and cost competitiveness. The Asian market is developing due to its huge domestic consumer base, such as in China, India, and Middle East. Every firm wants to show their presence in these markets in order to take advantage of the ecosystems developed by the semiconductor industry. However, policies regarding entering a country for doing business vary widely. There are some countries that are open to doing business and have policies to support friendly foreign direct investment. However, many others have barriers for bureaucratic and political reasons. On the one hand, stringent policies could be one of the most important criteria in deciding the location of a fabless firm. But, on the other hand, lower cost could be an even more attractive criterion for opening a fabless firm.

Cost: Total cost assessment requires a holistic view of costs across the enterprise over time, including direct and indirect cost elements [6–8]. Cost competitiveness is the core strength in order to deliver high quality design using talent from local areas with developed ecosystems, such as Taiwan or China. Both countries are low cost providers of engineering talent. However, costs for software design in semiconductors are higher than those for hardware design. Some of this is due to an increase in applications for multimedia phones, but a scarcity of software designers in West, and availability of clusters of semiconductor industries makers Asian market that are more favorable for fabless firms. It has become increasingly costly to bring people from diverse locations.

Communications could be categorized as transfer of goods, transfer of people, and transfer of ideas. On the basis of the above criteria, in fabless firms there could be movement of people from place to place for face to face communications and transfer of ideas through virtual meetings.

3.2.2.3 Third Level: Sub Criteria

Sub Criteria for Engineering Talent

Proximity to Universities [1]: Excellent graduate and post graduate student are a basic requirement for R&D firms. This is equally applicable to fabless firms, in which highly competent individual are required in order to perform research and product development. Proximity to good universities that are providing programs in relevant fields is thus a critical issue for fabless firms.

Attractive to Skilled Professional: Industries usually cluster around the cities to take advantage of talent pools [1, 9]. Additionally, engineers often look for the cities where they can switch between similar companies. Cities need to have good reputations within the technical community to be attractive for skilled professionals.

Quality of Life: There are different dimensions which can be discussed for quality of life such, as health services, cost of living, housing, personal services, recreational facilities, living environment, educational services, crime, and cultural facilities [1].

Culture of Innovation: Culture of innovation is an important concern and also a significant criteria for managers [10]. Fabless firms require a greater number of people who can do research and can turn research into innovation. For managers, innovation concern for an R&D location is 50 % higher than for experts who are non-managers.

Sub Criteria under Market Development

Proximity to Headquarters: Proximity to headquarters facilitates communication, especially for R&D, marketing, and manufacturing. Intraorganizational dislocation could be a reason for failure of an organization and barriers to innovation [11]. 88 % of American organizations have their R&D facility close to their headquarters. Since fabless firms are involved in R&D activities to greater extent than most other high technology companies, proximity to headquarters is an important factor for site selection.

Proximity to Foundries: Fabless firms rely on contract manufacturers to produce their designs [9]. Fabless semiconductor firms have been home to innovation for many fast growing industries in the computer and communication industries. Proximity to foundries can increase the source of production for competitive products by securing committed capacity and scheduling new products from foundry firms with shorter delivery times.

Access to Venture Capital: Young fabless firms require seed capital in order to establish new locations. The reputation of an area and success of previous entrepreneurs adds value for venture capital possibilities. These locations also attracts entrepreneurship-minded scientists and scholars [12].

Relationship to Competitors and Alliances: Strategic alliances are important criteria for fabless firms [1, 10, 13]. Firms accumulate the experience of local engineers to build up their own technological capabilities. Relationships with competitors increases the competitiveness of innovation and shortens delivery times for new designs. Alliances with equipment vendors improves their process technology.

Shift to Asian Market/ Market Growth Trend: Chip design is a process that creates the greatest value in the electronics industry [6, 14]. It has remained heavily concentrated in the United States. However, increasing domestic market development indicates bigger opportunity for new location of fabless firms to capture market share. Companies like General Electric, Harris Corp., IBM, Mitsubishi and Motorola started shifting their manufacturing activities to less expensive facilities in Taiwan, Malaysia, Singapore or China back in 2002. Table 3.11 in Appendix 1 shows that recently there have been an increasing number of Asian countries with steep growth for fabless firms.

Sub Criteria under Policy

Intellectual Property Protection: This criterion is closely linked with R&D activity [10]. Weak patent regimes could be a point for concern for a fabless firms in order to remain innovative with new designs. Intellectual property protection could play a significant role in deciding the location of fabless firms.

Openness of the Trade Regime: Restrictive trade regimes could be harmful, because of difficulties in activities, such as importing equipment, hiring personnel, and running the operations of a firm [10]. However, open trade regimes could provide a friendly market opportunity. This also helps in recognizing the demand for designs by consumer in that particular area.

Sub Criteria under Communication

Highway Transport: In order to minimize travel time to the location of fabless firms, efficient highway transport system is necessary [1]. Efficient highway transport system would reduce many key inconveniences.

Air Transportation: Face-to-face communications with alliances and financers is a significant activity for a business [1]. However, for fabless firms, transfer of ideas is sometimes difficult. Therefore, transfer of people, coupled with transfer of ideas, could be achieved with good airport transportation systems in an area.

Collaborative Tools: Organizations have become more distributed nowadays [15]. Virtual meetings are taking place most organizations, in order to reduce travel time and costs. Collaborative tools, such as teleconferencing and videoconferencing, remove the necessity travel overseas. Face-to-face meetings with customers, clients, and suppliers could be replaced with these virtual collaborative tools.

3.2.2.4 Fourth Level: Alternatives

Organizations engaged in establishing fabless firms that design semiconductor processes face a multitude of criteria which drive their location selection. These include the availability of researchers, engineers, and scientists who need a location where they can have good quality of life. Professional scientists and engineers want to live in cities where the amenities they value are available [1], costs are reasonable, their intellectual curiosity is fulfilled [10], and good schools are available for their children [1]. These companies also need to look at operating costs as a critical component of site selection and location retention. The other criteria for site selection are the availability university ecosystems and a cluster of other fabless companies and foundries. Government policy and market development trends are also criteria that impact the decision for the location of a fabless firm.

Based on these criteria, we selected six cities geographically dispersed on three continents for comparison. These cities are San Jose, CA; Stockholm, Sweden; Tokyo, Japan; Portland, OR; Hsinchu, Taiwan; and Haifa, Israel.

San Jose and Portland have a cluster of semiconductor industries and first-rate university ecosystems. The culture of innovation in the US is unparalleled in the rest of the world. Innovations originating from the US in the last century have had significant impacts on most of the high technology companies in the world. San Jose has large numbers of existing fabless firms [16]. Portland has also its share of high technology companies. For instance, Intel has its largest development fab in Portland [17].

Stockholm is also a city where many high technology industries operate. It has a developed university ecosystem coupled with quality of life which could attract engineers and scientists; an important criterion for the location of fabless firms [18].

Japan is a third biggest economy in the world, surpassed only by the US and China. Tokyo has many research facilities for semiconductor technology. Japan supplies more than 40 % of global NAND flash memory chips [19]. Japan is also a big supplier of chips that goes into electronic devices, such as smartphones, tablets, and PC's [20]. The culture of innovation, coupled with clusters of universities in Tokyo, makes it a good candidate for fabless firm location [21].

Taiwan is a major area for foundries. Many semiconductor industries operate there. For instance, recently Intel invested in ASPEED Technology Inc., a fabless company, to expand the company's research and development team and extend its cloud computing solutions [22]. Hsinchu has a large cluster of semiconductor companies, due to the presence of foundries, such as TSMC, UMC, Vanguard, and Win Semiconductors [13].

Israel is a country where many semiconductor companies are located. Among the three types semiconductor industries, fabless firms are most prominent in Israel [23]. Multinationals companies, such as Intel, Marvell, Freescale (Motorola), Texas Instruments, and Broadcom have operations in Israel. In addition, established local firms include Mellanox, DSP Group, EZchip, and Broadlight. Start-up firms, like Siverge, Siano, Altair, and Anobit are also involved in the fabless industry. Israel's policies are also conducive for high tech companies [23]. Therefore, Haifa was selected as one leading alternative for fabless firm location in this study.

3.3 Data Collection

After finalizing the model, the data quantification survey instrument was created to investigate the opinions of nine experts from different organizations in the semiconductor industry. Six responses were received. There were three experts from Intel, one expert from academia (who used to be a VP at Samsung), one expert from LSI logic, and one expert from Applied Materials. This panel of experts was chosen due to their wide knowledge, and for their many years of experience in the field of semiconductor manufacturing. The experts worked for companies that vary in size and represent the global cultural diversity. The low level of inconsistency in pairwise comparisons indicates that most of these experts in the field of semiconductor research and production generally were in agreement with each other these issues for the location of fabless firms.

The survey consisted of pairwise comparisons of the five criteria with respect to the objectives, pairwise comparison of the sub-criteria with respect to the criteria, and pairwise comparisons for the alternatives with respect to the sub-criteria. Some of the sub-criteria were removed from the survey based on the experts' feedback.

3.3.1 Quantitative Sub Criteria and Assumptions

Sub-criteria "Proximity to University"

The number of universities in each city is a quantitative criterion which can be found through online researches [24–29]. A scoring method was applied to evaluate each alternative, as shown below:

- For cities with 1–10 universities, the score is 1.0.
- For cities with 11–20 universities, the score is 2.0.
- For more than 20 universities, the score is 3.0.

Alternatives	San Jose	Stockholm	Tokyo	Portland	Hsinchu	Haifa
Score	3	2	3	2	3	1

Sub-criteria "Proximity to Foundries"

Similar to universities, the number of foundries in each alternative region can be found through online research [30]. Stockholm does not have any foundries. However, assumptions have been made because of the definition for the sub-criteria. Germany is the closest country to Sweden that has two foundries. Similarly, for Tokyo, Hsinchu and Haifa, the total number of foundries in their respective countries has been considered. However, for San Jose and Portland, the total number of foundries has been considered for these metro areas themselves.

Alternatives	San Jose	Stockholm	Tokyo	Portland	Hsinchu	Haifa
Number of foundries	2	2	3	2	4	2

Sub-criteria "Market Growth Trend"

The growth rate of each alternative is calculated based on the growth rate of each country [23, 31]. Countries such as Taiwan, Japan, Israel, and Sweden are relatively smaller than the United States. Therefore, each country's growth in fabless semiconductor design is considered based on growth within the city.

US	Europe	Japan	Taiwan	Israel
8.5 %	2 %	2 %	15 %	5 %

Table 3.1 Cost criterion

Cost	Alternatives						Sum
	San Jose	Stockholm	Tokyo	Portland	Hsinchu	Haifa	
Mean	0.20	0.23	0.22	0.15	0.09	0.10	
Reverse	5.0	4.3	4.5	6.7	11.1	10.0	41.7
Normalized	0.12	0.10	0.11	0.16	0.27	0.24	

Sub-criteria "Relationship with competitor/Alliances"

All the alternatives are scored equally due to fact that this sub criteria depends heavily on the type of company. The company could be either a small firm investing in a new area, looking for a low cost region; or it could be a large firm, looking for market presence in a new area. It could be a new firm that is looking for established ecosystems for education and suppliers, along with low cost. Therefore, in this study, all the alternatives were believed to have equal weight with respect to this sub-criterion, since there is no basis to correlate cities with "Relationship with Competitor/Alliances."

Reverse Criteria "Cost"

The survey for the cost criteria is based on the premise that, the higher the cost, the higher the score. As a result, the most expensive alternative gets the highest score. But, the nature of the location selection problem requires that the cheapest alternative get the highest score. To manage this, one more "reverse" step is inserted before the normalization step. A reciprocal is calculated for the original score from the pairwise comparison of each alternative. The results are normalized as the final score for the cost criterion (Table 3.1).

$$Reverse\ Score = \frac{1}{Original\ Score} \quad for\ every\ alternative$$

3.4 Results and Discussions

After gathering the expert inputs from the survey, the model produced the follow results for the six alternatives: Hsinchu, 18.8 %; San Jose, 18.6 %; and Portland, 18.4 %. Looking at these numbers, it is clear that these three cities received nearly equal weight for fabless firm location. Hsinchu is rated by the experts as a low cost location. Additionally, Hsinchu is very similar to San Jose and Portland for criteria such as engineering talent, quality of life, and openness to trade. San Jose has the highest score for sub-criteria including engineering talent, access to venture capital, and openness to trade. Portland has the highest score for quality of life and highway transportation. For other sub-criteria, San Jose and Portland are very close, except access to venture capital (Fig. 3.3, Tables 3.2 and 3.3).

3 Location Selection for Fabless Firms

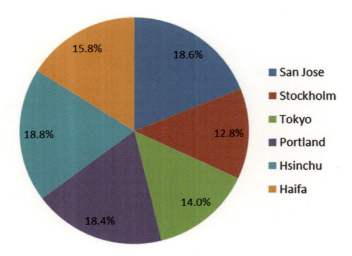

Fig. 3.3 Alternatives for fabless location

Table 3.2 Performance for alternatives

Performance Level	Alternatives
High	San Jose
	Portland
	Hsinchu
Medium	Haifa
Low	Stockholm
	Tokyo

Table 3.3 Final score of alternatives on all criteria and sub-criteria

Sub-criteria	San Jose	Stockholm	Tokyo	Portland	Hsinchu	Haifa
Proximity to university	0.0085	0.0057	0.0085	0.0057	0.0085	0.0028
Attract skilled professional	0.0239	0.0105	0.0134	0.0211	0.0144	0.0115
Quality of life	0.0178	0.0151	0.0098	0.0214	0.0160	0.0089
Culture of innovation	0.0246	0.0113	0.0164	0.0235	0.0133	0.0133
Proximity to headquarter	0.0017	0.0017	0.0017	0.0017	0.0017	0.0017
Proximity to foundries	0.0034	0.0034	0.0051	0.0034	0.0067	0.0034
Competitor/alliances	0.0033	0.0033	0.0033	0.0033	0.0033	0.0033
Access to venture capital	0.0122	0.0026	0.0053	0.0053	0.0033	0.0043
Market growth trend	0.0048	0.0011	0.0011	0.0048	0.0085	0.0028
Openness to trade	0.0140	0.0098	0.0112	0.0126	0.0119	0.0112
Intellectual property	0.0152	0.0144	0.0144	0.0144	0.0088	0.0120
Cost	0.0336	0.0292	0.0305	0.0448	0.0747	0.0672
Highway transport	0.0099	0.0089	0.0079	0.0109	0.0064	0.0054
Air transport	0.0091	0.0073	0.0086	0.0077	0.0068	0.0059
Collaborative tools	0.0038	0.0035	0.0033	0.0038	0.0035	0.0042
Final score	0.186	0.128	0.140	0.184	0.188	0.158

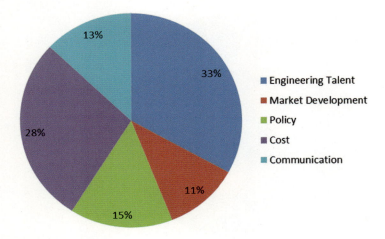

Fig. 3.4 Criteria score

Table 3.4 Final weights using HDM model for criteria and sub criteria

Criteria	Engineering talent	Market development	Policy	Cost	Communication
	0.33	0.11	0.15	*0.28*	0.13
Sub-criteria under each criteria	Proximity to university 0.0396	Proximity to headquarter 0.0099	Openness to trade 0.07		Highway transport 0.0494
	Attract skilled professional 0.0957	Proximity to foundries 0.0253	Intellectual property 0.08		Air transport 0.0455
	Quality of life 0.0891	Competitor/alliances 0.0198			Collaborative tools **0.0221**
	Culture of innovation *0.1023*	Access to venture capital *0.0330*			
		Market growth trend 0.0231			

Our model predicts that engineering talent has the highest impact on location selection for a fabless firm (33 %). Cost (28 %) is the second most important criterion. Market Development, Policy, and Communications have relatively similar impacts (Fig. 3.4).

Results for Criteria and Sub-Criteria

Table 3.4 shows that Culture of Innovation has the highest score under engineering talent. This makes sense, as fabless industries require highly educated personnel in order to be competitive. As far as market development is concerned, the results indicates that access to venture capital has the highest score for a new firm.

Table 3.5 Impact level of sub criteria

Impact level	Sub-criteria
High	Attract skilled professional
	Quality of life
	Culture of innovation
Medium	Openness to trade
	Intellectual property
	Highway transport
	Air transport
	Proximity to university
Low	Proximity to headquarter
	Proximity to foundries
	Competitor/alliances
	Access to venture capital
	Market growth trend
	Collaborative tools

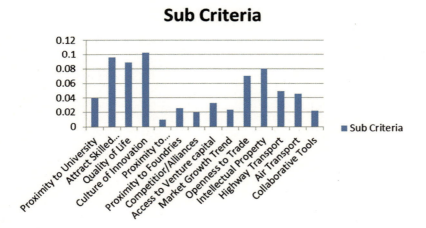

Fig. 3.5 Comparisons of sub criteria

However, for an established firm, proximity to foundries and market growth trend would be more important. This is especially true with shift in Asian markets to take advantage of well-established ecosystem for fabless firms, such as supply chain systems for tools required for fabless firms and availability of innovative engineering talent at low cost. Under policy, openness to trade and intellectual property are equally important. It is surprising to see that collaborative tools have the lowest score under communications. The low score of collaborative tools is indicator of the fact that even in today's information age, face-to-face meetings still remain the preferred mode of communication. Table 3.5 summarizes the impact level of each sub criteria on each alternative (Fig. 3.5).

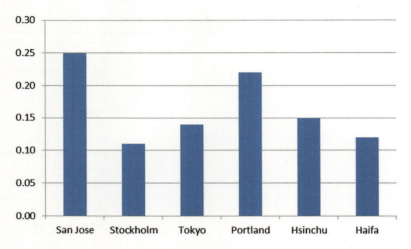

Fig. 3.6 Alternative score of sub-criteria—attracting skilled professional

Table 3.6 Performance of alternatives for sub-criteria of attract skilled professional

Performance level	Alternatives
High	San Jose
	Portland
Medium	Tokyo
	Hsinchu
Low	Stockholm
	Haifa

Horizontal Comparison of Alternatives by Sub-criteria

Attract skilled professionals: San Jose and Portland are the cities that have high ratings for attracting skilled professional. Stockholm and Haifa have the lowest rating in this sub-criterion. It is surprising to see that Stockholm, which is in the second position for higher education, has a low level of attraction for skilled professionals. There are a number of semiconductor firms that have opened branches in Stockholm due to its clean environment and excellent higher education system. However, the expert panel did not believe that this will be a sufficient reason to attract professional labor compared to Portland or San Jose. Israel also has several well-known universities. However, political instability makes it less attractive for many skilled professional (Fig. 3.6, Table 3.6).

Culture of Innovation: Portland and San Jose performed the best in this sub-criterion, followed by Tokyo, Haifa and Hsinchu. Stockholm performed poorly compared to other alternatives. Number of higher education institutions is a factor which makes a city a good candidate for culture of innovation. Therefore, it is surprising to see these results for culture of innovation. Portland has score of 2 for number of universities, which indicates that it has 10–20 higher education institutions.

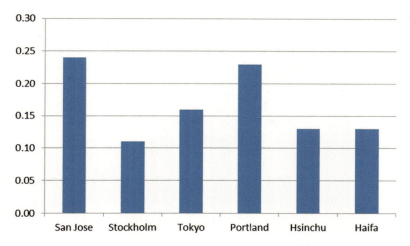

Fig. 3.7 Alternative score of sub-criteria culture of innovation

Table 3.7 Performance of alternatives under the sub-criteria of culture of innovation

Performance level	Alternatives
High	San Jose
	Portland
Medium	Tokyo
Low	Stockholm
	Hsinchu
	Haifa

Tokyo, Hsinchu, and San Jose have score of 3, indicating that all three cities have more than 20 higher education institutions in the surrounding area (Fig. 3.7, Table 3.7).

Access to Venture Capital: San Jose tops the list for access to venture capital. Tokyo and Portland are medium level. Others are slightly lower. There is a decreasing trend for accessing venture capital in the US, due to the economic crisis that began in 2008. However, a culture of innovation and a good higher education system, makes the US more attractive compared to any other country in the world. It will be interesting to see the results after 5–10 years. Will San Jose and Portland will remain at top in the list? (Fig. 3.8, Table 3.8)

Cost: Hsinchu and Haifa are at the top of the list of preferred locations with regards to the cost criteria for the location of fabless firms. Hsinchu has low cost labor pools, low cost of living, and established ecosystems for the semiconductor industry. Haifa has low costs and good relationships with the US, but political instability and the threat of war in the region tend to make this city less attractive for fabless firms (Fig. 3.9, Table 3.9).

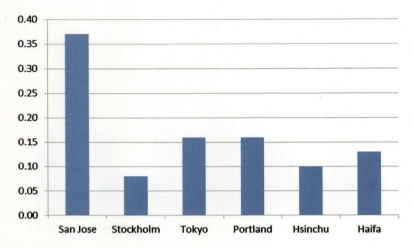

Fig. 3.8 Alternative score of sub-criteria—access to venture capital

Table 3.8 Performance of alternatives under the sub-criteria of venture capital

Performance level	Alternatives
High	San Jose
Medium	Tokyo
	Portland
Low	Stockholm
	Hsinchu
	Haifa

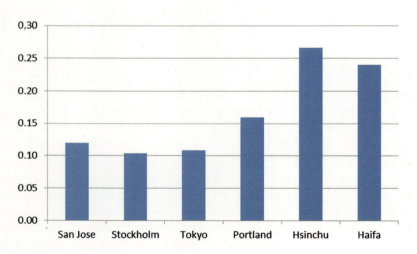

Fig. 3.9 Alternative score of criteria—cost

3   Location Selection for Fabless Firms

Table 3.9 Performance of alternatives under the sub-criteria of—cost

Performance level	Alternatives
High	Hsinchu
	Haifa
Medium	Portland
Low	Stockholm
	San Jose
	Tokyo

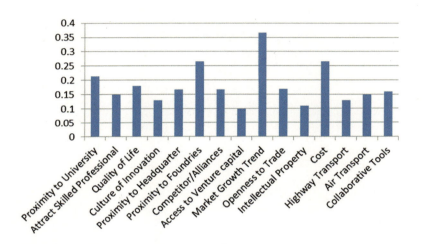

Fig. 3.10 Scores of all sub-criteria for alternative—Hsinchu

Vertical Comparison of Sub-criteria for each Alternative (Fig. 3.10)

Hsinchu: Leads the list. It has excellent Market Growth, Costs, and Proximity to Foundries. The disadvantages are Access to Venture capital and Intellectual Property (Fig. 3.11).

San Jose: Is excellent in the Access to Venture capital sub-criteria and also performs well in Culture of Innovation, Attracting Skilled Professionals, Proximity to Universities, and the sub-criteria under Policy and Communications. Cost is the only point that has a low rating (Fig. 3.12).

Portland: has good scores for all the sub-criteria and performs well in Attracting Skilled Professionals, Quality of Life, Culture of Innovation, and Highway Transport.

- Appendix 2 has detailed analyses of the horizontal and vertical comparisons for all the other alternatives.
- Appendix 3 includes results for pairwise comparisons done by experts.

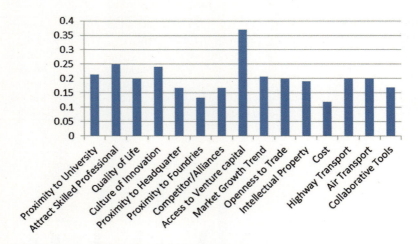

Fig. 3.11 Scores of all sub-criteria for alternative San Jose

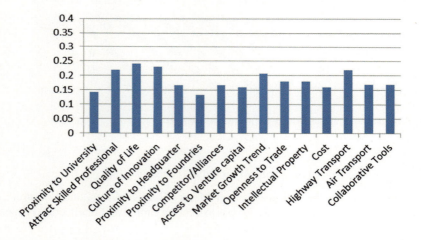

Fig. 3.12 Scores of all sub-criteria for alternative—Portland

3.5 Conclusions

The following conclusions have been made as a result of this research study:

- Engineering Talent has the highest impact on location selection for fabless firms. This will be a challenge for less developed countries, as they have limited pools of talented scientists and engineers. It also indicates that companies have to

locate fabless firms where professional employees are available or in places where there are high incentives for professional employees to relocate.
- Cost has the second highest impact on location selection for fables firms. Countries that want to attract fabless firms should find a way to reduce the cost of operations for these firms, including possible tax incentives.
- In the Market Development category, access to venture capital is the most important criteria for the selection of a location for fabless firms. However, this will vary according to the size of the company and also if a firm is either a new entrant or existing player in the fabless industry.
- Under the Policy criterion, both its sub-criteria had equal weight. However, it is important to note that Openness to Trade and Intellectual Property Protection are extremely import for securing innovative ideas and remaining competitive.
- In the Communications category, Highway and Air Transportation had higher weight than Collaboration Tools for site selection, which indicates that face-to-face communication is preferred over virtual meetings for process design and R&D activities.

Overall, the sub-criteria Attracting Skilled Professionals, Quality of Life, and Culture of Innovation have the highest impact. The sub-criteria Openness to Trade, Intellectual Property Protection, Highway Transport, Air Transport, and Proximity to Universities have medium level impacts. The sub-criteria Proximity to Headquarters, Proximity to Foundries, "Competitor/Alliances", Access to Venture Capital, Market Growth Trend, and Collaborative Tools had low impacts on the final alternatives.

This research created a generic model for location selection of a fabless semiconductor R&D firm. It used an Hierarchical Decision Model. This paper has discussed a detailed decision making process by identifying five key criteria and sub-criteria. However, the results may vary from company to company, according to the priorities that are set and by changing the weights for criteria and sub-criteria. There is trend in the semiconductor R&D industry for companies to prefer to acquire a firm, rather than to create a new firm. This gives leverage for existing market, time, money saved on human resources, and utilization of existing supply chains. Cost is an important criterion, which has the second highest weight in this research. This research could be extended with a separate model for the Cost criteria, which could be used for Make or Buy Decisions for fabless firms. This research provides a tool for decision making process for fabless firms which could be readily applied for any fabless company using experts in their respective fields.

Appendix 1

Table 3.10 Top 20 semiconductor sales leaders

2011 rank	2010 rank	2009 rank	Company	Headquarters	2009 ($M)	2010 ($M)	% Change	2011 ($M)	% Change
1	1	1	Qualcomm	U.S.	6,409	7,204	12 %	9,910	38 %
2	2	3	Broadcom	U.S.	4,271	6,589	54 %	7,160	9 %
3	3	2	AMD	U.S.	5,403	6,494	20 %	6,568	1 %
4	6	5	Nvidia	U.S.	3,151	3,575	13 %	3,939	10 %
5	4	6	Marvell	U.S.	2,690	3,592	34 %	3,445	−4 %
6	5	4	MediaTek	Taiwan	3,500	3,590	3 %	2,969	−17 %
7	7	7	Xilinx	U.S.	1,699	2,311	36 %	2,269	−2 %
8	8	10	Altera	U.S.	1,196	1,954	63 %	2,064	6 %
9	9	8	LSI Corp.	U.S.	1,422	1,616	14 %	2,042	26 %
10	10	11	Avago	Singapore	858	1,187	38 %	1,341	13 %
11	13	12	MStar	Taiwan	838	1,065	27 %	1,220	15 %
12	11	13	Novatek	Taiwan	819	1,149	40 %	1,198	4 %
13	15	16	CSR	Europe	601	801	33 %	845	5 %
14	12	9	ST-Ericsson[a]	Europe	1,263	1,146	−9 %	825	−28 %
15	16	15	Realtek	Taiwan	615	706	15 %	742	5 %
16	17	17	HiSilicon	China	572	652	14 %	710	9 %
17	27	67	Spreadtrum	China	105	346	230 %	674	95 %
18	19	19	PMC-Sierra	U.S.	496	635	28 %	654	3 %
19	18	14	Himax	Taiwan	693	643	−7 %	633	−2 %
20	21	–	Lantiq	Europe	0	550	N/A	540	−2 %
21	33	30	Dialog	Europe	218	297	36 %	527	77 %
22	22	21	Silicon Labs	U.S.	441	494	12 %	492	0 %
23	29	20	MegaChips	Japan	445	337	−24 %	456	35 %
24	23	24	Semtech	U.S.	254	403	59 %	438	9 %
25	24	23	SMSC	U.S.	283	397	40 %	415	5 %
Top 25 total		–	–		38,242	47,733	25 %	52,076	9 %
Non-top 25 fabless		–	–		11,091	14,781	33 %	12,811	−13 %
Total fabless		–	–		49,333	62,514	27 %	64,887	4 %

Source: Company reports, IC Insights' *Strategic Reviews Database*
[a]Represents the 50 % share not accounted for by ST

3 Location Selection for Fabless Firms

Table 3.11 Top 20 semiconductor sales leaders ranked by growth

2011 rank	Company	Headquarters	2010 ($M)	2011 ($M)	% Change
1	Spreadtrum	China	346	674	95 %
2	Dialog	Europe	297	527	77 %
3	Qualcomm	U.S.	7,204	9,910	38 %
4	MegaChips	Japan	337	456	35 %
5	LSI Crop.	U.S.	1,616	2,042	26 %
6	MStar	Taiwan	1,065	1,220	15 %
7	Avago	Singapore	1,187	1,341	13 %
8	Nvidia	U.S.	3,575	3,939	10 %
9	HiSilicon	China	652	710	9 %
10	Semtech	U.S.	403	438	9 %
11	Broadcom	U.S.	6,589	7,160	9 %
12	Altera	U.S.	1,954	2,064	6 %
13	CSR	Europe	801	845	5 %
14	Realtek	Taiwan	706	742	5 %
15	SMSC	U.S.	397	415	5 %
16	Novatek	Taiwan	1,149	1,198	4 %
17	PMC-Sierra	U.S.	635	654	3 %
18	AMD	U.S.	6,494	6,568	1 %
19	Silicon Labs	U.S.	494	492	0 %
20	Himax	Taiwan	643	633	−2 %
21	Xilinx	U.S.	2,311	2,269	−2 %
22	Langiq	Europe	550	540	−2 %
23	Marvell	U.S.	3,592	3,445	−4 %
24	MediaTek	Taiwan	3,590	2,969	−17 %
25	ST-Ericsson[a]	Europe	1,146	825	−28 %
Top 25 total			47,733	52,076	9 %
Non-top 25 fabless			14,781	12,811	−13 %
Total fabless			62,514	64,887	4 %

Source: Company reports, IC Insights' *Strategic Reviews Database*
[a]Represents the 50 % share not accounted for by ST

Appendix 2: Results of Alternative Score on Criteria and Sub-Criteria

Alternatives have been analyzed horizontally and vertically in order to know the how each sub criteria is affecting alternatives. Additionally effect on alternative will be different if location for fabless R&D firm are changed due to change in weight for criteria and sub criteria

Quality of Life: Portland exceeds all other alternatives. Due to Portland's environment friendly policies and good available infrastructure for semiconductor makes this city perfect candidate for quality of life. San Jose, Stockholm and Hsinchu are at medium level. Tokyo and Haifa are low in the sub-criteria. Tokyo low rating could be attributed to high density population, and high cost of living (Fig. 3.13, Table 3.12).

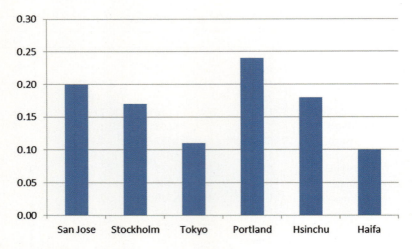

Fig. 3.13 Alternative score of sub-criteria quality of life

Table 3.12 Performance of alternatives under the sub-criteria of quality of life

Performance level	Alternatives
High	Portland
Medium	San Jose
	Stockholm
	Hsinchu
Low	Haifa
	Tokyo

Market Growth Trend: Hsinchu exceeds all others greatly. Portland and San Jose are nearly at same level. Performance of Stockholm and Haifa is not very attractive for opening a fabless firm in these cities (Fig. 3.14, Table 3.13).

Intellectual Property: Hsinchu rated lowest. Haifa is the second lowest alternative. Others are on the same level in performance in the sub-criteria (Fig. 3.15, Table 3.14).

Vertical Comparison of Sub-criteria for each Alternative (Fig. 3.16)

Stockholm: is good at Quality of Life, Competitor/Alliances, Intellectual Property and Transportation, but suffers a low score in Market Growth Trend, Access to Venture capital and Cost (Fig. 3.17).

Tokyo: is good at sub-criteria of Proximity to University and Proximity to Foundries, but has the disadvantages of low Market Growth Trend and low Quality of Life and Expensive Cost (Fig. 3.18).

Haifa: in Israel is low in majority of sub-criteria, but gets a good score in Cost.

3 Location Selection for Fabless Firms

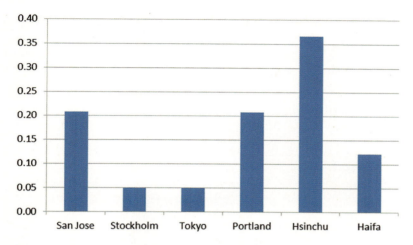

Fig. 3.14 Alternative score of sub-criteria market growth trend

Table 3.13 Performance of alternatives under the sub-criteria of market growth trend

Performance level	Alternatives
High	Hsinchu
Medium	San Jose
	Portland
Low	Stockholm
	Tokyo
	Haifa

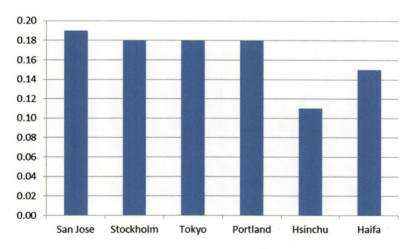

Fig. 3.15 Alternative score of sub-criteria intellectual property

Table 3.14 Performance of alternatives under the sub-criteria of intellectual property

Performance level	Alternatives
High	San Jose
	Portland
	Stockholm
	Tokyo
Medium	Haifa
Low	Hsinchu

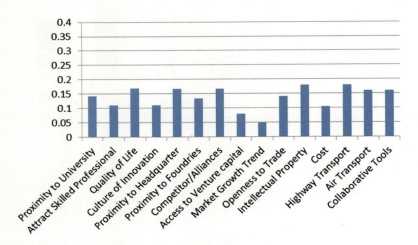

Fig. 3.16 Scores of all sub-criteria for alternative Stockholm

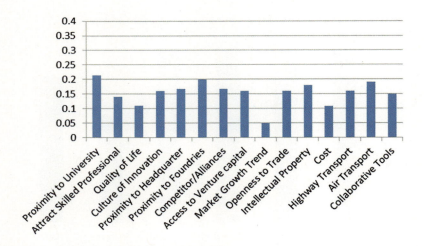

Fig. 3.17 Scores of all sub-criteria for alternative Tokyo

3 Location Selection for Fabless Firms

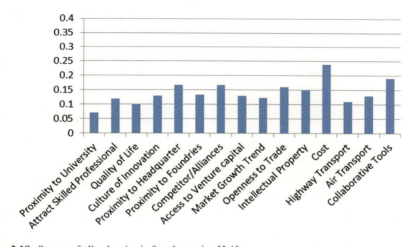

Fig. 3.18 Scores of all sub-criteria for alternative Haifa

Appendix 3: Pairwise Comparisons by Experts: PCM Software Results

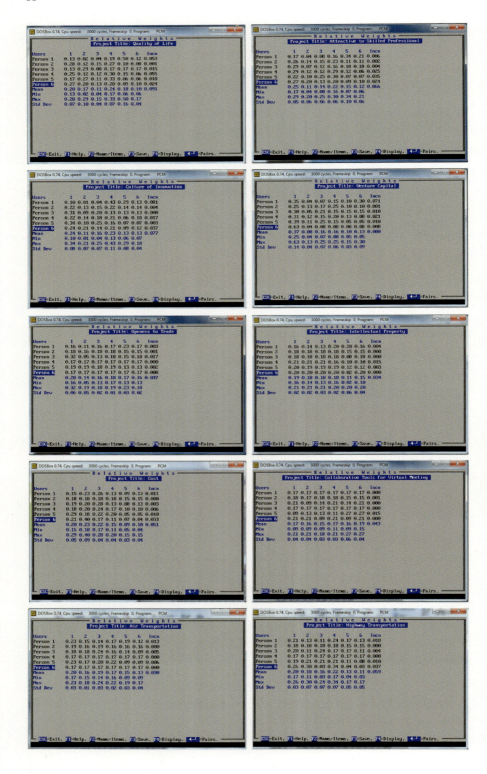

References

1. Malecki EJ (1987) The R&D location decision of the firm "creative" regions—a survey. Technovation 6:205–222
2. Manners D (2011) Fabless sector underperforms. http://www.electronicsweekly.com. Accessed 26 April 2011 [Online]. http://www.electronicsweekly.com/blogs/david-manners-semiconductor-blog/2011/04/fabless-sector-underperforms.html. Accessed 31 May 2012
3. U.S.-based Companies Held 12 of the Top 25 Fabless Spots in 2011. IC Insights (12 April 2012) [Online]. http://www.icinsights.com/news/bulletins/USbased-Companies-Held-12-Of-The-Top-25-Fabless-Spots-In-2011/. Accessed 31 May 2012
4. Qualcomm opens office in Cairo (6 May 2012) [Online]. http://comm.ae/qualcomm-opens-office-in-cairo/. Accessed 31 May 2012
5. Culpan T (2011) MediaTek to acquire Ralink in NT$18.2 billion share swap. Bloomberg 16 March 2011 [Online]. http://www.bloomberg.com/news/2011-03-16/mediatek-to-acquire-ralink-in-nt-18-2-billion-share-swap-1-.html. Accessed 31 May 2012
6. Ernst D (2005) Complexity and internationalisation of innovation: why is chip design moving to Asia? Int J Innov Manag 9(1):47–73
7. Rebuilding business strategies of genera electric machinery/ semiconductor manufacturers. Economic and Industrial Research Department Development Bank of Japan, Japan, 2008
8. Brummet RL, Flamholtz EG, Pyle WC (1968) Human resource management—a challenge for accountants. Account Rev 43(2):217–224
9. Macher JT, Mowery DC (2008) Innovation in global industries: U.S. firms. National Academic Press, Washington, DC
10. Kumar N (2001) Determinants of location of overseas R&D activity of multinational enterprises: the case of US and Japanese corporations. Res Policy 30:159–174
11. Brown C, Linden G (2005) Offshoring in the semiconductor industry: a historical perspective. University of California Berkeley, Berkeley
12. Balconi M, Fontana R (2011) Entry and innovation: an analysis of the fabless semiconductor business. Small Bus Econ 37(1):87–106
13. Yuan BJC, Chang CY, Lo MC (1998) Strategies of semiconductor industry in Taiwan. IEMC\'98 Proc., pp. 541–545
14. Breznick A (2002) U.S. chip industry continues struggle. 18 November 2002 [Online]. http://www.bizjournals.com/triangle/stories/2002/11/18/focus2.html. Accessed 20 May 2012
15. Maznevski ML, Chudoba KM (2000) Bridging space over time: global virtual team dynamics and effectiveness. Organ Sci 11(5):473–492
16. Fabless Manufacturing. Boogar lists [Online]. http://www.boogar.com/resources/electronics/fabless_manufacturing5.htm. Accessed 10 May 2012
17. Intel Global Manufacturing Facts [Online]. http://download.intel.com/newsroom/kits/22nm/pdfs/Global-Intel-Manufacturing_FactSheet.pdf. Accessed 10 May 2012
18. Ranking reveals world's top countries for higher education. Wall Street J (10 May 2012) [Online]. http://www.marketwatch.com/story/ranking-reveals-worlds-top-countries-for-higher-education-2012-05-10. Accessed 10 May 2012
19. Burt J (2011) IT & network infrastructure news. eWeek (11 May 2011) [Online]. http://www.eweek.com/c/a/IT-Infrastructure/Japan-Earthquake-Could-Be-Blow-to-Semiconductor-Industry-157469/. Accessed 10 May 2012
20. Fan CY (2011), Applying K-means clustering and technology map in Asia Pacific-semiconductors industry analysis. IEEE. pp. 1043–1047
21. Kishi T, Takemura M, Kadohira T (2011) Nanotechnology and green innovation in Japan. Strength Fract Complex 7:5–12
22. ASPEED receives funding led by intel capital (30 Aug 2011) [Online]. http://www.intel.com/pressroom/capital/pdfs/PortcoAspeed.pdf. Accessed 10 June 2012
23. Gradman S (2011) An overview of the Israeli semiconductor industry. October 2011 [Online]. http://il.mofcom.gov.cn/accessory/201201/1326371902770.pdf. Accessed 10 May 2012

24. List of colleges and universities in California [Online]. http://en.wikipedia.org/wiki/List_of_colleges_and_universities_in_California. Accessed 5 June 2012
25. List of colleges and universities in Oregon [Online]. http://en.wikipedia.org/wiki/List_of_colleges_and_universities_in_Oregon. Accessed 5 June 2012
26. List of universities in Sweden [Online]. http://en.wikipedia.org/wiki/List_of_universities_in_Sweden. Accessed 5 June 2012
27. List of Israeli universities and colleges [Online]. http://en.wikipedia.org/wiki/List_of_universities_in_Israel. Accessed 5 June 2012
28. List of universities in Japan [Online]. http://en.wikipedia.org/wiki/List_of_universities_in_Japan. Accessed 5 June 2012
29. List of universities in Taiwan [Online]. http://en.wikipedia.org/wiki/List_of_universities_in_Taiwan. Accessed 5 June 2012
30. List of semiconductor fabrication plants [Online]. http://en.wikipedia.org/wiki/List_of_semiconductor_fabrication_plants. Accessed 5 June 2012
31. U.S.-based Companies Held 12 of the Top 25 Fabless Spots in 2011 [Online]. http://www.icinsights.com/news/bulletins/USbased-Companies-Held-12-Of-The-Top-25-Fabless-Spots-In-2011/. Accessed 20 April 2012

Part II
Technology Evaluation

Chapter 4
FCC Regulation of the Video Navigation Device Industry: A Benefit-Cost Analysis Using a Dynamic Kano Concept

Jay Justice

Abstract In the 2010 National Broadband Plan, the FCC recommended a new regulatory course for video navigation devices to replace the ineffective CableCARD regime. The vertically integrated nature of these consumer devices has dampened the progress of innovation and specifications for which consumers should come to expect. This paper frames the features and specifications of video navigation devices in a dynamic Kano concept that qualitatively estimates customer demands before and after regulation. Through an integrated benefit-cost model, industry analysts can quantitatively gauge whether society will benefit from further FCC orders, or if these actions simply drive up the rates and complexity for consumer access.

4.1 Introduction

On March 16, 2010, the Federal Communications Commission (FCC) released "Connecting America: The National Broadband Plan", which recommends the framework that the United States should pursue in the upcoming decade in order to develop and strengthen its broadband infrastructure. The FCC created this plan as required by Congress' American Recovery and Reinvestment Act of 2009 in order to stimulate a struggling economy. The Plan lays out goals and recommends government regulation on the broadband industry that can help achieve those objectives. One of the potential problems that the FCC has identified, and intends to correct, is the lack of competition in the video navigation device industry. In the Code of Federal Regulations (CFR), the FCC defines video navigation devices as "Devices such as converter boxes, interactive communications equipment, and other equipment used by consumers to access multichannel video programming and other

---

J. Justice (✉)
Intel Corp., Santa Clara, CA, USA
e-mail: jay.justice@intel.com

services offered over multi-channel video programming systems" [9]. The Broadband Plan further defines these devices "to broadly include set-top boxes, digital video recorders (DVRs), and home theater PCs (HTPCs)" [10]. With the influx of continued innovation, this set of devices will likely grow to include items such as video game consoles [31] and other hybrid multipurpose tuners.

Citing innovation through competition in other industries, such as personal computers and mobile devices, the FCC notes a lack of similar advancement in the set-top box market. They reference Dell'Oro Group's Set-Top Box report, which shows that as of 2008, only two set-top box manufacturers (Cisco and Motorola) controlled 92 % of the market [10]. The FCC derives that this problem is an effect of the overwhelming majority of consumers leasing rather than buying devices. The Plan says that between July 2007 and November 2009, 97 % of deployed set-top boxes, were leased through Multi-channel Video Programming Distributors (MVPDs), rather than purchased from a retail source. As of August 2009, CableLabs has only certified 11 set-top boxes in accordance with FCC regulations. When comparing this number to the over 850 mobile devices that manufactures have certified for wireless networks, there appears to be obstacles that prevent potential competitors from entering the market.

The FCC has made two recommendations in the Broadband Plan to stimulate competition in video navigation devices. The first of these is Recommendation 4.12, which proposes a new video distribution topology, which would require a residential gateway to separate the MVPDs network from the consumer's home video network. The second of these is Recommendation 4.13, which calls for fixes to current CableCARD issues that industry members must implement before the end of 2010. This paper presents a benefit-cost model that the FCC and other industry participants can use to predict and measure the effectiveness of these new recommendations. We also analyze the shortcomings of the initial integration ban and offer recommendations to prevent similar deficiencies from negatively effecting further legislation.

4.2 Literature Review

Many academic papers cover the effects of regulation and standardization on the telecommunications industry. The sizable capital investment costs are a tremendous barrier for market entry. Several papers analyze government mandated functional and structural separation designed to promote competition. Howell, Meade, and O'Connor correlate structural separation in telecommunications companies to the experiences of electric utilities [23]. Meidan reviews the effects that standardization entities have had on the market for customer premise equipment (specifically the effects of CableLab's standardization of the cable modem) [4]. This paper concentrates on a market entry barrier that has arisen from a vertical integration scheme. De Fontenay and Gans show how vertical integration by a monopolist allows greater industry profits at the expense of consumers [19]. Buehler and Schmutzler demonstrate how vertical integration produces an "intimidation" effect, which leads to decreased investment from competitors [2]. Contrary to the results of anti-vertical integration research, Lee, Katayama, and Oh conclude that consumers are "always better off" with a vertically integrated telecommunications market [25]. Matsubayashi uses a telecommunications example to show that in some conditions, vertical integration can be beneficial to both the consumer and the integrated firm [27]. While many academic papers have concentrated on various aspects of vertical integration, few have concentrated specifically on the market for video navigation devices.

Kano, Takahashi, and Tsuji first published their customer demand attribute model in the mid 1980s. Many publications have expanded on this idea often calling it the "Kano Model" or "Kano Concept" [24]. Maltzer et al. contrasts the differences between the linear and symmetrical Importance-Performance Analysis with the non-linear and asymmetrical Kano Model [28]. Li et al. recommends using a combination of the Kano model along with AHP, rough set theory, and scale method to determine the most precise priority of customer requirements [26]. Xu et al. introduces an analytical Kano (A-Kano) model that includes indices for further quantification of customer needs [38]. Little research has attempted to quantify the value gained by society when Kano analysis indicates increasing customer demands over time.

4.3 Framing Regulation Using a Dynamic Kano Concept

The Kano concept captures the consumer's voice/mind at a single moment in time. This paper asserts that in a competitive high-tech market, customers will expect increased feature sets and better specifications over time. This will result in a downward shift of features and specifications in the Kano diagram, which is indicative of value gained by society. This paper defines this idea or progressive customer demands as a Dynamic Kano Concept. When market strategies (such as vertical integration) stifle competition, the progress of the Kano shift dampens. The goal of regulating these markets is to promote competition, which if successful, will lead to a downward shift in the Kano diagram and ultimately provide society with value. A comparison between this value gained and the cost of regulation becomes the basis for the benefit-cost model presented in this paper.

One can categorize the features of a video navigation device using the Dynamic Kano Concept. In this graph (Fig. 4.1), the horizontal axis represents the fulfillment of product requirements. The vertical axis measures customer satisfaction. The three plots on the graph represent the relationships between different levels of customer needs and implementation of the corresponding features. Basic Needs are the unspoken features that customers expect to have. If those features are present in the product, the customer is indifferent. However, if the features are missing, the customer becomes quickly dissatisfied. Performance Needs are the features and specifications that are directly proportional to customer satisfaction. When the device

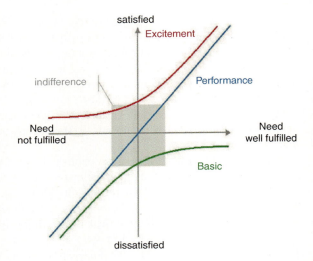

Fig. 4.1 The Kano concept

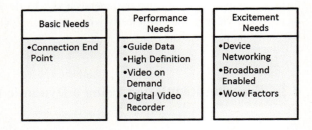

Fig. 4.2 Customer needs for a video navigation device

manufacturer implements these features, they rely on the Voice of the Customer as a guideline. Excitement Needs are the differentiators that will draw consumers to a product based on innovation that they did not expect. If device manufacturers implement these features, end users quickly become satisfied. However, if those features are not present, the consumer is indifferent. Both Basic Needs and Excitement Needs rely on the Mind of the Customer's unspoken and unknown demands.

Through the evaluation of video navigation devices currently available to consumers, eight primary features stand out as differentiators for providing value (Fig. 4.2). Only one feature fulfills the consumer's Basic Needs. As a Connection End Point, the device must be able to receive, tune, and decrypt the services to which the customer subscribed. Different audio and video connectors may be available depending on the other features of the box, but consumers will expect common connectors for their given application.

This paper argues that four features currently define the consumer's Performance Needs. Guide Data is a feature that gathers information from either the Internet or the MVPD's middleware to show a table of upcoming programs. Users often prefer different implementations of the guide data between devices, such as the ability to show more programs and channels per screen, or the option to view data for only the channels to which they have subscribed. Some inexpensive devices such as Digital Transport Adapters (DTAs) do not include any Guide Data. The ability to display High Definition programming is the second Performance Needs feature. Although nearly all television sets currently available at retail can support HD broadcasts, a large deployment of Standard Definition sets remain that have no need for a HD device. As SD sets become less prevalent, High Definition should become a basic feature on set-tops. The FCC currently only allows SD DTAs as an exception to the integration ban, but many service providers are currently lobbying for an exception on HD DTAs as well. Video on Demand (VOD) is a third Performance Needs feature that allows consumers to access free or pay-per-view content from the service provider. The fees for VOD access are generally included with a provider's subscription fees. This feature does not exist in DTAs, and will not be available in retail devices until the industry deploys a reliable two-way standard. The fourth Performance Needs feature is a Digital Video Recorder (DVR). The specifications and features of a DVR can vary in different ways, such as storage capacity, number of tuners, and commercial skipping. As of this writing, most leased DVRs can only record around 20 h of HD content, with no option for expansion. Many consumers willing to purchase retail DVRs point to this lack of capacity as one of the primary reasons for making the investment.

This paper points to three Excitement Needs features that are rarely available in leased devices. First, Device Networking is the ability to share video, music, and other multimedia files between devices in the home. This includes sharing recorded content from a DVR to other set-tops or computers in a residence, as well as playing files from a networked storage device to the set-top. Some leased devices include partially implemented Device Networking, but recorded content is only limited to other leased devices. The second Excitement Needs feature this paper identifies is having a Broadband Enabled device. This includes the ability to access features such as Internet Video, Social Networking, and Web Browsing directly from the video navigation device. While retail manufacturers have begun integrating these features in their devices, they are mostly absent in leased devices. Integrating video navigation devices with broadband features appear to be a primary driver in the Broadband Plan's recommendations. This paper will generalize the final Excitement Needs feature as Wow Factors. This funnel for innovation seeks to integrate features that consumers are not expecting. Such features may integrate the device with HD optical drives, gaming systems, home automation, and future technologies that only exist in innovator's imaginations at present. As competition drives innovation, Wow Factors will differentiate products and provide society with options that were not previously available.

Customer needs are dynamic, and when it comes to technology, they often change at a swift pace. Over time, Excitement Needs become Performance Needs, and Performance Needs become Basic Needs. The FCC correctly identifies that the changing Voice and Mind of the Customer is largely ignored in the current leased Set-top Box market. Other than choosing some basic features of the device to lease or switching between service providers, there is little power that consumers have when choosing between specifications or advanced feature sets.

Fig. 4.3 Changes in customer satisfaction in competitive market

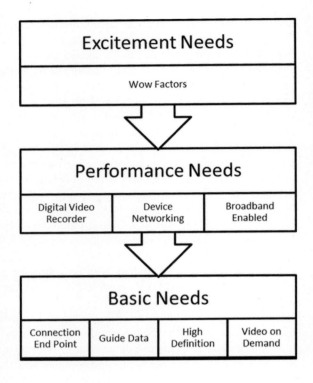

The competition between MVPDs has not been enough to spur innovation that will keep up with the shifting demands of consumers. Although the CableCARD regime has failed to correct this problem, the FCC's new recommendations show they are determined to drive competition and innovation using regulation.

A successful implementation of FCC regulations will result in more choices in video navigation devices on the market that fulfill increasingly demanding customer needs (Fig. 4.3). The funnel of Wow Factors generically fulfill Excitement Needs, so they will continue to appear in novel products and some of those features will catch on to become performance factors. Customers should expect the choice to pay for different levels of Device Networking and Broadband Enabled features as these options move from being Excitement Needs to becoming Performance Needs. While DVR features and specifications will likely continue to fulfill Performance Needs, greater competition will result in more choice in specifications such as larger storage capacities. Guide Data, High Definition, and Video on Demand should become customer expectations to fulfill Basic Needs with FCC regulation. The FCC has already made one unsuccessful attempt with Tru2Way to address the issue of retail devices not having access to the MVPD's VOD or Guide Data. As the population of SD-only consumers continues to fade away, HD capable devices will persist in becoming the expected standard. All these factors provide a qualitative framework for measuring whether society benefits from FCC regulation.

4.4 Benefit-Cost Analysis

The FCC appears to primarily drive its' decision to regulate the video navigation device industry on heuristic ideals rather than a data driven approach. While the FCC intends that regulation will lead to increased competition and innovation, they present no underlying data model to predict the outcomes of their actions. If the FCC is incorrect in their assumptions, consumers ultimately absorb the fees associated with regulation without any benefit to their video lifestyle. Since the initial attempt by the FCC has proven unsuccessful, they should provide analysis that is more concrete before subjecting the industry and public to an additional round of regulation. This paper provides a model that both the FCC and industry participants can use to analyze projected costs and balance those against estimated benefits to society.

A Benefit-Cost Analysis weighs the potential advantages that society gains from a project against the cost accumulated while implementing the solution. When the Benefit/Cost ratio is greater than 1, the analysis justifies the regulatory agency's actions. If the Benefit/Cost ratio is less than 1, the benefits to society do not justify the regulation. In this analysis, the Benefits are the value gained by society from the regulation and the Costs are the burden to society added by projects driven due to regulation.

$$\textit{Benefit to Cost Ratio for FCC Regulation} = \frac{\textit{Value of Regulation}}{\textit{Cost of Regulation}} \quad (4.1)$$

We will define the Value of Regulation as the summation of the product of the Consumer Value per Device multiplied by the number of devices sold for each type of device. This paper argues that there are currently four primary types of devices: SD STBs, HD STBs, SD DVRs, and HD DVRs. Regulation will result in a different value to society for each device type. Market analysis reports will predict the number of devices sold for each category.

$$\textit{Value of Regulation} = \sum_{k=0}^{n} \left(\textit{Consumer Value per Device}\right)_k * \left(\textit{Devices Sold}\right)_k \quad (4.2)$$

The Consumer Value per Device is the difference between the product of the pre-regulated Annual Lease Fees and the Expected Life of the Device (in years) minus the cost of the Retail Device. The Annual Lease Fees are the typical unregulated costs that a consumer would spend during the course of a year for a given device. The Expected Life in Years is the average length of time that the consumer would use the retail product. If the user is unable to switch the device between competing service types (Cable to Satellite to IPTV), the expected life in years would decrease. In addition, new encoding formats or communication protocols would have an adverse effect on the expected life. The product of the Annual Lease Fees and the

$$Consumer\ Value\ for\ HD\ STB = \$120 * 4 - \$100 = \$380$$

$$Annual\ Value\ of\ HD\ STB\ Regulation$$
$$= Consumer\ Value\ per\ HD\ STB * HD\ STBs\ Sold$$
$$= \$380 * 10{,}000{,}000 = \$3.8\ Billion$$

Fig. 4.4 HD STB example

$$Consumer\ Value\ for\ HD\ DVR = \$192 * 4 - \$500 = \$268$$
$$Annual\ Value\ of\ HD\ DVR\ Regulation$$
$$= Consumer\ Value\ per\ HD\ DVR * HD\ DVRs\ Sold$$
$$= \$268 * 13{,}000{,}000 = \$3.5\ Billion$$

Fig. 4.5 HD DVR example

Expected Life in Years would be the amount the consumer would spend if they chose the leasing route. The Device Cost is the amount a consumer would pay at retail for the owned device. A positive Consumer Value per Device means that buying a device at retail is less expensive. A negative value means that leasing is less expensive.

$$\begin{aligned}Consumer\ &Value\ per\ Device \\ &= (Annual\ Lease\ Fees)*(Expected\ Life\ in\ Years) \\ &\quad - Device\ Cost\end{aligned} \quad (4.3)$$

The first example (Fig. 4.4) implementing these equations centers on the Consumer Value per Device of HD Set-top Boxes (non-DVR). If a device were being leased for $10 per month, the Annual Lease Fee would be $120 ($10 per month * 12 months per year). For this example, we estimate that the Expected Life of the device will be 4 years. Consumers can currently purchase retail HD STBs for tuning broadband video for around $100. It is reasonable to believe that a competitive market would likely yield similar STBs at this Device Cost. Plugging the data for this example into Eq. 4.3 shows that each HD STB purchased at retail would have a $380 value to consumers versus leasing a similar product. If retailers sell ten million HD STBs in the United States in a given year, the regulation will lead to a $3.8 Billion annual savings to American consumers.

In the second example (Fig. 4.5), we will look at the value of regulating HD DVRs. For devices the MVPD leases for $16 per month, the Annual Lease Fee is $192. We will continue to use an Expected Life of 4 years in this example. Unlike HD STBs, there is currently a selection (albeit limited) of HD DVRs available to purchase at retail. The current prices of these devices start around $600 and increase based on specifications. Retail prices will likely need to drop further before consumers switch from their current month-to-month payments. Some sales models offer the device for a lower amount, but then add a monthly

4 FCC Regulation of the Video Navigation Device Industry... 81

>Annual Benefit of FCC Regulation
>= Annual Value of HD STB Regulation
>+ Annual Value of HD DVR Regulation
>= $3.8 Billion + $3.5 Billion = $7.3 Billion

Fig. 4.6 Total annual benefit to society

fee that brings the cost of ownership significantly higher than the original purchase price. Analysts would likely expect that the average sales price of a HD DVR would decrease as more competitors enter the market. For the purposes of this example, we will assume that regulation leads to an average device cost of $500. Once again using Eq. 4.3, we calculate that the ability to purchase a HD DVR has a $268 value to consumers. If analysts expect retailers to sell 13 million HD DVRs in the United States over the period of a year, this will capture an annual savings of $3.5 Billion for consumers (Fig. 4.5).

This paper will not include example calculations for standard definition devices. Although regulation may lead to a short-term value to American consumers, the rapidly decaying sales of these devices will not affect the Benefits to Cost Ratio as dramatically as high definition devices. By the time FCC regulation could affect the retail market, there would likely be very little demand. Hence, the estimated annual benefit of FCC regulation in these examples would be the sum of the annual values for each HD device, which is $7.3 Billion (Fig. 4.6).

The FCC and industry standards organizations funded by device manufacturers and MVPDs would directly pay for the costs association with this regulation. Indirectly, American television consumers and taxpayers will pay these costs. Taxpayers directly fund the FCC as they run the legal and administrative branches of the program. Device manufacturers will look to recoup their investments through future sales of video navigation devices. Since leased devices will become a competitive market, MVPDs will face the harshest direct financial shortfall in the form of lost revenue streams from device leases. Higher subscription fees may be a result as MVPDs look to recover some of their losses, but competition between service providers should keep prices from dramatic increases. The ability for consumers to purchase their own video navigation devices could have a positive effect on service subscription revenues. Many subscribers that have discontinued services may return to MVPDs because of the newly perceived value from a competitive device market. Alternately, many users may choose to stick with their subscriptions rather than letting them go, because they have already made an investment in devices that have not yet reached an acceptable payback period.

Analysts could use the costs associated with implementing the CableCARD regime to estimate what the cost will be to employ the AllVid solution. The NCTA estimates that the cable industry has invested around $1 billion in order to meet the FCC's original integration ban [21]. The figures for the AllVid solution would likely be higher since they intend to include all devices for Satellite and Telephone video services along with the cable industry. Comparing these costs to the figures we used in the previous examples would yield a Benefit to Cost Ratio of at least 2, and that only includes the benefits accrued in the first year.

4.5 CableCARD: The First Round of FCC Regulation

Recommendation 4.13:

> On an expedited basis, the FCC should adopt rules for cable operators to fix certain CableCARD issues while development of the gateway device functionality progresses. Adoption of these rules should be completed in the fall of 2010.

For a better understanding of Recommendation 4.13, it is crucial to review the previous attempt the FCC made to stimulate competition in the video navigation device market. The Telecommunications Act of 1996 was the first time Congress made a major revamping of the Communications Act of 1934. The stated goal of the 1996 modification was "to promote competition and reduce regulation in order to secure lower prices and higher quality services for American telecommunications consumers and encourage the rapid deployment of new telecommunications technologies" [33]. Section 629 specifically addresses the competitive availability of MVPD services and the devices used to navigate those services. This section states that the FCC will work with industry standard-setting organizations to adopt the regulations that will assure competition of services and devices, but will not prevent MVPDs from continuing to offer devices as long as MVPDs state charges to consumers separate from video access fees and do not subsidize those charges. This section also states that deregulation would only occur when the FCC deems the market for MVPD services and video navigation devices is competitive or the elimination of the regulations would be in the public's best interest.

Pursuant to the Telecommunications Act of 1996, the FCC issued a Notice of Proposed Rule Making (NPRM) [12] and began collecting comments from standards organizations, MVPDs, device manufacturers, and device retailers. In June 1998, the FCC filed a Report and Order [15] stating the new rules for the video navigation device market based on the comments and replies they received from the previous NPRM. The FCC encapsulated these rules in Title 47 CFR 76.1204 [6]. The primary goal outlined in the Order was to separate the conditional access functions from the other purposes of the device. The Order laid out two deadlines. By July 1, 2000, MVPDs must make necessary changes to their networks to separate security functions from Customer Premises Equipment (CPE). By January 1, 2005, MVPDs could no longer distribute new CPE with integrated security functions. The Order states that after the industry reaches the first deadline, the FCC will re-evaluate the second deadline to assess the appropriateness given the market conditions.

The FCC included an exception in the 1998 Order that exempted video navigation devices for Direct Broadcast Satellite (DBS) systems (Cable's biggest competitor). The Commission reasoned that DBS consumers could already purchase their equipment through unaffiliated sources, while the DBS supplier manages security by providing a Smart Card separate from the device. The other differentiator is that DBS equipment can be operated anywhere in the continental United States, while security integrated cable equipment can only be operated on the Cable provider's network. Thus, if the customer moves to a different city, they can still use their currently owned DBS equipment.

One of the advantages in the timing of the new rules was that most MVPDs were at the beginning of an analog to digital video transition. The shift to digital would allow the video industry to use their RF bandwidth more efficiently, and ultimately provide consumers with new technologies and services such as High Definition video and Video on Demand. This changeover required all new equipment in video distribution networks. The original Report and Order did not exclude analog equipment from the integration ban. The FCC received requests for reconsideration from multiple sources, stating that the inclusion of analog equipment in the new separable security rules would only slow down the digital-to-analog conversion. In May 1999, the FCC released an Order on Reconsideration excluding analog equipment from the integration ban [13].

Through a series of meetings concluding in 2002 held by the National Cable and Telecommunications Association (NCTA) and the Consumer Electronics Association (CEA), the country's largest cable Multiple Service Operators (MSOs) and consumer electronics manufacturers came to a consensus regarding a video delivery technology model for unidirectional digital cable products that would satisfy the FCC's integration ban. In December 2002, the group submitted a Memorandum of Understanding (MOU) to the FCC, which details a "plug and play" system, based on the Dynamic Feedback Arrangement Scrambling Technique (DFAST) and associated licensing agreements [37]. The agreement makes CableLabs the administrative body responsible for governing DFAST licenses. The MOU states that the DFAST licensing fee is not to exceed $5,000 and continued discussions will take place toward the development of a bidirectional receiver specification. The FCC took note of the voluntary cooperation between the consumer electronics and cable television industries and responded with a Further Notice of Proposed Rulemaking in January 2003 [8]. In this NPRM, the FCC sought comments on the proposed DFAST system and associated licensing model. In September 2003, the FCC released a Second Report and Order, in which they labeled the new technology "Digital Cable Ready" [16]. The Report and Order also adopts the unidirectional model proposed in the previous MOU. The corresponding request for comments sought to validate if CableLabs was the appropriate administrative body for the new Point of Deployment (POD) specifications, since the country's largest cable providers fund the organization. This document is also the first time that the FCC recognizes that, for marketing reasons, the NCTA will now refer to all POD devices as "CableCARDs", which is a term trademarked by CableLabs and standardized in SCTE28, SCTE 41, and CEA-679.

Due to the prospect of an agreement between the NCTA and CEA for a bi-directional access model, the FCC felt it was in the public's best interest to delay the deadline on the integration ban. In June 2003, they amended CFR 76.1204 to delay the deadline 18 months to July 1, 2006 [17]. By 2005, the video industry began considering a software-based conditional access solution that would prevent the need for the physical CableCARD. This new solution promised to reduce the complexity of content security and lower the prospective cost to implement the integration ban. The FCC considered the arguments of industry lobbyists and amended

CFR 76.1204 once again to provide another 12-month extension to the deadline [18]. On July 1, 2007, 30 months after the original deadline, the FCC's integration ban took effect.

Since the initial FCC Report and Order, various entities have submitted challenges against the new rules to the United States Court of Appeals. In April 2000, General Instrument Corporation (later bought by Motorola) petitions that syntax concerning the term "converter boxes" in the FCC order "jeopardizes" the security of the MVPD's network (GIC v FCC and USA [36] USCA 98-1420). In May 2006, Charter Communications made a similar argument as General Instrument concerning the use of the term "other equipment" (CC and A/NC v FCC and USA [34] USCA 05-123). In April 2008, Comcast Corporation petitioned that the integration ban is slowing down the analog-to-digital transition due to the increased expense of "low-cost integrated boxes" (CC v FCC and USA [35] USCA 07-144). In all three of these cases, the Court of Appeals found reason to deny the petitioner's requests.

In December 2009, the National Cable and Telecommunications Association provided a summary report to the FCC on the availability of commercial navigation devices [22]. This report states that since the integration ban took effect, the top ten MSOs serving 90 % of the nation's cable subscribers have deployed over 17,751,000 operator-owned set-tops, while only deploying about 456,000 CableCARDs. With an estimated program cost of around 1 billion dollars, the cost of the CableCARD initiative averages about $2,200 per card deployed. In April 2010, the FCC released a Fourth Further Notice of Proposed Rulemaking [7]. In this notice, the FCC states that the CableCARD regime has not been successful in meeting the goals of the integration ban and they propose rules for fixing those shortcomings until a successor technology becomes available.

4.6 The Failure of CableCARD Leads to the AllVid Approach

Recommendation 4.12:

The FCC should initiate a proceeding to ensure that all multichannel video programming distributors (MVPDs) install a gateway device or equivalent functionality in all new subscriber homes and in all homes requiring replacement set-top boxes, starting on or before Dec. 31, 2012.

As part of the FCC's Omnibus Broadband Initiative (OBI) to gather data and views in preparation for the National Broadband Plan, they released a Public Notice in December 2009 searching for comments on video device innovation [14]. Rather than stressing the competitive gap in the video devices market, the FCC focuses on the potential innovations that could take advantage of the continually evolving broadband network. The Notice includes several indicators that the FCC will now begin considering successor technologies to CableCARD. This document poses four questions to its potential audience:

1. "What technological and market-based limitations keep retail video devices from accessing all forms of video content that consumers want to watch?"
2. "Would a retail market for network agnostic video devices spur broadband use and adoption and achieve Section 629's goal of a competitive navigation device market for all MVPDs?"
3. "Can the home broadband service model be adapted to allow video networks to connect and interact with home video network devices such as televisions, DVRs, and Home Theater PCs via a multimedia home networking standard?"
4. "What obstacles stand in the way of video convergence?"

In April 2010, the FCC released a Notice of Inquiry [11] requesting comments as they embarked on their plans to meet the National Broadband Plan recommendation 4.12. The Commission cites two reasons why the retail market for video navigation devices is still not competitive. The first reason is that there are few added features in retail devices to make up for the loss of bidirectional features available in integrated devices such as Video on Demand. The second reason is that consumers cannot move their devices between competing MVPDs. In order to address these CableCARD shortcomings, the Notice introduces the AllVid concept, which treats the MVPD network as a separate entity from the consumer's home delivery system. The document labels consumer devices that can connect between different MVPD services, "smart video devices". There are two different topologies presented in the AllVid concept for connecting smart video devices to an MVPD network. In one approach, each device has an individual adapter. In the other method, consumers would use a single adapter gateway to connect all devices in the home to the MVPD network. The document specifies that the methodology that becomes the standard will become the successor to CableCARD.

FCC Commissioners Copps, McDowell, Clyburn and Baker, have all admitted that the CableCARD initiative has proven to be unsuccessful [1, 3, 5, 29]. McDowell points out that technological innovation has outpaced the government's ability to keep up, so every time they have approached convergence on a decision, a promising technology on the horizon has prevented mandates from occurring. Chairman Julius Genachowski goes on to list four advantages that the proposed AllVid concept will have over the current CableCARD regime [20]. First, the new technology platform will enable consumer electronics manufacturers to create devices that can transparently switch between competing video services. Second, the added separation of the gateway allows MVPDs to innovate and upgrade their distribution systems without the need for new customer premises equipment. Third, consumers will benefit from increased choice driven by growing competition in the retail CPE market. Finally, the AllVid concept promotes increased broadband adoption in the spirit of the National Broadband Plan as innovation continues to link television services with Internet content.

This paper points to four reasons why the initial integration ban failed and analyzes what the responsible parties need to do in the second round of rulemaking to avoid the same pitfalls. The first reason why the CableCARD regime failed is that the resultant devices were unable to switch between major service access types. When the FCC released satellite operators from the integration ban, the resultant regulation only affected devices connecting to cable networks. Since the devices have no requirement for modular components to switch between networks, consumers forfeit provider flexibility when they purchase a retail device. In the second round of rulemaking, the FCC should ensure the new solution has modular components that can easily switch between networks.

The second problem encountered by the CableCARD platform was that the pace of technology advancement outpaced the FCC's tempo for decision-making. Every time the FCC approached a major milestone in the initiative, a disruptive technology loomed on the horizon with much greater potential than the current plan provides. Device manufacturers and consumers waited for a stable platform to materialize, while the FCC continually pushed back deadlines while considering new technologies. Rather than trying to evolve regulation at the same rate as technology progression, the FCC should consider incremental phases that would coincide with the lifecycle of products. A standards regulation phase would provide both device manufacturers and consumers with a predictable window of when new products will enter the market and how long before forthcoming platforms will become available.

The third issue that hindered the acceptance of CableCARD is consumer education on the platform. Cable companies have developed complex pricing and installation schemes that may have indirectly discouraged customers from purchasing their own equipment. Due to a lack of marketing, the general population is often unaware of the availability of customer owned devices and the advantages they provide. Ultimately, the FCC needs to create a budget for promoting education on future regulatory platforms, rather than relying on device retailers and Cable companies to provide the details.

The final predicament this paper identifies as a source of failure for the CableCARD regime is that the regulation resulted in little availability for inexpensive retail devices. Manufacturers and retailers may have overestimated what consumers are willing to pay for customer owned equipment. Televisions with integrated devices made a brief appearance on the market, but the added feature generally included a significant price jump. Smaller profit margins were likely a distracter for manufacturers in pursuing a low-cost limited-feature product line. Since there was never a truly competitive market, lower-cost models never surfaced. The FCC has no rights to price control in a competitive market, but they can encourage consumers through incentives such as the digital converter coupon they provided during the analog-to-digital transition. These types of incentives may entice more device manufacturers to enter the market, jumpstarting a more competitive atmosphere.

4.7 Further Cost Considerations

Whether IPTV, Cable, or Satellite, most MVPD systems rely on a distributed software model for the user's experience. Middleware is the software platform that integrates several interfaces in the digital head-end, such as linear video content, conditional access, Video on Demand, Operations Support Systems (OSS), and the customer premises equipment. Rather than having the software on the customer's set-top communicate directly to these various devices in the head-end, the set-top downloads applications from a middleware server for user interfacing. This means that for middleware-centric equipment, the manufacturer of the navigation device does not develop most of the user-interface software running on the equipment. Some of these applications include, the interactive program guide, DVR controls, channel mapping, automated pay-per-view billing, and other innovative services. In international DVB standards, the Multimedia Home Platform (MHP) is a set of software standards developed to integrate these functions. From CableLabs, the OpenCable Applications Platform (OCAP) serves this function. OCAP standards are largely based on MHP [32].

One example of a proprietary middleware system is Microsoft's MediaRoom, which they first announced for IPTV distributors in June 2007. Rather than implementing MHP or OCAP, Microsoft developed a new open platform called Mediaroom Presentation Framework. With these ASP.net-based libraries, developers can use familiar tools to port internet experiences such as social networking and email directly to the video navigation device [30]. Similar to MHP and OCAP, this is another vehicle for innovation, but there may be some confusion over what the industry driver is for third party companies to take advantage of this platform.

On the smart-phone platform, both Apple and Google have already developed successful business models where users buy into a device and then continually add to and update the applications that run on the device through micro-transactions supported by either advertising or fee-per-application. Porting a similar model to the middleware solution, would likely result in a wave of third-party innovation that the FCC so desperately desires.

Consumers rarely realize their equipment leasing fees also go toward the capital and service fees of the middleware and other head-end equipment, such as the conditional access system. Due to the analog-to-digital transition and the latest changeover to MPEG-4 AVC encoding, most MVPD's have recently completed major overhauls of their head-end equipment and are several years away from the break-even point. Depending on the MSO's coverage area, the capital expenditure for a middleware platform can reach several hundred dollars per customer. One of the problems facing the MVPD, is where do they charge for the middleware expenses? If they bundle those charges with the service, they are forcing consumers that have purchased their own video navigation device to pay for something for which they are not using. Thus, the charges go to consumers through their lease prices on the set-top. If Motorola or Cisco were to sell their devices directly to customers, then there would probably still have to be a separate charge for use of the middleware and other head-end equipment. This capital expenditure model justifies agreements for device manufacturers to distribute their set-tops only through the MVPD (rather than making them available at retail outlets).

For many consumers, the question remains, why are they unable to purchase the same piece of equipment from their service provider that they are currently leasing? Logically, if a consumer is willing to spend several hundred upfront dollars on the equipment, they will likely feel obligated to stick with that service provider until they near an acceptable break-even point on their original investment. This break-even point would likely occur long after the customer's introductory pricing has expired, which would keep consumers from swapping between different service providers every other year. For example, a new customer may sign up for a discounted bundle that expires after 12 months. This same customer has the option to purchase an HD-DVR for $400 or lease it for $16 per month. When the price of their services returns to the normal billing amount after a year, they may wish to switch to a competitor in order to start a new 12 months of discounted fees. If the customer has leased their equipment, they will have spent a total of $192 on equipment fees. However, if the customer purchased the same piece of equipment, they will likely recognize that they are $202 in the hole. This argument would be analogous to saying that the inability to purchase equipment leads to increased customer choices in most service pricing schemes that MVPDs currently implement (thus, less customer loyalty). In addition, if the equipment were to malfunction after a warranty period, it would be up to the customer to fix or replace, rather than the service provider. Furthermore, if new technologies emerged such as encoding algorithms or media formats that require new hardware, the consumer would be stuck without the upgrades until they decide to lease or purchase a new box. These three reasons would all be strategic reasons why MVPDs should provide a sales option to consumers for video navigation devices. Providing this option would not directly address the FCC's integration ban goals, but would likely quell some of the unrest surrounding the MVPD control of video navigation equipment.

4.8 Conclusion

This paper uses a Dynamic Kano Concept to perform a qualitative analysis on video navigation device features, to point out how regulation should result in innovation leading to greater consumer value and satisfaction. The concurrent benefit-cost analysis compares the value gained by society through regulation against the cost of the initiative. While the results of this analysis may justify regulation, poorly executed rulemaking will not achieve those results. We have seen how the CableCARD initiative was defensible, but ultimately unsuccessful. The FCC must avoid similar pitfalls in this second round of rulemaking to achieve the expected results from this analysis.

The technology behind the AllVid gateway will continue evolving over the next several months. The currently proposed deadline may seem aggressive, given the length of time that the CableCARD initiative took and the increased complexity.

In order to meet these deadlines, agreement between the private and public sectors on the platform's details must come about expeditiously. Those interested in further research should continue monitoring FCC proceeding 97-80, "Implementation of the [33], Commercial Availability of Navigation Devices", to monitor the major proposals and agreements between the affected parties as the initiative continues to evolve. Given the cooperative spirit between device manufacturer and MVPDs while developing CableCARD, and the overall drive of the FCC to increase competition, the industry will likely implement the AllVid concept. The remaining questions are how long will it take, and will it truly lead to increased device competition and innovation.

References

1. Baker M (2010) Statement of commissioner Meredith A. Baker. Filed with FCC on 21 April 2010
2. Buehler S, Schmutzler A (2004) Intimidating competitors—endogenous vertical integration and downstream investment in successive oligopoly. http://ideas.repec.org/p/soz/wpaper/0409.html. Accessed 14 Jan 2013
3. Clyburn M (2010) Statement of commissioner Mignon L. Clyburn. Filed with FCC on 21 April 2010
4. Cohen-Meidan M (2013) The effects of standardization process on competition: an event study of the standardization process in the US cable modem market. Telecommun Pol, 31(10–11): 619–631. http://econpapers.repec.org/RePEc:eee:telpol:v:31:y::i:10-11:p:619-631. Accessed 14 Jan 2013
5. Copps M (2010) Statement of commissioner Michael J. Copps. Filed with FCC on 21 April 2010
6. FCC (2010a) Code of federal regulations title 47 Part 76 Section 1204 (47CFR76.1204). Multichannel video and cable television service—availability of equipment performing conditional access or security functions
7. FCC (2010b) Fourth further notice of proposed rulemaking, FCC 10-61, 21 April 2010
8. FCC (2003a) Further notice of proposed rulemaking, FCC 03-3, 10 Jan 2003
9. FCC (2004) Multichannel Video and cable television service—definitions. 47CFR76.1200
10. FCC (2010c) National broadband plan—download the plan. pp.18–66. Available at: http://www.broadband.gov/download-plan/
11. FCC (2010c) Notice of inquiry. FCC 10-60, 21 April 2010
12. FCC (1997) Notice of proposed rulemaking, FCC 97-53, 20 Feb 1997
13. FCC (1999) Order on Reconsideration, FCC 99-95, 14 May 1999
14. FCC (2009) Public notice: comment sought on video device innovation. NBP Public Notice #27, DA09-2519, 2009 Dec 3
15. FCC (1998). Report and order, FCC 98-116, 24 June 1998
16. FCC (2003b) Second report and order and second further notice of proposed rulemaking, FCC 03-225, 9 Oct 2003
17. Federal Register (2003) Commercial availability of navigation devices. 68, No. 116: 35818–35822
18. Federal Register (2005) Commercial availability of navigation devices. 70, No. 11: 36040–36053
19. De Fontenay CC, Gans JS (2004) Can vertical integration by a monopsonist harm consumer welfare? Int J Ind Org 22(6):821–34. http://ideas.repec.org/a/eee/indorg/v22y2004i6p821-834.html. Accessed 14 Jan 2013

20. Genachowski J (2010) Statement of Chairman Julius Genachowski. Filed with FCC on 21 April 2010
21. Goldberg N (VP and General Counsel for NCTA), E.P. to F.S.M.H.D. (2009a) FCC filing (Nov.18, 2009).
22. Goldberg N (VP and General Counsel for NCTA), E.P. to F.S.M.H.D., 2009b. Letter to FCC Secretary Marlene H. Dortch "Re: CS Docket No. 97-80 (Commercial Availability of Navigation Devices)". Filed with FCC on 22 Dec 2009
23. Howell B, Meade R, O'Connor S (2010) Structural separation versus vertical integration: lessons for telecommunications from electricity reforms. Telecommun Pol 34(7):392–403. http://dl.acm.org/citation.cfm?id=1833895.1833910. Accessed 14 Jan 2013
24. Kano N, Seraku N, Takahashi F, Tsuji S (1984) Attractive quality and must-be quality. Hinshitsu (Quality, J Jpn Soc Quality Control) 14(2):39–48
25. Lee D, Katayama H, Oh H (1997) Vertical integration in the telecommunication market. Comput Ind Eng 33(3–4):841–844. http://dx.doi.org/10.1016/S0360-8352(97)00262-3. Accessed 14 Jan 2013
26. Li Y et al (2009) An integrated method of rough set, Kano's model and AHP for rating customer requirements' final importance. Expert Syst Appl 36(3):7045–7053. http://dx.doi.org/10.1016/j.eswa.2008.08.036. Accessed 14 Jan 2013
27. Matsubayashi N (2013) Price and quality competition: the effect of differentiation and vertical integration. Eur J Oper Res. Elsevier. http://www.amazon.com/Price-quality-competition-differentiation-integration/dp/B000PDT0VW. Accessed 14 Jan 2013
28. Matzler K et al (2004) The asymmetric relationship between attribute-level performance and overall customer satisfaction: a reconsideration of the importance–performance analysis. Ind Mark Manag 33(4):271–277. http://www.researchgate.net/publication/222673151_The_asymmetric_relationship_between_attribute-level_performance_and_overall_customer_satisfaction_a_reconsideration_of_the_importanceperformance_analysis. Accessed 5 Nov 2012
29. McDowell R (2010) Statement of commissioner Rober M. McDowell. Filed with FCC on 21 April 2010
30. Microsoft Corp (2010b) Microsoft mediaroom: platform and extensibility FAQ. http://www.microsoft.com/Mediaroom/LearnMore/Briefs/PlatformExtensibilityFAQ.aspx. Last accessed 11 May 2010
31. Roshak T et al (2008) Television viewing on gaming consoles. U.S. Patent no. 20080167128, 10 July 2008
32. Simpson W (2006) Video over IP: a practical guide to technology and applications. Focal Press, Amsterdam, Boston. http://www.amazon.com/Video-Over-Technology-Applications-Professional/dp/0240805577. Accessed 14 Jan 2013
33. Telecommunications Act of 1996 (1996) Pub. LA., p. No. 104–104, 110 Stat. 56
34. USCA (United States Court of Appeals) (2006) Charter Communications, Inc. and Advance/Newhouse Communications v. Federal Communications Commission and United States of America. , No. 05-123
35. USCA (United States Court of Appeals) (2008) Comcast Corporation v. Federal Communications Commission and United States of America. No. 07-144
36. USCA (United States Court of Appeals) (2000) General Instrument Corporation v. Federal Communications Commission and United States of America. 98-1420
37. Vogel C et al (2002) Memorandum of understanding among cable MSOs and consumer electronics manufacturers, Filed in FCC Docket 97-80 on 12 Dec 2002
38. Xu Q et al (2009) An analytical Kano model for customer need analysis. http://journals.ohiolink.edu/ejc/article.cgi?issn=0142694x&issue=v30i0001&article=87_aakmfcna. Accessed 14 Jan 2013

Chapter 5
Technology Assessment: Energy Storage Technologies for Wind Power Generation

Yulianto Suharto and Tugrul U. Daim

Abstract The problems in generation imbalance for wind power require multi-criteria analysis for the decision makers. In addition to the required multi-criteria analysis, there is also a problem of uncertainty inherent in future changes as a result of interdependence among these criteria. To counter this two problems, this paper describes a systematic approach of Bayesian causal maps and systematic probability generation method. Bayesian causal maps, which is built from causal maps, is used to develop a proposed framework on scenario-based assessment of energy storage technologies for wind power generation. Causal maps provides a rich representation of ideas, through the modeling of complex structures, representing the chain of arguments, as networks.

5.1 Introduction

In real-world decision problems, decision maker(s) utilize the available information for making analysis and reaching decisions. The process of data analysis and decision making can be considered as a prediction process. Liu [1] mentions that in general there are two types of tasks in this process, which require different approaches: (1) classification which is concerned with deciding the nature of a

---

A prior version of this paper was included in the conference Proceedings of PICMET 2013.

Y. Suharto (✉)
Portland State University, Portland, OR, USA
e-mail: ysuharto@gmail.com

T.U. Daim
Engineering and Technology Management Department,
Portland State University, Portland, OR, USA
e-mail: tugrul@etm.pdx.edu

particular system given the features, which usually produces *labeled* data; (2) causal prediction which is concerned with the effect of the changes in some features to some other features in the system.

The later process—causal prediction—is more related to causal inference which is concerned with the degree of change of features in the prediction process. This change would directly or indirectly alter some of the features in the data. Hence, Causal Maps (CM) considered being applicable for this purpose [2]. According to Nadkarni [3], since CM represent domain knowledge more descriptively than other models such as regression or structural equations, they are more useful as a decision tool.

Uncertainty can be caused by incomplete or noisy information, the conflict among criteria, the uncertainties in subjective judgment, and different preferences among different decision makers and so on. Better decision making can be achieved if the uncertain interrelations among these decision elements can be explicitly modeled and reasoned with rather than ignored by some unrealistic assumptions or summarized out by subjective weighting schemas or heuristic rules [4].

A Bayesian networks (BN) is a graphical model that encodes relationships among variables in the system. Spiegelhalter et al. [5] argue that BN has several advantages for data analysis: (1) BN readily handles situations where some data entries are missing, (2) BN can be used to model causal relationships, and hence can be used to gain understanding about a problem domain and to predict the consequences of intervention, and, (3) BN is an ideal representation for combining prior knowledge (which often comes in causal form) and data since the model has both causal and probabilistic semantics.

BN can be constructed through two different approaches—data-based approach and knowledge-based approach [6]. The data-based approaches use conditional independence between variables of interest of Bayes nets to induce models from data. The knowledge-based approach uses expert's judgment in constructing Bayesian networks. The knowledge-based approach is especially useful in situations where domain knowledge is crucial and availability of data is scarce.

5.2 Causal Map (CM)

In order to understand the effect of the change(s), decision maker(s) must have some mechanisms that can discover the cause and effect relations from the data set. Causal Map (CM) is widely known to approach such a problem. Eden [2] defines CM as a "directed graph characterized by a hierarchical structure which is most often in the form of a means/end graph". In the last decades, CM have been widely used to construct a framework and represent major factors, knowledge and conditions that influence decision making process [6, 7].

Causal relationships can be either positive or negative, as specified by a '+', respectively a '−', sign on the arrow connecting two variables. The variables that cause a change are called cause variables and the ones that undergo the effect of the change are called effect variables [8].

CM provide a rich representation of ideas, through the modeling of complex structures, representing the chain of arguments, as networks [2, 3]. Often times the last stage of intervention process is to identify and agree to a set of potential strategic options. In some cases, the preferred direction may emerge naturally from a process of negotiation; in others further, more or less formal, analysis to evaluate the options and to understand their impacts on the goals could be helpful [9]. CM can provide us to look at the problem more extensively than other decision tools which consider causal relations, such as regression. CM has been widely used in international relations, administrative science, political science, sociology, policy analysis, organizational behavior and management [1–3, 6, 9–11].

One major concern that needs to be addressed in CM is that CM is not easy to define and the magnitude of the effect is difficult to express in numbers. In general, CM is constructed by gathering information from experts. These experts are more likely subjectively express themselves in qualitative rather than quantitative terms [8]. Kosko [12] introduced the concept of Fuzzy CM (FCM) to overcome the problem. FCM represents the concepts linguistically with an associated fuzzy set. FCM is a signed directed graph that allows feedback and employs concepts (nodes) and weighted edges between concepts [13]. The degree of relationship between concepts in an FCM is either a number in [0; 1] or [−1; 1], or a linguistic term, such as 'often', 'extremely', 'some', etc. [8].

5.3 Bayesian Networks (BN)

5.3.1 Definition

Bayesian networks (BN), are widely used for knowledge representation and reasoning under uncertainty in intelligent systems [14, 15]. In the eighteenth century, Bayes' Theorem is developed by Thomas Bayes (1702–1761); since then the theory had a major effect on statistical inferences. The probability of a cause is inferred by Bayes Theorem when effect of cause is observed. The theorem was expanded in time. It has been used as a cause and effect diagram since the end of twentieth century [16]. Some of the advantages in using Bayesian Networks (BN) are: (1) BN can handle incomplete data sets, (2) BN focus on causal relationship and then facilitate the combination of background knowledge and experimental data in a way that the process can avoid over fitting problem [3, 5].

BN is a model in which events are connected to each other with probabilities. This model can be anything (e.g., economic reasons, vehicle parts, ecosystem, etc.) which can be modeled with Bayes. If the probabilities of events which affect each other are known exactly, the achievements are closer to the true results [17]. In a BN, the nodes in the networks (e.g., decision criteria and sub-criteria, factors that influence them) are treated as random variables that are connected by directed arcs indicating probabilistic dependencies between them. The networks structure also called as the Bayesian Causal Map, together with Conditional Probability Tables (CPT) associated with each node provide a compact representation of the joint probability distribution of all variables. A suite of algorithms have been developed for probabilistic inference with BN, especially those which, when some variables' values have been observed, compute the posterior probabilities of others [4]. The ability to infer posterior probabilities makes it possible to examine various scenario-based analysis under uncertainty.

BN is a directed acyclic graph (DAG) which means there are no cycles. In other word, BN is a probabilistic graphical model that restricts the graph to be directed and acyclic. Other models such as Markov random fields (MRFs) have no such restrictions [18, 19]. If there is a link between A and B (A→B) we say that B is a child of A and A is a parent of B [20, 21]. In BN, a link from node A to node B does not always imply causality. It implies a direct influence of A over B and the probability of B is conditioned on the value of A [22, 23].

5.3.2 Prior and Conditional Probabilities in BN

The direction of the arrows in BN can be explained with causality as long as arrows do not cause an endless loop. The advantage in comparison to other statistical models such like regression is that casualty can supply missing information and details as well as bringing the priorities and key factors into focus [11]. Besides, the networks are constructed in such a way that in the beginning all factors have the same certainties.

If A and B are the occurrences of two factors Bayes rule is defined as follows:

$$P(B\mid A) = \frac{P(A\mid B)P(B)}{P(A)} \qquad (5.1)$$

Where, P(A) gives the probability of the occurrence of factor A and P(A|B) is the probability of the occurrence of A when B event is occurred. Hence, the link from node A to node B means that factor A has a direct affect on factor B. Furthermore, the probability of B depends on the probability of A [24].

The uncertainty of the interdependence of the variables is represented locally by Conditional Probability Distribution (CPD) that represents $P(X_i|Pa(X_i))$, where $Pa(X_i)$ denotes the parents of X_i. An independence assumption is also made with BN that X_i, given its parents $Pa(X_i)$, is independent of any other variables except its descendents. The graphical structure of BN allows an unambiguous representation of interdependency between variables [4]. This, together with the independence assumption, leads to one of the most important features of BN: the joint probability distribution of $X = (X_i, \ldots, X_n)$ can be factored out as a product of the conditional distributions in the network,

$$p(X_1,\ldots,X_n) = \prod_i \left(p(X_i \mid Pa(X_i)) \right) \qquad (5.2)$$

BN helps us to observe whole structure of factor interactions from a graph. This is the way marginal and conditional probabilities of the factors can be computed by marginalizing over the joint [25].

There are four different ways to generate conditional probabilities in BN:

1. Using historical data. This approach involves transforming continuous data into discrete data.
2. Noisy OR model, which is the most classic approach. Noisy OR model is utilizing canonical (parameterized) distributions [14, 26]. This approach can only handle the cases where the states of nodes are binary and the parents of variables are assumed to be independent.
3. Direct input by the expert. With the increase of states of a variable, estimating probabilities directly to all states at one time may inevitably involve biases and inaccuracies
4. Using pair-wise comparisons as proposed by Monti and Carenini [27]. In this method, experts only need to deal with two states instead of all the states of a variable at a time when they give their judgments on the states' probabilities. Hence, the biases of judgments could be reduced significantly and the consistency of judgments could be easily maintained. However, Monti and Carenini's work were limited to generate the conditional probabilities of a node/variable with a single parent, while in Bayesian networks a node can have multiple parents.

Chin [28] proposed a method called systematic probability generation to overcome certain limitations, particularly in generation of conditional probabilities. It is similar to Saaty's AHP, but the details are different according to the types of nodes. The following summarizes the way of assessing the dependence relationship between nodes in BN.

5.3.2.1 Prior Probabilities for Root Node (Node Without Any Caused/Parent Nodes Linked to It)

Suppose there are n states $x_1, x_2, \ldots, x_n$ of a node N_i which has no parent, and the probability of each state x_i, $P(x_i)$ need to be specified. When the number of the states is small, then direct input of probabilities by experts may still be feasible. However, when the number of the states is growing, this approach may causes biases and inaccuracies. Here, Saaty's AHP approach can be implemented.

Pairwise comparisons are carried out across potential states of the node with respect to the possibility of occurrence using a scale of 1–9. For instance, the question for pairwise comparisons in this category can be specified like: "Given root node N_1 and its states x_1 and x_2, which state is more likely to occur and how much more likely?". Similar to Saaty's AHP, the relative priorities of the potential states are then derived from the maximum eigenvector.

5.3.2.2 Conditional Probabilities for Node with Single-Parent

The same procedure as for the root node is applied based on the number of states of the parent node. As shown in Fig. 5.1, suppose that node A, with its states x_1 and x_2, has a single parent node A_1, with its states x_3 and x_4, the question for pairwise

Fig. 5.1 BN with single parent node

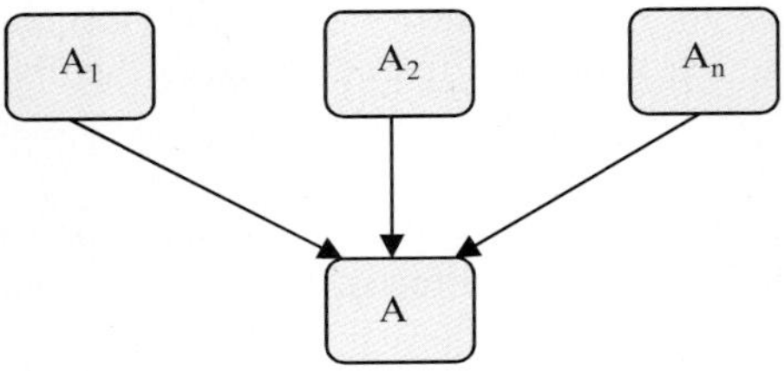

Fig. 5.2 BN with multiple parents

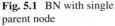

comparisons in this category can be specified like: "if A_1 is in the state of x_3, comparing the node A's state x_1 and x_2, which one is more likely to occur and by how much more likely, how about if A_1 is in the state of x_4?". The conditional probability table is constructed by keeping the relative priorities together.

5.3.2.3 Conditional Probabilities for Node with Multiple-Parents

For a node related to multiple parents, pairwise comparisons are conducted with respect to the potential states of each parent node. The conditional probabilities are calculated by normalizing the product of relative priorities that correspond to the combinatory states of parents.

As shown in Fig. 5.2, when a node A has multiple parents of $A_1, A_2\ldots$ and A_n, as suggested by Kim and Pearl [29], its probability conditional on $A_1, A_2\ldots$ and A_n can be approximated by:

$$P(A \mid A_1, A_2, \ldots, A_n) = \alpha P(A \mid A_1) P(A \mid A_2) \ldots P(A \mid A_n), \quad (5.3)$$

where α is a normalization factor that is used to ensure $\sum_{a} \in {}_A P(a \mid A_1, A_2, \ldots, A_n) = 1$.

5.3.3 *Probabilistic Inferences*

Probabilistic inferences about variables in the model can be drawn once a BN is constructed. The conditionals given in BN representation specify the prior joint distribution of the variables. If we observe or learn about the values of some variables, then such observations can be represented by tables where we assign 1 for the observed values and 0 for the unobserved values. Then the product of all tables (conditionals and observations) gives the (un-normalized) posterior joint distribution of the variables. Thus, the joint distribution of variables changes each time we learn new information about the variables.

Fig. 5.3 Graphic representation of BN

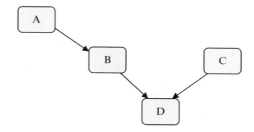

A simple system such as in Fig. 5.3 illustrate the concept of probabilistic inferences in BN. If there is an arc pointing from A to B, we say A is a parent of B. For each variable, we need to specify a table of conditional probability distributions, one for each configuration of states of its parents. Figure 5.1 shows these tables of conditional distributions—P(A), P(B|A), P(C) and P(D|B,C).

A fundamental assumption of a BN is that when we multiply the conditionals for each variable, we get the joint probability distribution for all variables in the networks. For Fig. 5.3, we make assumption that:

$$P(A,B,C,D) = P(A)*P(B|A)*P(C)*P(D|B,C) \qquad (5.4)$$

One can read these conditional independence assumptions directly from the BN graph as follows. Suppose we pick a sequence of the variables such that for all directed arcs in the networks, the variable at the tail of each arc precedes the variable at the head of the arc in the sequence. Since the directed graph is acyclic, there always exists such a sequence. In Fig. 5.3, one such sequence is A B C D. Then, the conditional independence assumptions can be stated as follows. For each variable in the sequence, we are assuming that it is conditionally independent of its predecessors in the sequence given its parents. The essential point here is that missing arcs (from a node to its successors in the sequence) signify conditional independence assumptions. Thus the lack of an arc from A to C indicates that C is independent of A; the lack of an arc from B to C indicates that B is independent of C; and the lack of an arc from A to D indicates that D is conditionally independent of A given B and C [3].

5.4 Transforming Causal Maps to Bayesian Causal Maps

Both BN and CM are causal models that represent cause–effect beliefs of experts. However, there are some differences in the two approaches to modeling that need to be addressed if we are to transform CM to Bayesian causal maps. These differences are discussed in the following paragraphs.

5.4.1 Conditional Independencies

Pearl [14] states that a networks model can be either a dependence map (D-map) or an independence map (I-map). In a D-map, an arrow between two variables in the model implies that the two variables are related. However, a lack of an arrow between variables does not necessarily imply independence between the two variables. An I-map, on the other hand, implies that concepts found to be separated are indeed conditionally independent, given other variables. Hence, CM is a D-map since CM is a directed graph that depicts causality between variables and also in CM an arrow between two variables implies dependence. However, the absence of an arrow between two variables in CM does not imply a lack of dependence. There is a possibility that the absence of the arrow resulted from the lack of articulation of the expert's judgement. It does not necessary imply that the expert believes that the variables to be independent [6].

BN, on the other hand, is an I-map. Hence, an absence of arrow from a variable to its *child* indicates conditional independence between the variables. Thus, when we want to transform CM to BN, it is important to ensure that the lack of links between the concepts in the causal map implies independence and the presence of links between concepts implies dependence [3, 6].

5.4.2 Reasoning Underlying Cause–Effect Relations

It is believed that from a logic or reasoning process standpoint, individuals perceive cause–effect relationships based on two types of reasoning: deductive and abductive [3]. A reasoning is called deductive if we reason from causes to effects. Abductive reasoning, on the other hand, happen when we reason from effects to causes.

A distinction between deductive and abductive reasoning behind the causal linkages is essential to establish accurate directions of linkages in CM. The emphasis in deriving CM should be on the causal theory underlying the causal statements rather than the language used [3, 9].

5.4.3 Direct vs. Indirect Relations

In CM a direct link between two variables does not guarantee a direct relationship between the two variables. It just implies a relation between the two variables that can be either direct or indirect. This distinction is important to identify conditional independencies in the CM [3, 6, 9]. Figure 5.4 illustrates the distinction of direct and indirect relationship and how a lack of distinction affects conditional independence assumptions in a CM.

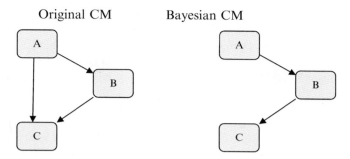

Fig. 5.4 Direct vs. indirect relations

In Fig. 5.4 on the Original CM, both A and B affect C while in the Bayesian CM, there is no linkage between A and C, implying that A affect C strictly through B. If we have complete information of B, any additional information of A will be irrelevant in making inferences about C.

5.4.4 Circular Loop and Reciprocal Influences Are Not Permitted in BN

As explained in the previous paragraph, CM is directed graphs that characterized by an acyclic structure. However, circular relations or causal loops destroy the hierarchical form of a graph. Circular relations in the CM violate the acyclic graphical structure required in BN. It is therefore essential to eliminate circular relations to make CM compatible with BN. Causal loops can exist for two reasons. First, they may be coding mistakes that need to be corrected. Second, they may represent dynamic relations between variables across multiple time frames [2, 3, 5, 6, 9, 30].

5.5 Designing a Roadmap Topology Using Bayesian Causal Map Approach

A procedure to design a roadmap topology using Bayesian causal maps approach can be summarized into two steps [3, 6, 31]:

1. Qualitative modeling, which consist of: data elicitation; derivation of CM; and modification of CM to design a roadmap topology using Bayesian causal maps approach
2. Quantitative modeling, which involve the derivation of the parameters of Bayesian causal maps

Data-based or knowledge-based approaches or a combination can be used for data elicitation purpose. Hence, literature review and/or expert's opinion are used to determine the variables of interest for constructing the original CM. Based on the elicitate data, the next step is to construct an original CM. In the last step of the qualitative modeling, the CM of the expert is modified—using the approaches of transforming CM to BN as explained in the above paragraphs with regards to: conditional independencies, reasoning underlying the link between concepts, distinction between direct and indirect relations, and eliminating circular relations—to eliminate biases that result from the use of textual analysis and to make the structure of the CM compatible with BN. In the qualitative modeling phase, the parameters of the Bayesian causal maps are derived using probability-encoding techniques [3].

In order to modify CM into a roadmap topology using Bayesian causal maps approach, the two most widely used methods are structured interviews and adjacency matrices [3, 9, 16, 28]. In structured interviews, the experts are provided a list of paired concepts as well as different alternative specifications of the relation between the concepts in the original map. The experts are then instructed to choose an alternative to specify the direct relation between the pair of concepts. Adjacency matrices, on the other hand, experts are provided the concepts in the form of an adjacency matrix, where the rows represent causes and columns represent effects. The experts are asked to enter '0' (no relation), '+1' (positive relation), or '−1' (negative relation) in each cell to specify the relation between two concepts in the matrix. These two structured methods help in removing the four modeling biases relating to the construction of Bayesian causal map.

For the last step, once the structure of the Bayesian causal map is constructed, numerical parameters of this modified structure need to be assessed so that the propagation algorithms in the Bayesian networks can be used to make inferences [6, 16]. For this purpose, data-based (historical data) and knowledge-based approaches (expert's opinion) can be utilized to get the parameter (prior and conditional probabilities of the variables of interest).

5.6 Case Study: Energy Storage Technologies for Wind Power Generation

This section describes the construction of Bayesian causal maps for a specific case study in energy storage technology for wind power generation [32, 33]. First, the paper illustrates how to construct the qualitative structure of a Bayesian causal maps from CM. Additional information—collected from experts to address the modeling issues discussed in Sect. 5.4.1 as well as to derive the numerical parameters of the Bayesian causal map—was also presented here. Second, Bayesian networks software called Netica® is also introduced to draw probabilistic inferences in a Bayesian causal maps.

5.6.1 The Goal: Choosing the Right Energy Storage Technology

The decision faced for the presented case study here is what type of energy storage technology should the decision maker(s) choose among these alternatives: pump hydro storage (PHS), sodium sulfur battery (NaS), and compressed air energy storage (CAES) to overcome the limitation of wind power generation. A completed study regarding the chosen storage technology can be seen in our previous study [32, 33].

Wind power shares the major drawbacks of most renewable energy generation alternatives: higher costs and inconsistency of power generation. Wind power is available at the whim of nature: it can only be generated when the right amount of wind is blowing. If the wind is calm or too light, the wind turbines will not generate any electricity. When the wind is blowing at a high speed, the turbines must be slowed or shut down to avoid damages to the system [31].

Power balancing requirements resulting from the intermittency of wind power suggest using energy storage assistance to improve overall generation and load characteristics. The problems in generation imbalance for wind power require multi-criteria analysis for the decision makers. The role of the system analyst is to develop scenario-based analysis and to analyze the decision and suggest a recommendation.

5.6.2 Procedure for Constructing a Bayesian Causal Map

The procedure involves qualitative and quantitative modeling which describe as follow.

5.6.2.1 Qualitative Modeling

Three activities are conducted in this phase: data elicitation; derivation of CM; and modification of CM to design a roadmap topology using Bayesian causal maps approach.

Step 1: Data Elicitation

Through literature review and expert's validation, we observed that there are 18 variables representing technical factors, economical factors, environmental factors, and social factor. The seven technical factors are efficiency, maturity, capacity, lifetime, durability, technology risk and autonomy. The economical factors are represented by capital costs, O&M costs, economic risk, R&D budget and recurrent costs. The environmental factors are represented by air pollution, water pollution, and wildlife impacts. The social factor is represented by social risk. All of these factors are defined in Table 5.1 [33].

Table 5.1 Variables in energy storage technology

Variables	Description
Efficiency	The ratio between released energy and stored energy
Maturity	The development phase of the storage technology such as early concept, prototype, demonstration, or commercialization stage
Capacity	The quantity of available energy in the storage system after charging
Lifetime	The length of time that the storage unit can be used
Durability	The number of times the storage unit can release the energy level it was designed for after each recharge
Autonomy	The maximum amount of time the system can continuously release energy
Investment costs	The total costs include the purchase of land, buildings, construction and equipment to be used in the storage unit
Operations and maintenance costs	The costs include two main parts: a fixed one, rated power and a variable part depending on its annual discharged energy
Recurrent costs	The cost per unit energy divided by the cycle life
Air pollution	The contamination of the atmosphere by noxious gases and particulates
Water pollution	The drainage of the waste water into natural water bodies
Wildlife impacts	The effects on nature and wildlife
Social risk	Risks arising from environmental problems or social discontent surrounding a project
Technology risk	Risk associated with technical aspect of the proposed project
Environmental regulations	A set of regulations of state and federal statutes, and common-law principles covering air pollution, water pollution, hazardous waste, the wilderness, and endangered wildlife
Economic risk	The risk that the project's output will not generate sufficient revenues to cover operating costs and to repay debt obligations
Willingness to Invest	The company's willingness to invest on a project given different kind of risks associated with the project
R&D	Budget allocated by the company for research and development
Storage technology decision	Selection of a energy storage technology among Sodium Sulfur Battery Storage, Compressed Air Energy Storage, and Pump Hydro Storage for balancing reserves in Northwest area

Step 2: Derivation of CM

Adjacency matrix—as explained in Sect. 5.5—is presented to three power administration authorities of Oregon State and three active members of Energy Nusantara (Indonesia Renewable Energy Community). The experts are instructed to specify the relation between two concepts in the matrix. Then the six responses are combined by taking the mode of the expert's responses. The complete adjacency matrix is presented in Table 5.2. This process resulted in the original of CM as shown in Fig. 5.3.

The matrix is read from row to column. For example, life time affects O&M cost negatively which means that if life time of the energy storage increases O&M cost will decrease. Equipped by the adjacency matrix shown in Table 5.2, we developed our original CM as shown in Fig. 5.5. Figure 5.5 indicates that each nodes in the original CMs in most cases have reciprocal influences with one another, something that is not allows in developing Bayesian causal maps [3].

Step 3: Modification of CM to design a roadmap topology using Bayesian causal map approach

Utilizing approaches as explained in Sect. 5.4 when we want to convert the CM into BN—by looking at four basic requirements: conditional independencies; reasoning underlying the link between concepts; distinction between direct and indirect relations; and eliminating circular relations—the original CM then converted into Bayesian causal maps. The final result of this processes is shown in Fig. 5.6.

5.6.2.2 Quantitative Modeling

Pairwise comparison are carried out across all states of the nodes with respect to the possibility of occurrence using a scale of 1–9. In this step, the parameters of the Bayesian causal maps—which consist of marginal probabilities and conditional probabilities—are assessed using systematic probability generation method developed by Chin [28]. After all the marginal and conditional probabilities are calculated, the final step is to do a scenario-based assessment of the energy storage technology options.

Step 1: Conditional probabilities assessment

The conditional probabilities of analysis criteria are generated after the likelihood of the states of each node was evaluated by pairwise comparisons. Experts are interviewed and pairwise comparison judgments are applied. Three different cases are presented here according to the type of comparisons. The rest of the nodes were calculated in the same manner.

Case one deals with the root/no-parent nodes. Pairwise comparisons were carried out among the states of the node. The relative priorities of the potential states can be generated from the maximum eigenvector and the relative priorities were derived as prior probabilities. The pairwise comparison matrix and the marginal probabilities for the node *Capacity* are shown in Table 5.3.

As for the case two, nodes having a single-parent node, pairwise comparisons were conducted among the states of the node with respect to each possible state of its parent node. The pairwise comparison matrices and the conditional probabilities for the node *Life Time* are shown in Table 5.4. Table 5.4 shows the final pairwise comparison matrix for the node *life time* when the its parent node *durability* is in the state of *low*. Similarly, we can get the probability of states of node *life time* on the condition that the state of its parent node *durability* is *medium* and *high*. The result is summarized in Table 5.5.

For the last case, nodes with multiple-parent nodes, pairwise comparisons were performed among the states of the node with respect to the all states of each parent node. The node *water pollution* is presented here as an illustration on how to use the systematic probability generation method. As shown in Fig. 5.6, the node *water pollution* (*WAP*) has two parents, node *environmental regulations* (*ENR*) and node

Table 5.2 Interrelation of energy storage technology factors

	Efficiency	Maturity	Capacity	Lifetime	Durability	Autonomy	Investment costs	O&M costs	Recurrent costs	Air pollution
Efficiency	0	1	0	0	0	1	1	0	0	0
Maturity	1	0	0	0	0	0	0	0	0	0
Capacity	0	0	0	0	0	0	1	0	0	1
Lifetime	0	0	0	0	0	0	0	−1	−1	0
Durability	0	0	0	1	0	1	0	1	0	0
Autonomy	0	0	0	0	0	0	0	1	1	0
Investment costs	−1	0	0	0	0	1	0	0	0	0
O&M costs	0	0	0	0	0	0	1	0	0	0
Recurrent costs	0	0	0	0	0	0	0	0	0	0
Air pollution	0	0	0	0	0	0	0	0	0	0
Water pollution	0	0	0	0	0	0	0	0	0	0
Wildlife impacts	0	0	0	0	0	0	0	0	0	0
Social risk	0	0	0	0	0	0	0	0	0	0
Technology risk	0	0	0	0	0	0	1	0	0	0
Economic risk	0	0	0	0	0	0	0	0	0	0
Willingness to invest	0	0	0	0	0	0	1	0	0	0
R&D	1	1	0	0	1	0	1	0	0	0
Environmental regulations	0	0	0	0	0	0	1	0	0	−1

[a]Storage technology decision: pump hydro storage (PHS), sodium sulfur battery (NaS), and compressed air energy storage (CAES)

5 Technology Assessment: Energy Storage Technologies for Wind Power Generation

Water pollution	Wildlife impacts	Social risk	Technology risk	Economic risk	Willingness to invest	R&D	Environmental regulations	Health and safety	Storage technology decision[a]
0	0	0	0	0	0	−1	0	0	0
0	0	0	−1	0	0	−1	0	0	1
1	0	0	−1	0	1	0	0	0	0
0	0	0	0	0	0	0	0	0	0
0	0	0	−1	0	0	0	0	0	0
0	0	0	0	0	0	0	0	0	0
0	0	−1	0	−1	−1	0	0	0	0
0	0	0	0	1	0	0	0	0	0
0	0	0	0	1	0	0	0	0	0
0	1	0	0	0	0	0	1	0	0
0	1	0	0	0	0	0	0	0	0
0	0	1	0	0	0	0	0	0	−1
0	0	0	0	0	0	0	0	0	−1
0	0	0	0	0	0	0	0	0	−1
0	0	0	0	0	0	0	0	0	−1
0	0	0	0	0	0	1	0	0	0
0	0	0	0	0	0	0	0	0	0
−1	0	0	0	0	0	0	0	0	0

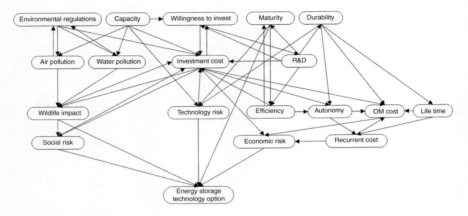

Fig. 5.5 Original CM

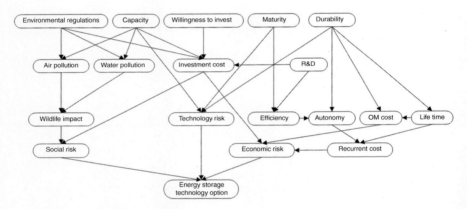

Fig. 5.6 Bayesian causal maps

Table 5.3 Pairwise comparison matrix for the node *Capacity*

Capacity	Low	Medium	High	*P* (capacity)
Low	1.000	0.333[b]	3.000[a]	0.258
Medium	3.000[a]	1.000	5.000[a]	0.637
High	0.333[b]	0.200[b]	1.000	0.105
		Inconsistency index[c]		0.037

[a]Expert's judgments
[b]Reciprocal of the expert's judgment
[c]The inconsistency index is less than 0.10, so no correction of judgments is needed

5 Technology Assessment: Energy Storage Technologies for Wind Power Generation

Table 5.4 Pairwise comparison matrix for node *life time* conditional on *durability* is *low*

Life time	Low	Medium	High	P (durability)
Low	1.000	0.333	4.000	0.073
Medium	3.000	1.000	9.000	0.256
High	0.250	0.111	1.000	0.671
		Inconsistency index		0.002

Table 5.5 Probabilities of *life time* conditional on *durability's* different states

Life time	Durability =L	Durability =M	Durability =H
Low	0.073	0.111	0.655
Medium	0.256	0.667	0.250
High	0.671	0.222	0.095

Table 5.6 Probabilities of *water pollution* conditional on *environmental regulations'* different states

Water Pollution	Environmental regulations =R (relaxed)	Environmental regulations =S (stricter)
Low	0.122	0.682
Medium	0.320	0.216
High	0.558	0.102

Table 5.7 Probabilities of *water pollution* conditional on *capacity's* different states

Water Pollution	Capacity =L	Capacity =M	Capacity =H
Low	0.648	0.570	0.196
Medium	0.230	0.333	0.311
High	0.122	0.097	0.493

capacity (*CAP*). Hence, we need to get the *P(WAP|ENR)* and *P(WAP|CAP)* first. The probabilities of node *water pollution* conditional on each parent are shown in Tables 5.6 and 5.7.

The next step would be computing the probabilities of node *water pollution* conditional on the state combinations of both its parent nodes using Eq. (5.3). For example, when node *environmental regulations* is on the state of *Relaxed* (*R*) and *capacity* is on the state of *Low* (*L*), then using Eq. (5.1) we can compute the probability of *water pollution* is *L* given the *environmental regulations* is *R* and the *capacity* is *L*:

$$P(WAP = L \mid ENR = R, CAP = L) = \alpha P(WAP = L \mid ENR = R) P(WAP = L \mid CAP = L)$$

Table 5.8 Probabilities of *water pollution* (*WAP*) conditional on different state combination of *environmental regulations* (*ENR*) and capacity (*CAP*)

ENR	Relaxed			Stricter		
CAP	L	M	H	L	M	H
L	0.358	0.302	0.060	0.877	0.826	0.532
M	0.333	0.463	0.250	0.099	0.153	0.267
H	0.308	0.235	0.690	0.025	0.021	0.200

Since α is a normalization factor, then:

$$\alpha = \frac{1}{\begin{array}{l}P(WAP = L \mid ENR = R)P(WAP = L \mid CAP = L) \\ +P(WAP = M \mid ENR = R)P(WAP = M \mid CAP = L) \\ +P(WAP = H \mid ENR = R)P(WAP = H \mid CAP = L)\end{array}}$$

From the above equations, we can get the following result:

P(WAP=L|ENR=R, CAP=L)=0.358
P(WAP=M|ENR=R, CAP=L)=0.334
P(WAP=H|ENR=R, CAP=L)=0.308

Similarly, the probabilities of the state of the node *WAP* conditional on the other state combinations of its parent nodes can also be generated and the final results are shown in Table 5.8.

Using the three cases as explained above, the Conditional Probability Table (CPT) of the other nodes with or without parent nodes in the Bayesian causal maps can be specified similarly. The CPT then used to compute all prior probabilities of all nodes in the Bayesian causal maps using Eq. (5.4). The number of nodes was large and each calculation of the prior probabilities was so complex that manual work was unrealistic. Hence, a graphical software package, Netica, was utilized and the final prior probability is shown in Fig. 5.7.

Step 2: scenario-based assessment of the energy storage technology options

A graphical software package, Netica [17] is utilized to make probabilistic inferences using sum propagation. The sum propagation computes the marginal probabilities of all the model variables and updates the marginals with all additional evidence received about other variables [3, 6, 16], . In this case study, we can evaluate each energy storage technology options under different scenarios.

The scenarios were defined in consultation with the experts, and they represent situations in which the experts believe that there will be future changes in the society, technology changes, internal changes, and unambiguous prescriptions for energy storage technology option in the energy literature. At the beginning of the case study we mentioned that the energy storage technology options are limited only to three options: pump hydro storage (PHS), sodium sulfur battery (NaS), and compressed air energy storage (CAES). Each option can be represented by

5 Technology Assessment: Energy Storage Technologies for Wind Power Generation

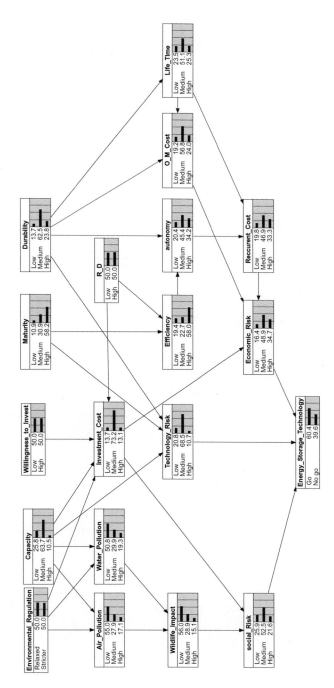

Fig. 5.7 Bayesian causal maps with prior probabilities

Table 5.9 Prior and posterior probabilities under two different scenarios

Nodes	Prior probabilities	Posterior probabilities in Scenario 1[a]	Posterior probabilities in Scenario 2[b]
1. *Social risk*			
Low	0.27	0.45	0.22
Medium	0.50	0.22	0.24
High	0.23	0.33	0.54
2. *Technology risk*			
Low	0.02	0.04	0.17
Medium	0.89	0.94	0.35
High	0.09	0.02	0.48
3. *Economic risk*			
Low	0.18	0.19	0.23
Medium	0.48	0.56	0.27
High	0.34	0.26	0.50
4. Energy *storage technology option 1*[c]			
Go	0.56	0.64	0.47
No go	0.44	0.36	0.54

[a]Scenario 1: *environmental regulation* is relaxed, *R&D budget* is high and *willingness to invest* is high
[b]Scenario 2: *environmental regulation* is stricter, *R&D budget* is low and *willingness to invest* is low
[c]Energy storage technology option 1, CAES: *capacity* is medium, *maturity* is medium and *durability* is high

specifying the state of three nodes: maturity; capacity; and durability. Each energy storage options has specification as follow:

– CAES: *capacity* is medium, *maturity* is medium and *durability* is high.
– PHS: *capacity* is high, *maturity* is high and *durability* is high.
– NaS: *capacity* is low, *maturity* is medium and *durability* is medium.

We specify two different scenarios and demonstrate how our inferences on energy storage technology option change depending on the different scenarios. Scenario one is set to be in a favor condition, in which *environmental regulation* is relaxed, *R&D budget* is high and *willingness to invest* is high, whereas scenario two is completely the opposite: *environmental regulation* is stricter, *R&D budget* is low and *willingness to invest* is low. This information is used to compute the posterior probabilities of the nodes directly affecting the decision of energy storage technology. Table 5.9 shows the prior probabilities of the three nodes directly affecting energy storage technology decision when all other variables, except capacity, maturity and durability) in the map, as shown in Fig. 5.7, are unknown.

When the scenario 1 is simulated on the Bayesian causal maps, the posterior probability of *social risk*=low increases from 0.27 to 0.45, and the posterior probability of energy storage technology option of *Go* is increases from 0.56 to 0.64. Under this conditions, the right decision is to select product option 1, which is

Table 5.10 Prior and posterior probabilities of energy storage technology option under two scenario

	States	CAES	PHS	NaS
Prior probabilities	Go	0.56	0.68	0.52
	No go	0.44	0.32	0.48
Scenario 1	Go	0.64	0.42	0.50
	No go	0.36	0.58	0.50
Scenario 2	Go	0.47	0.51	0.67
	No go	0.54	0.49	0.33

CAES. When scenario two is simulated, the posterior probability of *social risk* = high increases from 0.23 to 0.54, that of *technology risk* = high jump from 0.09 to 0.48 and that of *economic risk* = high increases from 0.34 to 0.50. The posterior probability of energy storage technology option of *No Go* is increases from 0.44 to 0.54. This implies that in scenario two, the right decision is to reject energy storage technology option 1, CAES.

Similarly, we can use the same procedure as described above to evaluate energy storage technology option two (PHS) and three (NaS) under scenario 2. Table 5.10 summarized all the posterior probabilities of energy storage decision under the two different scenarios. Table 5.10 shows that under scenario 2, the highest probability of state *Go* is for energy storage technology option 3, NaS. The posterior probability of energy storage technology option 3, NaS = Go is increases from 0.47 to 0.67. This is implies that in scenario 2, the right decision is to go with energy storage technology option 3, NaS.

5.7 Summary, Conclusion and Limitation

Two formal procedures are used in this study. Firstly is the use of a graphical structure of Bayesian causal maps introduce by Nadkarni [3]. Bayesian causal maps combine the strengths of causal maps and Bayesian networks and reduce the limitations of both. Secondly, a systematic probability generation method, as an extension to the work of Kim and Pearl [29], to compute the conditional probability table. One of the biggest advantage of the proposed method is that once the Bayesian causal maps is validated, analytical results can be updated easily with minimal involvement of experts, since the data are totally reusable and new finding or new data can be added and analyzed through support from the software system.

Bayesian causal maps provide a framework for representing the uncertainty of variables in the map as well as the effect of variables. Using concepts from the literature on causal modeling and logic [9, 14, 16], Bayesian causal map clarify the cause–effect relations depicted in the causal maps. They depict dependence between variables based on causal mapping approach (D-map) as well as a lack of dependence between variables based on the Bayesian networks approach (I-map) [3, 6, 9, 12, 14, 16].

References

1. Liu Z (2001) Causation, Bayesian networks, and cognitive maps. Zidonghua Xuebao/Acta Autom Sin 27(4):552–566
2. Eden C (2004) Analyzing cognitive maps to help structure issues or problems. Eur J Oper Res 159(3):673–686
3. Nadkarni S (2001) A Bayesian network approach to making inferences in causal maps. Eur J Oper Res 128(3):479–498
4. Watthayu W, Peng Y (2004) A Bayesian network based framework for multi-criteria decision making. Proceedings of the 17th international conference on multiple criteria decision analysis, pp. 6–11
5. Spiegelhalter DJ, Dawid AP, Lauritzen SL, Cowell RG (1993) Bayesian analysis in expert systems. Stat Sci 8(3):219–241
6. Nadkarni S (2004) A causal mapping approach to constructing Bayesian networks. Decis Support Syst 38(2):259–281
7. Sahin S, Ulengin F, Ulengin B (2006) A Bayesian causal map for inflation analysis: the case of Turkey. Eur J Oper Res 175(2):1268–1284
8. Lazzerini B, Mkrtchyan L (2010) Risk analysis using extended fuzzy cognitive maps. 2010 international conference on intelligent computing and cognitive informatics. pp. 179–182
9. Montibeller G, Belton V (2006) Causal maps and the evaluation of decision options—a review. J Oper Res Soc 57(7):779–791
10. Eden C, Ackermann F, Cropper S (1992) The analysis of cause maps. J Manag Stud 29(3): 309–324
11. Siau K, Tan X (2005) Improving the quality of conceptual modeling using cognitive mapping techniques. Data Knowl Eng 55(3):343–365
12. Kosko B (1986) Fuzzy cognitive maps. Int J Man-Machine Stud 24:65–75
13. Huang Y, Ni L, Miao Y (2009) A quantum cognitive map model. 2009 fifth international conference on natural computation. pp. 28–31
14. Pearl J (1988) Probabilistic reasoning in intelligent systems: networks of plausible inference. Morgan Kaufmann, San Francisco, CA, 552
15. Nilsson NJ (1996) Artificial intelligence: a modern approach. Artif Intell 82(1–2):369–380
16. Neapolitan RE (2009) Chapter 5—Foundations of Bayesian networks. In: Probabilistic methods for bioinformatics: with an introduction to Bayesian networks. Morgan Kaufmann, Burlington, MA
17. Norsys Software Corp (2011) Netica™ application. pp. 85–133
18. Mortensen EN (2006) Real-time semi-automatic segmentation using a Bayesian network. In: 2006 IEEE computer society conference on computer vision and pattern recognition, vol. 1 (CVPR'06). pp. 1007–1014
19. Doong SH, Shu-Chun Ho (2011) Construct a sequential decision-making model: a dynamic Bayesian network perspective. Proceedings of the 44th Hawaii international conference on system sciences. pp. 1–10
20. Zeng Y, Xiang Y, Pacekajus S (2008) Refinement of Bayesian network structures upon New Data.pdf. 2008 IEEE international conference on granular computing, GRC 2008. pp. 772–777
21. Jingjing L, Yan P, Ting Z (2008) The application of Bayesian network in the performance evaluation and decision-making system. 2008 IEEE international conference on networking, sensing and control. pp. 180–183
22. Thibault G, Bonnevay S, Aussem A (2007) Learning Bayesian network structures by estimation of distribution algorithms: an experimental analysis. 2007 2nd international conference on digital information management. pp. 127–132
23. Alpaydin E (2004) Introduction to machine learning (Adaptive computation and machine learning), vol. 5, no. August. The MIT Press, Cambridge, MA, pp 233–237

24. Changliang X, Zhanfeng S (2009) Wind energy in China: current scenario and future perspectives. Renew Sustain Energy Rev 13(8):1966–1974
25. Trucco P (2008) A Bayesian belief network modelling of organisational factors in risk analysis: a case study in maritime transportation. Reliab Eng Syst Safe 93(6):845–856
26. Lemmer JF, Gossink DE (2004) Recursive noisy OR—a rule for estimating complex probabilistic interactions. IEEE Trans Syst Man Cybernet B 34(6):2252–2261
27. Monti S, Carenini G (2000) Dealing with the expert inconsistency in probability elicitation. IEEE 12(4):499–508
28. Chin K-S, Tang D-W, Yang J-B, Wong SY, Wang H (2009) Assessing new product development project risk by Bayesian network with a systematic probability generation methodology. Expert Syst Appl 36(6):9879–9890
29. Kim JH, Pearl J (1983) A computational model for combined causal and diagnostic reasoning in inference systems. Proceedings of the eighth international joint conference on artificial intelligence. pp. 380–385
30. Heckerman D (1999) A tutorial on learning with Bayesian Networks. In: Learning in graphical models. MIT Press, Cambridge, MA, pp 301–354
31. Daim T, Kayakutlu G, Suharto Y, Bayram Y (2010) Clean energy investment scenarios using the Bayesian network. Int J Sustain Energy(November):1–16
32. Daim TU, Suharto Y (2012) Storage technology portfolio for integrating wind power generation storage technology portfolio for integrating wind power generation. In: Encyclopedia of energy engineering and technology. Taylor and Francis, New York, NY, pp 1–9
33. Daim U, Li X, Kim J, Simms S (2013) Evaluation of energy storage technologies for integration with renewable electricity: quantifying expert opinions. Environ Innovation Soc Transitions 3:29–49

Chapter 6
Hexavalent Chromium Substitution

David Tucker, James Eastham, Joe Smith, and Sumir Varma

Abstract From razor thin tool blade coatings to shiny custom motorcycle parts, hexavalent chromium (Hex-chrome) has historically been the coating of choice for a vast array of industrial applications. Hex-chrome has many advantages over other coating alternatives including hardness, corrosion resistance, coefficient of friction, process maturity, and economic factors. Existing Hex-chrome process technologies are simple and well understood in the industry.

Recent reports and media coverage have brought Hex-chrome into the spotlight. Increased environmental and regulatory pressure on existing Hex-chrome has created a need for companies to investigate alternative coatings. In 1988 [15] Hexavalent Chromium was declared a carcinogen and since has received additional scrutiny and regulation. Recent advances in coating technologies and process methods look to provide feasible alternatives to existing processes while providing Hex-Chrome free options. However, evaluating these potential alternatives is difficult as information from vendors is not easily obtained the decision process is not well documented.

In this project, the team provides a history of hard chromium coatings. We discuss the issues emanating from hard chromium and traditional application

---

D. Tucker (✉)
New Kinpo Group, Portland, OR, USA
e-mail: david.tucker@pdx.edu

J. Eastham
TriQuint Semiconductor, Portland, OR, USA
e-mail: jeastham@pdx.edu

J. Smith
Blount International, Portland, OR, USA
e-mail: Joe.Smith@blount.com

S. Varma
Tri Quint Semiconductor, Portland, OR, USA
e-mail: Sumir.Varma@tqs.com

processes. Various alternatives are discussed in detail, many of which are considered "Nano-coatings" due to their tiny architecture and deposition methods.

A criteria analysis/decision matrix is provided which provides:

- Multiple selection criteria/key metric scoring (harness, coefficient of friction, corrosion resistance)
- Consideration of cost of ownership
- Environmental impact factors
- Priority weighting of factors (cost vs. environmental)
- Visual results for ease of analysis, helps technology managers prepare for Hex-chrome alternative evaluation

In researching this topic, the team was unable to find such a decision model. The team adds to the existing body of knowledge by establishing this model and providing guidance regarding the model inputs. Although a fully comprehensive decision matrix could not be developed, due to limitations in available data, the team provides a detailed overview of each replacement technology and guidelines for making decisions in the future when such information is available.

6.1 Introduction

6.1.1 Overview

From razor thin tool blade coatings to shiny custom motorcycle parts, Hexavalent chromium (also called "Hex-Chrome") has historically been the coating of choice for a vast array of industrial applications. Hex-chrome has many advantages including maturity and cost. In 1988 Hexavalent Chromium was recommended a carcinogen by NIOSH (National Institute for Occupational Safety and Health) [15]. Since this time Hexavalent chromium has received additional scrutiny and regulation. Traditional chrome plating processes and materials are no longer deemed safe and present many hazards to workers and the environment. Government regulations and increasing safety concerns have risen to a point where companies are investigating replacement materials for existing processes which use Hex-Chrome.

Increased environmental and regulatory pressure on existing Hex-chrome has created a need for companies to investigate alternative coatings. Recent advances in coating materials and process methods look to provide feasible alternatives to existing processes. However, evaluating these potential alternatives is difficult as information from alternative vendors is not easily obtained and the decision process is somewhat complicated. Evaluating Hex-chrome alternatives is complex; a need for a decision model exists. In this project, we provide a history of hard chromium coatings and discuss the issues emanating from hard chromium and traditional application processes. Various alternatives are discussed in detail, some of which are considered "Nano-coatings" due to their tiny architecture and deposition methods.

A criteria analysis and decision matrix was developed, providing guidance to managers and engineers who need to make chrome replacement decisions. Although a fully comprehensive decision matrix could not be developed, due to limitations in available data, the team provides a detailed overview of each replacement technology and guidelines for making decisions in the future when such information is available.

6.1.2 Summary of Contributions

In researching this topic, the team was unable to find such a decision model. The team adds to the existing body of knowledge by establishing this model and providing guidance regarding the variables. Although a fully comprehensive decision matrix could not be developed, due to availability of quantifiable data, the team provides a detailed overview of each replacement technology and establishes guidelines for making decisions in the future when such information is available. Example model implementation is shown in following sections for a specific application (piston rod). The team also developed a scenario analysis which looks at hex-chrome material alternatives weighted by environmental and cost driven preferences.

6.2 History and Background Information

6.2.1 History of Chromium and Electrolytic Plating

The element chromium (Cr) was discovered in 1797 by Louis Nicolas Vauquelin [19]. A professor of chemistry and pharmacology, Vauquelin detected chromium in the mineral crocoite or red lead ore from Siberia. Chromium by itself is a lustrous, grey metal of high hardness and corrosion resistance, and is the only elemental solid that is antiferromagnetic. It is said to be the 21st most abundant element in the earth's crust and is typically mined from chromite in South Africa, Kazakhstan, India, Russia, and Turkey.

The study of chromium and its properties eventually led to its use as an alloying element in a variety of metals including stainless steel. Approximately 85 % of mined chromium is used in metal alloys [18], but its useful qualities also make it an excellent choice for chromate conversion and surface coatings on various substrates. Electroplating, which is the deposition of a thin layer of metal onto a cathode, was invented in 1839 with patents issued in 1840 [17]. Soon after, chrome began to be used as a surface coating, although it was not a widely adopted surface coating for industrial uses until the 1920s.

Due to its versatility as a surface coating and its excellent properties and characteristics, chrome plating has been used extensively throughout the world for a variety of industrial and commercial applications. Chrome plating can be applied at a variety of thicknesses from thin coatings of less than 0.0001" to thick coatings of 0.030" or more. Thick chrome plated coatings are often used to "build-up" worn part surfaces, which allows for rebuilding and resurfacing of parts to bring them back to their original part dimensions. From aircraft components, hydraulic actuators, and other wear components to gun barrels, hand tools and automotive trim, Chrome has been the surface coating of choice for almost a century.

There are several different surface preparations that utilize chromium, but the focus of this paper and analysis will be on those concerning electrolytic deposition on steel. The two main types of electrolytic chromium deposition on steel substrates are referred to as decorative chrome plating and hard chrome plating (also known as functional or industrial chrome plating). The variations in chemicals and processes for these two surface coatings impart unique and specific surface coating characteristics.

Decorative chrome plating typically has a thin layer of bright nickel underneath the chrome layer. This undercoat contributes to the lustrous surface of decorative chrome plating and also improves corrosion and tarnish resistance. As indicated by its name, decorative chrome is typically selected for its aesthetic appeal. It is often used as a coating for automotive bumpers, bicycles, plumbing fixtures, and other consumer products where visual appeal and tarnish resistance are desired.

Functional chrome coating often has a dull, gray appearance and imparts many desirable physical properties. These include high hardness, abrasion and wear resistance, corrosion and chemical resistance, as well as high adhesion strength. These attributes make hard chrome a suitable surface coating for engine components, hydraulic cylinders, cutting tools, and a multitude of other items. As mentioned previously, hard chrome plating is also used extensively to repair worn parts and tools. This is very common for expensive components used in heavy equipment and ships. A large consumer of this service is the U.S. Department of Defense.

Chrome electroplating is well understood since it has been around for nearly a century. The process is relatively simple and inexpensive. However, it is not without issue. Chrome electroplating is normally considered a line-of-sight plating process. This means that there must be a clear and direct path between the cathode (part to be plated) and the anode for movement of electrical current. This makes fixturing and positioning of small parts difficult, and plating of holes is very challenging. The distribution of chromium on part surfaces can be inconsistent when compared to other surface coating technologies, and the electrical efficiency of this process is very low.

6.2.2 Health, Safety, and Environmental Issues

Although chrome plating is very versatile and indispensable as an industrial surface coating, it does have major drawbacks of which health, safety, and environmental concerns top the list. Most hard chrome plating processes use plating solutions that contain hexavalent chromium which is a known carcinogen and mutagen [2]. Contact with chromic acid can cause dermatitis, and in severe cases, ulcers or burns on the skin. Prolonged inhalation of fumes or mist can result in ulcers and perforation in the nasal septum and esophagus. Hexavalent chromium is also extremely toxic if taken orally. Once reaching the bloodstream, hexavalent chromium causes damage to the kidneys, liver, and blood cells [2].

During the electroplating process, large amounts of hydrogen gas are produced at the anode/solution and cathode/solution interfaces. The evolution of hydrogen gas results in the formation of tiny hydrogen gas bubbles. As these bubbles reach the surface of the plating solution and burst, they create a fine mist of plating chemistry. Once airborne, the risk of these chemicals coming in contact with workers and being released into the atmosphere is high. Precautions must be taken to mitigate worker and environmental risks involving airborne hexavalent chromium. This commonly involves the enclosure of open plating tanks and the addition of air handling equipment to draw mist and vapors from the surface of the plating solution where it is pulled into a scrubber system which removes all chemicals and gases before releasing the air in to the atmosphere.

In addition to equipment needed to reduce airborne chemicals, people working near plating chemicals must also wear extensive PPE (personal protective equipment) to reduce or eliminate direct contact with plating chemicals. Plating chemicals have a very low pH (near 0) and, as stated above, can cause burns along with other long-term reactions. Common PPE includes safety goggles or face shields, water-proof and chemical resistant gloves, aprons, sleeves, and leg spats with shoe covers. To prevent workers from carrying contaminated clothing home with them, it is often recommended that all clothing and PPE worn while working around plating chemicals is left at the job site.

Chrome plating also creates a lot of toxic waste as everything that comes in contact with the plating solution must be decontaminated and disposed of as toxic waste. All fluids involved in the plating process must be treated before disposal. This includes water used to rinse plating solution from parts. This fluid is typically sent to an in-house water treatment facility where a filter press removes all solids, and then the remaining fluid is analyzed and treated to neutralize its pH before sending to the sewer system or to a waste disposal site.

6.2.3 Safety and Environmental Regulation

1970 was a pivotal year for worker and environmental protection. It was in this year that President Richard M. Nixon signed executive orders to create Occupational Health and Safety Administration (OSHA) and Environmental Protection Agency (EPA) [9, 16]. In 1975, National Institute of Occupational Safety and Health (NIOSH) documented the carcinogenic effects of water-insoluble Cr(VI) compounds, and in 1988 they recommended that all Cr(VI) compounds be considered occupational carcinogens [15]. In 1998, EPA's Integrated Risk Information System (IRIS) classified hexavalent chromium as a known human carcinogen via inhalation [11].

Formerly known as the Federal Water Pollution Control Act, the Clean Water Act was reorganized and expanded in 1972 with additional amendments and renaming in 1977 [12]. During this same timeframe the Clean Air Act of 1970 and its amendment in 1990 were enacted. These acts gave the EPA the authority to limit emissions of pollutants affecting air and water quality [10]. Since the formation of these entities, scientists have studied the toxicity of hexavalent chromium. Armed with this information, OSHA and EPA have continued to set and update regulations to safeguard the environment and people.

As previously mentioned, regulations mandated by OSHA and EPA create the need for extensive equipment and processes meant to protect workers, the community, and the environment. Industry has come up with some ingenious methods to reduce the risk of working with hexavalent chromium plating solutions, but these are only successful when used properly. To ensure conformance to regulation requires constant monitoring of systems, processes, and working environments. All these precautions add cost to chrome plating operations. This additional cost has put many smaller plating facilities out of business, but hasn't been great enough to deter larger facilities from using chromium-based plating chemicals up to this point.

Regulation of hexavalent chromium and electrolytic chromium plating has raised public awareness of its harmful qualities. This has resulted in many stories, investigative news reports, and law suits regarding standards violations and contaminated lands and water near industrial sites. Public consciousness and recent interest in care for the environment, sustainable energy and products, and other "green" technologies may end up being the tipping point for a major reduction in hexavalent chromium plating. Regardless of what "tips" the use of hexavalent chrome, it is clear that it will not always be a viable surface coating technology.

6.2.4 Economic Issues and Trends

Initially, the team expected to see downward trends related to hex-chrome manufacturing and production due to regulatory trends. However, through literature review and research the team discovered that upward trends in manufacturing are continuing. The data suggests that Companies are simply pushing more of their manufacturing and production to developing countries.

Since the turn of the century, costs of high grade chromium have been increasing. Figure 6.1 shows an increase from roughly 6,000\$/t in 2000 to almost 10,000\$/t in 2010 [5]. Production capacity, shown in Fig. 6.2, in developed countries has been flat to down, while developing countries have seen increased production [3, 5, 24, 25].

There are multiple reasons for this switch of roles, both economic as well as environmental. Environmentally, the maximum respiratory limit in China for Chromium exposure is 0.05 mg/m^3. This is 2.5 times the same limit in the US. (0.02 mg/m^3) and 3 times the EU limit (0.015 mg/m^3) [24]. This means that workers can be exposed to higher levels of Chromium in a plant atmosphere in China than in the US or EU. Combining this with significantly lower costs of labor and transportation have led to

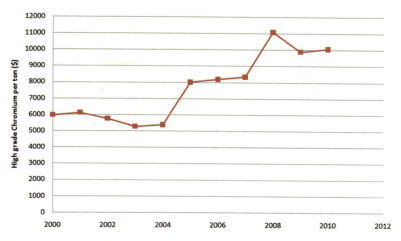

Fig. 6.1 Historical cost of chromium per ton in USD

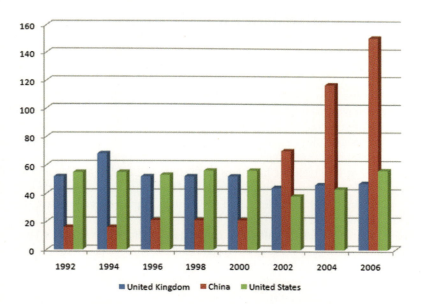

Fig. 6.2 Historical production capacity for China, United Kingdom and United States 1992–2006

multiple new manufacturing facilities in China. For example, there are slightly more than 1,000 manufacturing facilities in the entire US, while there are more than 800 facilities in the Pearl River Delta area of China alone [1, 7].

This leads to the disposal factor of Chromium waste. China has more than six million tons of Chromium waste awaiting disposal [13], which is roughly twice the worldwide production of Chromium per year. By comparison, the total Chromium

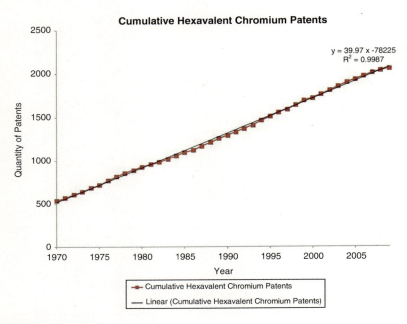

Fig. 6.3 Patent data trend

waste within the US in 2009 was only 7,500 t [6]. The point can be made that the environmental waste impact of Hexavalent Chromium in developing countries does not carry as much concern as in developed countries and companies are finding ways to get around these restrictions by moving their manufacturing to countries with lower environmental regulations. However, environmental regulations covering the usage of Hexavalent Chromium in developed countries are becoming more restrictive. There are regulatory movements underway to restrict imports of products manufactured with Hex chromium and even exemptions for areas like defense are being denied [26, 27].

There are many available alternate materials to replace Hexavalent Chromium for multiple uses; however these are typically highly proprietary, as they're basically variations in the chemical and elemental properties of Chromium. Because of this proprietary nature, there is not a lot of data available in the public domain regarding the usage and industrial experience of these materials. Which, has essentially led to a "Catch-22" situation where the lack of workplace data has slowed down the adoption of these new materials which, in turn has restricted the creation of an industrial need for widespread usage of the technology.

6.2.4.1 Patent and Article Data

Figure 6.3 illustrates the data that was collected using the Patent Search method as illustrated in Appendix 2. When the data is plotted in cumulative fashion, as shown in Fig. 6.3, the information exhibits a linear upward trend-line. This trend would

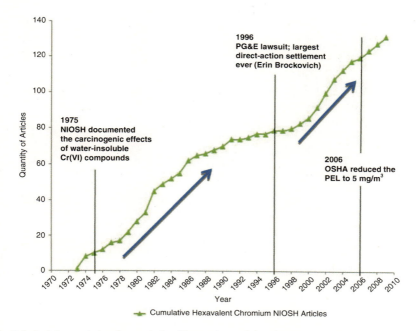

Fig. 6.4 Article trend showing periods of increasing articles (*blue arrow*) after major regulatory events

infer that the developments with respect to standard Hexavalent Chromium have continued without interruption from outside forces.

Figure 6.4 illustrates the data that was collected using the article search method as defined in Appendix 1.

As indicated by the above data, the first NIOSH article occurred in 1974; this article documented the carcinogenic effects of water soluble hexavalent chromium compounds. The research in the field has continued since the publishing of the initial article, although the data does exhibit distinct S curve trends. The first S curve appears to originate from the publishing of the initial article. Then as indicated by the plot, the interest plateaus. Then in 1996, the articles published continue to rise after settlement of the PG&E lawsuit. Therefore, the data suggests that as more research and exposure is completed, the regulatory environment with respect to Hex-Chrome is likely to increase as well.

6.2.5 Summary

A Force Field analysis was used to visually study the forces *for* change and the forces *against* change. Figure 6.5 shows the results of this analysis. We see that most of the forces for changing to alternate materials are environmental regulation

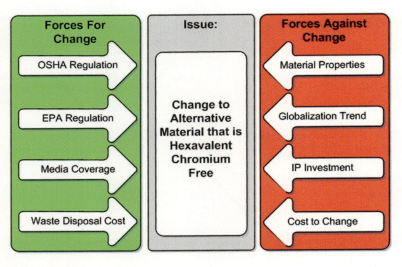

Fig. 6.5 Force field analysis

based. The only economic based force for change is the cost of chromium waste disposal. Of the forces against change, they're primarily economically driven.

Eventually, a tipping point will be reached where the environmental impact outweighs the economic advantages. At the current time it is easier to invest in equipment to meet safety and environmental regulations, or to move production to developing countries. Environmental regulations covering the usage of Hexavalent Chromium in developed countries are becoming restrictive. If past events are a predictor for future events we expect chromium will eventually be regulated to the point where it is not feasible in most applications. In the past other hazardous materials (e.g. lead, mercury, and halogens) followed a similar regulatory and environmental trajectory.

In summary, companies are currently finding ways around regulation but regulatory trends indicate that eventually alternatives must be considered. As with other materials, hex-chrome will be very difficult for companies to use.

6.3 Decision Model

6.3.1 Overview

Prior to implementation in software, the team developed a mathematical model. An overall score is established for each alternate material type as well as the process of record (standard hex-chrome). The overall score, called the "selection material rating score" is a function of the priority given to the category (i.e. hardness, corrosion resistance, friction coefficient, environmental cost, economic cost). The model provides an overall score for each material type as well as visual charts (bar charts) for easy material comparisons.

6.3.2 Functional Description

The evaluation process takes several steps. First, the user determines the application as the criteria weighting is highly dependent on the specific application. Next, a benchmark (control) must be selected; in our case we chose the existing hex-chrome process. The evaluation model compares alternate materials to the benchmark. Identifying performance criteria is the next step; our team chose hardness, corrosion resistance, friction coefficient, environmental cost, and economic cost. Selecting the materials to evaluate is the next step.

Our team chose various alternatives as described in future sections. Next, a priority must be assigned to each of the performance criteria for the given application. For example, if hardness is the most important factor for a given application, then hardness would be given a higher score (weight) than the other performance criterion. After assigning proper weighting, scoring guidelines must be established. Depending on what information is available, different scoring approaches may be selected. Future sections of this paper discuss the scoring guidelines out team used in detail. An evaluation scenario must be selected next in order to properly evaluate alternatives. In some applications cost might be the primary driver. In this case, a "cost driven" scenario would be selected. The final step in the process is the ranking materials step using the evaluation model. Once ranked, the user would move to a feasibility stage with the selected material(s). Since the material would still need to be proven in a real-world application, this step is beyond the scope of this project. The process as stated is flowcharted in Fig. 6.6.

6.3.3 Detailed Description

The mathematical model is shown below. A selection total ranking is calculated for each material (S_i) which is the summation of the weighted performance criteria $P_j C_{i,j}$ for all the criteria scores.

$$S_i = \sum_{j=1}^{n} P_j C_{i,j} \quad \forall i, j \tag{6.1}$$

Where
S_i = Selection Material Rating Score for material i
P_j = Priority for Criteria j
$C_{i,j}$ = Criteria Score j for Material i
n = Number of Selection Criteria

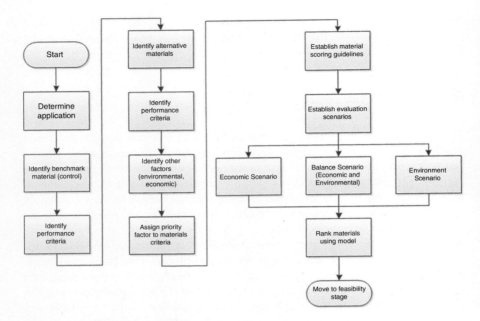

Fig. 6.6 Evaluation process flowchart

6.4 Data Gathering and Model Implementation

6.4.1 Material Selection Criteria

The component that was chosen for the material selection analysis was a hydraulic piston rod. Hydraulic pistons are used in several applications such as vibration dampening in automobiles, mechanical movement of objects such as lift stations, and compression applications such as waste collection [4].

In order to analyze hydraulic piston rods effectively, the several criteria were selected that were necessary for performance and functionality of the component. Table 6.1 identifies the selection criteria with respect to product performance.

In addition to the above required criteria, additional criteria that were nonphysical or mechanical properties were analyzed. These properties are of importance, since the evaluator since it is the responsibility of the evaluator and management to predict and anticipate internal and external market forces when making decisions. Table 6.2 identifies the additional selection items that were weighted in the decision analysis.

In order to analyze the non-Hexavalent Chromium materials several assumptions needed to be made with respect to the selection criteria as listed above. Assumptions are needed because of data availability and the qualitative nature of the available data. In the situation were raw data is available, the raw data will supersede the assumptions, and be used in the selection methodology. However, when unavailable the assumptions will lead the selection.

6 Hexavalent Chromium Substitution

Table 6.1 Selection criteria

Material property	Description
Surface roughness	Material having the capability of a smooth surface.
Surface hardness	Adequate hardness to prevent wear from the friction and contact with mating components during operation.
Corrosion resistance	Ability of the coating to resist corrosion.

Table 6.2 Additional selection criteria

Material property	Description
Material cost	The cost of ownership should be similar to the current material and process
Environmental cost	The cost incurred by the environment for the use and disposal of products and by-products should be lower than the current material

6.4.2 Criteria and Priority Scoring

We used a priority scale of 1 (not important), 2 (somewhat important), and 3 (very important). For the rating scale, we used a similar scoring method: 0.5 (property not listed in datasheet), 1 (bad), and 3 (good).

6.4.3 Criteria and Material Analysis Assumptions

In order to test the functionality of our decision model, some assumptions were established. If material data was not available from the manufacturer for the alternate material, the assumption was the given property was less than that of hex-chrome. The environmental cost and impact of the alternative material was considered to be less than that of hex-chrome. The material cost for the alternative material was considered greater than the cost of hex-chrome.

6.4.4 Alternate Materials Evaluated

The alternative materials were chosen based on the explicit identification that the materials were hexavalent chromium free in the marketing brochures, and material specifications sheets. The material information was searched and compiled utilizing information that was publicly available on the internet. Table 6.3 identifies the alternate materials that we evaluated in the analysis, specifically, the manufacturer, product name, and web address.

Table 6.3 Potential materials

Manufacturer	Product name	Web address
A Brite	Enviro-Alloy	http://www.abrite.com/acs.htm
Shining Surface Systems	Mettex 6	http://www.surface-systems.com/
U.S. Chrome	Hard TriCom	http://www.uschrome.com
Integran	Nanovate CR	http://www.integran.com
Sub-one	InnerArmor	http://www.sub-one.com

Table 6.4 Material summary

	Material type				
Material property	Enviro-Alloy	Mettex 6	Hard TriCom	Nanovate CR	InnerArmor
Corrosion resistance	Good[a]	NA	Good	Good	Good
Hardness	NA[b]	Good	Good	NA	Good
Coefficient of friction	NA	Good	NA	Good	Good
Environmental cost	Good	Good	Good	Good	Good

Bad = material property less than chrome
[a]Good = material property equal to or greater than chrome
[b]NA = material property data not available

6.4.5 Strengths and Weakness

In order to analyze the materials, the strengths and weaknesses were recording from all the material data sheets identified for analysis. Appendix 3 lists all the strength and weakness tables collected for the materials analyzed. Table 6.4 summarizes the strengths and weaknesses of the subject materials, as they relate to the criteria identified for the hydraulic cylinder.

Additional assumptions:

1. If listed as strength the performance is equal to or better than the traditional Hexavalent Chromium product.
2. If a physical performance characteristic is not listed, then the physical property is less than traditional Hexavalent Chromium.

6.4.6 Model Implementation and Results

Five alternative materials were compared to the standard existing Hexavalent chromium process. These five materials were evaluated using the mathematical model outlined above. The initial evaluation consisted of five primary factors as described above: surface roughness, surface hardness, corrosion resistance, cost, and environmental impact. An overall score was calculated for each potential replacement which is the summation of each of the weighted (priority) criteria scores. These scores were then compared to each other for a cursory decision. As previously discussed, the goal of this project was to build a decision process, rather than a conclusive decision analysis, due to limitation of alternative coating data.

6 Hexavalent Chromium Substitution

		Enviro-Alloy		
Chemical Property	Priority	Value	Rating	Score
Corrosion Resistance	3	Good	3	9
Physical Property	Priority	Value	Rating	Score
Hardness	3	Not Listed	0.5	1.5
Mechanical Property	Priority	Value	Rating	Score
Coefficient of Friction	3	Not Listed	0.5	1.5
Economic	Priority	Value	Rating	Score
Economic Cost	1	Bad	1	1
Environmental	Priority	Value	Rating	Score
Environmental Cost	3	Good	3	9
		Total Score		22

Fig. 6.7 Enviro-Alloy model results

The decision model was implemented using MS-Excel version 2007. Input cells were created which allow engineers and managers to enter data for each vendor and view the results visually in easy to read charts.

Data was used for each alternative based on information obtained from the manufacturer's data-sheets or input was empirically decided based from research. The following example illustrates a typical output results (Fig. 6.7), for Enviro-Alloy.

6.5 Scenario Analysis

In order to analyze the implication of economic and environmental criteria on material selection, the methodology of scenario analysis was utilized. For the material selection process, three separate scenarios of the model stated above were conducted and compared.

For the analysis, the priority levels of the Environmental and Economic factors were altered from a high (value of 3) to low (value of 1) level, and the resulting preferred material was determined mathematically. Figure 6.8 titled Scenario Analysis Summary identifies the three different scenarios that were utilized for the decision model and corresponding priority levels. Note: all other material criteria were held constant for the evaluation.

6.5.1 Cost Scenario

A cost driven scenario is defined as a high priority value on economic costs, and low priority value on environmental costs. Under this scenario the preferred material of choice is standard Hexavalent Chrome. Figure 6.9 titled Cost Driven Scenario Model Output, illustrates the results of the model under a cost driven scenario.

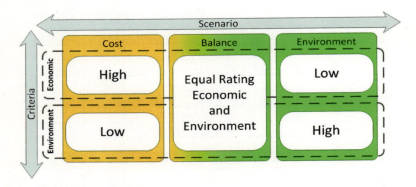

Fig. 6.8 Scenario analysis summary

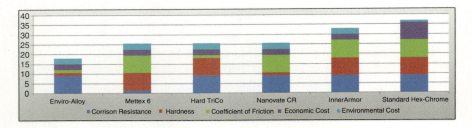

Fig. 6.9 Cost driven scenario model output

6.5.2 Balanced Scenario

A Balanced scenario is defined as setting the economic costs are equal to the environmental costs. Under this scenario the preferred material of choice is either standard Hexavalent Chrome or the InnerArmor material. Figure 6.10 titled balanced scenario model output, illustrates the results of the model under a balanced scenario.

6.5.3 Environmental Scenario

An environmental driven scenario is defined as a high priority value on environmental costs, and low priority value on economic costs. Under this scenario the preferred material of choice is InnerArmor. Figure 6.11 titled Environmental Scenario Model Output, illustrates the results of the model under an environmental driven scenario.

6 Hexavalent Chromium Substitution

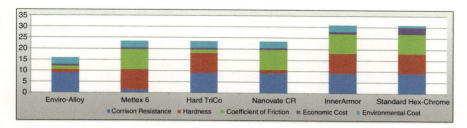

Fig. 6.10 Balanced (environment=cost)

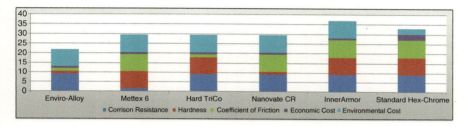

Fig. 6.11 Environmental driven scenario output

6.5.4 Conclusion

From a pure cost standpoint, existing Hex-chrome is the most cost effective followed by InnerArmor. Currently Hex-chrome is not the best choice when environmental criteria are considered. InnerArmor looks to be the best choice in this category followed by three other alternate vendors. When a balanced scenario is analyzed, where cost and environmental impact are both considered, InnerArmor and the existing Hex-chrome appear to be the best choices.

6.6 Conclusion and Recommendations

6.6.1 Project Summary

In this project, the team provided a history of hard chromium coatings. We discussed the regulatory, environmental, and economic issues emanating from hard chromium. Various alternatives are discussed in detail, many of which are considered "Nano-coatings" due to their tiny architecture and deposition methods. An evaluation model/decision matrix was developed. This model evaluates various alternatives using a multiple selection criteria along with weighted scoring and scenario analysis. The team added to the existing body of knowledge by establishing this model and providing guidance regarding the model inputs.

6.6.2 Future Direction

As data becomes available, scoring factors should be a gradient of the actual values. For example, the model could support actual hardness data for each material normalized to the baseline (hex-chrome). Weighting factors could also be added to the model to comprehend additional factors such as professional, organizational, and other factors. This expanded model is shown below:

$$S_i = \sum_{j=1}^{n} k_j P_j C_{i,j} \quad \forall i,j \tag{6.2}$$

6.6.3 Concluding Remarks

In this project, the team provides a history of hard chromium coatings. We discussed the issues surrounding hard chromium and traditional application processes. Various alternatives were discussed in detail, and a decision matrix/evaluation model was developed.

Appendix 1: Article Search Methodology

In order to understand the future of hexavalent chromium, a article search was conducted using data that is available on the National Institute for Safety and Health (NIOSH) website. The NIOSH site provided an internal search engine that was used to data mine the information on the site. Table 6.5 identifies the search criteria that was utilized to search the website.

Table 6.5 Article search criteria

Find results: with all the words	Issue date: start	Issue date: end
Chromium, hexavalent	January	December

For each of the above searches the years that were analyzed were from year 1970 to year 2009 (inclusive). For each of the samples the issue date was changed for both the Start and End values to represent the year of interest.

For Example:

Entry (1) January 1980 and December 1980
Entry (2) January 1981 and December 1981

For each of the samples, the number of articles published was recorded in the responding data set.

Appendix 2: Patent Search Methodology

In order to understand the future of hexavalent chromium, a patent search was conducted using data that is available on the United States Patent and Trademark (USPTO) website. The search engine that was used to data mine the information on the USPTO site was Google patents [14]. Through Google patents, data was collected using the following search criteria (Table 6.6).

For each of the above searches the years that were analyzed were from year 1970 to year 2009 (inclusive). For each of the samples the issue date was changed for both the Start and End values to represent the year of interest.

For Example:

Entry (1) January 1980 and December 1980
Entry (2) January 1981 and December 1981

For each of the samples, the number of patents issued was recorded in the responding data set. In order to obtain the y-intercept for the number of patents issued before 1980, data set was searched without an opening Issue date, and with the closing date of December 1979.

Table 6.6 Patent search criteria

Find results: with all the words	Find results: without the words	Document status	Issue date: start	Issue date: end
Hexavalent chromium	Trivalent	Issued	January	December

Appendix 3: Alternate Materials Strengths and Weaknesses

Table 6.7 Material: Enviro-Alloy strengths and weaknesses [20]

Strengths	Weaknesses
Corrosion resistance Electrical throw Coverage	No data listed

Table 6.8 Material: Mettex 6 strengths and weaknesses [21]

Strengths	Weaknesses
Hardness Heat treat hardness Friction coefficient Surface roughness Throwing power Covering power Current efficiency Deposition rate	Wear rate

Table 6.9 Material: Hard TriCom strengths and weaknesses [22]

Strengths	Weaknesses
Hardness Wear resistance Fatigue debit Thermal stability Corrosion resistance Coverage	No data listed

Table 6.10 Material: Nanovate CR strengths and weaknesses [23]

Strengths	Weaknesses
Friction coefficient Sliding wear Corrosion protection Fatigue debit High temp durability Deposition frequency Throughput Energy consumption Bath stability	No data listed

Table 6.11 Material: InnerArmor strengths and weaknesses [8]

Strengths	Weaknesses
Hardness Corrosion resistance Coefficient of friction Coverage/uniformity Thinner application Environmental	No data listed

References

1. Chinasavvy (2013) Metal and plastic chrome plating|ChinaSavvy. http://www.chinasavvy.com/industrial/plating.php.
2. Grevatt P (1998) Toxicological review of hexavalent chromium (CAS No. 18540-29-9) in support of summary information on the Integrated Risk Information System (IRIS)
3. Kogel JE, Trivedi NC, Barker JM (2006) Industrial minerals & rocks: commodities, markets, and uses. Society for Mining Metallurgy, Littleton, CO, p321
4. LIGON (2013) Hydraulic cylinder applications by industry and application. http://www.hydrauliccylindergroup.com/hydraulic-cylinder-industries-applications/index.htm
5. Papp JF (2009) 2007 minerals yearbook. Chromium (advanced release)
6. Papp JF (USGS), Mersdorf L (2010) Mineral industry surveys. Chromium (February)
7. Sherwood BJ (2010) Regulations, unfair competition: a double-edged sword—metal finishing. http://www.metalfinishing.com/view/14562/regulations-unfair-competition-a-double-edged-sword/
8. Sub-One (2011) InnerArmor coatings for hard chrome replacement. http://www.sub-one.com/ind_hardchrome.html
9. US EPA O EPA History (1970–1985)
10. US EPA O of A and R History|Clean Air Act|US EPA
11. US EPA O of IA and A (2010) Chromium-6 in drinking water (EPA815-F-10-005)
12. US EPA O of P Summary of the Clean Water Act
13. Xin C, Baoyin S (2010) Completing disposal of chemical waste by year end. China Daily 1
14. Google. http://www.google.com/?tbm=pts
15. CDC—Hexavalent Chromium—NIOSH Workplace Safety and Health Topic
16. OSHA 35-year milestones. http://www.osha.gov/as/opa/osha35yearmilestones.html
17. Electroplating (2011) Wikipedia, the free encyclopedia. http://en.wikipedia.org/w/index.php?title=Electroplating&oldid=417176360
18. Chromium (2011) Wikipedia, the free encyclopedia. http://en.wikipedia.org/w/index.php?title=Chromium&oldid=418872185
19. Nicolas-Louis Vauquelin (French chemist)—Britannica online encyclopedia. http://www.britannica.com/EBchecked/topic/624185/Nicolas-Louis-Vauquelin
20. A Brite Company—Technology of tomorrow for today's plating industry. http://www.abrite.com/
21. Shining Surface Systems. http://www.surface-systems.com/
22. US Chrome—Hard chrome plating, chrome alternatives and cylinder repair. 5 US Locations. http://www.uschrome.com/tricom_cobalt_ds.html
23. Magnetic shield & magnetic shielding—Integran Technologies, Inc. http://www.integran.com/services/nanovate-em-magnetic-shield-coating/
24. Institute of Health and Consumer Protection Chemicals Bureau I-21020 Ispra (VA) (2005) Chromium trioxide, sodium chromate, sodium dichromate, ammonium dichromate and potassium dichromate: summary risk assessment report. Institute of Health and Consumer Protection Chemicals Bureau I-21020 Ispra (VA), UK
25. (2006) Minerals yearbook 2006. Area reports. International: 2–22
26. (2007) European Union denies exemption for the use of hexavalent chromium for electrical/electronic equipment—metal finishing. http://www.metalfinishing.com/view/2575/european-union-denies-exemption-for-the-use-of-hexavalent-chromium-for-electrical-electronic-equipment/
27. (2009) DOD forcing the hex-chrome alternative issue—metal finishing. http://www.metalfinishing.com/view/2596/dod-forcing-the-hex-chrome-alternative-issue/

Part III
Research and Development

Chapter 7
Exploring Adoption of Services Delivered Through Information Technology: Case of Mobile Services

Nuri Basoglu, Tugrul U. Daim, and Banu Kargin

Abstract Better services are best developed by understanding the requirements and needs of the users. In this study, our intention was to shed some light on the process of mobile service adoption and preference by investigating value added services especially for information services. The study started with background research to identify factors determining the adoption of mobile services; then continued with qualitative studies. After these studies, an experimental study was conducted. During the experimental study, a conjoint analysis had been conducted. During conjoint analysis, product preference factors were explored. Our results show that service cost and service speed were the most critical factors. Mobile technologies are gaining more popularity and diffusing into every aspect of our life. Value Added Services (VAS) have a huge impact on consumers' usage patterns and has become a significant differentiator across the operators. These led to new opportunities in innovation of differentiating services.

7.1 Introduction

Mobile service adoption can be attributed to several effective factors: personal, social or level of technology. Before exploring the mobile service adoption factors, foundation of theories and previous studies on technology adoption were explored.

N. Basoglu (✉)
Izmir Institute of Technology, Izmir, Turkey
e-mail: nuribasoglu@iyte.edu.tr

T.U. Daim
Engineering and Technology Management Department,
Portland State University, Portland, OR, USA
e-mail: tugrul@etm.pdx.edu

B. Kargin
Turkcell, Istanbul, Turkey
e-mail: Banu.Kargin@turkcell.com.tr

A number of theories have been developed to help explain the concept of technology adoption [1, 2]. In summary, theoretical models that aim to clarify the relationship between consumer attitudes, intentions, and actual use include the Theory of Reasoned Action (TRA) [3], the Theory of Planned Behavior (TPB) [4], Innovation Diffusion Theory [5–8], the Technology Acceptance Model (TAM) [9, 10] and Unified Theory of Acceptance and Use of Technology (UTAUT) [11].

Kauffman and Techatassanasoontorn [12] explored different adopter categories and factors that affect adoption decisions of digital wireless phones from 46 developed and developing countries from 1992 to 2002 and found that digital wireless phone adoption patterns did not follow a normal distribution and did not map exactly into Rogers' five adopter categories. Another study has been conducted by Lal et al. [13] regarding the usage of mobile wireless. The paper intended to look at how homeworkers used mobile phone for social interaction purposes. In-dept, semi-structured interviews were conducted for small sample. The finding suggested that significant number of homeworkers (employees who work from home) actually use mobile wireless to communicate with relatives outside designated work hours. It shows that the importance of mobile wireless are increasing from time to time. Lal and Dwivedi [14] also conducted research regarding the usage of mobile phones. They investigated the usage of mobile phones to stay connected to work "anytime, anywhere". The paper attempted to uncover whether homeworkers actually remain connected as indicated. Semi structured interviews were conducted and the findings suggest that actually homeworkers took various actions in order to control their contactability outside the work domain.

Scupola [15] conducted research in adoption of e-commerce in SME's in the perspectives of Denmark and Australia. The paper highlighted similarities and differences of SMEs of those count4ries. Literature review and questionnaires were conducted in Danish and Australian Companies. The findings suggest that both countries have similar significant factors that affecting SME's e-commerce adoption and implementation. Although differences still exist for some part. Tan et al. [16], wrote a paper to investigate the demographic characteristics of Small and Medium Enterprises (SMEs) in adopting ICT by looking at the benefits, barriers and the intention. Questionnaires were distributed to collect the data. The results show that regardless year of business and internet experiences, SMEs would adopt ICT. The study is applicable only to the setting of SMEs in southern Malaysia. The topic of technology adoption in SMEs is not actually new. Research has been conducted back in 2006 by Zeimpekis and Giaglis [17] in which they examined the implementation of telematics use in SMEs in Greek Market. The research found that the adoption of telematics was still low in Greece however they realized the importance of mobile services. It is undeniable that the operators are looking toward this direction and already starting to make strategic decisions. Aleke et al. [18] also looked into the adoption of ICT in developing country. It is expanded the scope of what Tan, et al. did in 2010. They used focus group that consists of 27 agribusiness proprietors to examine how social augmented parameters impact the effective adoption of ICT in Southeast Nigeria. The findings suggest that a balance between efforts in designing ICT and social factors need to be maintained in order to ensure successful diffusion of innovation.

Seneler et al. [19] conducted a study on adoption of online services. The study was focusing on factors that affect the attitude towards using online services. Through series of literature research and focus group, the study concluded that usefulness and ease of use are affecting the "intention to use" in the case of online services. Not only that, acquaintances, commercials, and self-efficacy also identified as positive factors. The study is expected to give insight to the developers of online services on factors that matter, so that people will actually use online services. Ozkan et al. [20] explored similar issues by looking at the adoption of e-payment status. The adoption of e-payment systems correlate with the adoption of online services. The findings of this research concluded that security, trust, perceived advantage, assurance seals, perceived risk and usability were important factors for customers to use e-payment. Similar study with Ozkan et al. [20] was conducted earlier by Khalifa and Shen [21]. The examined the factors that affect the adoption of B2C mobile commerce. Technology Acceptance Model and Theory of Planned Behavior (TPB) were developed and empirically tested. The results showed that technology characteristics variables are important in the adoption of mobile commerce.

Standing, et al. [22] studied electronic markets in the resource engineering sector. The paper looked at economic, social, political and cultural factors and their interconnections in the transition of companies into global e-markets. It concluded that the implementation of ICT will allowed the incremental growth of suppliers in the global electronic market. The implementation of ICT can reduce the transaction cost which made the electronic market more desirable. Al-maghrabi et al. [23] looked at e-shopping in Saudi Arabia as the manifestation of adoption of ICT. This research complement and add research insight to what Seneler (Seneler 2010) and Ozkan (Ozkan 2010) did. A structural equation model was used to prove that usefulness, enjoyment and subjective norm are determinants of online shopping. Abbasi et al. [24] also investigated the topic of Technology Acceptance to complement Al-maghrabi et al. [23] work. The finding suggested that social belief along with management support and user experience influenced individual's perceptions in adopting IT technologies.

As identified through the review of literature, the adoption of mobile devices and services depends on several factors and is difficult to assess. Therefore, we propose and demonstrate a prototype based approach for this objective.

7.2 Methodology

7.2.1 Research Model

Personalization may be defined as a powerful tool that enables consumers to select the content, presentation and functionality of the service according to their unique needs and preferences. According to the needs of consumers, personalization seems to be a desired feature. This is also mentioned by Carlsson et al. [25] such that dimensions of communication which involve personalization predict the use of some mobile services.

The effect of personalization on preference was investigated by Kargin and Basoglu [26] in 2006. One of their significant findings is that personalization has a direct impact on usefulness and an indirect impact on attitude via usefulness. Making it unique to the individual in various ways is an important part of any service. Consumers should feel services are unique to them. Bouwman et al. [27] also indicated that the characteristics (personalization) of mobile services will affect the future use or adoption of mobile services.

H1: Personalization significantly and positively influences the preference of the mobile service user.

Content is a major factor for the performance of such services. Grantham and Tsekouras [28] reviewed the recent diffusion literature and indicated that services should not focus on one single attributes or products. In other words, the contents (attributes) should be rich in order to lead users to adopt the mobile services.

Content correctness, content delivery time, content quality, content quantity, and content provider are the ingredients of content. In literature, Gilbert et al. [29] also focus on importance of the content aspect of services. According to their findings, one key barrier to attracting a critical mass of adopters is the lack of compelling content [29]. In 2005, Repo emphasized on construct of content in his study of User Applications of Mobile Multimedia [30]. Muthaiyah [31] cited on useful applications and premium content which will lead to consumer demand.

H2: Content of services significantly and positively influences the preference of the mobile service user.

Cost is another aspect of mobile services which can be compared with the value of services. Users compare costs and benefits of services and try to find a relative advantage over other services. Service costs are also researched by [32]. They found that financial costs are significant barriers to the use of mobile services [32]. Additionally, Hong et al. [33] examines the "Perceived Cost" in his model.

Mallat [34] found that premium pricing will be a barrier for users to adopt mobile payments. Kim et al. [35] researched the adoption of Mobile Internet and found that cost plays important role in the adoption of the mobile internet. Turel et al. [36] contribute by conducting research in the adoption of mobile services and found that price (cost) is critical driver in adoption decision.

H3: Cost significantly and negatively influences the preference of the mobile service user.

In conjoint test, different screen sizes are offered in different scenarios. Two types of screen size are offered: Handsets with large and small size screens (large: 176×208 pixels—small: 96×68 pixels). In 2003, Yamakawa and Matsumoto emphasized handset features during adoption of mobile internet services. They called this construct "size and form factors" in their integrating framework. They called these type factors as facilitating conditions for the demand side [37].

H4: Screen size of mobile terminal positively and significantly influences the preference of the mobile service user.

7 Exploring Adoption of Services Delivered Through Information Technology... 143

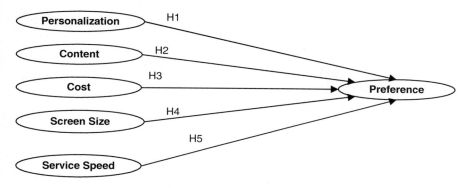

Fig. 7.1 Mobile service conjoint framework

Table 7.1 Mobile service conjoint framework hypotheses

Hypotheses	Dependent variable	Independent variable	Relationship
H1	Preference	Personalization	Positive
H2		Content	Positive
H3		Cost	Negative
H4		Screen size	Positive
H5		Service speed	Positive

In 2004, Pagani used speed of use as a construct in her model [38]. According to the result of the study, speed of use is the most important determinant of adoption of multimedia mobile services. Results also showed that speed of use is more appreciated by young people. In addition to Pagani, Hung et al. [39] revealed that connection speed influences attitude formation towards WAP usage.

H5: Service speed positively and significantly influences the preference of the mobile services user (Fig. 7.1).

Research hypotheses for conjoint constructs drawn from the research framework have been summarized in Table 7.1. These factors may positively or negatively influence user's preference. The main goal of this conjoint analysis is to identify a hierarchy of importance of the critical factors influencing the adoption and preference of mobile services.

During conjoint analysis, a mobile pharmacy service was described in terms of a number of attributes. Mobile pharmacy service provides the nearest pharmacies' information depending on the user's current location. To use this service, the user sends a message from his/her phone by writing "PHARMACY" to the short number of 1111. The mobile service is described in terms of personalization, content, cost, screen size and service speed. Then, each attribute was broken down into a number of levels (Table 7.2):

The hypotheses were explained separately and the relationships between the research constructs for each hypothesis have been indicated in the following pages.

Table 7.2 Attribute levels

Attribute	Levels
Personalization	Exist—not exist
Content	SMS—detailed SMS—MMS
Cost	Inexpensive (0.25 YTL)—expensive (1 YTL)
Screen size	Large (176×208 pixels)—small (96×68 pixels)
Service speed	Fast (1 min)—slow (8 min)

Table 7.3 Research studies

Study	Date	Sample	Remarks
Interviews	Dec. 2006	12	12 questions, 28 constructs
Brainstorming	Mar. 2007	10	19 constructs
Expert focus group	Apr. 2007	11	2 questions, 28 constructs
Pilot study	May 2007	8	35 questions, 18 constructs
Experimental study	May 2007	102	35 questions, 18 constructs

7.2.2 Data Collection

This study was part of a series of research projects. In addition to the literature review, qualitative studies including interviews, brainstorming sessions, and an expert focus group study via e-mail were employed to build and test the research hypotheses. In addition to these studies, different constructs of the final research framework were tested via different pilot studies. In the final step, a quantitative study was conducted. In the development process of the framework and survey scale for this study, a series of empirical studies were administered. Table 7.3 summarizes these studies.

Qualitative studies started with the literature survey. For this purpose, studies about mobile services and theories about research models were investigated in depth. In the References section, you may find detailed information about references.

In terms of qualitative studies, interviews, brainstorming and expert focus group study were conducted. Face to face, semi-structured, in-depth interviewing with mobile service users were also employed. The goal of the interview was to deeply explore the participants' point of view, feelings and perspectives about mobile services. In this sense, in-depth interviews yielded a lot of information. The data for the current research was extracted from interviews concerning the adoption factors of mobile services, especially information-based services. Users were categorized as experienced and novice users according to their usage level of mobile services and number of different services they had. The minimum selection criterion for participants was experience on SMS use. Experience on SMS use was estimated to be necessary to be able to discuss the adoption factors of more advanced mobile services. The interviewees were aged between 25 and 35. Six of the respondents were male, and eight of them were female. Users were also categorized as experienced and novice users according to their service usage experiences and number of different services they use. Each interview was audio recorded; notes were taken and each of them took approximately 1 h. Interviews were reported after each meeting.

After interviews, a brainstorming session was conducted to generate new ideas and new constructs about mobile service adoption. Brainstorming was usually considered a task of divergent thinking, and the ideas produced in most research on brainstorming were counted and scored [40]. Brainstorming is a specific technique developed by Alex F. Osborn who introduced the modern brainstorming session in 1938 as a means of using the brains to storm a problem [41]. Before the brainstorming session, a brainstorming plan was developed. It was ensured that everyone participating in the brainstorm session understood and agreed with the aim of the session. The brainstorming session was carried out with ten people. Four of the participants were experienced users. The average age of the group was 28, and the education level was university or above. Four of the participants were male, and six of them were female. When scheduling the meeting, a brief explanation of the problem and history of the study was given. This helped participants prepare mentally for the session and focus on the particular issue. When inviting individuals to the session, people with different backgrounds and degrees of expertise were chosen. The rules of brainstorming were explained before the session. The brainstorming session lasted approximately 1 h and ten participants were invited to the meeting. Some of the participants were experienced in mobile service usage, some of them were not. During the meeting, notes were taken and the whole meeting was video-recorded. A whiteboard was used for brainstorming since ideas were written on the whiteboard. After the session, the brainstorming notes were edited, the ideas were arranged and the video was watched again.

After the brainstorming session, an expert focus group study was conducted via e-mail to verify the constructs and their importance levels. This element of the study was carried out with 11 people who have experience with mobile service usage and also 6 of them were employees in telecommunication sector. Average age of the expert group was 28 and education level was high (university degree or above). Three of them were male, and eight of them were female. The study had two questions. The first question tried to measure the importance levels of construct group. The second question was about selecting the most important constructs during mobile service usage or design. The results of this study can be found in the findings section.

7.2.3 Conjoint Alternatives

The main goal of the experimental study was to obtain knowledge and inputs about mobile service adoption and design. Conjoint analysis and a questionnaire were used as data collection methods for this study. For the mobile service conjoint framework, conjoint analysis was selected to evaluate service alternatives. In a real purchase situation, consumers do not make choices based on a single attribute.

Consumers examine a range of features or attributes and then make judgments or trade-offs to determine their final purchase choice. Conjoint analysis examined these trade-offs to determine the combination of attributes that will be most satisfying to the consumer. In other words, by using conjoint analysis, a company can determine the optimal features for their product or service. In addition, conjoint analysis will identify the best advertising message by identifying the features that are most important in product or service choice.

The experimental study was conducted via a portable application which was coded in Microsoft Excel with Visual Basic. The application includes three different screens. The first screen aims to collect user demographics. Demographic questions include gender, age, education and mobile service experience years. The second and last screens were designed to test the framework which was mentioned in the framework section. In detail, the second screen was designed to identify a hierarchy of importance of the critical factors influencing the design and the adoption of mobile services. By using this screen, the mobile service conjoint framework was tested. For this purpose, conjoint analysis was conducted. Conjoint analysis is a statistical technique used to determine how people value different features that make up an individual product or service. SPSS Conjoint software package was selected for analysis. It uses the full-profile (also known as full-concept) approach, where respondents rank, order, or score a set of profiles, or cards according to preference. Each profile describes a complete product or service and consists of a different combination of factor levels for all factors of interest. Depending on the conjoint analysis method, a mobile pharmacy service was described in terms of a number of attributes (constructs in this study); namely personalization, content, cost, screen size and service speed. Then, each attribute was broken down into a number of levels.

An SPSS Conjoint method was used to generate alternatives with these attributes and its levels. SPSS conjoint generated 64 alternatives for five attributes and their levels in a traditional way. In order to decrease the number of alternatives, fractional factorial designs were used. Finally, SPSS Conjoint formed eight alternatives (Table 7.4). Each alternative had different attribute levels and therefore represented a different service or product. One of the alternatives was modified after a pilot study. Participants offered a new alternative which was somehow different from one of the alternatives. After the evaluation of this alternative, it became one of the alternatives feasible for the design that meets the needs of consumers. All these alternatives were called scenarios during the experimental study.

Users were asked to rank these eight alternatives (see Fig. 7.2). These alternatives were presented as a classical card view. And each card could be ranked easily by the help of choice buttons. Users may rank cards from 1 to 8. "1" is for the most desirable one, "8" is for the least desirable one. Each card has a detailed button on it. User can click this button and see all details of the related alternative.

The items of this instrument and the instrument itself were examined via a pilot study. This pilot study was done with ten people. According to comments from the pilot group, the instrument was modified. After the pilot study, the experimental study was conducted with 102 people. The data from this study was collected in a

7 Exploring Adoption of Services Delivered Through Information Technology...   147

Table 7.4 Conjoint alternatives generated by SPSS

Alternative #	Speed	Cost	Screen size	Other characteristics
1	Low	High	Small	Detailed SMS Personalization
2	Low	Low	Small	MMS
3	High	Low	Large	SMS Personalization
4	High	Low	Large	Detailed SMS
5	High	High	Large	MMS Personalization
6	High	High	Small	SMS
7	Low	High	Large	SMS
8	High	Low	Small	SMS Personalization

Rank	Speed	Cost	Screen	Other		Rank	Speed	Cost	Screen	Others
1 (a)	Slow	Expensive	Small	Personalization Detailed SMS — Detail/Select		5 (e)	Fast	Expensive	Large	MMS Personalization — Detail/Select
2 (b)	Slow	Cheap	Small	MMS — Detail/Select		6 (f)	Fast	Expensive	Small	SMS — Detail/Select
3 (c)	Fast	Cheap	Large	SMS Personalization — Detail/Select		7 (g)	Slow	Expensive	Large	SMS — Detail/Select
4 (d)	Fast	Cheap	Large	Detailed SMS — Detail/Select		8 (h)	Fast	Cheap	Small	SMS Personalization — Detail/Select

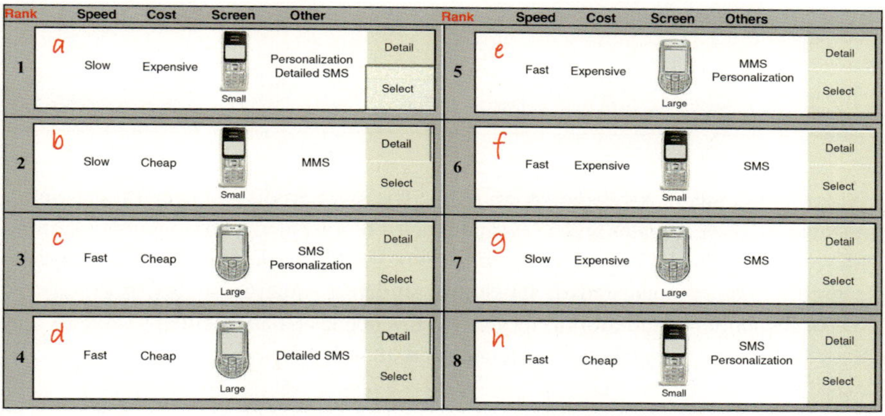

Fig. 7.2 Screen-shot of alternative selection screen

Microsoft Office Excel worksheet. After collecting, the data was sorted, transposed and arranged and became SPSS suitable. Then the organized data was transferred to an SPSS file for analyses.

7.3 Results

7.3.1 *Profile of Experimental Study Users*

The profile of respondents is presented in Table 7.5. This table represents all the frequency analysis conducted on demographic variables. Only mobile service experience construct was regrouped. The results indicate that our sample was

Table 7.5 Profile of respondents

Range	Frequency	Percentage	Cumulative percentage
Gender			
Female	44	43	43
Male	58	57	100
Age			
21–25	50	49	49
26–30	41	40	89
31–40	11	11	100
Education			
High school	1	1	1
University student	16	16	17
Undergraduate	45	44	61
Graduate	40	39	100
Mobile service experience			
≤2 years	25	25	25
>2–4 years	25	25	50
>4–6 years	21	21	70
>6–8 years	21	21	91
>8 years	9	9	100

predominantly aged between 26 and 30. The gender distribution of the study subjects was 43 % females and 57 % males. This represented a homogeneous sample with regard to gender. The educational level of the respondents was high. The sample predominantly consisted of university students, undergraduates or graduates. 25 % of respondents had mobile service experience less than or equal to 2 years and only 9 % of respondents had experience more than 8 years.

7.3.2 Results of Mobile Service Conjoint Analysis

The mobile service conjoint framework hypotheses were tested via conjoint analysis of SPPS conjoint module. Using conjoint analysis, we tried to answer questions such as: Which attributes are important or unimportant to the respondents? What levels of product attributes are the most or least desirable in the respondents' mind? What is the market share of preference? During analysis, the average importance values for attributes and utility scores for attribute levels were calculated. According to the results, the attribute "speed" showed the greatest range with the resulting average importance score of 37.5, while the attribute "personalization" showed the smallest range with the resulting average importance score of 8.29. The range of the utility values (highest to lowest) for each factor provides a measure of how important the factor was to overall preference. Factors with greater utility ranges play a more significant role than those with smaller ranges. Table 7.6 provides a measure of the relative importance of each factor known as an importance score or value. The values are computed by taking the utility range for each factor

Table 7.6 Average importance score of attributes

Attribute	Average importance score
Speed	37.47
Cost	34.87
Content	10.49
Screen	8.88
Personalization	8.29

Table 7.7 Utility scores

Attributes	Levels	Part-worths utility	Std. error
Speed	Fast	1.102	0.051
	Slow	−1.102	0.051
Cost	Inexpensive	1.026	0.044
	Expensive	−1.026	0.044
Screen	Small	−0.261	0.044
	Large	0.261	0.044
Personalization	Exists	0.244	0.044
	Not exist	−0.244	0.044
Content	SMS	−0.338	0.059
	Detailed SMS	0.279	0.067
	MMS	0.059	0.067
(Constant)		4.309	0.045

separately and divide by the sum of the utility ranges for all factors. The values thus represented percentages and have the property to add up to 100. The calculations were done separately for each subject, and the results are then averaged over all the subjects. Average importance scores of all attributes can be seen in Table 7.6.

Table 7.7 shows the utility (part-worths) scores and their standard errors for each factor level. Higher utility values indicate greater preference. As expected, there is an inverse relationship between costs and utility, with higher cost corresponding to lower utility (larger negative values mean lower utility) (Fig. 7.3).

In addition to summarizing the average utilities, which were explained above, each respondent's utility calculations were done separately. Fiwas not the most important factor as opposed to overall preference of our sample. For this respondent, content (36 %), speed (29 %), screen (19 %), cost (14 %) and personalization (2 %) are important in the written order. Content is the most important factor in service purchase as it has the highest range of utility values. Content is followed in importance by the speed of the service. Based on the range and value of the utilities, we can see that personalization was relatively unimportant to this respondent. Therefore, advertising which emphasizes personalization would be ineffective. This person would make his or her purchase choice based mainly on content and then on the speed of the service. Marketers could use the information from utility values to design products and/or services which come closest to satisfying important consumer segments. This technique, therefore, could be used to identify market opportunities by exploring the potential of product feature combinations that are not currently available. Table 7.8 shows average importance scores of attributes for the selected respondent (Fig. 7.4).

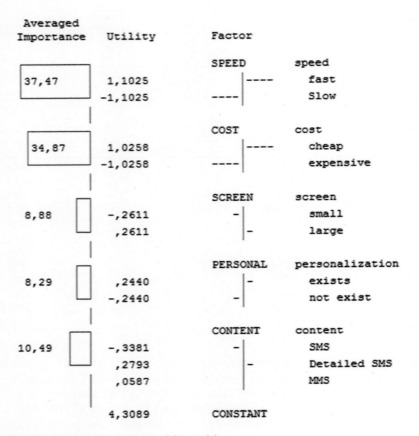

Fig. 7.3 Results of mobile service conjoint model

Table 7.8 Subject II's average importance score

Attribute	Average importance score
Content	36.21
Speed	28.78
Screen	19.18
Cost	13.91
Personalization	1.92

Depending on the conjoint scores, market shares for all alternatives were calculated (see Table 7.9).

Alternative 4 was chosen as the most preferred alternative. The attribute levels of Alternative 4 can be seen in Table 7.10. In the light of these facts, it can be said that Alternative 4 will obtain more market share than others.

Alternative 3 and Alternative 8 followed the Alternative 4, respectively. Their market shares were very close to Alternative 4.

7 Exploring Adoption of Services Delivered Through Information Technology... 151

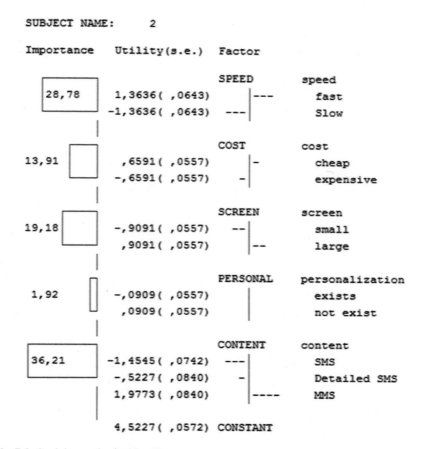

Fig. 7.4 Conjoint result of subject II

7.3.3 Sample Clustering

In addition to the models of the study, mobile service adoption factors were also explained by the sample clustering method. For that reason, different cluster analyses, having two, three and four clusters, were tried. These cluster analyses were done depending on service attributes such as speed, cost and depending on technology and personality characteristics such as experience, innovativeness and enjoyment. In this part of the study, cluster analysis with four clusters was explained in depth. The names given to the clusters are subjective and they may be changed.

The most important and interesting results were obtained with cluster analysis having four samples. This cluster analysis was done depending on service attributes which were used in conjoint analysis. Number of cases in each cluster is 10, 36, 20, and 36, respectively (see Table 7.11).

Table 7.9 Alternatives and market shares

Card	Speed	Cost	Screen	Personalization	Content	Rank 1	2	3	4	5	6	7	8	Average score	Market share (%)
Alternative 4	Fast	Inexpensive	Large	Not exist	Detailed SMS	**35**	27	25	8	5	2	0	0	6.73	19
Alternative 3	Fast	Inexpensive	Large	Exist	SMS	25	**40**	23	7	7	0	0	0	6.60	18
Alternative 8	Fast	Inexpensive	Small	Exist	SMS	22	17	**34**	13	10	1	1	4	6.08	17
Alternative 5	Fast	Expensive	Large	Exist	MMS	13	4	12	29	**30**	9	2	3	4.95	14
Alternative 2	Slow	Inexpensive	Small	Not exist	MMS	2	8	2	26	10	**34**	12	8	3.79	11
Alternative 6	Fast	Expensive	Small	Not exist	SMS	2	3	2	15	25	**33**	20	2	3.54	10
Alternative 1	Slow	Expensive	Small	Exist	Detailed SMS	3	2	3	4	7	14	**36**	33	2.44	7
Alternative 7	Slow	Expensive	Large	Not exist	SMS	0	1	1	0	8	9	31	**52**	1.86	5

7 Exploring Adoption of Services Delivered Through Information Technology... 153

Table 7.10 Attribute levels of alternative 4

Card	Alternative 4
Speed	Fast (1 min)
Cost	Inexpensive (0.25 YTL)
Screen	Large (176 × 208 pixels)
Personalization	Not exist
Content	Detailed SMS

Table 7.11 Number of cases in clusters

Clusters	Number of cases
SMS addict	10
Price-sensitive	36
MMS addict	20
Speedy	36

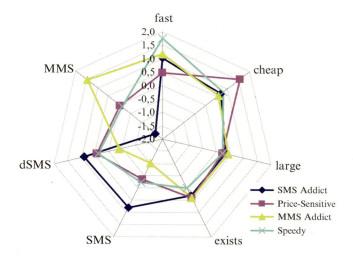

Fig. 7.5 Cluster analysis result with four clusters (service attributes)

The first of these clusters was named SMS addicts. The results showed that they prefer SMS (Short Messaging Service) and detailed SMS instead of MMS. Second cluster represented the price-sensitive users. The most significant differentiator of this cluster is that they prefer lower prices. In addition to this, getting a quick reply from the service is not an important factor. And also, they are indifferent to content, screen size and personalization features. The Third cluster was called MMS (Multimedia Messaging Service) addicts. They preferred messages with pictures and sounds, namely MMS instead of SMS. They are indifferent to cost. It can be more or less. The last cluster represented speedy users. They would like to get a response from the service quickly. Personalization and large screen size are not very important for this cluster. The details of the analysis can be seen in Fig. 7.5 and Table 7.12.

Table 7.12 Results of cluster analysis with four clusters (service attributes)

Attribute	Level	F	Sig.	SMS addict	Price-sensitive	MMS addict	Speedy
Speed	Fast	41.900	.000	1.01	0.46	1.15	**1.74**
Cost	Inexpensive	28.390	.000	0.70	**1.59**	0.58	0.81
Personalization	Exists	4.490	.005	0.30	0.40	**0.40**	−0.01
Content	SMS	24.690	.000	**0.80**	−0.37	−1.05	−0.23
Content	Detailed SMS	16.180	.000	**0.90**	0.41	−0.40	0.35
Content	MMS	98.220	.000	−1.70	−0.05	**1.45**	−0.12

7.4 Research Synthesis

The results for conjoint analysis reveal that speed, cost and content are the most important factors to overall mobile service preference. During the design of value added services, operators should consider the factors identified and tested in this theoretical framework in depth. The Speed problem may be resolved with employing new high speed technologies. Cost is another important factor. Users prefer low costs. In addition to offering low cost, different payment methods can be searched such as credit card payment or partial payment. Some services may be offered as free for trial or loyalty purposes.

In terms of part-worth utilities, alternatives which have fast, inexpensive, detailed SMS, large screen and personalization features were preferred. Although screen size was not a direct characteristic of service, large screens were preferred by users during the service usage. This is an important insight to handset producers and operators. Operators may force handset manufacturers to produce handsets which are compatible with services.

In terms of market shares for alternatives, alternative 3 and alternative 8 were the followers of the alternative 4. All three alternatives have high-speed capability, and they are inexpensive. Table 7.13 displays the alternative levels of the most preferred alternatives:

According to these results, it is understood that services delivered via SMS based platforms will obtain more market shares than others.

According to results of the cluster analysis, different segments have been defined. Communication and marketing programs should be varied based on different segments. For example, *SMS Addict* segment prefers to receive text messages, instead of MMS. Text-based services can be offered to them such as text-based information services. On the other hand, *MMS addicts* prefer services that include pictures, images or sounds. Downloadable contents such as video or wallpaper may be marketed to them. Additionally, new services should be advertised to them via MMS instead of SMS.

It is considered that findings of this study will contribute to the mobile service adoption literature. This research provides insights for mobile service and product

Table 7.13 The most preferred alternatives

Card	Speed	Cost	Screen	Personalization	Content
Alternative 4	Fast	Inexpensive	Large	Not exist	Detailed SMS
Alternative 3	Fast	Inexpensive	Large	Exist	SMS
Alternative 8	Fast	Inexpensive	Small	Exist	SMS

managers during service design and requirement phases in the telecommunication industry. Value added services' marketing experts will also gain some additional insights about users' behaviors, needs and preferences. They may use them in their marketing activities accordingly.

During this study, many limitations were encountered. First of all, sample size of 102 was appropriate, but having a larger sample size would provide more beneficial and fruitful results. However, due to the burden of answering time in the application, the return rate fell below the estimations. Secondly, the respondents of the study represented people between 21 and 40 years of age. This may be seen as a limitation. However, since value added services target young generation, it was acceptable, particularly since results did not draw conclusions outside this demographic.

In addition to this, the experimental study was conducted only in Turkey, so culture effect could not be estimated. It is also limited with Istanbul, there is no other city. Further studies in mobile service adoption area would extend this study. Adoption factors should analyzed on larger samples from different cultures. In this way, the effect of culture may be estimated.

7.5 Conclusions

Some technology forecast studies show that mobile systems will gain more popularity and will diffuse into different parts of our life. Better services will be best developed by understanding the requirements of the potential users. In this study, our intention was to shed some light on the process of mobile service adoption by investigating and understanding factors affecting the users' preference and intention.

The results for conjoint analysis reveal that speed, cost and content are the most important factors to overall mobile service preference. In terms of part-worths utilities, alternatives which have fast, inexpensive, detailed SMS, large screen and personalization features were preferred.

As a result of market-share analysis, alternative 4 was selected as the most preferred service. Alternative 4 provides quick response to users (after querying, response delivers in 1 min). It is relatively inexpensive and displayed in large screen.

For this alternative, content is delivered via detailed SMS which provides more and detailed information, but it does not include a map. This alternative does not include personalization option. This may be a result of desire for simplicity. Users may think that if it does not have personalization option, it will be simple.

Further studies in mobile service adoption area may include the extension of the models with different constructs. Moreover, constructs should be analyzed on larger samples from different cultures. By this way, the effect of culture may be estimated.

The framework developed for this research was beneficial for further empirical studies in this area. Extension of this study should include analyzing new constructs on more advanced value added services such as video-downloading and Mobile-TV. Their adoption process may include different factors. Additionally, due to rapid changes in the mobile service and telecommunication environment, following the sectors of telecommunication and value added services will be very beneficial for understanding the dynamics in this turbulent marketplace.

Appendices

Interview Questions (English)

1. Do you follow technology closely? Do you use a new technology, product or service right after its launch or do you wait until others use and adopt it?
2. In the same medium, which do you prefer? The Internet over PC or mobile phone? Why?
3. Did you use any mobile services? (Logo Melody, Chat, News Package etc.)
4. Which mobile service do you use most? How long have you been using this service? Do you remember the first mobile service you have used?
5. What do you think is the most important feature of the mobile service that makes it popular? Does usage occur randomly, or consciously? Does it occur willingly and in a planned way?
6. Is there any location based services that you've used recently? What is the most favorite feature of this service? When and in which conditions and situations did you use it?
7. Do you feel comfortable using this service?
8. Do you think this service adds value to your life?
9. What other LBS applications or services would you like to use?
10. Is there any other new feature(s) you wish were offered by any LBS?
11. Any other comments?

7 Exploring Adoption of Services Delivered Through Information Technology... 157

Main Screen of Experimental Study

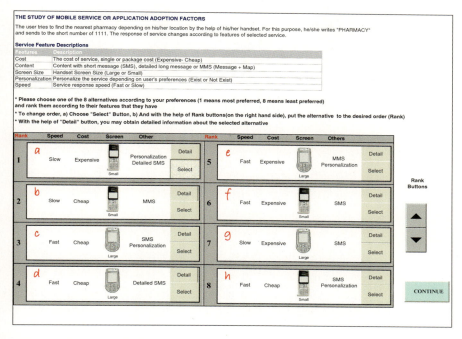

Fig. 7.6 Experimental study—main screen

Table 7.14 Steps of alternatives

Alternatives	Attributes	Step 1	Step 2	Step 3	Step 4
Scenario 1	Slow, expensive, small-screen, personalization, SMS	User writes a message from his small-screen-size phone "PHARMACY" to the number 1111 to learn the nearest pharmacy.	Answer is received via SMS after 8 min. User gets bored. Message is long thus needs scrolling in a small-screen-size phone.	If the user wants, he/she can request personalized messages such as, if he has a car, driving instructions are provided. If not, walking path is provided.	The service is expensive and user is surprised to see such a high price on the bill. The price of service is 1 YTL
Scenario 2	Slow, inexpensive, small-Screen, MMS	User writes a message from his small-screen-size phone "PHARMACY" to the number 1111 to learn the nearest pharmacy.	Answer is received via MMS after 8 min. The message contains a colored map of the nearest pharmacy but since the screen is small, it cannot be seen clearly. User gets bored because he got the message in 8 min.	User cannot ask for personalized messages.	The price is not high and user is pleased to see a reasonable amount on the bill. The price of service is 0.25 YTL.
Scenario 3	Fast, inexpensive, large-screen, personalization, MMS	User writes a message from his small-screen-size phone "PHARMACY" to the number 1111 to learn the nearest pharmacy.	Answer is received via MMS quickly in 1 min. The message contains a colored map of nearest pharmacy and it can be seen clearly in the big screen.	If the user wants, he/she can request personalized messages such as, if he has a car, driving instructions are provided. If not, walking path is provided.	The price is not high and user is pleased to see a reasonable amount on the bill. The price of service is 0.25 YTL.

7 Exploring Adoption of Services Delivered Through Information Technology...

Scenario 4	Fast, inexpensive, large-screen, SMS	User writes a message from his small-screen-size phone "PHARMACY" to the number 1111 to learn the nearest pharmacy.	Answer is received via SMS quickly in 1 min. Message is long but no need to scroll.	User cannot ask for personalized messages.	The price is not high and user is pleased to see a reasonable amount on the bill. The price of service is 0.25 YTL.
Scenario 5	Fast, expensive, large-screen, personalization, MMS	User writes a message from his small-screen-size phone "PHARMACY" to the number 1111 to learn the nearest pharmacy.	Answer is received via MMS in a minute. The message contains a colored map of nearest pharmacy and it can be seen clearly in the big screen.	If the user wants, he/she can request personalized messages such as, if he has a car, driving instructions are provided. If not, walking path is provided.	The service is expensive and user is surprised to see such a high price on the bill.
Scenario 6	Fast, expensive, large-screen, SMS	User writes a message from his small-screen-size phone "PHARMACY" to the number 1111 to learn the nearest pharmacy.	Answer is received via SMS quickly in 1 min. Message is long but no need to scroll.	User cannot ask for personalized messages.	The service is expensive and user is surprised to see such a high price on the bill. The price of service is 1 YTL.
Scenario 7	Slow, expensive, large-screen, SMS	User writes a message from his small-screen-size phone "PHARMACY" to the number 1111 to learn the nearest pharmacy.	Answer is received via SMS after 8 min. User gets bored. Message is long but no need to scroll.	User cannot ask for personalized messages.	The service is expensive and user is surprised to see such a high price on the bill. The price of service is 1 YTL.
Scenario 8	Fast, inexpensive, small screen, personalization, SMS	User writes a message from his small-screen-size phone "PHARMACY" to the number 1111 to learn the nearest pharmacy.	Answer is received via SMS quickly in 1 min. Message is long but no need to scroll.	If the user wants, he/she can request personalized messages such as, if he has a car, driving instructions are provided. If not, walking path is provided.	The service is expensive and user is surprised to see such a high price on the bill. The price of service is 1 YTL.

Alternatives 4 of Experimental Study

SENARYO - D

Step1: User requests information about the nearest pharmacy by using his large screen handset (Writes Pharmacy, sends to the short number of 1111)

```
TO: 1111
PHARMACY
```

Step2: The response is received after 1 minute with a long and detailed SMS. The response was very fast. The user could easily get the needed information.

```
FROM: 2737
The nearest pharmacies are following: Beyoglu Tepebasi Pharmacy, 02123553555; Zumrutevler ISTIKLAL Pharmacy: 02124546345; Asmalımescit YENI Pharmacy 02123645567. For more info, send the name to 1111.
```

Step3: User can not request customized information based on his/her preferences.

Step4: User is pleased with the cost of the service. The cost was within the budget of user. The service price is 0.25YTL per usage.

Fig. 7.7 Experimental study—scenario-D's screen shot

References

1. Kleijnen M, de Ruyter K (2003) Factors influencing the adoption of mobile gaming services, Mobile commerce: technology, theory, and applications. Idea Group Publishing, Hershey, PA, pp 202–217
2. Mennecke B, Strader T (2003) Mobile commerce technology, theory and applications. Idea Group, Hershey, PA
3. Ajzen I, Fishbein M (1980) Understanding attitudes and predicting social behaviour. Prentice-Hall, Englewood Cliffs, NJ
4. Ajzen I (1991) The theory of planned behaviour. Organ Behav Hum Decis Proc 50(2):179–211
5. Agarwal R, Prasad J (1998) A conceptual and operational definition of personal innovativeness in the domain of information technology. Inform Syst Res 9(2):204–215

6. Agarwal R, Prasad J (1997) The role of innovation characteristics and perceived voluntariness in the acceptance of information technologies. Decis Sci 28(3):557–581
7. Moore G, Benbasat I (1991) Development of an instrument to measure the perceptions of adopting an information technology innovation. Inform Syst Res 2(3):192–222
8. Rogers EM (1993) Diffusion of innovations, 3rd edn. Free Press, New York
9. Davis FD, Bagozzi RP, Warshaw PR (1989) User acceptance of computer technology: a comparison of two theoretical models. Manag Sci 35(8):982–1003
10. Davis FD (1989) Perceived usefulness, perceived ease of use, and user acceptance of technology. MIS Quart 13(3):319–340
11. Venkatesh V, Morris MG, Davis GB, Davis FD (2003) User acceptance of information technology: toward a unified view. MIS Quart 27(3):425–478
12. Kauffman RJ, Techatassanasoontorn AA (2009) Understanding early diffusion of digital wireless phones. Telecommun Policy 33(8):432–450
13. Lal B et al (2009) Homeworkers' usage of mobile phones; social isolation in the home-workplace. J Enterprise Inform Manag 22(3):257–274
14. Lal B, Dwivedi YK (2010) Investigating homeworkers' inclination to remain connected to work at "anytime, anywhere" via mobile phones. J Enterprise Inform Manag 23(6):759–774
15. Scupola A (2009) SMEs' e-commerce adoption: perspectives from Denmark and Australia. J Enterprise Inform Manag 22(1):152–166
16. Tan KS et al (2010) Internet-based ICT adoption among SMEs: demographic versus benefits, barriers, and adoption intention. J Enterprise Inform Manag 23(1):27–55
17. Zeimpekis V, Giaglis GM (2006) Urban dynamic real-time distribution services: insights from SMEs. J Enterprise Inform Manag 19(4):667–388
18. Aleke B et al (2011) ICT adoption in developing countries: perspectives from small-scale agribusinesses. J Enterprise Inform Manag 24:68–84
19. Seneler CO et al (2010) An empirical analysis of the antecedents of adoption of online services: a prototype-based framework. J Enterprise Inform Manag 23(4):471–438
20. Ozkan S et al (2010) Facilitating the adoption of e-payment systems: theoretical constructs and empirical analysis. J Enterprise Inform Manag 23(3):305–325
21. Khalifa M, Shen KN (2008) Explaining the adoption of transactional B2C mobile commerce. J Enterprise Inform Manag 21(2):110–124
22. Standing C et al (2010) Managing the transition to global electronic markets in the resource engineering sector. J Enterprise Inform Manag 23(1):56–80
23. Al-maghrabi T et al (2011) Antecedents of continuance intentions towards e-shopping: the case of Saudi Arabia. J Enterprise Inform Manag 21(1):85–111
24. Abbasi MS et al (2011) Social influence, voluntariness, experience and the internet acceptance: an extension of technology acceptance model within a south-Asian country context. J Enterprise Inform Manag 24(1):30–52
25. Carlsson C, Carlsson J, Hyvönen K, Puhakainen J, Walden P (2006) Adoption of mobile devices/services – searching for answers with the UTAUT. Institute for Advanced Management Systems Research, Finland, 6, 132
26. Kargin B, Basoglu N (2006) Adoption factors of mobile services. International conference on mobile business (ICMB'06), 41, Copenhagen
27. Bouwman H, Carlsson C, Moline-Castillo F, Walden P (2007) Barriers and drivers in the adoption of current and future mobile services in Finland. Telemat Inform 24(2):145–160
28. Grantham A, Tsekouras G (2005) Diffusing wireless applications in a mobile world. Technol Soc 27(1):85–104
29. Gilbert AL, Han H (2005) Understanding mobile data services adoption: demography, attitudes or needs? Technol Forecast Soc Change 72(3):327–337
30. Repo P (2005) User applications of mobile multimedia. Proceedings of the PICS workshop at Ubicomp 2005, Tokyo
31. Muthaiyah S (2004) Key success factors of 3rd generation mobile network services for M-Commerce in Malaysia. Am J Appl Sci 1(4):261–265

32. Carlsson C, Hyvönen K, Repo P, Walden P (2005) Asynchronous adoption patterns of mobile services. Proceedings of the 38th annual Hawaii international conference on system sciences (HICSS'05), 7, 7
33. Hong S, Tam K, Kim J (2006) Mobile data service fuels the desire for uniqueness. Commun ACM 49(9):89–94
34. Mallat N (2007) Exploring consumer adoption of mobile payments—a qualitative study. J Strategic Inform Syst 16(4):413–432
35. Kim HW, Chan HC, Gupta S (2007) Value-based adoption of mobile internet: an empirical investigation. Decis Support Syst 43(1):111–126
36. Turel O, Serenko A, Bontis N (2007) User acceptance of wireless short messaging services: deconstructing perceived value. Inform Manag 44(1):63–73
37. Yamakawa P, Matsumoto M (2003) Lessons learned from the adoption of MobileInternet services in Japan. Proceedings of IAMOT conference, Nancy, France
38. Pagani M (2004) Determinants of adoption of third generation mobile multimedia services. J Interact Market 18(3):46–59
39. Hung S, Ku C, Chang C (2003) Critical factors of wap services adoption: an empirical study. Electron Comm Res Appl 2(1):42–60
40. McGlynn RP, McGurk D, Effland V, Johll N, Harding D (2004) Brainstorming and task performance in groups constrained by evidence. Organ Behav Hum Decis Process 93(1):5–87
41. Osborn AF (1963) Applied imagination: principles and procedures of creative problem-solving, 3 revisedth edn. Charles Scribner's Sons, New York, NY

Chapter 8
Risk Management in Research and Development: A Case Study from the Semiconductor Industry

Ramin Neshati and Tugrul U. Daim

Abstract This paper reviews a completed product development project at a semiconductor manufacturing firm. The data gathered is organized using a Risk Categorization Framework and Behavior Model. Key questions explored include the unpredictable nature of R&D as related to semiconductor manufacturing and the manner in which risk can be better managed in an R&D setting. The research was accomplished through an action research methodology. The researchers have been a part of the development team for over 2 years starting with the planning of the product and ending with the launch of the product. A post launch process helped gather the final data used in this paper

8.1 Model Building

As high-technology markets battle a "civilized war" [5] R&D managers continue to radically shift corporate strategies to better align business units, centralize operations, and narrow product launch windows [13]. The ultimate goal of these strategic maneuvers by technology managers is to focus acute attention on financial returns [7] in the hopes of further empowering their own positions as guardians of enormous investments, beholden only to the shareholders whom they ultimately serve. While these strategies may be essential for business operations, they tend to create new challenges for project managers by promoting an environment where unforeseen risks can materialize from a variety of sources. These unforeseen risks

---

R. Neshati (✉)
Intel Corporation, Hillsboro, OR, USA
e-mail: ramin.neshati@intel.com

T.U. Daim
Engineering and Technology Management Department,
Portland State University, Portland, OR, USA
e-mail: tugrul@etm.pdx.edu

can strain an organization's flexibility to use unique and heretofore underexplored methodologies in order to avoid project failures and to thereby drive it towards institutionalized rigidity and ineptitude [13].

Using data collected from interviews with project managers in technology firms across multiple geographies [11,17], researchers in the field of technology management have introduced a unique framework for identifying and assessing risk [3]. This framework, styled the *"Risk Categorization Framework and Behavior Model,"* identifies classes of risks and provides guidance to technology managers to choose the appropriate response and behavior to uniquely mitigate each category of risk. Prior to this, conventional wisdom held that traditional frameworks encompassed individual risk items, whereas the newly introduced framework consolidates risk into manageable categories and behaviors, thus simplifying the need to identify every risk and ensuring that heretofore latent or undiscovered risks will be comprehended, characterized and mitigated as opposed to going undetected.

8.1.1 Risk Categorization Framework and Behavior Model

As seen in Table 8.1 below, this newly posited Risk Categorization Framework and Behavior Model identifies and characterizes two major divisions of risks: 'Inside' risks and 'Outside' risks.

Inside risks are those that are under the direct influence of the project manager and which are traditionally taught in standard management programs. Cule et al. [3] further divide these risks into two behavior categories: Self Assessment and Task Control. Self Assessment behaviors refer to characteristics of the project manager. They describe the manner in which the project manager assesses her skills when confronted with questions such as: "Do I have the competence to thoroughly assess risk?" or "Do I lack the appropriate people skills to be a successful communicator?" or "Can I manage change effectively?" and so on. Task Control behaviors refer to what the project manager can directly control and is generally considered to be the textbook approach to project management [3]. This category relates to questions such as: "Have I staffed the appropriate personal for the project?"; or "Is the technology stable?"; or "Should I outsource?" and so on.

Outside risks, by contrast, are those that are not under the complete influence of the project manager and are the kinds of risks that are not traditionally taught in standard management programs. Cule et al. [3] further divide these risks into two distinct behavior categories: Client Relationship and Environment Monitor. Client Relationship behaviors refer to activities that the project manager can not directly control, but over which she maintains some degree of influence. In this context, the client refers to the people internal to a company with whom the project manager deals [3]. These internal personnel are the key stakeholders who essentially define the successful outcome of a project. They include executive managers, division managers and other project managers. Environment Monitor behaviors refer to activities over which the project manager has no control and no influence.

Table 8.1 Risk categorizing and behavior model from company data under study

Inside risk	
Self	Task
• *Inadequate communication* 　1. One voice was not utilized in communicating issues 　2. Deviations of design in Manufacturing not communicated to tech marking and thus to customers • *Inadequate planning* 　1. Lack of foresight 　　• Made decisions without data 　　• Made poor projections 　　• Goals copied from a different project without understanding the differences 　　• Failure to collect and analyze product design requests for other products see overlap and leverages 　　• Key pieces not taken seriously early on the process 　2. Setting unrealistic goals and expectations 　3. Documenting issues early	• *Inadequate communication* 　1. Different engineers presenting data in different formats 　2. Inconsistent reworks 　3. Too little time to work • *Inadequate planning* 　1. Inadequate Resources (human and equipment): Increase head count to support major project 　2. New methodology needs to be certified 　3. Different test environments causes unforeseen/uncomprehensible issues in the real factory 　4. Planning systems were out synch between Manufacturing and Production Planning
Outside risk	
Client	Environment
• *Inadequate communication* 　1. Customer 　　• Customers not notified of key issues 　2. Get firm commitments from stakeholders about reviews; they need to be done regularly 　3. Division not engaged early enough 　4. Requirements not established or tracked 　5. Clear expectations not set • *Inadequate planning* 　1. Underfunding of development 　2. Priority cause tester resources and engineers to be assigned to higher priority issues 　3. Changed launch plans 　4. Freeze requirements	• *Inadequate planning* 　1. Organizational changes before the product was released 　2. "Preemption" of higher priority projects 　3. Roadmap changes

Examples include: corporate takeovers, time sensitive markets and organizational changes (i.e., layoffs) and so on. Cule et al. [3] recommend that project managers constantly monitor the environment for deviations, by working more closely with marketing personnel and by maintaining access to industry trade journals. Like many other researchers [6,8,11,16], Cule et al. [3] stress the importance of establishing a contingency plan.

8.2 Methodology

The data used in this paper was obtained from a postmortem presentation to executive staff at a semiconductor manufacturing company. Managers representing various functional and cross-group organizations gave presentations that summarized the project into two bipolar extremes of performance during the development timeframe of a specific product such as: "What we did well?" and "What we could improve upon?"

To populate the behavior model, the data was *grounded* for recurring themes. Grounded theory, also known as 'emergent' or 'action' research, is a qualitative methodology based on the assumption that theory is concealed in data, to be discovered through iterative sampling and analysis [21]. Two themes emerged: communication and planning. These themes were used as categories in each of the quadrants from the Cule model: Self, Task, Client and Environment. The key data items were placed under the theme categories according to their risk pattern from Table 8.1. Table 8.1 shows the populated Risk Categorization Framework and Behavior Model using this data.

8.2.1 *Communication*

Employees prefer open and honest communication [9,19]. Whenever communication is found to be failing, it can be costly to an organization. For example, at HP, two engineers at two different sites geographically apart were working independently for several weeks on a printer problem. Their goal was to prove throughput consistency across different media. At the end of their tests, they discussed their results. Not surprisingly, these results were found to be inconsistent. After some analysis it was determined that there was confusion over the definition of the problem (specifically, on the limit breakpoints used to control the ink flow). This highlights a distinct lack of communication. Some of the tests had to be performed again, resulting in several weeks of wasted output and effort.

In order to establish a common theme among researchers concerned with project management practices, Schultz et al. [18] pooled together a list of research factors that were critical for success in project management. About the importance of communication they wrote:

> Adequate communication [is where] sufficient information is available on project objectives, status, changes, organizational coordination, clients' needs, and so forth. Further, formal lines of communication have been established between the project team and its clients and between the team and the rest of the organization.

Oz and Sosik [12] interviewed executives at software development companies and collected both quantitative and qualitative data. Using this data, they produced a list of five major factors that could contribute to project risks. They hypothesized and proved that poor project management skills and lack of corporate leadership were positively related to poorly communicated goals and deliverables. Furthermore, about communication they wrote:

> ...poor communication within a project team, between developers and users, and between the development team and senior management, can increase the likelihood of project failure.

Thus, using the data from Table 8.1 above, we hypothesize the following:

> H1: Inadequate communication can lead to unnecessary project risk and inefficiencies such as delays, repeated work and so on.

8.2.2 Planning

Successful teams need successful plans. Good planning practices, with a good set of goals and metrics create good estimates [9]. Likewise, inadequate planning practices, such as bad estimates, cause market delays, scope redefinitions and feature creep, as well as budget issues, Pinto [13]. Writing on the importance of planning, Pinto and Kharbanda [16] state that the:

> ...essence of efficient project management is to take the time to get it as right as possible the first time. "It" includes the schedule, the team composition, the project specifications, and the budget. There is a truism that those who fail to plan are planning to fail.

In order to be effective in this effort, it is important to create a contingency plan early in the process. By doing so, disruptions to key projects can be minimized [8,15,16]. Thus, using the data from Table 8.1 we hypothesize the following:

> H2: Inadequate planning can lead to unnecessary project risk and inefficiencies such as delays, repeated work and so on.

8.3 Discussion

We focused on the key issues as they relate to the four behaviors in the life of a project manager. While the intent of this paper is not to cover every item on the Risk Categorization Framework and Behavior Model (see Table 8.1), the general themes will be reviewed below.

8.3.1 The Self Assessment

As discussed earlier, Self Assessment behaviors refer to characteristics of the project manager that can be directly influenced. It is often hard to be critical of one's own behavior in the absence of an honest feedback mechanism. Once the self assessment is complete, it is even harder to change one's behavior for the common good. Project managers can get accustomed to a particular mode of operation and any involuntary impetus for behavior modification can be viewed with suspicion. Thus, project managers tend to fall into the 'comfort zone' trap. See the result of the analysis in the *SELF* quadrant in Table 8.1 for additional context.

8.3.2 Inadequate Communication

From the data, it appears that some of the project managers failed to effectively collaborate on changes. The problem appears to be the failure to use a consensus-based approach along with a common set of assumptions and semantics (sometimes known colloquially as 'one voice') to communicate design changes to the different divisions and customers. For example, the manager of one of the units (validation) stated the following:

> One voice was not utilized in communicating with validation on issues. The most damage occurred when a change in design was not properly communicated to the rest of the team. This was noticed by customers who were not notified of the key issues. They thought the company was hiding something.

In order for an organization to be effective, consistent and clear communication, for both internal and external clients, should come from one voice [2]. Further, the one voice needs to emanate from a strong and respected leader who understands how to tailor the message to the situation and avoid the "Mushroom Principle of Management" [16]. This management principle is thus named as it refers to keeping the employee base in the dark and regularly fed with manure.

8.3.3 Inadequate Planning

The project managers made several mistakes due to inadequate planning. While re-use is an important strategy and can reduce the amount of workload on subsequent products, some project managers neglected to verify whether the methodologies were aligned with the product plan. To make matters worse, the "lack of foresight" on the part of these project managers led to the unfortunate integration of negative experiences and poor projections from previous projects.

8.3.4 The Task Control

As discussed earlier, Task Control behaviors are under the direct control of project managers. For more on this context, see the *TASK* quadrant in Table 8.1.

8.3.5 Inadequate Communication

Whenever communication is consistent among different divisions and teams in R&D environments, misunderstandings about goals, objects and development issues are greatly reduced [20]. In our case, a manager in manufacturing states:

> Different engineers [are] presenting data in different formats [;. we need to] standardize templates for better data collection.

Now, it is often the case that designs may need to be changed or reworked during the course of the project. These planned alterations are important in the course of the project and they must be carefully anticipated and managed. If done incorrectly, they can become expensive and lead to unnecessary project delays. The reader is referred to in the HP printer engineers example cited earlier in this paper. To effectively manage planned alterations and rework cycles, project managers must:

1. Reduce avoidable repetitions [1]
2. Engage as many cross functional teams as possible [14]

Another example may be necessary to clarify this point. After conducting interviews with expert engineers, a project manager determines that certain issues cannot be resolved due to inadequate or old software. In an attempt to formulate a solution, the project manager engages a software engineer to discuss alternatives with other engineers on the project. Afterwards, the software engineer is surprised to learn that the problems in question were not related to the software but to some other elements of the project that were imported from previous projects. These elements were not suited well to this project and needed to be updated. No one adequately researched the root cause of the problem, as the prevailing attitude from the majority of the project engineers was that it was either not important enough, or that they did not have sufficient time to look into it. The urge to keep "hammering" onward to produce products creates a mental barrier for addressing this problem in a timely manner. This type of communication problem has been discussed before by Hallum and Daim [4]. The authors believe that managers and engineers have a different sense of urgency and priority for problem identification and resolution.

8.3.6 Inadequate Planning

The data suggest that the project managers inadequately planned the product development cycle. Possibly, managers incorrectly forecasted both personnel and equipment and tools requirements [11]. Additionally, managers may not have aligned the various organizations, such as R&D labs with product validation or the factory.

Finally, these project managers may have allowed the integration of unproven methodologies during the production cycle [3]. Better planning could have mitigated these problems, since they are all seemingly within the project manager's sphere of control.

8.3.7 The Client Relationships

As discussed earlier, Client Relationship behaviors refers to activities that the project manager cannot directly control, but may be able to influence. See the *CLIENT* quadrant in Table 8.1 for further context.

8.3.8 Inadequate Communication

According to the research conducted by Keil et al. [11], failure to adequately communicate with the customer has been rated as the second most important risk factor that a project may face, the first being the lack of commitment by senior management. In short, if the customer does not perceive a value from the project then the project is a failure [16]. To rectify this issue, a manager offered a simple, yet insightful observation:

> Set expectations with customers up front. If they don't like the product, better to know that up front and change the plan.

8.3.9 Inadequate Planning

Pinto and Kharbanda [15] puts it bluntly: "If you want to fail ignore the stakeholders." In the case examined here, the engineers who worked in R&D with well-developed timelines were continually frustrated by having to hit "a moving target." Their frustration stems from uncontrolled schedule slips, anxiety over project cancellation and its attendant consequences (such as layoffs, etc.). Although it is not clearly stated in the data, the failure to freeze the requirements possibly could be attributed to the low confidence and trust among the key stakeholders [10]. Nevertheless, uncommitted schedules, shrinking budgets and the loss of key personnel to higher priority projects may inevitably lead to project cancellations.

8.3.10 The Environment Monitoring

As discussed earlier, Environment Monitor behavior refers to activities that the project manager cannot directly control or influence; however, they still need to be monitored. See the *ENVIRONMENT* quadrant in Table 8.1 for more context.

8.3.11 Inadequate Planning

Organizational changes are seemingly uncontrollable. Pinto [14] suggests that "project managers and their teams need [to be protected]" from the "change in players" so that their focus can remain on their primary managerial duties. Organizational changes can destroy the positive relationship that project managers painstakingly cultivate with senior management [3,16]; they must start over and rebuild.

The data in this study suggests that both organizational and product priority changes occurred during the development timeframe. In fact, the product was "preempted" [11] to other higher priority projects. To ease the impact of these difficulties, project managers need to develop contingency plans, monitor the environment, and update the plan as necessary [3,6,8,11,16].

8.4 Conclusions

The project failures analyzed in this paper increased risks as shown in the behavior model in Table 8.1. Project mangers need to be aware of these types of risks and be alert to risk mitigation strategies. As we have seen in this case, communication and planning were the two recurring themes and problem areas that were gleaned directly from the data. These issues lead to many ancillary problems as discussed above. Thus, the original H1 and H2 hypotheses shown below have been partially proven:

H1: Inadequate communication can lead to risk and unnecessary delays
H2: Inadequate planning can lead to risk and unnecessary delays

The above hypotheses should be further analyzed in future studies using quantitative methodologies and corroborated with the application of the model referenced in this paper to additional cases. According to Pinto and Kharbanda [15], "it is through these past failures that we gain experience and wisdom to push on towards successful conclusions." Companies that conduct project analysis, such as postmortems referenced in this paper, are to be commended for their determination to learn from mistakes in order to not repeat them.

References

1. Boehm B, Basili R (2001) Victor. Software defect reduction top 10 list. Computer, January 2001, pp. 135–137
2. Christian PH (1993) Project success or project failure: it's up to you. IM. p. 8
3. Cule P, Schmidt R, Mark K (2000) Strategies for heading off is project failure. Inform Syst Manag 17(2):65
4. Hallum D, Daim TU (2009) A hierarchical decision model for optimum design alternative selection. Int J Decis Sci Risk Manag 1(Special issue):2–22

5. Davidow WH (1986) Marketing high technology: an insider's view. Free Press, New York
6. Tesch D, Kloppenborg TJ, Erolick MN (2007) IT project risk factors: the project management professionals perspective. J Comp Inform Syst 47(4):61
7. Germeraad P (2003) Measuring R&D in 2003. Res Technol Manag 46(6 (Special Issue)):47–56
8. Tom Gosselin (1993) Negotiating with your boss. Training and Development (May)
9. Harvard Management Update (2000) Why some teams succeed (and so many don't)
10. Inganas M, Marxt C (2007) Measuring the science-to-market gap—the case of new energy technologies. Int J Innov Technol Manag 4(4):457–478
11. Keil M, Cule PE, Lyytinen K, Schmidt RC (1998) A framework for identifying software project risks. Commun ACM 41(11):76–83
12. Oz E, Sosik JJ (2000) Why information systems projects are abandoned: A leadership and communication theory and exploratory study. J Comp Inform Syst 41(1):66
13. Pinto JK (2002) Project management 2002. Res Technol Manag 45(2):22
14. Pinto JK (1997) The power of project management. Industry Week 246(15):138
15. Pinto JK, Kharbanda OP (1996) How to fail in project management (without really trying). Bus Horizons 39(4):45
16. Pinto JK, Kharbanda OP (1995) Lessons for an accidental profession. Bus Horizons 38(2):41
17. Schmidt R, Lyytinen K, Keil M, Cule P (2001) Identifying soft-ware project risks: an international Delphi study. J Manag Inform Syst 17(4):5
18. Schultz RL, Slevin DP, Pinto JK (1987) Strategy and tactics in a process model of project implementation. Interfaces 17(3):34
19. Shirahada K, Niwa K (2007) Future-orientated mindset's contribute to management of corporate R&D personnel motivation in Japan. Int J Innov Technol Manag 4(4):375–392
20. (2007) Wyeth Pharmaceuticals: spurring scientific creativity with metrics. Product #: 607008
21. Glaser BG, Strauss AL (1967) The discovery of grounded theory: strategies for qualitative research. Aldine, Chicago

Chapter 9
Technology Standards Development: A Framework

Ramin Neshati and Tugrul U. Daim

Abstract Distributed Innovation and inter-company collaborative development have become prevalent modes of operation for some technology-intensive firms which rely on them to reduce their investment outlays while concomitantly preserving their technology leadership positions within their respective industries. Technology standards development has become a key enabler for achieving these seemingly bipolar objectives. The de facto model that exemplifies this trend can be summed up as: 'collaborate, standardize, compete!'

Under the rubric of a proposed technology standards development paradigm derived from extant practice, we examine the case of the Universal Serial Bus (USB) technology. By probing the reasons and the processes for the creation of technology standards such as USB, we explore the underlying methods by which firms collaboratively pool intellectual assets while maintaining their competitive edge. Our model identifies and describes the environmental forces that influence technology standards development and sheds lights on governance issues that emanate from such activities. Experiential observations point to opportunities and challenges that call for the deft management of standards-related investments and activities by pace-setting technology firms.

Several shortcomings have surfaced from this study, such as the need for metrics to measure the degree to which technology standards contribute to business objectives, the development of efficient methods to engender collaboration across large multinational corporations, the impact of standards on new product development and the effects of globalization on standards development in emerging economies.

R. Neshati (✉)
Intel Corporation, Hillsboro, OR, USA
e-mail: ramin.neshati@intel.com

T.U. Daim
Engineering and Technology Management Department,
Portland State University, Portland, OR, USA
e-mail: tugrul@etm.pdx.edu

9.1 Introduction

In the fast-paced and chaotic milieu of technology development, no longer can a single firm operate—to borrow a phrase from the seventeenth century British poet John Donne—as 'an island, entire of itself.' Owing to the massive investment requirements of ecosystem infrastructures to enable market growth, most technology-intensive firms find it necessary to work in partnership with other firms, including their direct competitors, to pool their resources and to lessen their investment burdens in order to survive and thrive. The phenomenon of Distributed Innovation and the collaborative development of technology via an ecosystem constitute the foundational paradigms that are explored in this study.

Researchers in the field of business strategy and technology management have, in recent times, noted a persistent pattern affecting large technology-intensive firms in the Personal Computer (PC) and Consumer Electronic (CE) industries. It appears that most of these firms find it difficult to register sustained revenue and profit growth as markets mature and saturate with their products and services [1]. This growth-stall trend that affects many large technology-intensive firms has been documented in the literature and its impact has been analyzed in recent studies [2, 3]. Here, we will also consider whether the development, promulgation, and adoption of technology standards can enable firms to achieve incremental growth and thereby gain or retain competitive advantage.

To precisely define the scope and reach of this study, some nomenclature clarifications are in order. We define 'technology' as the application of tools to solve problems that extend human potential for the benefit of society. We define 'standard' as establishment of a norm [4]. Thus, a 'technology standard' is the application of tools using an established norm to solve problems that extend human potential for the benefit of society. Hariharan (1990) gives an alternative definition in which a 'technology standard' is said to be a model, a specification or a design with a dominant market position in the industry for its product class [5]. This latter definition is more appealing owing to its focused delineation of the term standard—namely, a specification with a dominant position within the industry—which we will adopt in this paper. Throughout this study, therefore, a technology standard refers to the development of a technical specification which is in turn implemented by the promoters and adopters of said specification, and instantiated in products that are introduced in various technology-driven markets such as consumer electronics, enterprise computing, information technology and so on, by the members of those ecosystems.

The question inevitably arises: Why develop technology standards in the first place? The short answer can be traced back to Donne's 'an island, entire of itself' metaphor. A more illuminating answer is provided by Cline et al. (2008) in that standards accelerate technology adoption by enabling "the timely deployment of value-added functionality, followed by the broadest possible industry support for the necessary infrastructure to deliver the next level of innovations" [6]. Further, anytime a certain technology can be instantiated in multiple different ways with dissimilar interface points, there is the potential for a proliferation of disparate methods for accomplishing the same task or end result. This proliferation in turn can lead to inefficiencies and lower returns for the firm, confusion and higher costs for the consumer, or both. Another raison d'être for technology standards development is offered by Gawer (2000) in that standards setting invariably spawns complementary innovations that enhance the value of interoperable products emanating from a horizontally disintegrated ecosystem [7].

The premise of this study is centered on standardization as a facilitator of simplicity, cost reduction, and interoperability between products from different vendors participating in a business ecosystem, thus engendering market growth and better business prospects for all participants in the standards activity. By the same token, standardization cannot militate against innovation and value-added differentiation. Simply meeting the minimum requirements of a standard can be viewed as 'good enough' and thus serve as a disincentive to take on the harder challenge of innovating around and above the interface points defined by the standard. There is a crucial tension between differentiation through innovation and 'vanilla' standardization which we will explore further in this paper.

A technology standard is generally developed and maintained by an organization formed from a collection of representative firms or entities operating within that industry. In the PC and CE industries, for instance, there are a number of standards developing organizations with varying levels of openness, authority, influence, charter, and function. In this context, openness refers to the degree of availability of participation to an individual, an entity, a representative firm, or a governmental agency. A formal Standards Developing Organization (SDO) may operate under the aegis and sponsorship of a national organization or completely independently, and may have representation from a variety of institutions or individuals. Examples of SDOs include IEEE, ANSI, and so on. Furthermore, an International Standards Developing Organization (ISDO) typically operates at the multi-national level with representation determined by a national organization or governmental bureau, and generally carries a high level of legitimacy and influence. Examples of ISDOs include the ISO and the ITU. With the advent of personal computing in the early 1980s, a steady shift has occurred toward the creation of special-purpose, focused, and agile types of standards developing organizations, commonly referred to as Special Interest Groups (SIGs). Figure 9.1 in Appendix 1 depicts the trend towards the stabilization of SDOs and the linear growth of SIGs over time. As can be seen, SDO formation has been relatively stable since the 1970s while the formation of SIGs has seen an ascending linear growth since the 1980s. By construction, a SIG is an informal and decentralized standards developing consortium. As an incorporated, legally recognized entity, a SIG may operate as a mutual-benefit corporation, a non-profit corporation with by-laws, a governing board, or the elected officers of a board [8]. In the state of Oregon, for instance, a SIG is legally recognized by state statute such as 501(C)(6) [9]. A SIG may be open or closed with respect to its acceptance of participants, but it is invariably focused on a narrow scope of technology development.

This may be one reason for the proliferation and popularity of SIGs in recent times. A more thorough comparison between SIGs and SDOs is shown in Table 9.1 in Appendix 1. The gist of this comparison yields a useful insight: The informal and relatively fast-paced nature of SIGs, in contrast to SDOs, is more responsive to business needs. This may be a reason for the growing popularity of SIGs over SDOs. Commenting on the reasons that induce technology firms to cooperate on standards activities, Chiesa and Toletti (2003) assert that the SDO represents the ultimate evolution of a collaborative structure due to its ability to retain broad representation of vested firms in the industry [10]. The same is true for a SIG. This coming-together of a disparate collection of participants to develop a standards-based business association and commercial collaboration is referred to as an ecosystem. Notably, this feature—an ecosystem to facilitate commerce—is absent in the SDO framework.

The most compelling feature of SIGs is their ability to channel mutually-beneficial collaboration towards the development of complementary and interoperable products with robust attention paid to the verification of compliance to the agreed-upon standard by the SIG's participating members. While the SIG itself may not be invested in a commercial enterprise, yet it must facilitate the proper conditions to benefit its members, all of whom are presumably invested and intensely interested in commerce. Also, it should be noted that the collaborative innovation emanating from SIGs is inherently different from that which is present in the open innovation environment. The latter occurs in the absence of formal planning or centralized organization and does not always operate according to the business needs of its consumers. The former is a planned, organized activity with clear and specific objectives that are linked to the business imperatives of its stakeholders [11]. Indeed, open innovation is a very complex phenomenon that draws upon many research streams, including globalization, technology intensity, technology fusion, new business models, and knowledge leveraging. A thorough treatment of the open innovation phenomenon is beyond the scope of this study.

9.1.1 Research Questions

We consider three important questions that comprise the core of this paper. These questions are as follows:

(a) Why and how do PC and CE technology firms create standards?
(b) Can these technology firms protect their intellectual assets while sharing knowledge and expertise with industry ecosystems? Furthermore, will such knowledge sharing help or hinder their competitiveness and growth potential?
(c) Are standards organizations such as SIGs suitable vehicles for promoting collaborative innovation in technology-intensive industries?

We will explore and answer these questions through the course of this study.

9.1.2 Methodology

Both qualitative and quantitative methodologies are employed here. A review and assessment of the academic literature on the phenomenon of Distributed Innovation (DI) and a brief case study on the creation of the Universal Serial Bus (USB) technology comprise the qualitative methodologies in this paper. The quantitative methods consist of the identification of distinct and relevant factors for technology standards development gleaned from a survey of experts in the field of technology management and the subsequent pair-wise comparisons between these factors using a PCM software tool to derive rank ordering and the assignment of priorities to these factors. Other statistical analysis is performed as well. The qualitative and quantitative methodologies are employed independently of each other.

9.1.3 Literature Review

In the academic literature, DI is described as the act of collaboration among and between several firms to develop and sustain technological innovations for the benefit of all. Sawhney and Prandelli (2000) maintain that the trend towards the adoption of DI has accelerated in recent years as a result of the dilemma in which the knowledge required to compete in the technology industry has continued to diversify even as disparate markets collide; at the same time, technology firms have constricted their knowledge base around their core competencies in order to compete more effectively [12]. One such collision is currently occurring between the Personal Computer (PC) and the Consumer Electronics (CE) industries. This gap, between diversification on the one hand and specialization on the other, has created an opportunity for increased collaborative innovation, which is dubbed Distributed Innovation (DI). We frame technology standards development as an extension of DI, given that the end result is beneficial to a group or an ecosystem of firms and requires cross-company collaboration before its potential benefits can materialize and be realized commercially. Addressing the importance of an ecosystem to collaborative innovation within the framework of technology standards development activity from an R&D perspective, Horn (2005) highlights the central importance of an ecosystem in bringing together technological inventions and capabilities with business and societal needs [13]. Horn further acknowledges some of the problems inherent in establishing successful ecosystems, namely overcoming the 'not invented here' mentality and the coordination of technological innovations in order to enable value added differentiation. In this vein, R&D activities are better harvested when technology standards development is managed to be 'in tune with the marketplace.'

Expanding on the theory of organizational ecology, Ozsomer and Cavusgil (1999) contend that DI can be extended to study the competitive behavior of PC firms before and after the release of technology standards. They find that firm behavior before the release of technology standards can be characterized as positive interdependence or mutualism but that after a standard is released firm behavior shifts towards negative interdependence or full competition. These researchers contend that the net effect of competition decreases as adoption of technology standards increases and caution technology managers to promote strategies that rapidly expand the user base of standards-based products and services [14]. In analyzing the impact of technology standards on New Product Development (NPD), Sahay and Riley (2003) concluded that NPD is greatly influenced by the volume and pace of technology standards. These researchers distinguish between 'customer interface' standards and 'compatibility' standards. The former determine the pattern of interaction between the user and the product, such as the Microsoft Windows operating system, while the latter define the fit and interaction between components within a product or between various products [15]. Thus, firms that develop customer interface standards demonstrate strong appropriability and an affinity towards proprietary interfaces, while firms that develop compatibility standards demonstrate weak appropriability and a penchant for open interfaces. These researchers advise managers to account for the differences between customer interface and compatibility standards on resource allocation for new product development, as these decisions may impact the firm's market competitiveness.

Much of the literature on the impact of standards development on product and process innovation borrows from the groundbreaking work of Utterback and Abernathy (1975), in which they established patterns of innovation within technology firms and developed various models to explain the rate of innovation of products and processes on the basis of the firm's chosen business and competition strategy [16]. One of the main upshots of this research suggests that technology firms race to propagate their own implementation of a technological innovation in order to establish a de facto standard which others will have to emulate. In applying the Utterback and Abernathy model to the firm's strategic alliances, Mauri and McMillan (1999) found that technology-intensive firms form alliances as the level of technology complexity and cross-dependencies increase [17]. Their findings buttress the Utterback and Abernathy product and process innovation models and contradict a large body of research which contends that technology firms avoid alliances to protect their intellectual assets from potentially exploitative and opportunistic behaviors of their rivals, partners, and others in their ecosystem.

The importance of technology standards development for the purpose of reinvigorating the US economy and renewing the competitiveness of US technology firms cannot be overemphasized. Burnside and Witkin (2008), while confirming the futility of the 'go-it-alone' approach, point to alarming statistics concerning the decline of US technological prowess [18]. For instance, measured as a percentage, in 2004 the US was overtaken in the issuance of science and engineering degrees by China, Japan and Ireland. Further, in 2005 US R&D as a percentage of GDP was below that of China, Ireland, Russia and the EU. These researches contend that the lack of an Intellectual Property (IP) licensing model between university R&D and the industry is the key obstacle in maintaining a steady flow of technological innovation and business collaboration. Echoing similar sentiments, Pisano and Shih (2009) draw a bleak picture of the gradual decline of the US technology industry in its inability to produce its own innovations and inventions [19]. These researchers call for focused research and development as well as closer collaboration between business, academia and government to restore US technological competitiveness. This advice hearkens back to a couple of decades ago when a similar alarm was sounded over America's declining prowess in semiconductor manufacturing, which ultimately gave birth to the collaborative arrangement called Sematech [20]. Sematech is a consortium of the leading semiconductor manufacturing firms that pool their research and development in a collaborative manner for the benefit of all of its members [21]. Clearly, collaborative innovation is not alien to American technology firms. However, the evolving process of technological change has a profound effect on the development, diffusion, and adoption of technology standards. In studying the increasingly rapid pace of technological innovation, Coyle (2005) found that technology standards can pace innovation by providing stability in a time of constant change [22]. Thus, standards defining organizations must maintain a steady beat rate of technological innovation and reach across other standards defining organizations for coordination and influence to build dependence pyramids. Using these standards, firms can specialize in the development of tools and other technology-based products to enable the development of more advanced innovations and applications. For instance, semiconductor makers rely on a host of sophisticated factory tools, such as reliability and measurement equipment, to streamline and automate their operations. In turn, these tools may be based on certain standards in order to engender multiple sourcing and choice. Thus, technology standards facilitate competition as well as innovation.

In a seminal study on the diffusion of competing standards in two-sided markets, Sun and Tse (2006) found that network effects overshadowed technological superiority in determining the outcome of conflicting standards, in that strong network effects locked in an inferior standard even though a superior standard was available [23]. This implies that in defining technology standards new entrants must have superior technologies or financial resources to succeed as latecomers or when there is already a standard in place. By coining terms such as 'single-home' (i.e. the adoption of one standard by a firm) and 'multi-home' (i.e. the adoption of multiple standards by a firm) these researchers draw distinctions between the 'Dynamic System' and the 'Differential Game' models. One clear implication from this study is particularly instructive: The tendency to multi-home will result in multiple standards, but within the context of the Differential Game model there will be a gradual convergence of multiple standards towards a harmonious steady state. This bringing of a potentially chaotic environment into focus and creation of predictability facilitates the requisite and organic evolution of a business ecosystem. Thus, a firm that is contemplating investing in technology standards development or participating in an existing standards activity can have a better sense of its potential payback. Riley (2007) likens technology standards to elements of a competitive strategy and offers a conceptual framework for the successful pursuit of technology standards [24].

An interesting, but often overlooked, point about the willingness and funding of personnel for technology standards development activity is raised by Blind (2006) who contends that standards work results in the flow of R&D primarily from large, well-funded and resourced firms to smaller and less-resourced counterparts [25]. The implication being that industry leaders with high R&D output must be wooed by the standards developing ecosystem with favorable licensing terms as incentive to counterbalance the net outflow of R&D output from large to small firms. Another implication is related to the resource requirements of technology standards development. Large firms are more able to afford assigning their talented employees to these tasks while the same may not be true for small or medium-sized firms. Thus, the latter may be chronically under-represented in influencing the direction of technology standards development which may necessitate external policies, such as governmental or regulatory, to goad these firms into active participation and positive contribution. In a related stream of research, Waguespack and Fleming (2009), examined the role of startup firms in technology standards development and found that participation in standards activities greatly accelerated a 'liquidity event' [26]. The surprising finding here is that technology adoption, per se, was not the sole benefit for the startup but that simply attending standards organization meetings and conferences provided a sufficient level of exposure to exert influence, establish relationships with others in the ecosystem, and thus gain traction for the startup firm's technological innovations. This important finding highlights the impact of relationships within technology standards developing regimes. Consistent with this finding, Harryson (2008) reports on the importance of relationship management for startup firms to balance technological explorations with industrial exploitations [27]. An implication of this study suggests that by building relationships, R&D managers can establish bridges to 'previously disconnected disciplines and areas of value creating activities to drive creativity, innovation and entrepreneurship.'

The academic literature on technology standards development is somewhat scant as of this writing but it is beginning to get the attention of researchers. The main threads from the literature review in this study can be summarized as: (1) the practice of Distributed Innovation and the interdependence of firms when pooling intellectual assets towards a common cause; (2) the legal and regulatory environment for collaboration; and (3) the necessity, complementarity, and network effects of robust business ecosystems. With this review of the germane academic literature behind us, we proceed to formulate a proposed framework for the pursuit of technology standards development.

9.2 Framework

To outline a framework for the development of technology standards, we begin with a consideration of the necessary key attributes and elements that are important in this endeavor. With the aid of a survey instrument and a blind survey of a randomly selected set of technology managers in the greater Portland metropolitan area—all of whom participate in technology standards development to varying degrees—we have identified the following six attributes and characteristics of technology standards development as being significant and consequential for managers in technology-intensive firms:

1. Cost of development
2. Functionality and usability
3. Compatibility with existing standards and infrastructures
4. Strategic synergy with business objectives
5. Longevity of technology standards
6. Leadership opportunities afforded the firm by virtue of its investment in standards

These managers were asked to identify the top attributes and success metrics for the pursuit of technology standards development by their respective firms. The attributes that were consistently singled out were then enumerated from the survey responses, resulting in the list of six attributes shown above. In a follow-up survey of the same set of technology managers, the respondents were asked to compare and rate these six factors for relevance and importance using the pair-wise comparison method. The result of this exercise is shown in Table 9.2 in Appendix 1, and the survey data appears in Appendix 2.

Notably, our survey respondents rated 'compatibility with existing standards and infrastructures' as the highest priority consideration in the development of technology standards, followed closely by 'functionality and usability' as well as 'strategic synergy with business objectives.' Contrary to our expectations, 'cost of development' and 'longevity' of technology standards were rated lower, tied for fourth place in the rankings, with 'leadership opportunities...' bringing up the rear. The key learning from the analysis of the results of this survey highlights the importance of continuity, through generational compatibility, when developing technology standards. Specifically, our survey respondents identified temporal congruency as the most important characteristic in the development of technology standards. A cursory reflection of a popular extant technology standard bears out this finding. Consider, for example, the recent success of the Blu-ray optical disc technology that has effectively superseded the incumbent DVD [28]. Compatibility with the existing digital video disc format as well as superior bit rate scalability are two of the most commonly cited reasons for the success of this new technology by its proponents.

Using the top three priority factors identified by our survey—compatibility, functionality and strategic synergy—we now offer a general model for the development of technology standards that addresses aspects of each factor.

9.2.1 Model Definition

The paradigm proposed in this paper is patterned after the so-called 'five forces' model that drive competition as originally identified and described by Porter [29]. In Porter's model, these competitive forces—threat of new entrants, threat of substitutes, bargaining power of buyers, bargaining power of suppliers, and rivalry among competitors—inform the nature and intensity of competition within an ecosystem. Depending on the strength and direction of these forces, competing firms can formulate strategies to outmaneuver their rivals and manage their business interests. Fortunately, Porter's model is sufficiently malleable and can be used to describe the dynamics within the technology standards development process. Our modified five forces model, derived from Porter's work, is shown in Fig. 9.2 in Appendix 1. In the context of technology standards development, the five forces are defined as: Business objectives, market requirements, alternative technologies, industry ecosystem, and standards strategy.

Business objectives are unique to each firm that decides to participate in a standards development organization, such as SDO or SIG. In effect, each firm must have a viable business interest in the development of the technology standard in question and to manifest these interests through objectives that are tangibly connected with the performance of the firm. These objectives do not need to be made known beyond the confines of the firm itself, but their existence is necessary for without clear and measurable business objectives a firm's participation in technology standards development is likely to be an inefficient and wasteful activity.

Market requirements drive the definition and the boundaries of the standards activity in question. Depending on the depth and breadth of these requirements definitions, a standards activity can either flower or flounder. Crisp, well-articulated requirements can channel attention and focus on solving immediate and important problems, thus enabling the participants in the standards development activity to respond to market requirements and to recoup their investments in a timely, efficient and gainful manner. By contrast, lack of clear requirements can plunge the standards development group into a potentially endless spiral of iterative, inefficient and divergent activities relative to the original goals.

Alternative technologies act as the counterbalance to the need for investment in the pursuit of technology standards development. Before a new technology standard is contemplated, the question must be posed as to whether existing alternatives can be used to solve the same problem or to respond to emerging market requirements. If an objective assessment of the available alternatives does not turn up viable options or substitutes, then investment in the standards development activity in question can be justifiably pursued. At times, an alternative technology may exist but it could be deficient for the future needs of the industry. In such a case, the assessment of the alternative technologies must also address the feasibility of extending the existing technology to meet market requirements.

Industry ecosystem refers to a multitude of technology-intensive firms that exist in a dynamic and chaotic milieu. Together, the ecosystem members at once define as well as take advantage of technology standards through commercial enterprise. These firms may constitute suppliers, customers, complementors, competitors, leaders, followers, component providers, platform builders, and so on. The important aspect of the ecosystem is the provision of choice in offering an interoperable suite of products and services that add value and enhance the appeal of the technology standard.

Ecosystem members endeavor to deliver products that meet a minimum bar for compliance and quality, seamless interoperability, and future evolutionary compatibility.

Standardization strategy lies at the core of our model and is comprised of four main components that delineate the key considerations in the pursuit of technology standards development by any firm joining a standards developing body. These considerations include: Scope definition, intellectual property rights management, execution and exit strategy.

- The scope identifies the range and extent of the technology to be standardized and defines the tasks and activities that are necessary in the development of the standard. These may include authoring technical specifications, developing marketing communications and press relations, observing regulatory and governmental laws, and developing a robust suite of compliance and interoperability rules and tools to measure adherence to the technology standard by those firms with commercial interests. In defining the scope it is important that the standard establish the necessary and sufficient functions to meet market requirements as well as to allow for differentiation by providing hooks and headroom for extensions by those firms that wish to offer enhanced capabilities above the minimum requirements of the standard.
- Intellectual Property (IP) is a complex and consequential aspect of the strategic decision to participate in technology standards development as it provides a uniform metric for measuring returns on innovation. There are many options available, ranging from the decision to not participate and not disclose any IP to one of full participation and the royalty-free (RF) licensing of all IP rights to any and all takers. The IP model that is generally used in most of the SIGs today is dubbed 'reasonable and non-discriminatory' (RAND), or a variant thereof. In short, this model allows for the licensing of the relevant IP by its holder to the members of the standards developing body (SIG, SDO or other) under terms that are deemed reasonable, that is they cannot be too harsh to drive any licensee out of business, and non-discriminatory, in that no potential licensees will be discriminated against or be given prejudicial treatment by the licensor. Consistent with the IP model outlined here, Hemphill (2007) posits a patent strategies matrix for de jure technology standards development [30]. Another important consideration of the choice of an IP model is the size of the firm. Participating in technology standards activities can increase the difference between large and small firms' incentives to litigate, rather than the relative value of their patents. According to Simcoe, Graham and Feldman (2009), since specialized technology providers cannot seek rents in complementary markets, they find the need to defend IP more aggressively once it has been incorporated into an open platform [31].
- Execution strategy addresses the choice of the organization in which to participate for the purpose of developing a technology standard, as well as the level and intensity of participation. As has been mentioned, there are many types of standards developing organizations and alliances such as SDO, SIG and others. Before joining an organization, careful consideration should be given to the legal obligations of memberships in these organizations, particularly with respect to IP

disclosure or licensing requirements. Once a firm has decided to join, it must also decide the level at which it should participate, whether it should participate as a full-fledged voting member or as an observer, whether it should populate the organization's governing body, such as board of directors or functional equivalent, or simply confine its participation to the technical specification development committees, and other tactical considerations.

- Exit strategy is equally important to all of the above considerations and must be contemplated before the decision to join a technology standards developing organization. In general, the firm must anticipate its position within the technology defining body once its initial objective has been accomplished. This is important since industry standards defining bodies can live for a long time and may deviate from the strategic intent and objectives of many of its members over time. A key consideration in formulating an exit strategy can be the provision of termination or expiration contingencies in the organization's bylaws. Another consideration can be the transfer of the technology standard from an incubatory organization, where the technology is initially defined, to a more permanent standards maintenance organization for long-term support and evolutionary updates of that technology.

Having outlined our generalized model, we now proceed to apply the case of the Universal Serial Bus (USB) technology to this model.

9.2.2 Model Application: The Case of USB

In the early 1990s peripheral devices that connected to a PC platform such as scanners, printers, personal digital assistants, and video cameras, each had their own complicated installation procedure. In fact, many such connections required the complete shutdown of the system, manual installation of the hardware and requisite software, and a restart of the entire system followed by post-installation adjustments, before a simple data transfer could take place between the PC and the peripheral device such as a printer. This level of functional malleability and expandability was both the boon and the bane of the PC.

With the growing popularity of the PC as a desktop printing and communications platform and the ever-increasing demand for connectivity with the burgeoning worldwide network of PC systems called the Internet, a faster and more convenient method of connecting and interacting with devices was needed without the hardship and the inefficient interruptions of the PC shutdown and reboot sequence. In recognizing this problem, Intel Corporation contributed technology from its research facilities to enable the low-cost and high-speed connectivity of peripheral devices to the PC platform with the ease of plug-and-play simplicity [32]. In fact, Intel spearheaded the formation of a group of influential industry leaders in developing an industry specification with royalty-free IP licensing that would be made available to all adopters of this technology. The technology was dubbed the Universal Serial

Bus, or USB for short. Intel implemented the USB technology in its chipset products and hosted many interoperability events to facilitate the adoption of this technology by other members of the growing USB ecosystem in peripheral devices and software. Ultimately, the USB Implementers Forum (USB-IF) was formed in 1995 and later incorporated as a stand-alone industry standards organization to support and accelerate the market and consumer adoption of USB-compliant products. Today, USB is a household name and is the preferred connectivity standard for nearly all major CE and PC devices being produced worldwide. The list of devices that implement USB connectivity continues to grow and expand [33].

The generational compatibility and easy-to-use functionality of the USB technology standard have facilitated an expanding list of CE devices to connect and disconnect with the PC platform without requiring complicated installation procedures to be performed by the consumer. Progressively, the USB standard has displaced older and competing means of connectivity such as the parallel port, IEEE 1394, or FireWire technology. In 2007, *Maximum PC* magazine named USB the premier PC technology innovation of all time [34]. Notably, this accolade puts USB ahead of the Intel Pentium processor or the Microsoft Windows operating system.

In applying our generalized model to the case of the USB technology standard, using our proposed framework, we consider the following elements: Business objectives, market requirements, alternative technologies, industry ecosystem and standardization strategy. The resulting model application is shown in Fig. 9.3 in Appendix 1.

Business objectives: The goal here is to accomplish PC and CE connectivity with ease in a progressively efficient, low-cost and performant manner.

Market requirements: The market requires an open standard that is accessible to a variety of hardware and software vendors, in order to facilitate a robust ecosystem of interoperable products and services. Furthermore, the market requires a technology that is easy to adopt without arduous IP licensing and royalty obligations.

Alternative technologies: At the time when USB was being contemplated, there were existing technologies, such as the parallel and serial ports, but these alternatives were deemed to be 'out of gas' as their performance and ability to transfer large amounts of data was limited and restrictive of the overall performance of the platform. Additionally, there were other technologies, such as 1394/FireWire, but owing to their proprietary nature and onerous licensing and royalty terms, the industry was loathe to adopt these technologies.

Industry ecosystem: At the time of the introduction of the USB technology, there existed a healthy and thriving ecosystem comprised of Original Equipment Manufacturers (OEMs), Independent Hardware Vendors (IHVs), Operating System Vendors (OSVs), Independent Software Vendors (ISVs), as well as a plethora of device and tools vendors. This ecosystem came together through the leadership and influence exerted by a few industry vanguards such as Intel and Microsoft to form and propel the broad adoption of the USB technology and its subsequent maintenance and evolution.

Standardization strategy: The scope consists of specifications to enable easy and compatible PC-to-device connectivity. This requires a simple interface between hardware and software to ensure consumer-friendly attachment points, without the need for complex installation or post-installation procedures. The IP policy is crucial in ensuring the rapid adoption and instantiation of the standardized technology. As its original author and proponent, Intel decided to contribute the USB technology under royalty free (RF) IP licensing terms to all members of the USB ecosystem. For its execution strategy, Intel opted for a two-stage technology transfer model. This model is depicted as Fig. 9.4 in Appendix 1. Intel acted as the technology incubator and released its initial specification to a group of like-minded proponents of the technology called the USB Promoters Group. This group of companies came together under legal provisions much like a SIG for the express goal of refining and endorsing a set of specifications to enable the implementation and compliance of the USB technology standard. After the accomplishment of these goals, the USB technology transferred to the USB Implementers Forum (USB-IF), another industry standards body much like a SIG, for the express purpose of promotion, maintenance and evolution of the technology. In effect, the USB ecosystem interacts and interfaces with the USB-IF to facilitate interoperable product development and the pursuit of commerce.

9.3 Discussion

Technology standardization continues to evolve over time. Recently, we have witnessed a gradual weakening in the dissonance between the different approaches to standards development in the computing, communications, and consumer electronics industries, as these previously isolated technology domains have collided and blended together. The PC industry has historically been unregulated, market-driven, and has shown a preference for informal standardization bodies, such as SIGs or ad-hoc alliances. By contrast, the CE industry has historically been regimented and regulated through governmental oversight and has thus exhibited a strong preference for more formality in standards development, such as the SDO or the ISDO format. Thus, it is possible to hypothesize (**H1**) that in the near future we can anticipate and observe a strengthening of SIG structures with increasing formality and rigor, and we may equally expect that SDOs adopt a more business-friendly stance through shorter specification development cycles and increased attention to product instantiation and compliance issues.

The assertiveness of developing economies such as China, India, and Brazil, constitutes another mega-trend on the horizon. These economies, previously absent from the Western-dominated technology standards development sphere, will increasingly exert influence and seek out their place on the global stage of international standards developing organizations. It is possible to hypothesize (**H2**) that in the near future we can anticipate and observe the formation of local technology standardization bodies that are housed and sponsored in these emerging economies.

Finally, the growing sensitivity to the rapid decay of our global environmental and the rise of the 'green' movements across will undoubtedly have an impact on technology standards development. For example, energy efficiency, lead-free components, and other such concerns will begin to exert their influence in the direction and scope of technology standards development. It is possible to hypothesize (**H3**) that the increasing awareness and demand for conservation of energy in computing, communications, and consumer electronics platforms and devices will lead to the need for enhanced and sophisticated standards in managing energy delivery and energy consumption.

Moreover, some clearly discernible trends in IP policy cannot escape our attention. IP rights management has become a highly visible issue in recent times, owing to some high-profile patent infringement cases. The choice of the IP model in technology standards development depends in large part on the scope of the technology in question, the preferences of the ecosystem participants and the predilections of those implementing the technology in question. In addition, the different approaches and emphases on IP rights management between the developed and the developing economies around the globe will become more pronounced and fraught with management challenges and possibilities. In this vein, it is possible to hypothesize (**H4**) that in the near future we will witness a noticeable movement towards the adoption of royalty-free IP rights policies. There are many opportunities for policy innovations in this regard such as ex ante disclosure of licensing terms, the durability of licensing commitments, the formation and nature of patent pools, and related concerns.

In the course of the development of technology standards, the authors of this study have compiled both experiential and strategic lessons worthy of citation in this study. The most important lesson is related to the existence of entrenched, 'legacy' technologies. These technologies are usually extremely difficult to dislodge with the introduction of new technology standards as the existing infrastructures and ecosystem are deeply vested in the recoupment of their initial investments and in continuing to milk cash cows. Furthermore, breakthroughs and disruptive technology innovations need business justification followed by massive enabling investments to achieve traction. The development of such technology standards has historically consumed inordinate amounts of resources and heavy lifting. Finally, a strategy to 'lift all boats' by way of technology standards is not always in the best interest of the lead sponsor as it may easily enable its competitors without requiring them to invest equally in the development of the standard. To mitigate this weakness, most technology standardization advocates prefer hooks and harnesses to enable them to innovate above the standard for differentiation and value-added functionality in order to create distance between themselves and their competitors and imitators.

Strategically, any participation in standards development activities must support a business objective. This truism is often taken for granted or not taken seriously by engineers and technologists whose main aim is to innovate and develop technologies. Thus, a large amount of technology standardization effort often is left on the table without commercial exploitation or instantiation because the business imperatives of the company were incongruent with the effort of its employees that produced the technology standard. Moreover, a firm must ensure that only its top skills and sophisticated, mature human resources are tapped for participation in standards developing bodies. This is crucial as the protection of the firm's crown jewels—its IP portfolio—is at stake and could easily be jeopardized or compromised if the caliber of participants is lacking the requisite training in group dynamics, effective communication, IP law, influencing skills, and related proficiencies.

9.4 Future Research

In this study we outlined three research questions as follows:

- Why and how do PC and CE technology firms create standards?
- Can these technology firms protect their intellectual assets while sharing knowledge and expertise with industry ecosystems? Moreover, will such knowledge sharing help or hinder their competitiveness and growth potential?
- Are standards organizations such as SIGs suitable vehicles for promoting collaborative innovation in technology-intensive industries?

As a result of this study we know that technology standards are created through a variety of standards organizations and bodies, such as SIGs and SDOs, to facilitate technology diffusion and to advance the business objectives of the sponsoring firms. Secondly, we have noted that technology firms must balance their business imperatives to effectively compete while sharing critical intellectual properties that are used to develop technology standards. Thirdly, we have observed that standards developing organizations can pose challenges for technology managers as industries with differing disclosure and regulatory cultures collide and converge.

Each of the four hypotheses posited in the discussion section above, (**H1–H4**) merit further exploration and empirical scrutiny through field work, longitudinal studies, ethnographic observations, and so on. In addition, some of the other findings in this study point to the need for scholarly examination of additional topics such as:

1. Success metrics to measure the achievement of business objectives in driving technology standards.
2. Efficient methods to coordinate the desired objectives and results across large, multinational corporations and ISDOs.
3. The effects of technology standards on new product development (NPD) and the market impacts of dominant designs on horizontal industries.
4. The effect of globalization and culture on technology standards development and the emergence of new economies.
5. Geographic and cultural differences in technology standards development. For instance, a comparative study of the market-oriented, industry-led model prevalent in the US with the government-influenced model prevalent in the EU and Japan, and the government-funded and directed model prevalent in China.

Contributions in any of the above areas will greatly enhance and round-out the existing knowledge base on technology standards development, diffusion, and adoption in the coming decades.

Appendix 1: Exhibits

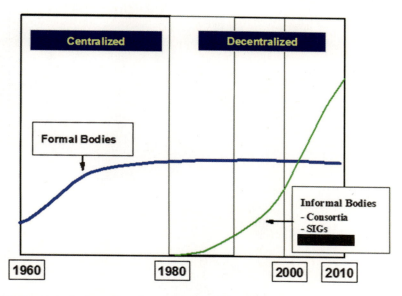

Fig. 9.1 Trends in the formation of centralized SDOs and decentralized SIGs [35]

Table 9.1 Comparison between SDOs and SIGs [35]

	SDO (e.g. IEEE)	SIG (e.g. PCI)
Focus	Architectural purity	Product interoperability
Scope	Broad	Narrow
Sponsor	Government	Business
Outcome	Predictable	Predictable
Mode of operation	Formal	Informal
Pace of operation	Slow	Fast
Order	Before implementation	With implementation
Verification	Rare	Robust
Time horizon (years)	5–10	2–5

Table 9.2 Survey results of factors influencing technology standards development

PCM results	Cost	Usability	Compatibility	Synergy	Longevity	Leadership
Max	0.21	0.24	0.26	0.19	0.23	0.15
Min	0.09	0.14	0.17	0.13	0.10	0.08
Mean	0.16	0.19	0.20	0.17	0.16	0.12
Std dev	0.04	0.03	0.03	0.02	0.04	0.02
Rank	4T	2	1	3	4T	6

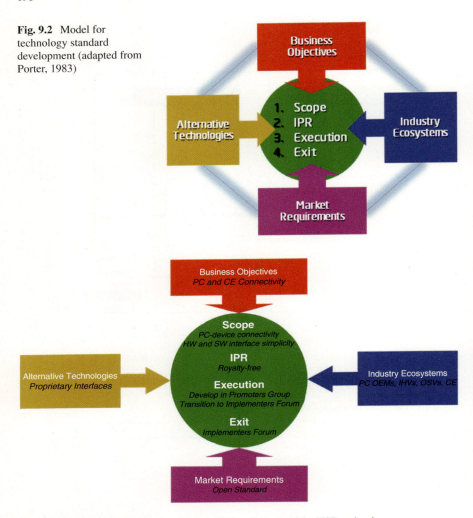

Fig. 9.2 Model for technology standard development (adapted from Porter, 1983)

Fig. 9.3 Standards development model applied to the case of the USB technology

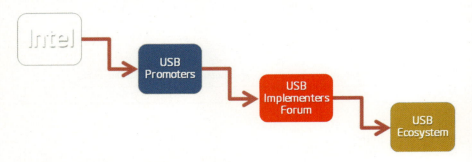

Fig. 9.4 The USB technology transfer model

9 Technology Standards Development: A Framework

Appendix 2: Data

Survey data from eight technologists in the greater Portland metropolitan area are shown below. Names and company affiliations are not reproduced in deference to requests for anonymity. The PCM software tool was used to obtain priority results.

Factors in standards development
PCM data
Decision criteria
S1 = cost
S2 = usability
S3 = compatibility
S4 = synergy
S5 = longevity
S6 = leadership

	S1–S2	S1–S3	S1–S4	S1–S5	S1–S6	S2–S3	S2–S4	S2–S5	S2–S6	S3–S4	S3–S5	S3–S6	S4–S5	S4–S6	S5–S6
Respondent 1	40 60	40 60	50 50	50 50	70 30	60 40	60 40	40 60	60 40	55 45	60 40	60 40	60 40	70 30	70 30
Respondent 2	40 60	30 70	50 50	50 50	60 40	60 40	60 40	60 40	60 40	45 55	60 40	60 40	50 50	70 30	70 30
Respondent 3	55 45	50 50	60 40	65 35	60 40	40 60	40 60	40 60	60 40	50 50	60 40	55 45	65 35	65 35	60 40
Respondent 4	50 50	20 80	60 40	50 50	70 30	50 50	60 40	50 50	70 30	60 40	60 40	70 30	50 50	50 50	80 20
Respondent 5	40 60	30 70	60 40	50 50	60 40	60 40	60 40	40 60	60 40	50 50	60 40	55 45	50 50	60 40	60 40
Respondent 6	40 60	40 60	50 50	50 50	50 50	50 50	60 40	70 30	70 30	50 50	50 50	70 30	70 30	60 40	60 40
Respondent 7	30 70	30 70	30 70	30 70	50 50	60 40	60 40	60 40	60 40	50 50	30 70	70 30	50 50	50 50	70 30
Respondent 8	60 40	50 50	50 50	60 40	70 30	50 50	60 40	70 30	60 40	60 40	60 40	50 50	70 30	50 50	40 60

PCM results

	S1	S2	S3	S4	S5	S6
Max	0.21	0.24	0.26	0.19	0.23	0.15
Min	0.09	0.14	0.17	0.13	0.1	0.08
Mean	0.16	0.19	0.2	0.17	0.16	0.12
Std dev	0.04	0.03	0.03	0.02	0.04	0.02

References

1. Corporate Strategy Board (1998) Stall points: barriers to growth for the large corporate enterprise. The Corporate Advisory Board, Washington, DC
2. Keil D (2006) Limits to firm growth: a pilot study. Unpublished paper, Department of Engineering and Technology Management, Portland State University
3. Neshati R (2009) Towards a theory of growth stall in technology-intensive firms. Paper submitted in fulfillment of independent study requirements, Department of Engineering and Technology Management, Portland State University
4. http://ade.state.az.us/standards/technology/Rationale.pdf
5. Hariharan S (1990) Technological compatibility, standards and global competition. Doctoral dissertation, University of Michigan, Ann Arbor
6. Cline K, Grindstaff L, Grobman S, Rasheed Y (2008) Innovating above and beyond standards. Intel Technol J 12(4):255–267
7. Gawer A (2000) The organization of platform leadership. Doctoral dissertation, Massachusetts Institute of Technology
8. http://www.pcisig.com/membership/about_us/Articles_of_Incorporation/
9. http://www.leg.state.or.us/ors/
10. Chiesa V, Toletti G (2003) Standard-setting strategies in the multimedia sector. Int J Innov Manage 7(3):281–308
11. Gassman O (2006) Opening up the innovation process: towards an agenda. R&D Manage 36(3):223–228
12. Sawhney M, Prandelli E (2000) Communities of creation: managing distributed innovation in turbulent markets. Calif Manage Rev 42(4):24–54
13. Horn PM (2005) The changing nature of innovation. Res Technol Manage 48(6):28–33
14. Ozsomer A, Cavusgil ST (1999) The effects of technology standards on the structure of the global PC industry. Eur J Market 34(9/10):1199–1220
15. Sahay A, Riley D (2003) The role of resource access, market considerations, and the nature of innovation in pursuits of standards in the new product development process. J Prod Innov Manage 20(5):338–355
16. Utterback JM, Abernathy WJ (1975) A dynamic model of process and product innovation. Omega 3(6):639–656
17. Mauri AJ, McMillan GS (1999) The influence of technology on strategic alliances: an application of the Utterback and Abernathy model of product and process innovation. Int J Innov Manage 3(4):367–378
18. Burnside B, Witkin L (2008) Forging successful university-industry collaborations. Res Technol Manage 51(2):26–30
19. Pisano GP, Shih WC (2009) Restoring American competitiveness. Harv Bus Rev 87(7/8):114–125
20. Alic JA (1991) Policy issues in collaborative research and development. Int Trade J 6(1):63–88
21. http://www.sematech.org/
22. Coyle K (2005) Standards in a time of constant change. J Acad Librarianship 31(3):280–283
23. Sun M, Tse E (2006) The diffusion of competing technology standards. Academy of Management (Best Conference Paper)
24. Riley D (2007) Factors affecting the pursuit of standards: a theoretical framework. Market Rev 7(2):139–154
25. Blind K (2006) Explanatory Factors for Participation in Formal Standardisation Processes: Empirical Evidence at Firm Level. Economics of Innovation & New Technology 15(2):157–170
26. Waguespack DM, Fleming L (2009) Scanning the commons? Evidence on the benefits of startups participating in open standards development. Manage Sci 55(2):210–223

27. Harryson S (2008) Entrepreneurship through relationships—navigating from creativity to commercialization. R&D Manage 38(3):290–310
28. http://us.blu-raydisc.com/#/pages/whatisblu
29. Porter ME (1983) Note on the structural analysis of industries. HBS case 9-376-054
30. Hemphill TA (2007) Firm patent strategies in US technology standards development. Int J Innov Manage 11(4):469–496
31. Simcoe TS, Graham SJH, Feldman MP (2009) Competing on standards? Entrepreneurship, intellectual property, and platform technologies. J Econ Manage Strat 18(3):775–816
32. http://www.intel.com/technology/usb/
33. http://www.usb.org/home
34. http://www.maximumpc.com/
35. http://www.ibm.com/developerworks/library/pa-spec1.html

Part IV
International Aspects

Chapter 10
Managing Issues of IT Service Offshore Outsourcing Projects

Rosine Hanna, David Raffo, and Tugrul U. Daim

Abstract Western countries' information technology and software intensive firms are increasingly producing software and IT services in developing countries. Regardless of the swift advancement in offshore outsourcing, there are arrays of issues that must be investigated in order for companies to benefit from the offshore outsourcing. Numerous significant benefits can be accomplished through the successful management of offshore outsourcing. Critical issues are the challenges that can happen throughout the lifecycle of offshore outsourcing IT service projects. This research will investigate these critical issues throughout the whole lifecycle of executed offshore outsourcing projects in the IT service industry from the client managerial perspective.

10.1 Introduction

Information Technology (IT) service offshore outsourcing describes the transfer of IT services to an offshore outsourcing supplier (OOS) in a near or far away country. The services themselves are partially or totally transferred [1, 13, 34, 38, 48, 59]. IT offshore outsourcing is worth being researched because it has specific characteristics that distinguish it from the well researched field of IT outsourcing. IT service and software development offshore outsourcing is becoming a dominant paradigm in the IT service and software development industry [72, 75].

Western countries' information technology and software intensive firms are attracted to offshore outsourcing in developing countries because of the promised benefits of: lower costs, faster delivery speed, the ability to focus their in-house

---

R. Hanna (✉) • D. Raffo • T.U. Daim
Engineering and Technology Management Department,
Portland State University, Portland, OR, USA
e-mail: rosine@pdx.edu; raffod@pdx.edu; tugrul@etm.pdx.edu

IT staff on more higher value work, access to supplier resources, capabilities and process improvement [14]. IT outsourcing should not be viewed as a process that leads to instant success. Not all IT service and software development projects benefit from offshore outsourcing as half of the organizations that shifted processes offshore failed to generate the benefits they expected [23, 24, 48, 51]. The literature indicates that 20 % of offshore outsourcing software development contracts are cancelled in the first year, more than 25 % of all offshore outsourced software development projects are cancelled outright before completion and 80 % of offshore outsourcing IT projects overrun their budgets [39].

IT services and software development offshore outsourcing projects pose substantial issues and challenges to the client companies in managing these projects [20]. In IT service offshore outsourcing, delivery occurs under the additional condition of distance between the service supplier and the client in terms of physical distance, time zone differences or cultural differences. Additionally, complexity increases due to the higher degree of geographical dispersion among team members [36, 58, 72, 86]. Therefore, there is a need to investigate the critical issues of IT service offshore outsourcing projects from the client managerial perspective.

10.2 Sourcing Options

There are four major types of sourcing options for U.S. IT services and software development projects: (1) in-sourcing, (2) outsourcing, (3) off-shoring, (4) offshore outsourcing as shown in Figs. 10.1 and 10.2.

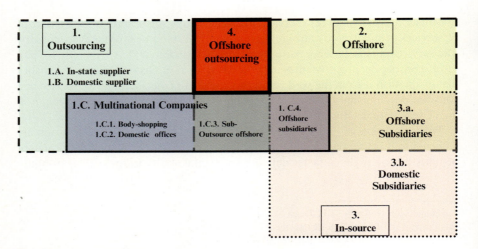

Fig. 10.1 Sourcing options

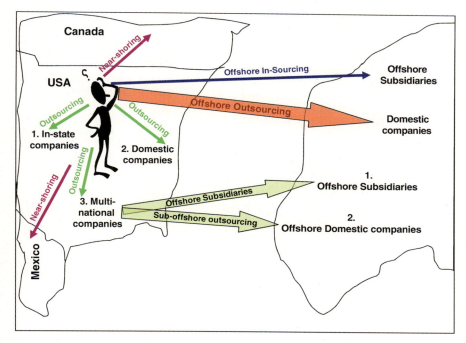

Fig. 10.2 Outsourcing and offshore options

1. *In-sourcing*: Decision makers decide to keep the IT services and software production in house on their own premises and in their home countries. Clients may also decide to build and operate their own facilities in domestic locations in their own country as domestic subsidiaries [13, 84].
2. *Outsourcing*: Decision makers decide to contract out part or all of a firm's IT services and software development to a domestic third party vendor [68]. The third party can be one or multiple domestic/national vendor or instate provider [35, 57].
    2.1 *Outsourcing with multinational companies*: Companies have their headquarters in high-wage countries open subsidiaries in low-wage countries to work on products and services for their domestic and global markets. Companies also can have their headquarters in low-wage countries open subsidiaries in high-wage countries to serve their local market(s) [63, 77]. For instance, some Indian enterprises set-up wholly owned facilities overseas to perform parts of the software development process. The most common practice is to perform systems analysis and design work at the customers' site while the rest of the development process is done from Indian and other locations of offshore development centers [41, 56]. Indian Firms hold a number of top ten positions across types of services offered. Key Indian players are Tata Consultancy Services (TCS), Wipro and Infosys as shown in Table 10.1.

Table 10.1 The top ten multinational companies and country of origin

Business services	Software development	Call centers
1. Hewitt Association *U.S.*	1. Tata Consultancy Services *India*	1. Convergys *U.S.*
2. ACS *U.S.*	2. Infosys Technology *India*	2. Wipro *India*
3. Accenture *U.S.*	3. Wipro *India*	3. ICICI OneSource *India*
4. IBM *U.S.*	4. Accenture *U.S.*	4. ClientLogic *U.S.*
5. EDS *U.S.*	5. IMB *U.S.*	5. 24/7 Customer *India*
6. Hewlett-Packard *U.S.*	6. Cognizant Technology Solutions *U.S.*	6. SR.Teleperformance *France*
7. Wipro *India*	7. Satyam *India*	7. eTelecare International *U.S.*
8. HCL Technology *India*	8. Patni Computer Systems *India*	8. SITEL *U.S.*
9. Tata Consultancy Services *India*	9. EDS *U.S.*	9. Teletech *U.S.*
10. WNS Global Services *India*	10. CSC *U.S.*	10. CustomerCorp *U.S.*

Source: National Association of Software and IT Service Companies (NASSCOM)—India's software regulatory board—http://www.nasscom.org, July 2002 [26]. Business Week (2006) [21]

Common workflows or delivery models that multinational companies such as Genpact, Accenture, IBM Services, Tata or any other outsourcing multinational companies (see Table 10.1) dispatch teams to thoroughly investigate the workflow of an entire IT department. The team then helps build a new IT platform, redesigns all processes, administers programs and acts as a virtual subsidiary. The contractor then disperses work among a global network of staff ranging from the U.S. to Asia and to Eastern Europe [21].

For instance, Tata Consultancy Services TCS is part of the Tata Group. TCS was founded in 1968 as a consulting service firm for the emerging IT industry. By 2006, TCS had expanded to become a global player with revenue over USD 2 billion with over 74,000 associates and 50 service delivery centers in 34 countries. TCS has developed a global delivery model in which tangible work is handled mainly by teams located remotely from clients, while a small team remains at the client's site. Usually, TCS's on-site and offshore teams conduct frequent interaction and collaboration with each other until a task is completed. TCS project teams based on-site, onshore, near-shore and offshore work together depending on the expertise and knowledge that reside within TCS's different locations. In an example beginning in late 2005, Netherlands based **ABN AMRO** Bank announced a USD 1.2 billion outsourcing contract with five providers. Tata Consultancy Services was one of the five and provides support and application enhancement services. The outsourcing project of the **ABN AMRO** Bank TCS contract consisted of three arrangements across three continents. Each arrangement type has an on-site component at the client site and a remote component somewhere else [64].

3. *Off-shoring*: Occurs when an organization moves work from one location to another location on a different continent [74, 75], researchers call it offshore in-sourcing and offshore subsidiaries [42].

4. *Offshore outsourcing*: Outsourcing of IT Services and software development work to a third party supplier located on a different continent than the client [74, 75]. This particular option has been quite prevalent in recent years and it will be examined in more detail.

10.3 Issues of IT Service Offshore Outsourcing Investigated in this Research

In offshore relationships, users and business analysts usually reside at the client side and technical analysts and developers tend to perform their work from offshore locations [48]. Large geographic distances substantially accentuate the complexity of coordination in such global set-ups and demand strategies for working efficiently [31]. Some of the most common challenges faced in offshore outsourcing projects relate to: over-expenditure, hidden costs [3, 41, 65, 82], communication problems, differences in project management practices, language barriers, time-zone differences, cultural differences, security and political issues and supplier site location [10, 47].

Raffo et al. [72] and Setamanit et al. [79, 80] identified the issues that affect the performance of offshore outsourcing for software development projects. Issues were identified and placed into three groups: fundamental issues, strategic issues and organizational issues as listed in Table 10.2, which will be described in further detail.

According to Raffo et al. [72] and Setamanit et al. [79, 80], fundamental issues, listed in Table 10.1, are directly impacted by the nature of all offshore outsourcing, including software development projects. These inherent obstacles can greatly impact the effectiveness of an project that has been outsourced offshore. However, by using an appropriate strategy and tool support, the project manager can mitigate the negative impacts of these issues. Communication issues could be caused by (1) inadequate informal communication and (2) loss of communication richness. Moreover, cultural and language differences are also identified as main challenges that affect the offshore outsourcing projects in many different ways. These include the effectiveness of communication and coordination, group decision making and

Table 10.2 Issues and challenges affecting the performance of offshore outsourcing for software development projects [72, 79, 80]

Fundamental issues	Strategic issues	Organizational issues

• *Communication issues*
  1. Inadequate informal communication
  2. Loss of communication richness
• *Coordination and control issues*
• *Cultural differences*
• *Language differences*
• *Time-zone differences*
	• *Development site location*
	• *Product architecture*
	• *Development strategy*
	  1. Module-based
	  2. Phase-based
	  3. Follow-the-sun
	• *Distribution overhead*
	• *Distribution effort loss*
		Team formulation
		Team dynamics
		  (*building trust*)

team performance. A project manager working on a project that has been outsourced, particularly offshore, should develop a plan to address these communication issues. Failure to do so, could negatively impact the success of the project; and perhaps worse, an underestimation of the importance of these issues may have a leave a project manager having regrets during a post mortem of the project.

One of the most important global software development challenges is related to the requirements phase of software development [70]. The requirements phase asks for a great deal of communication between the client team and supplier team [76], and is particularly acute in offshore outsourcing teams [61]. Prikladnicki et al. [69, 70] suggest face to face requirements elicitation as functional business requirements can easily be misunderstood due to the organizational, distance, cultural and language differences [61]. Even in stable business environments [9, 27, 33, 61] the need for detailed requirements [17, 78] are required to overcome the difficulties of global software development. Also, the level of familiarity (precedent requirements) with similar requirements seems to have a positive impact on a project [9, 83].

Building on the work of Raffo et al. [12] and Setamanit et al. [79, 80] and other researchers [15, 22, 29, 48, 61, 69, 78] in the area of issues and challenges of offshore outsourcing IT service projects, the most common issues and challenges were identified and compared to other sourcing options as shown in Table 10.3 below. As shown below, although offshore outsourcing approaches are common, they are certainly not without risk.

The main differences between "outsourcing" and "offshore outsourcing" of IT services and software development from a financial point of view are the labor costs and transaction costs [19, 49, 71]. When offshore outsourcing is chosen, the labor costs are typically lower while transaction costs are high. Transaction costs are associated with the overhead required to facilitate the interaction between the client and service provider. Khan et al. [41] states that when companies offshore outsource, labor costs are up to ten times lower than domestic outsourcing but the transaction costs are much higher and less certain than domestic outsourcing. These transaction costs can be up to 75 % of the total costs of offshore outsourcing. Transaction costs include communication costs, travelling costs, costs of poor quality and extra testing among others. These transaction costs are sometimes considered as hidden costs [41]. Therefore, in Table 10.3, offshore outsourcing has high degree of challenges on the cost vector, particularly related to hidden costs and cost overruns.

Outsourcing to domestic suppliers potentially has the advantage of personnel speaking the same language and within the same cultural background. The downside is that local outsourcing (for western companies) is expensive due to labor costs [49]. Previous research addressed the issue of knowledge transfer due to cultural and language issues. Indeed, cultural and language issues may exist with a domestic service providers, but the cultural, language, communication issues are much more significant with the offshore outsourcing service providers [4–6].

Issues associated with outsourcing with multinational companies are considered medium degree and similar to outsourcing with domestic suppliers. Often, multinational service suppliers have offices in the client's home region to help assist with

10 Managing Issues of IT Service Offshore Outsourcing Projects

Table 10.3 Issues/challenges level of sourcing options in terms of risk

Issues/challenges	In-sourcing USA offices	In-sourcing Offshore subsidiaries	Outsourcing National vendors	Outsourcing Multinational companies	Offshore outsourcing
Over expenditure/Hidden costs incurred by the client [4–6, 50, 52]	Low	Low	Medium	High	High
Difference in interpretation of project requirements between the client and the supplier [78]	Limited	Low	Medium	Medium	High
Poorly developed and documented requirements by the client company	Limited	Low	Medium	Medium	High
Poor tracking and managing requirement changes by the client company [78]	Limited	Low	Medium	Medium	High
Lack of a full communication plan between the client and the supplier [46, 72, 79, 80]	Limited	Low	Medium	Medium	High
Communication and coordination problems between the client and the supplier [32, 78]	Limited	Low	High	High	High
Language barrier [4, 10, 47, 67]	Limited	Low	Medium	Medium	High
Time-zone differences between the client and the supplier [4, 10, 47, 67, 82, 85]	Limited	High	Low	Low	High
Cultural differences between the client and the supplier [4, 10, 32, 41, 47, 60, 85]	Limited	Low	Medium	Medium	High
Incomplete and unclear contract [32]	N/A	N/A	Medium	Medium	High
Contract renegotiation and termination	N/A	N/A	Medium	Medium	High
Difference in project management practices between the client and the supplier	Limited	Low	Medium	Medium	High
Unable to measure performance of the supplier	Limited	Low	Medium	Medium	High
Supplier technical/security and political issues [3, 4, 32, 41, 55, 67, 85]	Limited	Low	Low	Low	High
No previous experience of the supplier	N/A	N/A	Medium	Medium	High
Lack of supplier standardized working methods	N/A	N/A	Medium	Low	High
Poor execution plan-timing of transition to supplier [47, 82]	Limited	Low	Medium	Medium	High

any communication or cultural issues with an overseas facility. In fact, once a decision has been made to outsource with a multinational company, negotiation of the contract and the agreement is commonly signed with the domestic offices of that multinational company [40, 41, 56]. In this arrangement, the domestic office holds legal responsibility for delivering the services according to the specifications in the contract ensuring that savings, service levels, and other outsourcing objectives are attained as stipulated in the contract [40]. All communications between client and the international company will generally be routed through the specialized technical and legal personnel at the domestic office. Therefore, international companies will be treated the same as the outsourcing vendor with the exception of more expensive contracts to deliver high quality services [56, 63, 64]. Development of IT services and software costs vary substantially across nations because of labor costs. The cost of offshore outsourcing in India is the same regardless of the location of the client, but the labor costs of body-shopping to the US entails higher costs due to the higher wages paid [56, 62].

For example, Indian vendors such as WiPro and Tata consultancy (TCS) (see Table 10.1) have recognized the need for closer, personal, day-to-day relationships with major customers and have opened offices and increased staff in North America to provide them [42]. In addition, due to political situations and potential risks of natural disasters [43, 44], many multinational companies are developing backup sites in places such as the Philippines and Canada where English fluency is common [42].

As IT services and software development have high degrees of interaction between the client and the service provider with more dynamic requirements the likelihood of issues to arise increases. Each individual client-service provider interaction has the opportunity for communication problems, cultural differences, language and time zone differences to create higher levels of challenges in offshore outsourcing compared with in-sourcing and outsourcing options [2, 4] as indicated in Table 10.3.

Offshore subsidiaries are developed to overcome some of the problems with offshore outsourcing of IT services and software development to third party suppliers. Many firms have committed themselves to offshore in-sourcing strategy to obtain the advantages of low-cost professionals [53, 73]. In this model, foreign technology workers are employees of U.S. based companies and receive the same training, software tools and development process guidelines as their western counterparts [73]. The main difference between these workers and domestic employees is salary [42, 73].

Researchers have found that offshore outsourcing of IT services and software development work poses considerably more challenges than domestic outsourcing as shown in Table 10.3. Offshore outsourcing is more challenging because of time zone differences [11, 25], the need for more controls [16, 45], distance and time-zone difference [30, 64], cultural differences [15, 37, 66, 73, 81], language problems [5, 6, 8], having to define requirements more rigorously [27, 28], difficulties in managing dispersed teams [64, 66], security and political issues [3, 41, 85] as in Table 10.3. The complexity of an outsourcing decision, and specifically an offshoring one, should not be underestimated. While cost is a major motivating factor in this decision, it is important, or even imperative, to consider costs beyond salary differential between two countries. Developing a plan that can be well executed to address the potential problems discussed here is a prudent step for any company considering offshore, or any type, of outsourcing as part of their strategy to deliver goods and services.

References

1. Agrawal V, Farrell D et al (2003) Offshoring and beyond. Mckinsey Quart 4:24–34, Special edition
2. Aspray W, Mayadas F et al (2006) Globalization and offshoring of software, a report of the ACM job migration task force. Association for Computing Machinery (ACM), USA
3. Barthelemy J (2001) The hidden costs of IT outsourcing. MIT Sloan Manage Rev 42(30): 60–70
4. Beulen E, Fenema PV et al (2005) From application outsourcing to infrastructure management: extending the offshore outsourcing service portfolio. Eur Manage J 23(2):133–144
5. Beulen E, Ribbers P (2003) IT outsourcing contracts: practical implications of the incomplete contract theory, Proceedings of the 36th annual Hawaii international conference on system sciences (HICSS'03). System Sciences, Hawaii
6. Bhalla A, Sodhi MS et al (2008) Is more offshoring better? An exploratory study of western companies offshoring IT-enabled services to S.E. Asia. J Oper Manag 26(2):322–335
7. Bhat JM, Gupta M et al (2006) Overcoming requirements engineering challenges: lessons from offshore outsourcing. Softw IEEE 23(5):38–44
8. Bock S (2008) Supporting offshoring and nearshoring decisions for mass customization manufacturing processes. Eur J Oper Res 184(2):490–508
9. Boehm B, Abts C et al (2000) Software cost estimation with Cocomo II. Prentice Hall, New York
10. Carmel E (1999) Global software teams: collaborating across borders and time zones. Prentice Hall, Upper Saddle River, NJ
11. Carmel E, Abbott P (2003) Configurations of global software development: Offshore versus nearshore, Proceedings of the 2006 international workshop on global software development for the practitioner. ACM, Shanghai, China
12. Carmel E, Agarwal R (2001) Tactical approaches for alleviating distance in global software development. IEEE Softw 18(2):22–29
13. Carmel E, Agrawal R (2002) The maturation of offshore sourcing of information technology work. MIS Quart Executive 20:65–78
14. Carmel E, Beulen E (2005) Governance in offshore outsourcing relationships. Offshore outsourcing of information technology work. Cambridge University Press, Cambridge
15. Carmel E, Tjia P (2005) offshoring information technology: sourcing and outsourcing to a global workforce. Cambridge University Press, Cambridge
16. Choudhury V, Sabherwal R (2003) Portfolios of control in outsourced software development projects. Inform Syst Res 14(3):291–314
17. Chrissis M, Konrad M et al (2006) CMMI: guidelines for process integration and product improvement. Pearson Education, Inc., Boston, MA
18. Cramton CD (2001) The mutual knowledge problem and its consequences for dispersed collaboration. Organ Sci 12(3):346–371
19. Dibbern J, Winkler J et al (2008) Explaining variations in client extra costs between software projects offshored to India. MIS Quart 32(2):333–366
20. Ebert C, Murthy BK, et al. (2008) Managing risks in global software engineering: principles and practices. IEEE international conference on global software engineering. Bangalore

21. Engardio P (2006) The future of outsourcing: How it is transforming whole industries and changing the way we work. Business Week (January 30): 50–58
22. Erber G, Sayed-Ahmed A (2005) Offshore outsourcing. Intereconomics 40(2):100–112
23. Ferguson E (2004) Impact of offshore outsourcing on CS/IS curricula. J Comp Sci Colleges 19(4):68–77
24. Ferguson E, McCracken D et al. (2004) Offshore outsourcing: current conditions and diagnosis. Executive Board of the ACM Special Interest Group on Computer Science Education (SIGCSE) Norfolk. ACM, Virginia, USA
25. Gokhale AA (2007) Offshore outsourcing: a Delphi study. J Inform Technol Case Appl Res 9(3):6–18
26. Gold T (2004) Outsourcing software development offshore: making it work. Auerbach Publications, New York
27. Gopal A, Mukhopadhyay T et al (2002) The role of software processes and communication in offshore software development. Commun ACM 45(4):193–200
28. Gopal A, Sivaramakrishnan K et al (2003) Contracts in offshore software development: an empirical analysis. Manage Sci 49(12):1671–1683
29. Greenemeier L (2002) Offshore outsourcing grows to global proportions. InformationWeek 56. doi: 8750-6874
30. Gupta S (2002) Demystifying offshore outsourcing despite the risks, the benefits can be great. CMA Manag 76(8):36–39
31. Han H, Lee J et al (2008) Analyzing the impact of a firm's capability on outsourcing success: a process perspective. Inform Manag 45(1):31–42
32. Hanna R, Daim T (2007) Critical success factors in outsourcing: case of software industry. Portland International Center for Management of Engineering and Technology (PICMET), Portland, OR
33. Herbsleb J, Grinter R (1999) Splitting the organization and integrating the code: Conway's law revisited. International conference on software engineering (ICSE99). Los Angeles, CA
34. Hirschheim R, Loebbecke C et al. (2005) Offshoring and its implications for the information systems discipline. Proceedings of the 26th international conference on information systems, Las Vegas, NV
35. Hoffmann T (1996) JP Morgan to save $50 million via outsourcing pact. Comp World 30(21):10
36. Holmström OH, Fitzgerald B et al (2008) Two-stage offshoring: an investigation of the Irish bridge. MIS Quart 32(2):257–279
37. Iacovou CL, Nakatsu R (2008) A risk profile of offshore-outsourced development projects. Commun of the ACM 51(6):89–94
38. Jahns C, Hartmann E et al (2007) Offshoring: dimensions and diffusion of a new business concept. J Purchasing Supp Manag 12(4):218–231
39. Kendall R, Post DE et al (2007) A proposed taxonomy for software development risks for high-performance computing (HPC) scientific/engineering applications. Software Engineering Institute, Pittsburgh, PA
40. Kern T (1997) The gestalt of an information technology outsourcing relationship: an exploratory analysis, Proceedings of the eighteenth international conference on information systems. Association for Information Systems, Atlanta, GA
41. Khan N, Currie WL et al (2003) Evaluating offshore IT outsourcing in India: supplier and customer scenarios, Proceedings of the 36th annual Hawaii international conference on system sciences. System Sciences, Hawaii
42. King W (2005) Outsourcing becomes more complex. Inform Syst Manag 22(2):89–90
43. King WR (2006) Offshoring decision time is at hand. Inform Syst Manag 23(3):102–103
44. King WR, Torkzadeh G (2008) Information systems offshoring research status and issues. MIS Quart 32(2):205–225
45. Kotlarsky J, Fenema P et al (2008) Developing a knowledge-based perspective on coordination: the case of global software projects. Inform Manag 45(2):96–108
46. Kraut R, Streeter L (1995) Co-ordination in software development. Commun ACM 38(3):69–81

47. Krishna S, Sahay S et al (2004) Managing cross-cultural issues in global software outsourcing. Commun ACM 47(4):62–66
48. Lacity M, Rottman JW (2008) Offshore outsourcing of IT work: client and supplier perspectives (technology, work and globalization). Palgrave Macmillan, New York
49. Lacity M, Willcocks L et al (2008) Global outsourcing of back office service: lessons, trends, and enduring challenges. Strategic Outsourcing Int J 1(1):13–34
50. Lacity MC, Hirschheim R (1993) The information systems outsourcing bandwagon. Sloan Manage Rev 35(1):73–86
51. Lacity MC, Willcocks LP et al (1996) The value of selective IT sourcing. MIT Sloan Manage Rev 37(3):13–25
52. Lacity MC, Willcocks LP (1995) Interpreting information technology sourcing decisions from a transaction cost perspective: findings and critique. Account Manage and Inform Technol 5(3–4):203–244
53. Laplante PA, Costello T et al (2004) Who, what, why, where, and when of IT outsourcing. IT Profess 6(1):19–23
54. Lawrence P, Karr J (1996) Technology spending and alliances: new highs in financial services firms. J Retail Bank Serv 17(3):45–52
55. Levina N, Ross J (2003) From the vendor's perspective: exploring the value proposition in information technology outsourcing. MIS Quart 27(3):331–364
56. Majumdar S, Simons K et al (2011) Body shopping versus offshoring among Indian software and information technology. Inform Technol Manage 12(1):17–34
57. McFarlan FW, Nolan RL (1995) How to manage an IT outsourcing alliance. Sloan Manage Rev 36(2):9–23
58. McIvor R (2000) A practical framework for understanding the outsourcing process. Supp Chain Manage Int J 5(1):22–36
59. Mirani R (2006) Client-vendor relationships in offshore applications development: an evolutionary framework. Inform Resour Manage J 19(4):72–86
60. Mohtashami M, Marlowe T et al (2006) Risk management for collaborative software development. Inform Syst Manage 23(4):20–30
61. Na K, Simpson JT et al (2007) Software development risk and project performance measurement: evidence in Korea. J Syst Softw 80(4):596–605
62. Niederman F (2004) IT employment prospects in 2004: a mixed bag. IEEE Comp Soc Publ 37(1):69–77
63. Niosi J, Tschang T (2009) The strategies of Chinese and Indian software multinationals: implications for internationalization theory. Ind Corp Change 18(2):269–294
64. Oshri I, Kotlarsky J et al (2008) Managing dispersed expertise in IT offshore outsourcing, lessons from Tata consultancy services. MIS Quart Executive 6(2):53–65
65. Overby S (2003) The hidden costs of offshore outsourcing. CIO Magazine (September 1): 1–13
66. Oza NV, Hall T et al (2006) Trust in software outsourcing relationships: an empirical investigation of Indian software companies. Inform Softw Technol 48(5):345–354
67. Pai AK, Basu S (2007) Offshore technology outsourcing: overview of management and legal issues. Bus Process Manage J 13:21–46
68. Palvia P (1995) A dialectic view of information systems outsourcing: pros and cons. J Inform Process Manage 38(3):265–267
69. Prikladnicki R, Audy J et al (2003) Global software development in practice lessons learned. Softw Process Improvement Pract 8(4):267–281
70. Prikladnicki R, Audy JLN et al. (2006) A reference model for global software development: findings from a case study. Proceedings of the IEEE international conference on global software engineering (ICGSE'06), Florianopolis
71. Qu Z, Brocklehurst M (2003) What will it take for China to become a competitive force in offshore outsourcing? An analysis of the role of transaction costs in supplier selection. J Inform Technol 18:53–67
72. Raffo D, Setamanit S (2005) A simulation model for global software development project. The international workshop on software process simulation and modeling, St. Louis, MO

73. Rao MT (2004) Key issues for global IT sourcing: country and individual factors. Inform Syst Manage 21(3):16–21
74. Rottman JW, Lacity M (2006) Proven practices for effectively offshoring IT work. Sloan Manage Rev 47(3):56–63
75. Rottman JW, Lacity M (2008) A US client's learning from outsourcing IT work offshore. Inform Syst Front 10(2):259–275
76. Sakthivel S (2005) Virtual workgroups in offshore systems development. Inform Softw Technol 47(5):305–318
77. Schwalbe K (2010) Information technology project management. Cengage Learning Inc, Boston, MA
78. Sengupta B, Chandra S et al. (2006) A research agenda for distributed software development. Proceedings of the 28th international conference on software engineering Shanghai, China. ACM, New York
79. Setamanit S, Wakeland W et al. (2006) Planning and improving global software development process using simulation. Proceedings of the 2006 international workshop on global software development for the practitioner (GSD '06), ACM, New York
80. Setamanit S, Wakeland W et al (2007) Using simulation to evaluate global software development task allocation strategies. Softw Process Improvement Pract 12(5):491–503
81. Smith HA, Mckeen JD (2004) Developments in practice XIV: IT outsourcing—how far can you go? Commun AIS 14:508–520
82. Tafti M (2005) Risk factors associated with offshore IT outsourcing. Ind Manage Data Syst 105(5):549–560
83. Tiwana A (2004) Beyond the black box: knowledge overlaps in software outsourcing. IEEE Softw 21(5):51–58
84. Trent RJ, Monczka RM (2005) Achieving excellence in global sourcing. MIT Sloan Manage Rev 47(1):24–32
85. Vogel D, Connolly J (2005) Best practices for dealing with offshore software development. Handbook of business strategy. Intertech Engineering Associates, Inc., Westwood, MA
86. Yalaho A, Nahar N (2009) The ICT—supported unified process model of offshore outsourcing of software production: exploratory examination and validation. Int J Innov Technol Manage 6(1):59–96

Chapter 11
Global New Product Development

Russell Watt

Globalization In the age of ubiquitous internet bandwidth, the development of a global market, coupled with rapid development of what once were underdeveloped countries and regions has led to many companies thinking and acting globally. This phenomenon has brought many new challenging facets of globalization to the surface in today's business world. These new challenges have to be managed effectively to succeed in the rapidly changing world. The areas of Technology Management and New Product Development have long been a significant area of interest for academic researchers and corporations, for fairly obvious reasons. New products are the key to continued profitable existence and growth for companies and exceptional versus ordinary technology management can be the difference between thriving and extinction. A perceived trend in new product development has become more prevalent in recent times; the trend of globalization of the development process. Stemming from efforts to develop better products faster, cheaper, and with greater market success, companies have looked to globalize their product development efforts. If a corporation is to start a global product development strategy, other more general issues in management related to management of technology in general must also be considered and understood to have a reasonable chance of success. This chapter will focus heavily on New Product Development in a global context while also addressing some larger issues related to Global Technology Management. Specifically this text will include (1) An overview of recent articles on Global New Product Development a framework to access the motivations and reasons to proceed on New Product Development Globalization Method as well as an assessment on the effectivity of its implementation; (2) an overview of articles on some aspects of Technology Management in a global context and a framework to evaluate addressing potential issues in this arena; (3) A review of a few product development cases at Xerox, a large multinational corporation who has globalized some of their

---

R. Watt (✉)
Nike, Inc.
Beaverton, OR, USA
e-mail: russ.watt@nike.com

product development efforts, and an evaluation of these case studies with the frameworks that have been created. The end result of this exercise will be an evaluation of current practice related to Global New Product development at Xerox, more specifically products with design responsibility residing at the Wilsonville, Oregon site, and identification of gaps between current practice and best practices identified through papers published in academia. Additionally, a discussion touching on the more generalized issues that can become relevant to global technology management in general will also be presented.

11.1 Introduction

The Xerox Wilsonville site is engaged in the practice of developing printers for the office market, and is part of the Global Technology Corporation familiar to most people. The majority of the activities on site are aimed at printers based on proprietary marking technology termed, Solid Ink. Solid Ink technology is similar to ink jet printing that is used by many participants in the printing market across many segments, but differs as it uses a wax based ink system rather than an aqueous based system. This difference offers some inherent advantages as well as challenges, both technically based and market centered. Like other industries, competition is fierce and significant cost and profitability pressures exist. One of the ways that Xerox has attempted to improve the cost structure and product portfolio offered, is to leverage other geographic locations, both within and external to captive Xerox resources.

The first specific case that will be examined from Xerox will include the products known as the *ColorQube 9200 series* of products. This development effort represented many firsts for the Xerox Solid Ink business. It was the first foray into the A3 paper size (the European equivalent to 11" × 17" paper size) market segment as well as being the first product developed by resources not solely located at the Wilsonville site. The development effort was global as two sites in North America, a single location in the United Kingdom and two sites in Southeast Asia were active and significant participants in the development effort. The second case study is another development effort that has yet to launch a product. The announcement of the product is forthcoming in the near future. Due to the timing of this writing and the product announcement, many details related to the development effort and product details will intentionally be left vague, the product will be a new entrant into a market space where Xerox has been an active participant. Lastly, a third case study will be viewed. Once again, this third case study is a branching out into new market space for Solid Ink Technology. This third case is somewhat different as the bulk of the development effort was done in Monroe Country, New York with content provided by Xerox Wilsonville and another overseas development partner. This third product has recently been announced to the public and is called the CiPress. It is a machine aimed at the production printing business which prints directly to paper while it is still on a roll at very high speeds, in excess of 500 ft/min.

Xerox, like many others, is a for profit business entity. Of course, many factors contribute to the profitability of a product and business. The focus of this work will be on the development efforts and not upon the execution of the marketing strategy. Although this execution and the marketing plan in general are significant contributors to the overall profitability of a product, this will not be examined in this work. The development process itself, including time to market considerations, NRE (Non Recurring Engineering) costs to develop the product and manufacturing transfer issues will be the focus of the work.

11.2 Global New Product Development Definition

The term Global New Product Development has been extremely prevalent in literature and management discussions. The form of the "globalization" can take many shapes and structures; simply purchasing foreign made components may be considered as the globalization of a product, but this practice is generally not what is meant by global development [1]. The output of development is the knowledge required to create a product or service that has value in the marketplace. This knowledge has many forms, but for the focus of this paper it will not include of parts or subsystems that are commoditized—readily available from more than one source. The structure by which an organization spreads out the responsibility of New Product globally can have many manifestations, but more than one geographic region must be represented to be global. An organization may choose to open a development office in a foreign region or it may elect to partner with another company with a development location in another region. Some researchers have defined Global New Product Development as "using a highly-distributed, networked development process facilitated by a fully digital PD [Product Development] system…. This practice may involve outsourced engineering work along with captive offshore engineering facilities." [2]. von Zedwitz and Gassmann developed their structural model of global research and development as illustrated in the following table [3] (Fig. 11.1).

To comply with this definition, the ownership of development resources is not constrained; development resources can be owned by the outsourcing or geographically expanding company or by another development partner altogether. In the following chart either option including offshore locations should be considered to be Global New Product Development, provided that there is substantial development work occurring at more than one location (Fig. 11.2).

Both of the following heuristics look at where resources are geographically located and who "owns" these resources. Global New Product Development Teams are not required to be "owned" or employed by the same firm to fit either of the above models. Many "simple" New Product Development approaches take the form of partnering with an offshore manufacturing location that is often owned by Contract Manufacturer (CM). In this scenario, the CM often leverages economies of scale with the purchasing of commodity components or purchasing agreements with subcontractors and has the opportunity to focus on supply chain logistics and optimization [4].

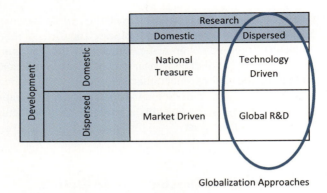

Fig. 11.1 von Zedwitz and Gassmann definitions of approaches

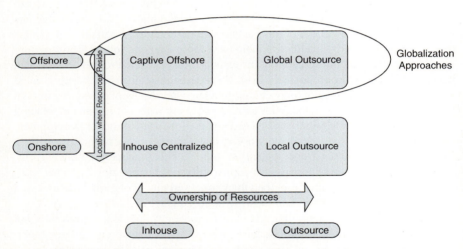

Fig. 11.2 Defining global new product development by location and ownership. Adapted from Eppinger and Chitkara [2]

11.3 Factors Considered in the Globalization Decision

Global New Product Development has been defined by others as the use of engineering or scientific resources from more than one geographic region and should not be confused with Global Product Development. In fact differences between market requirements can be one of the reasons to move towards a Global Product

Development Strategy. For example, video cassette recorders often have different formats and standards for transmissions, such as PAL, NTSC or SECAM. These standards are generally country or region specific [5]. If a company engaged in the manufacturing of VCRs is located in a region where PAL is the standard, it is reasonable that the depth of technical knowledge about another region's standard is lacking when compared to engineers and companies who reside and work where a different standard is in place. In the von Zedwitz and Gassmann model, this would be termed either a market driven or global R&D approach, depending on where the supporting technology-work related to the different content standards—research was done. The ability to find new ideas is one of the basic motivations for Global New Product Development and there are many examples for a domestic company finding new ideas abroad [6]. A further extension of the finding product ideas concept, is the concept of entering a new market. Some companies have the opening of a new office in a new region or country as part of the overall corporate strategy, from a market access point of view. This is often done as potential tariffs, taxes or other regulatory issues may also be avoided. Further, having a local office can help make a foreign company more attractive to potential local customers [7].

Without question, the increase in R&D spending has been significant as summarized by other researchers [8], but it would be inaccurate to conclude that the Globalization of New Product Development activities are a new phenomenon. Research and writing on global research and development was quite prevalent for more than a decade [9–11]. The underlying reasons as to why corporations choose to move to a global new product development strategy needs to be understood before a basis for comparison as well as how to develop a strategy to successful implement such a strategy. Certainly the potential benefits for a global new development strategy must outweigh the risks, and then the execution of the strategy must adequate to enable the net benefit to exceed the risks and costs of doing so. It is not a foregone conclusion that an outsourcing arrangement to leverage the labor rate differences between two regions will automatically offset the added management and logistics that are required for such a structure to be successful [12]. From a purely project management point of view; project quality, cost and schedule are primary deliverables for any project all which factor in to project success. A substantial report completed by the management consultants, McKinsey & Co., found that the impact to total profitability of a project that is completed 6 months late is a reduction in after-tax profits of 33 %—clearly showing the impact of reducing time to market for the profitability of a new product [13].

Many studies and theories have been presented regarding factors to consider when formulating a global product development strategy. Some factors that are frequently considered are related to the potential for lower costs, improved development process, access to new markets and access to technology [2, 3]. Another significant undercurrent leading to global new product development is simply related to which countries are producing more skilled workers. Statistics show that India, China and other countries in Asia are graduating more students formally trained in engineering and sciences than the United States and other first world countries [14]. With a heightened supply of technical professionals and a lower cost of living, the cost of an engineer in some of these countries is substantially less than the cost of an domestic engineer for an American company. The salary of an engineer in China or researcher, for example, was approximately one third of a comparable US salary in 2005 [15]. It has been noted by some researchers that the "labor arbitrage" between two countries or regions can be the sole reason for pursuit of a global product development strategy, especially for companies doing new product development work abroad and not basic or pure scientific research [16]. In addition to the savings from salaries, government policy in many developing companies have made direct foreign investment by US and other companies attractive from a taxation point of view as well as terms of government loans to be extremely attractive [17]. The innovation strategy of a country is often tied to new technology investments and can be the means for a government to try to elevated the standard of living for the an entire nation while also balancing other objectives. In the case of Malaysia, government policy was enacted to attempt to improve the standard of living while balancing environmental objectives [18].

Much of this economic policy is guided in an effort to create innovation clusters, geographic regions that specialize in specific industries [19]. The purpose of this clustering is to help with the sharing of knowledge and to establish centers of excellence in various industries and technologies [20]. Not all innovation clusters are located in developing countries, as most Americans are familiar with software and technology clusters in the Silicon Valley, the automotive cluster in and around Detroit, and Boston's Route 128 high tech cluster. Some researchers have argued that clusters are most effective when they are "tied" to other clusters to further knowledge [21]. Many companies are interested in participating in clusters, as there is the feeling that being geographically closer to areas where excellence in a particular science or technology is beneficial, and that there is a significant need to have a presence in that area for both marketing and brand awareness [22, 23]. As a result of clustering, it is very rare, perhaps even unheard of, for an automotive supplier not to have a presence in the Detroit area or a software company with a significant web presence to not have a Silicon Valley office. Porter and Stern conclude that a common innovation infrastructure that arises from technology clusters help to stimulate and drive overall innovation within a particular market segments [24].

Efficient Global New Product Development has the opportunity to shorten design cycles. Some of the potential benefits come simply form the use of more hours in the development day due to the difference in time zones. Just as "the sun never set on the British Empire", with a truly global development effort, it would be possible to effectively leverage a series of development sites so that value added work could be done 24 h per day. This perceived benefit must overcome the noted challenges in coordination, communication and cultural and time zone differences, among other challenges [16]. The basic desires of business, to reduce development costs, increase market reach and to shorten time to market for a new product are fundamental reasons why Global New Product Development has become a popular strategy [25].

Depending upon the structure of the offshoring arrangement, another potential benefit is freeing up of capital by the parent, or outsourcing, company. This is especially common when the globalization strategy is done by the use of a contract manufacturer in a low cost wage region or country. Especially as an outcome of the global financial crisis of 2010, many companies are more conservative in their new product development expenditures. When the offshore or outsource agreement takes development activities to an outside firm, it is possible that the financial arrangement will have the outsourcing company to invest in the development costs for a share of the product profits [26]. When this approach is taken, the outsourcer will now find a means to work on more projects than if the corporate R&D budget were the only access to development funds. Many times, this is an attractive route to pursue as it will virtually ensure that the development partner is truly interested in market success of the new product [27, 28].

It is clear that that the decision and factors to pursue a global new product development approach is an important decision. As previously noted, this structure of the arrangement can have substantially different depths. For example, Magna Steyr, a large automotive supplier with many development capabilities, has been hired to 'simply manufacture' vehicles with the Mercedes Benz nameplate in contrast to developing and engineering the ride and feel of BMW's X3 SUV [29]. The need and strategic intent of the outsourcing arrangement should be tailored to meet the specific situation. This may or may not include offshoring.

When a development partner is chosen, it is also of paramount importance to decide strategically which of the value creation activities will be handled away from the home office. This decision becomes a more important one, if the offshore resources are not controlled or owned by the same company. For example, Sony Ericsson has decided that only 'older' cell phone models would be manufactured by contract manufacturers and Porsche has determined that only the lower end models of their product portfolio were suitable for allowing another company to manufacture them [29]. When the partnership includes development work, many researchers have concluded that outsourcing the core technical competency of the business is a decision that should not be made [2]. It may be easy to conclude that a parent company owned development center in a foreign location would alleviate any and all concerns in this area, but this may not be the case. A region or country with a high level of technical competence may also experience a high level of employee turnover to competing firms. Development partnership agreements often occur in regions of technology clusters, which may create issues with knowledge management of critical concepts, which is often termed "Intellectual Property Leakage" [30].

In addition to the decision on whether or not to pursue a global new product development approach, considerations about where this globalization should be carefully thought out. There typically are a few 'hot spots' such as Bangalore, Moscow, Chengdu, Delhi or Shanghai, but failure to look beyond these 'hot spots' could be a serious mistake. Farrell has developed a framework to help identify specific factors to help select an appropriate location for offshore development. According to her work, the historical 'hot spots' often experience rapid increase in labor rates; and due to more foreign R&D and service work added to a developing region, the infrastructure may not be able support such rapid growth [31]. According to Farrell, making a bad decision with respect to location for an offshore location is very difficult to change due to the capital expense of the initial investment. Farrell further describes many reasons why some of the 'hot spots' such as Prague, Mumbai or China may not be the best choices for the long term. Her framework based on a series of factors such as risks from a political and policy angle as well as from natural disasters, total pool of skilled employees with appropriate language skills, accessibility to the local market and infrastructure such as power grid stability, IT bandwidth and transportation [31].

Many authors warn about the outsourcing of core competencies or core technologies, due to the strategic nature of inherently differentiated technology [2, 32, 33]. Fundamentally, a company should strive to excel in the technical area where it superior to its competitors, wherever this competitive advantage may lie. Outsourcing what should be a sustainable competitive advantage does not seem like a sound long term strategy. For example, Apple should think twice before outsourcing development related to user interfaces. If the globalization center is a captive center, being owned by the parent company, careful consideration should be taken before sending core competency work to another region. When a decision is to be made related to sending core technology development work abroad; factors to consider maybe the Intellectual Property policy and culture of a potential "host" nation and turnover rates among technical professional in the foreign nation. There certainly can be a number of other considerations, but is extremely sensitive decision that should not be based uniquely on potential cost savings on direct labor.

11.4 Efficiency of Global New Product Development

Logically, it seems unlikely that a corporation could transition from a self-contained development model to a global development organization overnight. Many key learning points are required to increase the likelihood of success with a global development effort. It seems that the majority of these could be broken down into two main areas: (1) Issues with moving to a distributed development model and (2) Issues dealing with the international nature of Global New Product Development. The ability to address potential issues in one or both of these areas will have a positive contribution to how well the new product development effort will be executed. Researchers have noted that some practitioners have acknowledge that foreign R&D investment is often expensive with respect to the cost of execution and may result in low project efficiency, but even with these beliefs, the potential of the approach is "underestimated and insufficiently exploited" [3].

It seems logical, that having an efficient local new product development process that is efficient and effective would increase the probability of exporting research and development work abroad. A large study by Kleinschmidt, de Brentani and Salomo has demonstrated this. Their study showed significant relationships between having a formal development procedure, strong management commitment and a strong local innovation culture to be related to positive financial performance of the new products and taking advantages of opportunities when they arise [34].

Their research took a case study approach on 387 global new product development efforts across many industries and geographies. It should also be understood that an accurate and honest assessment of these impendent variables should be considered when evaluating criteria to decide on the pursuit of a global new product development effort, and this assessment may not be totally obvious. Research has shown that the single most important factor in innovation is the actual corporate culture— and specifically the willingness to take risks, an orientation towards future markets and a willingness to cannibalize existing products. Often companies use the number of patents granted as a proxy for innovation, but the correlation between patents granted and radical innovation is quite low, which may not be an obvious conclusion to many technology managers [35]. The salient point is that in order to be successful in a global development strategy, you first need to examine the strengths and weaknesses of the current development paradigm before a globalization effort is undertaken. Further, when such an analysis is done, ensure that the measures of the efficacy of the NPD process are what are evaluated and not simply metrics that are simply easy to measure, such as the number of patents granted as a metric for innovation.

To truly measure the efficacy of a global new product development effort, clearly adherence to original time to market schedule and development budget are obvious metrics. Another reasonable metric will be a measure of commercial success such as market share or a financial metric such as gross profit. Further, given the circumstances, it should be reasonable to consider unplanned trips measured in either cost or time away from the home office for engineers or managers to spend 'bringing up' the offshore facility. Other considerations could be resolution time of complex design or manufacturing problems or manufacturing line uptimes. The key concept in measuring effectiveness of a globalized New Product Development is that the specific metrics have to be carefully selected, and well aligned with objectives.

11.5 Global New Product Development at Xerox

To further the basis of this work, examples of Global New Product Development of Xerox will be compared to findings highlighted in the academic literature. Three product development efforts will be used as test vehicles for concepts developed on Global New Product Development.

In addition to understanding what specific traits should be present to increase the probability for success in Global New Product Development, some understanding of the transition from domestic new product development to a global new product development is required. The path for Xerox, and specifically, Xerox Wilsonville started more than a decade ago. Prior to 2000, the Xerox Wilsonville facility was a part of Tektronix. Tektronix purchased a manufacturing facility in Northern Malaysia. This manufacturing facility became the manufacturing facility for all products that were developed by the then Corporate Printing and Imaging Division (CPID) of Tektronix. This action was motivated by the significant cost of labor benefit in moving manufacturing from Oregon to Malaysia. As this facility was owned by Tektronix, significant spending in the areas of IT infrastructure and employee training occurred. In early 2000, Xerox Corporation purchased the CPID division from Tektronix. The Malaysia facility was an asset that was part of that sale. The existing IT infrastructure was left largely untouched. In 2004, Xerox sold many manufacturing facilities to Flextronics, a global contract manufacturer based in Singapore, and named them as the global manufacturing partner for Xerox for all markets excluding the production market [36]. Very little could be seen as far as changes made to the Northern facility through these ownership changes. IT capability and connectivity between Malaysia and Wilsonville saw no noticeable impact. The Flextronics facility in Northern Malaysia manufactures complete printers for one of the market segments that Solid Ink printers participate in. Additionally, this facility performs some manufacturing processes and all functional tests for all printheads serving other markets. For needs in other market segments, completed and tested printheads from Northern Malaysia are shipped to other locations so that printheads can be integrated into those products. It appears that this approach has been taken for two main reasons. First, it appears that Xerox does not want to duplicate the capital expense for the equipment and facility needed to manufacture printheads. Second, the printhead is viewed as a core competence and a technology differentiator. Xerox has taken then approach to attempt to limit the number of facilities with access to process knowledge and the need technical expertise to test and manufacture it.

In a much more recent transaction, Xerox has sold off parts of their engineering services and some development capabilities to an Indian engineering services firm, HCL Technologies [37]. Some functions involved in this transaction are facilities that product prototype printed circuit boards and engineering design tool support as well as some software development and electrical engineering design groups. It appears as this transaction occurred for two reasons: (1) To eventually move this work to lower cost regions and (2) To establish a relationship with HCL so that their design resources could be used by Xerox if the need exists. HCL Technologies is an engineering services firm with substantial development capabilities. Xerox believes that HCL will be able to take over some of the engineering support services and tasks as well as take over some of the "basic" engineering that is not technology differentiators for the products and services that Xerox offers, all at a lower cost structure to Xerox. HCL Technologies has received rave reviews for its management practices that "puts employees first" and for their ability to meet customer's needs [38, 39]. Many engineers see this as a first step to seeing their jobs move to lower cost regions, resulting in fear and uncertainty in their job security. However, there is a very large and significant exception to this commonly held view. Engineers who work on printheads and ink do not share this opinion. They see these elements as a strategic part of the corporation's future and do not share the same fear.

As mentioned above, one of the reasons for corporations to begin a global new product development strategy is exposure to new markets. For Xerox, Asia has been a region where a substantial amount of foreign activity but this factor is not a consideration for Xerox. Xerox is a partner with Fuji Film Company in a joint venture,

Fuji Xerox. Fuji Xerox is a separate business entity who is the exclusive sales channel for Xerox products in Asia. With this arrangement, Xerox expanding through either a Xerox owned facility of through an outsourcing provider does not provide Xerox direct access to the new market.

11.6 Specific Case Studies in Global New Product Development at Xerox

11.6.1 Case 1: Globally Distributed Development Using Xerox Resources (Fig. 11.3)

The globalization of the product development has not stopped with the Northern Malaysia facility. A fairly recent product launch was the ColorQube 9200 and follow on 9300 series products. These products were the first foray of Xerox's proprietary Solid Ink Technology into the A3 market segment. The development sites for this product were spread out to three main sites, two in North America and one in Europe. Additionally, the manufacturing site for the product was chosen to be located in Southern Malaysia with the most technically challenging component, the printhead, was still to be manufactured and tested at the well-known facility in Northern Malaysia. The Southern Malaysia factory was not unknown to Xerox, as it was factory used for a number of black and white products developed elsewhere within Xerox. However, the factory was a new factory using the Solid Ink technology from Xerox. This southern facility experiences a high employee turnover rate when compared to the turnover rate in Northern Malaysia. Additionally, the IT connectivity between Southern Malaysia and Wilsonville is substandard when compared to the information flow between Wilsonville and Northern Malaysia.

11.6.2 Case 2: Partnered Offshore Development

Another project that is nearing launch has been a joint development of a new multifunction (print, copy and scan) device. In which Xerox partnered with an offshore company to assist with the development of a new product. The core technology of

Fig. 11.3 Xerox ColorQube 9200 series. Image from xerox.com

printheads and inks were re-used from other products while the partner company redesigned the rest of the product under the guidance of a team of engineers from Xerox Wilsonville. There had been two Xerox resources living abroad at the partner's site to help facilitate communication between the two companies and to give guidance to the local engineering resources. On an as needed basis, other resources from Xerox Wilsonville have been engaged to assist with technical problems. It seems as the quality of work performed has been of a high standard and the cost to Xerox has been quite favorable. The specific details of the development agreement are unknown, but the partner also sells the product under their company name in their home country while Xerox sells the product under a Xerox badge in other geographies. The development partner chosen was known to Xerox as they have been a long term supplier to Xerox for modules across many platforms and products. This approach has seemed to work fairly well with respect to adherence to original schedule and development budget. As this product is not yet launched, it is not yet known how successful it will be with respect to original business goals.

Although this project has gone well, there could be trouble in the future, if this model is used again. According to research done in the automotive industry, Xerox may be positioning itself to lose critical knowledge in how its products work and interact between modules and components. In a product that has a high degree of interdependencies, not understanding the components at a deep, intricate level related to how these components interact can often lead to problems that will be costly and difficult to address, at the integration stages of the project. Engineering the product as a system will require trade-offs and the engineers making these trade-offs need to understand the component capabilities as well as the system performance requirements [40].

In an outsourcing development model, many researchers have concluded that module partitioning is a good overall approach, but keeping the technical responsibility for design and development of the core technology, and the activities that have direct impact on product performance, should be an absolute must [2, 40]. The approach taken here does follow this advice, as the core technology of printheads and ink are still supplied by Xerox directly.

Establishing a level of trust is an important step in any joint development effort and doing so quickly is usually beneficial. Having a few collocated engineers is a smart decision, but it is also important that the specific individuals chosen have personal skills that will help to bridge two cultures. Having this trust is an important building block for a successful relationship, but joint innovation also requires knowledge sharing and the implementation of ideas not simply idea proposals [41]. Knowledge sharing, and especially knowledge sharing outside of the immediate workgroup is related to better performance in a globally distributed development model [42]. The basic arrangement between Xerox and this development partner helps to address some of the potential concerns that may exist between the sponsoring corporation and the development partner. Clearly, the development partner benefits from the success on the product (and not just the development project) as they will stand to benefit in building their brand with the product branded with their

Fig. 11.4 Xerox CiPress™ 500 continuous feed press. Image from xerox.com

company's logo in their home region. This helps to address a basic concern related to the motivation of the individual entities involved [43]. In this arrangement, there is clearly a reason to make a successful product and therefore there is some comfort knowing that the development partner has more to gain than learning knowledge from Xerox.

When this project began, Xerox identified a need to assign two individuals to largely serve as the conduit for information between the two organizations. Research has shown that additional workshops or forums to share knowledge have been shown to be beneficial [42]. There has also been a better definition of responsibilities between Xerox and the development partner with this product when compared to case 1 above. The use of a resource interface matrix, which specifically defines accountability and ownership of specific tasks, has helped in this area.

11.6.3 Case 3: Partnered Development in Production Space (Fig. 11.4)

The last example of Global NPD is the CiPress which has just been recently announced publically [44]. This product once again re-used printhead and ink technology that have been used in other already released products. The paper handling system was handed over to a development partner in Switzerland while the system software and other portions of the machine, specifically the marking hardware, was developed in Monroe Country, New York. Overall, the development effort went better than expected, but system complexity made some problem solving efforts non-trivial. This project had some inherent advantages over this first example case discussed, one of the largest is that the manufacturing of the product occurred in the same location as the majority of the product development. As this product is aimed at the Production Market, it is manufactured in Monroe Country, New York, in close proximity to most of the product design engineers as well as the individuals responsible for system integration. This proximity helped with the handoff between development engineers and manufacturing engineers as well as the opportunity to

Table 11.1 Global new product development summary for Xerox Solid Ink Technology

Case study	Potential labor rate savings	Overseas mfg.	Outsourced mfg.	Multiple development sites	Outsourced devel. effort
ColorQube 9200	Yes	Yes	Yes	Yes	No
#2 (yet to be announced product)	Yes	Yes	Yes	Yes	Yes
CiPress 500	No	No	No	Yes	Yes

establish relationships between individuals in these different, but interdependent functional areas. It is further supported by some research that organizations learn from previous Global NPD programs [45].

These three cases all represent slightly difference approaches to a distributed global new product development model. It is not required that there be a "one size fits all" approach to this overall trend within Xerox. In fact, IBM has taken the approach of different types of open innovation for different market segments, which are precisely what the three products represent—three difference segments in which Solid Ink Technology for Xerox participates in [25]. There are some other common trends that are seen in these three development approaches, one of the most concerning is the lack of a common database across all of these development teams to share product requirements and actual product performance during manufacturing.

Once again, this development effort kept core technology competencies of printheads and inks under the control of Xerox while practicing the reuse of these items from other projects. Reuse is a common practice that can aid in the development of new products as there is a substantial body of knowledge associated with the components or modules to be reused. Additionally, keeping the technology related to printheads and ink under the control of engineers and scientists thereby keeping the core technology within the corporation and not outsourced should be a long term benefit to xerox (Table 11.1).

11.7 Relevant Aspects of Technology Management

Technology Management is an important field onto itself, but some areas are quite significant when globalization is considered. Some of these topics will be examined in a similar fashion to the approach taken on Global New Product Development. Specifically, the aspects related to Intellectual Property and Virtual Teams will be examined. The broad topic of Virtual Teams has many subtopics such as communication and potential cultural issues that will be touched upon. Additionally, when global issues are involved, there certainly will be economic and development policy aspects will also be involved.

It is well known, and supported by data, than salaries in China and other developing countries, are less than salaries in other developed nations such as the United States and Western Europe. For this reason many companies have moved manufacturing and development activities to these lower cost regions as a method to reduce the cost to develop a new product. Additionally, there is evidence that may indicate that the government of China has been engaged in practices that may not be in adherence to World Trade Organization policies on free trade [46]. International Commerce rules and regulations prohibit "unfair" government involvement in the form of illegal loans and land gifts [47]. As an example of these claims, very recently, SolarWorld, a German company with North American Headquarters in Hillsboro, Oregon has filed a complaint with the United States Department of Commerce and the International Trade Commission making these claims of unfair business practices along with a consortium of solar companies [48]. Clearly, this potential issue has not been settled, but it is possible that if SolarWorld is successful in its filing, the cost structure of some goods and services from China may change eroding some of the cost benefits that exist today.

11.7.1 Intellectual Property Management

Intellectual Property laws are slightly different from country to country, and understanding the differences and their implications is of extreme importance for any organization wanting to protect IP as part of their sustainable competitive advantage. Recent changes in United States Law has changed the US from a 'first to invent' country to a 'first to file' country which is in line with more industrialized countries [49]. Although this change will make a significant step towards a more uniform Intellectual Property front, there are still many potential issues that have to be considered when either manufacturing or development is done offshore or with the assistance of a partner of some type. There have been fairly recent agreements between the United States and China on the Intellectual Property [50], but there is still some concern among some American executives and companies about piracy in China and other countries. It seems that Steve Ballmer, the former Microsoft CEO, is likely one of these executives. According to reports Ballmer believes that 2011 profits in China will be about 5 % of US profits despite having comparable sales of personal computers, and likely operating systems and application software, in both countries [51]. Could it possible this profit differential is due partly to software piracy?

When Intellectual Property Management is concerned, first it is important to understand that a cohesive patent strategy should be an integral part of the business strategy for any technology based business. Additionally, the strategy that is based solely on the number of patents granted is almost always a poor one. According to Bhatia and Carey, in addition to their opinions noted above, it is quite possible for a company to spend significantly less money on the cost of acquisition and maintenance of the patent portfolio and still increase revenue associated with the portfolio, as Hitachi has achieved [52].

Primarily due to labor cost savings, China has seems to be at the forefront of globalization movements of US based companies as well as forefront of Intellectual Property concerns. Before entering into any agreement or practice in another country it is very important to understand the laws and intellectual property rights in the country [53]. Failing to take this action is bluntly foolish and bordering on negligent for any technology manager. When a contract manufacturer or any other partner is brought on, it is important to ensure that the selection will protect a firm's intellectual property. Arruñada and Vázquez write:

> If a contract manufacturer tries to retain its services by offering to share other clients' trade secrets, assume that, somewhere down the road, it will do the same with your IP. [29]

It seems that Intellectual Property leakage is a real concern when these secrets are shared with manufacturing or other development partners. It would be prudent to make sure that appropriate steps, such as filing for patents or securing non-disclosure agreements, as well as understanding the enforceability of these filings and agreements are in order before work commences in a foreign country. In the specific area of Intellectual Property Management, Roy and Sivakumar conclude that a partnership agreement with an out of country firm should not be made from a purely short-term standpoint [54]. They believe that a longer term relationship between outsourcing companies and the outsourcing suppliers is fundamentally a safer approach in securing Intellectual Property. Additional research done suggests that the two objectives of reducing manufacturing costs and retaining adequate Intellectual Property protection can be addresses by a subset of manufacturing being done by captive resources rather than by outsourcing all manufacturing steps. The resulting developed framework also estimates the fraction of the IP claims are at risk for leakage given what specific steps are handled by a contract manufacturer. Given this estimate of leakage and the potential to save production costs, an optimization between these two competing objectives can be optimized for a given situation [30].

11.7.2 Virtual Teams and Communication

A globally dispersed presence will guarantee the need to establish of cross functional teams that are geographically dispersed. Teams in this format are often referred to as "virtual teams". For companies that do not have all employees physically located in the same place, the use of virtual teams has become common resulting in some inherent challenges that need to be addressed and overcome. What may be the first, and most obvious is communication. It is also imperative that a common goal is understood and communicated so that all parties can rally behind it. Further individual roles and responsibilities need to be defined in a manner that supports common goals [55]. Communication is one of management's fundamental responsibilities.

Efficient and effective communication can help with the some of the difficulties that can arise in multisite product development or multisite work teams. This communication should help bridge gaps between groups, whether they be manufacturing or development resources. Experts have warned that not having good information sharing, especially when it comes to revision control can be a significant problem in the global new product development arena [56]. Some researchers recommend having a shared database or source of record to eliminate errors and to ensure that all parties refer to the same data repository for reference [2].

Communication modes and their relationship to success in global development teams, have been studied for quite some time. The increase bandwidth of computer and telephony connectivity of today has unquestionably helped facilitate some of these asynchronous communication medium, such as email and shared data repositories. As such, these communication methods are often called "computer-mediated" communication. These mediums are termed as asynchronous as they do not require, nor do they lend themselves well to an immediate exchange of information between the communicating parties [57]. As trivial as it may appear, research has shown that training of team members about capabilities of various communication mediums can be significant factor in the effectiveness of the exchange of ideas [58]. Just as a shared data repository can help with sharing technical details, computer mediated communication can also assist in bridging a geographic gap with communication [59]. It has long been established that face to face communication is the benchmark that all other forms of communication is measured, but some studies have shown that video conferencing is equivalent in the ability to communicate over great distances [60].

Despite the increase of asynchronous communication tools that are readily available today, some individuals prefer face to face meetings, especially at the beginning of a new project. When IBM was developing what was to become the award winning family of laptop computers called the ThinkPad, numerous face to face meetings among the development community, despite being located at multiple locations around the world was one of the best practices of the development, as judged by the development team [61]. Some feel that face to face meetings maybe the best way to establish trust, which is a core value in learning to work together [26, 55]. Further, it seems that different cultures develop trust differently. According to Bailey; Asian, Latin American and Eastern European cultures typically spend more time to develop professional relationships when compared to Western Cultures [62]. The key point is that different cultural backgrounds impact work relationships differently. Having a "one size fits all" approach may not work, but establishing trust between work groups and individuals is unquestionably a good intermediate step to help with functional excellence [63].

As previously mentioned, cross-cultural virtual teams have been an active topic for researchers for quite some time. Some studies have identified points that are quiet salient in this context. Australian researchers gathered data to support than most members (80.3 % of respondents) of cross-cultural virtual teams admit that they change the way they speak when a part of cross-cultural virtual teams while 60.7 % change the way they write when communicating within the team. Some of the changes seem obvious, but in practice may not be. The top two verbal communication changes found in the study were "speaking more slowly/clearly" (53.3 % of respondents) and the "avoidance of slang/colloquialisms" (27.0 %). These changes, coupled with the data that 96.7 % of the respondents said that team telephone conferences were a media used for interaction meaning that these changes in behavior happen frequently [64]. Other problems can arise in the arena of communication stemming from cultural norms. An example given in the same study, explains that silence is largely interpreted in one of three ways, depending on culture and experience in cross cultural teams. The first interpretation of silence is frustration that other team members do not speak, the second is that some team members prefer to be invited into the conversation rather than "interrupt" and the third interpretation came from team members with more cross cultural experience who could indentify why the silence was occurring which resulted in them eliciting other team members to speak. To explain further, the second interpretation seemed to be relatively common among Asian team members and the more observant individuals fitting the third interpretation practiced allowing team members "think time" to digest and interpret the preceding comment to the silence before inviting other opinions [64]. This example of silence and its interpretation is fairly specific, but it demonstrates how different cultures may interpret the same thing differently. The effect could potentially be even more profound in an asynchronous communication medium, such as email especially when work hours are substantially different due to changes in time zones that can be commonplace in globally distributed teams [65]. It could be easy to believe how an email that is not replied to could be either a sign of agreement or that the recipient is not comfortable with expressing a contrary opinion [66].

Another potential difficulty in virtual teams can be a function of the makeup of the team. When a team is geographically dispersed, the likelihood of having individuals with different cultural backgrounds certainly is increased [67]. The research area of cross cultural teams has been quite rich in published papers and studies looking at the effectiveness of such teams and potential issues that may arise—highlighting a few of the issues here will hardly do the topic justice. A recurring mistake that organizations can make is holding on to an assumption that policies, procedures or practices that work in one region will be directly portable to another region that may have a different value structure that is rooted in its culture [62]. Often it is important to understand motivations and cultural tendencies to develop a fruitful working relationship. Having a different cultural background from others working in the same team may make this and understanding these differences are often the first step in finding a common ground and shared historical perspective [64].

Cultural differences also impact how individuals perceive others when an individual is acting under norms that are typical in their native culture but seemingly take on another meaning when interpreting actions or responses by an individual from a foreign culture. A good example is a Japanese "yes". Most Westerners interpret this reply as an agreement, but often a Japanese individual means to acknowledge the request intending to give an answer at a later time. Further cultural differences, such as religious and national holidays also impact the ability for teams to collaborate efficiently [67].

11.7.3 Xerox Global Technology Practices

Xerox has network of global research centers that are established in various technology hubs across the globe. The Palo Alto Research Center, PARC, is probably the most famous and is located in the heart of the Silicon Valley, a center for software and other high tech ventures. The newest center is located in Chennai, India which has rapidly become another technology center in the software arena. Other centers in the global network are located in suburban Toronto, Ontario Canada and Monroe County, New York. Xerox has generally located centers in geographic locations where the benefits of a technology cluster can be leveraged. It may seem odd that Monroe Country, New York is included in this listing, but it is geographically located in the American center of document and color science technology. Other important entities in the local vicinity are Kodak's World Head Quarters as well as the Munsell Color Science Lab located within Rochester Institute of Technology, which is widely regarding as the premier research lab in the area of color science.

Xerox has established a long term partnership with Flextronics as a manufacturing partner in Southeast Asia. The longevity of the relationship is a method that can be used to assist in intellectual property protection. This is done with the understanding that Flextronics is also an outsourcing provider to many of Xerox's largest competitors—so the "safety" of intellectual secrets should not be deemed as a topic without risk. Practices such as early filing of intellectual property as well as non-disclosure agreements are drawn up between Xerox, Flextronics, and suppliers to Flextronics. By having a long-term relationship, a level of trust between the organizations and individuals has a greater chance to be established. This trust can be another reason that confidential information is treated appropriately. Additionally, Xerox has retained legal representation in all countries where any type of development or manufacturing work to assist in understanding the local laws where business is being done. It is important, and a best practice to understand the local laws and policies where business takes place from an intellectual property point of view. As the arrangement with Flextronics is practiced, Xerox provides manufacturing process development, supplier quality engineering and supplier sourcing and technical problem solving when issues arise. Flextronics provides unskilled labor, purchasing power, logistics support and some process and quality engineering to monitor production processes. With this division of labor, Xerox still is able to maintain critical knowledge of inner workings of the manufacture of their products. It is quite important to note, that this arrangement is where the relationship evolved to, and not necessarily where it was originally planned to settle.

In the area of virtual teams and communication, there exist opportunities for improvement. First, there are some infrastructure issues between Xerox and the Southern Malaysia manufacturing facility which prohibits a shared data repository for technical information sharing as well as a general lack of standardized information formats to quickly convey important status updates. It was quite unfortunate that the issues was not foreseen and addressed before it hindered progress on issues related to production launch. The high turnover rate of technical staff in some of the Flextronics facilities also causes problems in establishing trust amongst team members as there seemingly are always changes in the team makeup due to staffing issues. The issues related to infrastructure connectivity also make the use videoconferencing or shared desktop meetings such as Skype problematic. The use of such communication tools that are readily available today have been found to be a "critical contingency" to help with the barriers and communication issues that can occur within virtual teams [66].

11.7.4 Conclusions and Management Implications

Of course Xerox is like any organization in that there will certainly be opportunities to improve. With any luck there will also be some items that the organization does well and has already starting to improve through its own learning cycles. In the area of Global New Product Development, Xerox has had some obvious successes and perhaps more importantly improvements from its first whole hearted endeavor in the practice. Specifically, in the cases under review for global product development Xerox management would agree that the efficiency of the development effort has been noticeable. Adherence to original project budget and schedule has appeared to improve. The motivations behind Xerox's global development efforts are readily found in academic literature.

For a variety of reasons, it seems that the Southern Malaysia facility has a number of opportunities for improvement. It seems that this opinion is held by a number of individuals at Xerox. Unfortunately, Xerox has found that Farrell was correct when she warned, "the inherent 'stickiness' of established offshore locations make it crucial to choose the right one the first time" [31]. Bluntly, Xerox is extremely hesitant to essentially start over with another Flextronics site given the time and effort that has already been invested at the current facility. If Xerox knew then what Xerox knows now, would this site been selected for the manufacturing? Hopefully, Xerox can objectively look at the current situation and remedy some of the issues in the near future. It may be premature to conclude that the Southern Malaysian site is no capable of producing products and to provide the service and support expected.

References

1. Santos J, Doz Y, Williamson P (2004) Is your innovation process global? MIT Sloan Manage Rev 45(4 (Summer)):31–37
2. Eppinger SD, Chitkara AR (2006) The new practise of global product development. MIT Sloan Manage Rev 47(4 (Summer)):22–30
3. von Zedtwitz M, Gassmann O (2002) Market versus technology drive in R&D internationalization: four different patterns of managing research and development. Res Policy 31(4):569–588
4. Kuei C-h, Madu CN, Lin C (2011) Developing global supply chain quality management systems. Int J Prod Res 49(15):4457–4481
5. Subramaniam M, Rosenthal S, Hatten K (1998) Global new product development processes: preliminary findings and research. J Manage Stud 35(6):773–796
6. Washburn NT, Hunsaker BT (2011) Finding great ideas in emerging markets. Harv Bus Rev 89(9/10):115–120
7. Bradley F, Meyer R, Gao Y (2006) Use of supplier-customer relationships by SMEs to enter foreign markets. Ind Market Manage 35(6):652–665
8. Jones GK, Teegen HJ (2003) Factors affecting foreign R&D location decisions: management and host policy implications. Int J Technol Manage 25(8):791
9. Ronstadt RC (1978) International R&D: the establishment and evolution of research and development abroad by seven U.S. multinationals. J Int Bus Stud 9(1):7–24
10. Kuemmerle W (1999) The drivers of foreign direct investment into research and development: an empirical investigation. J Int Bus Stud 30(1):1–24
11. Richard F (1997) The globalization of R&D: Results of a survey of foreign-affiliated R&D laboratories in the USA. Res Policy 26(1):85–103

12. Stalk G Jr (2006) The costly secret of China sourcing. Harv Bus Rev 84(2):64–66
13. Dilts DM, Pence KR (2006) Impact of role in the decision to fail: an exploratory study of terminated projects. J Oper Manage 24(4):378–396
14. Wadhwa V, Gereffi G, Rissing B, Ong R (2007) Where the engineers are. SSRN eLibrary
15. Von Zedtwitz M, Ikeda T, Li G, Carpenter R, Hämäläinen S (2007) Managing foreign R&D in China. Res Technol Manage 50(3):19–27
16. Tripathy A, Eppinger SD (2011) Organizing global product development for complex engineered systems. IEEE Trans Eng Manage 58(3):510–529
17. Lai H-C, Shyu JZ (2005) A comparison of innovation capacity at science parks across the Taiwan Strait: the case of Zhangjiang High-Tech Park and Hsinchu Science-based Industrial Park. Technovation 25(7):805–813
18. Gobble MM, Gwynne P (2011) Malaysia seeks economic success based on science and technology. Res Technol Manage 54(5):2–3
19. Martin R, Sunley P (2003) Deconstructing clusters: chaotic concept or policy panacea? J Econ Geogr 3(1):5–35
20. Fallah MH (2005) Technology clusters and innovation. Curr Iss Technol Manage Stevens Alliance Technol Manage 9(9):1–4
21. Engel JS, del-Palacio I (2011) Global clusters of innovation: the case of Israel and the Silicon Valley. Calif Manage Rev 53:27–49
22. Lecocq C, Leten B, Kusters J, Looy BV (2009) Do firms benefit from being present in technology clusters? Evidence from a panel of biopharmaceutical firms. SSRN eLibrary
23. Madsen AN, Andersen PD (2010) Innovative regions and industrial clusters in hydrogen and fuel cell technology. Energy Policy 38(10):5372–5381
24. Porter ME, Stern S (2001) Innovation: location matters (cover story). MIT Sloan Manage Rev 42(4 (Summer)):28–36
25. Chesbrough HW (2003) The era of open innovation. MIT Sloan Manage Rev 44(3 (Spring)):35–41
26. Nohria N, Huston L, Brown JS, Hagel J III, Lipman-Blumen J, Premji A (2005) Feed R&D—or farm it out? Harv Bus Rev 83:17–28
27. van de Vrande V, Vanhaverbeke W, Duysters G (2011) Additivity and complementarity in external technology sourcing: the added value of corporate venture capital investments. IEEE Trans Eng Manage 58(3):483–496
28. Arndt M (2009) The year in innovation. BusinessWeek.com: 7
29. Arruñada B, Vázquez XH (2006) When your contract manufacturer becomes your competitor. Harv Bus Rev 84(9):135–144
30. Kim JP, Hamza K, Saitou K (2009) Optimal outsourcing for intellectual property protection and production cost minimization. In IEEE International Symposium on Assembly and Manufacturing, 2009. ISAM 2009:124–129
31. Farrell D (2006) Smarter offshoring. Harv Bus Rev 84(6):84–92
32. Prahalad CK, Hamel G (1990) The core competence of the corporation. Harv Bus Rev 68(3):79–91
33. Hoecht A, Trott P (2006) Outsourcing, information leakage and the risk of losing technology-based competencies. Eur Bus Rev 18(5):395–412
34. Kleinschmidt EJ, de Brentani U, Salomo S (2007) Performance of global new product development programs: a resource-based view. J Prod Innov Manage 24(5):419–441
35. Larry Y (2007) Measuring the culture of innovation. MIT Sloan Manage Rev 48(4 (Summer)):7
36. Bulkeley WM (2001) Xerox to sell some plants to flextronics. Wall Street J Eastern Ed 238(66):B6
37. Xerox shifts 600 jobs to India firm [Online]. http://pqasb.pqarchiver.com/democratandchronicle/access/2380526151.html?FMT=ABS&FMTS=ABS:FT&date=Jun+21%2C+2011&author=Matthew+Daneman&pub=Rochester+Democrat+and+Chronicle&edition=&startpage=n%2Fa&desc=Xerox+shifts+600+jobs+to+India+firm. Accessed 14 Nov 2011
38. Nayar V (2010) Employees first, customers second. Chief Learn Officer 9(10):20–23
39. Kersnar J (2011) Outsourcing matures, slowly. CFO 27(2):39–40
40. Zirpoli F, Becker MC (2011) What happens when you outsource too much? MIT Sloan Manage Rev 52(2 (Winter)):59–64

41. Bidault F, Castello A (2010) Why too much trust is death to innovation. MIT Sloan Manage Rev 51(4 (Summer)):33–38
42. Cummings JN (2004) Work groups, structural diversity, and knowledge sharing in a global organization. Manage Sci 50(3):352–364
43. Boudreau KJ, Lakhani KR (2009) How to manage outside innovation. MIT Sloan Manage Rev 50(4 (Summer)):69–76
44. Xerox CiPress 500 Production Inkjet System: Product Detail—Buyers Lab Advisor [Online]. http://www.buyerslab.com/Advisor/Products/60824/Xerox/CiPress-500-Production-Inkjet-System. Accessed 12 Nov 2011
45. Sampson RC (2005) Experience effects and collaborative returns in R&D alliances. Strategic Manage J 26(11):1009–1031
46. Bradsher K (2010) On clean energy, china skirts rules. The New York Times (September)
47. Haley UCV, Haley GT (2008) Subsidies and the China price. Harv Bus Rev 86(6):25–26
48. SolarWorld leads charge against China trade practices|Sustainable Business Oregon [Online]. http://www.sustainablebusinessoregon.com/articles/2011/10/solarworld-leads-charge-against-china.html. Accessed 21 Oct 2011
49. Maier R (2011) House passes Leahy-Smith America Invents Act; US poised to move to a first-inventor-to-file system, adopt other changes to patent laws. Intellect Property Technol Law J 23(10):13–17
50. Patent Office, China Deepen Cooperation (2011) Chem Eng News 89(31): 30
51. Fletcher O, Dean J, Qi S (2011) Ballmer bares China travails. Wall Street J Eastern Ed 257(123):B1–B2
52. Bhatia V, Carey G (2007) Patenting for profits. MIT Sloan Manage Rev 48(4 (Summer)):15–16
53. Chapman JC, Ji L (2011) A brave new world: technology transfer to China. Licensing J 31(8):5–11
54. Roy S, Sivakumar K (2011) managing intellectual property in global outsourcing for innovation generation. J Prod Innov Manage 28(1):48–62
55. Monalisa M, Daim T, Mirani F, Dash P, Khamis R, Bhusari V (2008) Managing global design teams. Res Technol Manage 51(4):48–59
56. Amaral J, Parker G (2008) Prevent disasters in design outsourcing. Harv Bus Rev 86(9):30–34
57. Berry GR (2011) Enhancing effectiveness on virtual teams. J Bus Commun 48(2):186–206
58. den Otter A, Emmitt S (2007) Exploring effectiveness of team communication: balancing synchronous and asynchronous communication in design teams. Eng Construct Arch Manage 14(5):408–419
59. Berry G (2006) Can computer-mediated, asynchronous communication improve, team processes and decision making? J Bus Commun 43(4):344–366
60. Guo Z, D'Ambra J, Turner T, Zhang H (2009) Improving the effectiveness of virtual teams: a comparison of video-conferencing and face-to-face communication in China. IEEE Trans Profess Commun 52(1):1–16
61. Sakakibara K (1995) Global new product development: the case of IBM notebook computers. Harv Bus Rev 6(2 (Summer)):25–40
62. Bailey P (2010) Chess moves. T+D 64(12):56–61
63. Sarker S, Ajuja M, Sarker S, Kirkeby S (2011) The role of communication and trust in global virtual teams: a social network perspective. J Manage Inform Syst 28(1 (Summer)):273–309
64. Anawati D, Craig A (2006) Behavioral adaptation within cross-cultural virtual teams. IEEE Trans Profess Commun 49(1):44–56
65. Rutkowski A-F, Saunders C, Vogel D, van Genuchten M (2007) 'Is it already 4 a.m. in your time zone?' Focus immersion and temporal dissociation in virtual teams. Small Group Res 38(1):98–129
66. Montoya MM, Massey AP, Hung Y-TC, Crisp CB (2009) Can you hear me now? Communication in virtual product development teams. J Prod Innov Manage 26(2):139–155
67. Oertig M, Buergi T (2006) The challenges of managing cross-cultural virtual project teams. Team Perform Manage 12(1/2):23–30

Part V
Social and Political Aspects

Chapter 12
A Comparative Analysis of Career Growth Models in R&D Organizations

Sowmini Sengupta, Jorge Garcia, Nayem Rahman, and Daria Spatar

Abstract Firms that invest in developing cutting-edge technologies rely on leading technology practitioners to make innovations happen. These technology practitioners grow in their domain through continued discoveries which results in recognition of their work assessed through peer evaluations. These professional recognitions need to then translate into career growth for the practitioner within the firm in order for them to feel that their contributions are also valued by the company. Retaining technical talent is critical for the company in not only leveraging the skills of these individuals to achieve the company's goals but these technology practitioners also serve as role models for other, newer members in the firm. This study analyses the various models that companies use to manage the career growth of these critical individuals. The study found four predominant career models from studying literature as well as in practice. Using this information, the study then selected five companies in various leading technical fields to understand their approach to technical career growth. Their characteristics such as size of the company, research investment, etc. and predominant career growth ladders were compared and contrasted. This study gives managers of leading technology firms some rich information on managing the individuals in their organization.

Keywords Technical Career Growth • R&D • Management

S. Sengupta (✉) • J. Garcia • N. Rahman
Intel Corporation, Santa Clara, CA, USA
e-mail: jorge.l.garcia@intel.com; nayem.rahman@intel.com; sowmini.b.sengupta@intel.com

D. Spatar
Portland State University, Portland, OR, USA
e-mail: spatar@pdx.edu

12.1 Introduction

The organizations that emphasize on research and development (R&D) require outstanding professionals in the subject matter. Managing those resources is critical to conduct state-of the-art research and development, and manufacturing. It is important to understand what these R&D professionals want to achieve. If managers cannot comprehend their career growth needs they may end up losing those personnel. Organizations need to come up with career paths to retain and motivate workers. They need to make a balance between organizational needs and individuals' needs, and develop career paths accordingly [1]. This allows for achieving employee commitment and retention within the organization.

Professionals in R&D often have a desire to focus on a particular specialty on top of career orientations geared towards promotions [1]. Research scientists tend to care more about how their colleagues around the world think about their work than their immediate supervisor [2]. Organizations must make efforts to have R&D personnel achieve excellence in scientific discovery. A healthy, competitive environment needs to be maintained so that organizations can get most out of their R&D personnel's talents and capabilities.

An organization's R&D activities are different from the other functions within the organization. R&D encounters many challenges and uncertainties in terms for project duration, budget, and due to the uncertain nature of R&D results [2]. The R&D results aspect is very important. This requires that R&D personnel have a healthy research work environment, proper motivations, and adequate job satisfaction. R&D personnel need to have freedom of work, as opposed to being micromanaged.

In high-tech companies, R&D is the main driver of competitive advantage and growth [3]. Organizations invest huge amounts of money in R&D. Large companies, such as Intel, IBM, HP, Microsoft, and Siemens, spend billions of dollars on their R&D. A key managerial challenge is to make sure R&D investments are effectively translated into innovation to foster growth and competitiveness of the company [3]. Managers in R&D must ensure that scientists and researchers get logistics and managerial support to be successful [4, 5]. Managers needs to promote communication channels between R&D personnel and the rest of the relevant organization to keep employees engaged.

Given that the R&D department is such a vital part of high-tech organizations, career growth paths need to be designed effectively [6]. In this paper, we make an attempt to review the R&D career paths of some selected high-tech global companies in the US and suggest a career growth model that could be used by R&D organizations in different sized companies in different sectors. We make an attempt to provide details of career path hierarchy, training, logistic support, and incentives to be successful in different stages of R&D career paths. Chen et al. [7] argue that appropriate career development programs need to be developed to satisfy the requirements of R&D personnel at various stages of the career ladder.

The emergence of the Internet and communication technologies have made business organizations global. Innovation, research and development, and business have become much more competitive. R&D personnel in organizations need to stay competitive and organizations need to invest in R&D growth of employees. Organizations need to come up with a management framework for the sustainability of R&D departments. The framework for R&D management needs to allow employees to stay engaged, and the rest of the organization to perform efficiently.

R&D career paths might differ from one another depending on the size of organizations. Large organizations might have more hierarchical career ladders compared to small- and medium-sized organizations. To manage employees in large organizations, many processes need to be in place. This might make employee promotion growth overly bureaucratic. This needs to be streamlined to maintain employee morale and career growth. On the other hand, small companies might not be able to provide logistical support, such as state of the art research labs, or they might not be able to provide career growth opportunities. This needs to be addressed as well. In this paper, we will make an attempt to come up with career growth models for organization of different sizes. We attempt to provide detailed career growth models.

In this study, we will attempt to obtain information from selected companies to understand what their R&D personnel look for in career growth. On the other hand, we will also review what the management of these R&D organizations expects from the R&D personnel: How these organizations lay out career paths for R&D personnel; and what kind of training and growth opportunities they offer R&D personnel.

This paper is organized as follows: Sect. 12.2 briefly provides an overview of existing literature on this topic; Sect. 12.3 provides details of the research methodology; Sect. 12.4 discusses data collection and analysis; Sect. 12.5 summarizes and concludes the paper.

12.2 Literature Review

There are four major career paths described in the literature: (1) Linear, (2) Dual, (3) Hybrid, and (4) Project. The first one, the Linear Career Path, implies that a scientist is promoted to a managerial position. In this case, an individual gradually leaves his or her technical responsibilities [8]. One of the major downsides to this approach is that R&D organizations end up losing good scientists, who go on to become administrators [9]. Usually, in the organizations with linear career development, there is no way to grow if a person chooses to stay in a technical area of expertise. He or she eventually reaches a plateau, which leads to decreased efficiency and satisfaction [10].

Another career development model is called the "Dual Career Path" or "Dual Ladder System." It was introduced in late 1950s [11]. The dual approach lets an employee choose to grow either along a technical path or to pursue an administrative route. This gives more career opportunities within an organization that can lead to success. John P. Doherty, DuPont's director for U.S. compensation, commented on this type of system, saying: "We want to provide them with parallel routes so they can go into either track, whichever one is suitable for them as well as suitable from a business perspective in what [we] see as the strengths of particular employees [9]." It is notable that this approach did not find successful applications until the 1990s [12]. Nowadays, it is widely utilized in scientific and engineering companies [13]. Although the details may vary, the career paths are similar. Salary grades are equivalent across both ladders. An example of a dual career ladder is presented in the picture below. Some authors feel that this approach stimulates innovation among employees [14].

In 1991, Bailyn proposed the "hybrid career" system, which allowed employees to move among various career routes both sequentially and concurrently [15]. A study conducted by Allen and Katz [11] indicated that many R&D professionals would prefer neither management nor scientific paths, but would rather move from one project to another. Petroni called this approach "from project to project [15]."

In 2000, Petroni [15] did additional research on which career routes were most preferable for R&D specialists. The questionnaire was completed by 151 engineers and scientists. The findings showed that only 45 respondents had unequivocal preferences, whereas others expressed equal preferences for several career paths. Among those who had clear preferences, the managerial path had the highest score. On average, though, the technical route was the most preferable one, followed by the "from project to project" route. The managerial path was ranked the lowest. The author concluded that the Dual Career Path was not an effective approach for managing R&D professionals. Another finding by Chen et al. [16] concluded that career opportunities and rewards should be flexible to suit employees with different needs and aspirations.

It is notable that even though the Dual Ladder is one of the most widely used system, it is still criticized, because it does not provide equal opportunities for growth along the management paths and technological routes. Technical employees lack decision power, and a managerial career is more attractive and prestigious than a technical one [11, 15, 16]. Petroni et al. [14] in a recent study conclude that this system does not support employees' development as integration experts, or T-shaped people, which is requirement for open innovation. The authors propose an "open dual ladder" approach, which is described as following: "Graduates with a technical background start their career in the R&D division of a firm and can later move to other positions, including those that involve significant managerial responsibility." They also suggest that managerial training is an important part of this system to better prepare specialists for administrative positions.

Besides the four most common career development paths, there are several alternatives that are less widely used, but can be more suitable for certain companies. Strategic spin-off as an alternative to traditional R&D management has been proposed by Ferrary [3]. The main idea of this approach was that a parent company helps its researcher–entrepreneurs to create a spin-off and supports it in the beginning. The parent company could partner or acquire the spin-off if it turns out to be successful. Ferrary says that in case of strategic spin-offs, researcher-entrepreneurs were more innovative, creative and motivated, as they were not limited by bureaucracy and formalities of big company. They had more decision autonomy and got more social recognition. In order to encourage such career development, the parent company should provide entrepreneurial training and allow former employee to return back if a spin-off fails.

An alternative to the Dual Ladder called the "Knowledge lLadder" has been proposed by Debackere et al. [17]. The main determinants of career growth in this system were individual knowledge and competence. Salary and rewards were not directly connected to the hierarchy but to the employee's performance. The authors suggested that this would allow linking organizational development to personal evolution and growth.

Chen et al. [7] conducted a study to analyze how career development programs at R&D organizations fit employees' career needs and whether the gap between career needs and available programs affected satisfaction and turnover. More than 360 R&D personnel in the high-tech industry in the Hsinchu Science-based Industrial Park (HSIP) participated in the study. The results showed that gaps between available programs and employees' needs negatively affected job satisfaction and led to higher levels of turnover. The authors argued that there were a number of diverse groups within R&D organizations that had different career needs and expectations. Thus, there should be different career development programs to meet those needs. They proposed that managers should identify career needs at different career stages: Exploration, Establishment, Maintenance, and Disengagement. They should offer appropriate career development programs at each of these stages.

One of the major works on employees' aspirations and drivers was published by Edgar Schein [18] in 1970–1980. He identified following eight patterns that affected a person's career development: (1) Autonomy/independence; (2) Security/stability; (3) Technical-functional competence; (4) General Managerial Competence; (5) Entrepreneurial Creativity; (6) Service or Dedication to a Cause; (7) Pure Challenge; and (8) Life Style. He found out that most people would classify themselves into several groups, but in most cases, a person's decision about his or her career would be primarily dominated by one of the anchors. Bigliardi and Dormino [6] studied how career anchors corresponded with three career routes: Managerial, Technical and Project. More than 150 R&D specialists participated in their study. The results indicated that the managerial route had a strong positive correlation with managerial competence, entrepreneurial creativity, and pure challenge anchors. But, it had a negative correlation with technical–functional competence and security/stability anchors. The technical route was positively correlated with technical–functional and life style anchors. It was negatively correlated with the managerial competence anchor. The project route was correlated positively with the technical functional anchor, but negatively with managerial competence. They also found out that age was strongly related to security/stability, autonomy/independence and technical–functional anchors. The life style anchor was found to be the most important one, followed by technical–functional, and service/dedication. Managerial competence was the least preferable anchor. Based on these results, the authors suggested that a greater number of career opportunities should be offered in order to overcome the overly formalized ladder system. The same conclusion was made by Igbaria et al. [19]. They surveyed 78 R&D employees in New Mexico to study career orientations, job involvement, and satisfaction. The researchers found that the managerial and technical competence orientations got the lowest scores, whereas service, job security, and lifestyle had the highest priorities. Thus, they concluded that the dual career ladder did not provide a complete model to satisfy career needs and aspirations for R&D professionals. The authors proposed that additional career paths and appropriate reward systems should be developed.

Multiple research shows that a company not only needs to develop career paths, but also provide training to its employees [3, 20, 21, 22]. This would increase knowledge and skills, positively affect employees' attitude and job satisfaction, and increase efficiency and performance [20]. As Schein [18] points out, in addition to technical competence, employees need managerial and leadership skills, which could be developed through training and seminars. Also, trainings might have a positive effect on knowledge sharing among R&D professionals [22].

12.3 Methodology

Our approach was to review the career growth models and practices in companies with major R&D investments and make observations from the data collected from the study. We came up with three main focus areas to investigate. First, what kinds of questions are relevant to career growth in an organization? Second, what kind of organizations are good candidates for this study? Third, are there are other kinds of data about the organization itself that would influence the career model in practice.

12.3.1 Research Questions

We broke down these questions on career growth models into five main categories:

- The first objective for understanding the career growth model used in an organization is to understand if they are following any of the commonly known career growth model.
  - What kind of progression levels exist? What is the model in use by a company?

- Driving higher results requires not only innovation and expertise in a technical field, but also non-technical competencies, e.g. communication. Documented and readily available expectations remove ambiguity in interpretation. Hearing career success stories in the organization not only has the ability to inspire, but also to educate. So, our next set of questions focused on the information and resources available to employees so that they can understand, own, and drive their own career growth.
  - Are the requirements for each level documented? Is it divided into categories of competencies (Technical and Non-technical)? Are the R&D career path success stories available and shared? Is this information available to the employees?

- Continuous learning is key to the growth for any individual. Organizations that recognize and encourage on-going training will benefit not only from enhanced knowledge, but also from the motivation that the employee will gain.
   - What kind of training or career development programs do they provide (e.g. tuition re-imbursement, ad-hoc—internal and external—training classes, professional memberships, or attending conferences)?
- People are more successful when they are passionate about the job they do. Continuous education needs to be augmented with practice. Having an open environment where the employee can work on assignments in different roles will help them experiment and determine what types of jobs are the most desirable and in line with their personal growth. It also gives them an opportunity to practice and hone different skills.
   - What kinds of additional opportunities are provided for skills needed for career advancement (e.g. short-term assignments, or rotation programs)?
- A recognition pinnacle for any researcher is the ability to patent their innovation. However, the cost involved in patenting can be a challenge. An organization that wants to retain and grow innovators can benefit from supporting the financial impact of patenting for the individual.
   - Does the company encourage and support patent submissions?

12.3.2 Choosing the Organizations

Second, we had to decide what type of organizations we were interested in examining. Some of the industry giants in innovation had to be included in the study. As patents are a widely known measure of R&D innovation, we first picked a company with the highest number of patents in the last year, referred to from here on as Company A. Given that R&D investment is yet another widely publicized metric for a company, we next chose one of the top investors, referred to from here on as Company B. We decided that it would be useful to look at an industry beyond semiconductor and ICT, so we included one leading R&D investor in the energy sector, which is referred to as Company C. We also decided to include start-ups and academic research institutes to the study, as these are other common leading R&D avenues. These are referred to as Company D and Company E respectively.

12.3.3 Additional Data Points

Third, we felt it would be interesting to study other R&D data regarding the organization. We decided that R&D expenses, number of employees, and number of patents filed in 2012 would be useful information to correlate the career growth model against.

We collected R&D data from annual reports. We met with and discussed with one or more individual from the organization to cover the list of questions regarding the career development models and programs in practice.

12.4 Findings and Analysis

We studied five companies are in different sectors. We discovered a number of facts about these companies regarding their R&D career paths and career development opportunities.

12.4.1 Career Ladders

First, we define the various career ladder that have been identified in the literature which we will then identify each company against in the future sections (Figs. 12.1, 12.2, 12.3, and 12.4).

12.4.2 Company A

Company A is the number one company in the world, for the last 20 years, in obtaining patents. As such, it prides itself on encouraging and helping employees to submit patents, and provides resources to cover the legal, technical, and financial expenses associated with filing patents.

Company A close matches the hybrid career ladder. It allows its employees to remain technical/professional or move to management/executive ladders. Company A distinctly documents the technical and non-technical competencies and expectations for each level (Fig. 12.5).

Company A offers a variety of training programs to its employees in order to keep its workforce competitive and up to date. The main programs include the following:

Individual Development Plans—this is an annual activity used to identify future business commitments and opportunities to improve employee's skills. The manager and employee discuss career opportunities to identify areas of growth or gaps in the individual's repertoire.

Mentoring—each employee is encouraged to find multiple mentors for different areas, such as career growth, technical knowledge, business and client knowledge.

On Demand Learning—this is a customized training offered by professionals and managers in different areas of the company. The program allows individual employees to be trained in areas of development, new initiatives, or as an aid to re-skill the workforce.

Fig. 12.1 Linear Career Model [8]

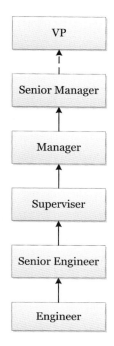

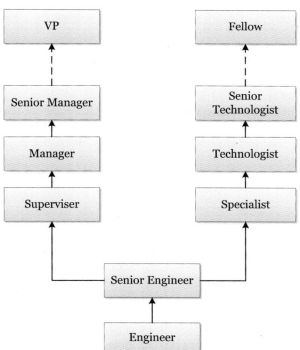

Fig. 12.2 Dual Career Model [11]

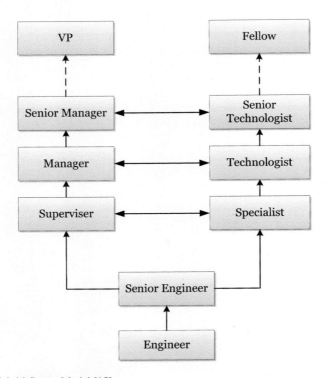

Fig. 12.3 Hybrid Career Model [15]

Foundation Competences—is an in depth training designed to grow workforce skill for future market shifts.

In addition to these unique training opportunities, Company A also offers career advice, tuition reimbursement, and "internal job markets." This is an internal jobs database allowing current employees to apply directly for existing positions available at Company A.

12.4.3 Company B

One of the R&D companies studied in this research was a semiconductor company. In 2012, this company spent more than ten billion US dollars in R&D. Each year, it releases a large number of cutting-edge products to the market. All this indicates that the company manages a large number of strong R&D personnel.

This company provides hybrid career paths for R&D employees. One path provides an R&D managerial ladder and the other path provides a pure R&D technical leadership ladder. In this dual path approach, both managerial and technical ladders have stages in their career paths. Expectations for each of the stages in the ladder

Fig. 12.4 Project Career Model [15]

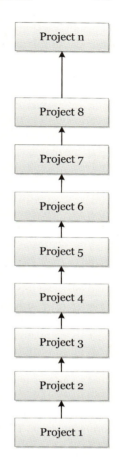

Fig. 12.5 Company A Career Model

demands varying levels of expertise. These technical ladders are used as tool for strategic development, systematically developing technical experts in accordance with strategic business needs. These technical ladders are also used as motivators, for promotions, for development, and as strategic planning tools. Technical ladders provide an exclusive career path for outstanding experts. Technical ladder distribution is driven by strategic business needs. The technical ladder nomination on different levels expresses the potential for a technical ladder career for an employee and is a sign of recognition of the employee's technical expertise.

In the managerial path, R&D managers are expected to assume both managerial and leadership role in driving the R&D personnel to achieve business expectations and contribute to the company's business and revenue growth. Management puts employees on different ladders in the technical career path. They are in charge of ensuring selection of technical employees for different ladders by carefully cross-checking nominations and reviewing technical ladder employees.

This company assists its R&D personnel and engineers in career advancements to allow them to acquire varied skill-sets. These include short-term assignments as rotation engineers, normally 6 months to 1 year.

Each year, this company allocates large amounts of money for employee career development in terms of internal and external training classes, attending professional conferences, and acquiring professional memberships.

This company provides tuition-reimbursement opportunities to its employees. This allows employees to take university classes to learn the latest tools and technologies and earn advanced degrees. This significantly helps employees to be productive and successful in their jobs. The company hires intern engineering students for summer jobs. Later, many of them join the company as full time employees.

The company also provides mentor and mentee partnerships as part of its mentoring program. By matching mentee's identified development areas and mentor's areas of expertise, this program allows employees broaden their skill-sets.

Company B also strongly encourages its R&D personnel and engineers to submit patent applications. For 2012, this company was granted 1,290 patents.

12.4.4 Company C

Company C is a leading solar panel manufacturer with a history of innovation. It is headquartered in Germany. In their 2012 annual report, the company listed 2,355 employees.

The company uses a linear career ladder currently. Career growth is managed carefully, and ongoing attention is given to every employee. Regular discussions happen between managers and employees in terms of career growth opportunities and potential for advancement. The company takes pride in supporting on-going education for every employee and has a tuition re-imbursement program. They also recognize the need for both theoretical learning and practical applications of knowledge. They encourage researchers to practice their skills and apply it to their manufacturing lines. Managing R&D with a global development viewpoint is considered a critical competency. Ongoing technical growth is encouraged by incentive programs such as bonuses. They also have an award called the Edison award. Patenting is encouraged and supported by the company. It is even mentioned in the annual report.

12.4.5 Company D

We conducted an interview with a representative of a small biopharmaceutical start-up company, which was founded in 2006. The company focuses on developing oncology treatments. In 2013, seven employees are engaged in R&D. Though the company does not have a formalized career development model, the employees are encouraged to expand their areas of expertise and acquire new knowledge and skills. Salary and rewards are mostly linked to individual's level of experience, competence, and performance. Based on this description, we have concluded that Company D employs a "knowledge ladder." The salary level is determined using a benchmarking service called Radford, which allows comparing aggregated information about different companies in biotech industry.

The company supports employees' aspirations to study and provides tuition reimbursement. In 2013, two employees were studying to get MBAs and their expenses were covered by the employer. The representative emphasized that the company is promoting and encouraging employees' desires to learn and grow professionally. He emphasizes that his role as an employer is to provide his employees with a valuable set of knowledge and skills that are in high demand in the market. The company has a patent that provides exclusivity for the medication they have developed. It also is actively managing two patent families, including 14 pending applications. The patents are results of teamwork, but if a researcher decides to file the patent on his/her own, the company will support the submission and processing costs.

The representative made the following observations about the dual ladder system:

There are people who are neither talented scientists nor great managers. So, they cannot successfully progress through either of those paths. These employees tend to stay in their positions for many years without any visible performance improvement. Managers have to make the decision on whether such employees are worth keeping. If a company does not have a clear and understandable system for personnel evaluation, such decisions might be considered subjective and unfair. Criteria for employees' evaluation should be identified and a process for promotion or termination of employment should be developed.

12.4.6 Company E

We also studied career paths in a public university that employs over 2,200 faculty members. The university provides a faculty track for those who teach, do research and service, and a track for those employees who only conduct research. The levels are similar and linked to rewards and salary. It can be concluded that this career development model is similar to a Dual Career Ladder found in R&D organizations.

The university offers classes to its employees at reduced price and also allocates some money to each department for external trainings. The patent submission is supported and all the decisions are made by high level of management.

12.4.7 Summary

A summary of the findings from the various companies discussed in this study is provided in Table 12.1.

Table 12.1 shows that there is a potential relationship between the types of career ladders, based upon both the industry and the number of employees. We also found that organizational development is critical in all sectors, so a management career path is imperative for all. Some organizations, however, do have the ability to also sustain a technical career path.

In our discussions, we also came across that fact that private and public organizations have different performance management methods and policies.

12.5 Conclusion and Future Work

This study is based on data collection from interviews and documents related R&D career paths in five organizations. We also conducted an extensive literature review. We identified several key areas that an organization should consider in developing its R&D career path. We observed that large organizations maintain hybrid or dual career path to allow R&D personnel to pursue a managerial or pure technical path. R&D personnel find job satisfaction in their career when they are encouraged and provided support to show excellence in terms of state of the art research work and scientific discovery. Adopting a continuous improvement processes in R&D career paths were found to be the strongest predictors of career aspiration in R&D organizations [23].

The R&D organizations need to provide employees with other professional development opportunities, such as tuition reimbursements, and training opportunities in latest tools and technologies. They need to promote and encourage employees' desires to learn and grow professionally. R&D organizations must encourage and support patent application submissions. In order to make sure R&D personnel are motivated at work and in their career growth, there must be a well-defined system for employee performance evaluation. This helps employees to know upfront what is expected of them by company management.

In this paper, we have come up with an R&D career growth model that R&D organizations might find beneficial. To make the R&D career growth model effective, senior executives need to champion it. Our career growth model should enable

12 A Comparative Analysis of Career Growth Models in R&D Organizations

Table 12.1 Summary of findings

Company	Category	Industry	Type	R&D expense	# of employees	# of patents	Type of career ladder	Documented expectations for each level	Training programs	Career development programs	IP submission support
Company A	Established	ICT	Commercial	$6.3B	434,246	6,478	Hybrid	Yes	Yes	Yes	Yes
Company B	Established	Semiconductor	Commercial	$10.1B	105,000	1,290	Hybrid	Yes	Yes	Yes	Yes
Company C	Established	Energy	Commercial	€29.1M	2,355	71	Single	Yes	Yes	Yes	Yes
Company D	Startup	Biotech	Commercial	$14.6K	12	1	Knowledge	N/A	Yes	Yes	Yes
Company E	Established	University	Education	N/A	2,289	33	Dual	Yes	Yes	Yes	Yes

R&D organizations to deliver operational excellence in terms of quality, efficiency, speed, and capacity to deliver scientific discoveries on cutting-edge technologies. Given that high-tech industries are fast moving, business conditions change fast and employee aspirations also change quickly. Therefore, career growth models need to be revisited periodically and improved as needed. As part of future research, we will work on sustainability metrics for an R&D organization's career path.

References

1. Lee H-W, Yen K-W (2011) A study of the relationship between work values and career orientation of employed in the high technology industry. Qual Quant 47(2):803–810
2. Clarke TE (2002) Unique features of an R&D work environment and research scientists and engineers. Knowl Technol Policy 15(3):58–69
3. Ferrary M (2007) Strategic spin-off: a new incentive contract for managing R&D researchers. J Technol Transfer 33(6):600–618
4. Post C, DiTomaso N, Farris GF, Cordero R (2009) Work–family conflict and turnover intentions among scientists and engineers working in R&D. J Bus Psychol 24(1):19–32
5. Yeh C (2009) Career needs of R&D personnel during the 'Maintenance' stage : a exploration study and a new scale. J Hum Resour Adult Learn 5:35–43
6. Bigliardi B, Dormio AI (2009) R&D personnel career routes : an exploratory study. J Technol Manage Innovat 4(1):8–21
7. Chen T-Y, Chang P-L, Yeh C-W (2004) A study of career needs, career development programs, job satisfaction and the turnover intentions of R&D personnel. Career Dev Int 9(4):424–437
8. Tremblay M, Wils T, Proulx C (2002) Determinants of career path preferences among Canadian engineers. J Eng Technol Manage 19(1):1–23
9. Thayer AM (1998) Dual career ladders. Chem Eng News 76(44):1–80
10. Connor GCO, Cocco J, Laverty T (2011) Corporate entrepreneurship, human capital, and the third career ladder. Corp Entrepreneurship 31(17):541–554
11. Allen TJ, Katz R (1986) The dual ladder: motivational solution or managerial delusion? R&D Manage 16(2):185–197
12. Epstein KA (1986) The dual ladder: realities of technically-based careers
13. Wu F-S, Haak R (2013) Innovation mechanisms and knowledge communities for corporate central R&D. Creativity Innovat Manage 22(1):37–52
14. Liu Y (2011) Building and analysis of iceberg model for innovation capability of R&D personnel in enterprises. 2011 International conference on management and service science, pp 1–3.
15. Petroni A (2000) Strategic career development for R&D staff: a field research. Team Perform Manag 6(3/4):52–62
16. Petroni G, Venturini K, Verbano C (2012) Open innovation and new issues in R&D organization and personnel management. Int Hum Resour Manage 23(1):147–173
17. Debackere K, Buyens D, Vandenbossche T (1997) Strategic career development for R&D professionals. Technovation 7(2):53–62
18. Schein EH (1996) Career anchors revisited: implications for career development in the 21st century. Acad Manage Exec 10(4):80–88
19. Igbaria M, Kassicieh SK, Silver M (1999) Career orientations and career success among research, and development and engineering professionals. J Eng Technol Manage 16(1):29–54
20. Kang Y-C, Fang C-H (2009) Developing a R&D competency framework to support training – a case study in Taiwan. 2009 International conference on management and service science, pp 1–4, Sep 2009

21. Adnan Z, Shah K, Ahmad J (2011) Direct influence of human resource management practices on financial performance in Malaysian R&D companies. World Rev Bus Res 1(3):61–77
22. Liu N-C, Liu M-S (2011) Human resource practices and individual knowledge-sharing behavior – an empirical study for Taiwanese R&D professionals. Int Hum Resour Manage 22(4):981–997
23. Ismail M, Ramly ES (2010) Career aspirations of R&D professionals in government research institutes and multinational corporations. Organ Markets Emerg Econ 1(2):32–47

Chapter 13
Researching Social Capital in R&D Management: A Case Study in High-Tech Industry

Songphon Munkongsujarit, Antonie Jetter, and Tugrul U. Daim

Abstract An increasing number of publications in R&D management embrace the concept of social capital to observe, measure, and explain very different phenomena, such as R&D knowledge diffusion patterns; research productivity on the individual, team, and regional levels; and the governance and structure of R&D alliances and partnerships. The various research findings are difficult to compare, contrast, and integrate, since no coherent definition of *social capital* exists. To close this gap, this paper proposes a framework for social capital in R&D management that describes three dimensions of social capital (structural, relational, cognitive) and their links to R&D knowledge transfer. The framework is theoretically derived from social science literature, in which the concept of social capital first originated, and the recent R&D management literature. The framework is subsequently used to guide the inquiry in a case study of a complex, multi-year knowledge transfer process between a university and a high-tech company. The case study shows the complex impact of all three social capital dimensions on R&D knowledge transfer and supports the proposed frameworks as a useful tool for R&D management research on social capital.

13.1 Introduction

The concept of *social capital* originated in sociology, but it is increasingly used in other contexts [62] and, as a result of the rise of social networking, even in everyday language [8, 24, 33]. A number of studies link the concept of social capital to R&D management.

S. Munkongsujarit (✉)
NSTDA, Klong Luang, Thailand
e-mail: songphon@hotmail.com

A. Jetter • T.U. Daim
Engineering and Technology Management Department,
Portland State University, Portland, OR, USA
e-mail: jettera@gmail.com; tugrul@etm.pdx.edu

Among others, research has been conducted on R&D knowledge diffusion patterns [21]; R&D outcomes of individuals and teams [47]; firm-level innovation [22, 46, 81]; technology management at the regional, national, and international levels [3, 35, 42]; and the governance and structure of R&D alliances and partnerships [5, 39].

However, to date studies have lacked a shared definition and operationalization of social capital, and study findings are difficult to integrate and assimilate. In order to close this gap, this paper develops a framework for social capital in R&D management that describes three dimensions of social capital (structural, relational, cognitive) and their links to R&D knowledge transfer. The framework is subsequently used to guide the inquiry in a descriptive case study of a complex, multi-year knowledge transfer process between a university and a high-tech company.

Section 13.2 reviews the social science literature on social capital as well as publications in R&D and technology management that use the concept of social capital. Section 13.3 builds on the literature review and develops an integrated framework for social capital and knowledge transfer: Sect. 13.3.1 describes the dimensions of social capital, Sect. 13.3.2 introduces a knowledge transfer model and discusses its relevance for R&D management, and Sect. 13.3.3 proposes an integrated social capital and knowledge transfer model. The purpose of the framework is to synthesize and organize the literature discussed in Sect. 13.2. By providing a preliminary theory on social capital in R&D, it further serves the practical purpose of guiding case study research. All case studies, unless they follow a purely ethnographic or grounded theory design, need to be preceded by the development of a preliminary theory [79]. The framework proposed in Sect. 13.3 provides such a preliminary theory and can be used for case studies that are targeted at exploration, description, or explanation [79]. In Sect. 13.4, the framework is used for a descriptive case study that reports on a knowledge transfer process between academia and industry. Section 13.5 discusses the case study finding in the context of this paper.

13.2 Literature Review

Social capital is widely understood as a form of capital that complements other production factors (such as labor and financial capital) and that consists of personal connections and interpersonal interactions [24]. Ostrom [61] defined *social capital* as the arrangement of human resources to improve the flow of future income. The author made a clear distinction between human capital and social capital. *Human capital* is defined as the knowledge and skills that individuals bring to the solution of any problem whereas *social capital* is defined as capital created by individuals spending time and energy working with other individuals to find better ways of making possible the achievement of certain ends that in its absence would not be possible [61].

The social capital concept has its roots in social science and has been independently developed by the French sociologist Pierre Bourdieu, the American sociologist James Coleman, and the American political scientist Robert Putnam. Their work in different fields has cumulated in the modern understanding of the phenomenon. Bourdieu investigated how the persistence of social class and established inequality leads to unequal access to resources. Based on Marxist theory, he theorized that economic capital, in the form of accumulated labor, is at the root of all other types of capital. Cultural (later named social) capital is derived from the social structure and the social structure is a result of economic capital. This explains the unequal academic achievement of children from different social classes and from different groups within social classes [10]. With the view of social capital as resources that result from social structure, Bourdieu defined social capital as follows: "Social capital is the sum of resources, actual or virtual, that accrue to an individual or a group by virtue of possessing a durable network of more or less institutionalized relationships of mutual acquaintance and recognition" [11].

Coleman also investigated the relationship between social inequality and academic achievement [24] and used rational choice theory, which assumes that individuals automatically act in ways that serve their own interests to integrate economic and social theory. Coleman [19] defined *social capital* as a function of the social structure that serves as a resource for its owners:

> Social capital is defined by its function. It is not a single entity, but a variety of different entities having two characteristics in common: they all consist of some aspect of a social structure, and they facilitate certain actions of individuals who are within the structure. Like other forms of capital, social capital is productive, making possible the achievement of certain ends that would not be attainable in its absence.

Building on Coleman's work, Putnam investigated the role of civic engagement in generating political stability and economic prosperity in society [24] and claimed that a strong decline in social capital in the U.S. had rendered much of urban America ungovernable [63, 65]. In Putnam's definition, "social capital refers to features of social organization, such as trust, norms, and networks, that can improve the efficiency of society by facilitating coordinated action" ([64], p. X). Putnam also contributed to the concept of social capital by introducing a distinction between the bonding (or exclusive) and bridging (or inclusive) aspects of social capital. The bonding aspect of social capital reinforces exclusive identities and maintains homogeneity while the bridging aspect of social capital brings together people from diverse social divisions, which leads to a better linkage to external assets and information.

Based on the foundational work on social capital by Bourdieu, Coleman, and Putman, several extensions to the theory have taken place. One of the research disciplines that may gain new insights into organization behavior, such as the R&D team, focuses on the concepts of social capital and social networks [13]. Product development has long been regarded as not only a technical but also a social process, especially in complex product development [49]. Burt further investigated aspects of social capital and proposed two additional concepts, namely structural holes and network closure. The concept of structural holes originated in the works of Granovetter [30, 31] on the strength of weak ties, which assumes that information in a social network is not uniformly distributed: strong ties provide a flow of homogenous information between strongly connected individuals while weak ties enable the transfer of heterogeneous and new information between connected individuals. Thus, individuals who have connections with weaker ties are likely to be able to access broader information. Weak ties between individuals in the network structure can be viewed as structural holes, which separate non-redundant sources of information between different groups of individuals. An individual whose relationships span across more structural holes, or bridges the holes between different networks, has broader and richer information access. Burt backed up his argument on the benefit of bridging structural holes with a number of empirical studies [14–16]. One of his studies, which looks at the networks around managers in a large American electronics company, explicitly points out that creativity and innovation are associated with networks of individuals and groups that span across structural holes [16]. Network closure—the second aspect of social capital introduced by Burt [15]—is critical to realizing the value that structural holes can provide: it creates closed relationships between individuals, promotes high level of trust in the network, and facilitates sanctions that prevent individuals from violating the norms of conduct. Network closure thus provides a reliable communication channel for information flow that makes it less risky for individuals in the network to collaborate, resulting in a reinforcement of strong ties. A number of studies support the argument that strong ties lead to less conflict and a more productive environment [45, 57].

Though structural holes (the bridging function of social capital) and network closure (the bonding function of social capital) focus on different network mechanisms, Burt concluded that both aspects of social capital are important and contribute to the performance of individuals and groups; bridging and spanning across structural holes is the source of added value while bonding and closure of the network is critical to realizing the value buried in the structural holes [15].

Burt's extensions of social capital theory are not the only one. In the management literature, Nahapiet and Ghoshal [56] presented one of the most relevant applications of social capital: their theoretical model explains the organizational advantage of the firm as a result of the interrelationships between social capital and intellectual capital. They defined *social capital* as "the sum of the actual and potential resources embedded within, available through, and derived from the network of relationships possessed by an individual or social unit" (p. 243) and suggested the use of a three-dimensional view of social capital, namely, the structural dimension, the relational dimension, and the cognitive dimension. Social capital facilitates the creation of new intellectual capital, which provides intangible assets and resources that determine the value and competitiveness of an organization. Nahapiet and Ghoshal [56] explicitly noted the similarity of their framework and the resource-based view of the firm proposed by Barney [7], which indicates that competitive advantage of the companies stems from their unique collection of resources (including physical resources, human resources, and organizational resources) that are rare, durable, imperfectly imitable, and non-tradable.

The link between knowledge creation, competitiveness, and various aspects of social capital is also researched in technology and R&D management. On the level of individuals and teams, Lee et al. [47] examined the impact of different aspects of an individual's human capital (education, work experience, and training) and social capital (level of interconnectedness, relationship, and shared expectations with others) on R&D outcome. The results of their work show that human capital and social capital complement each other. Dahl and Pedersen [21] investigated the effect of social networks on the R&D knowledge diffusion process. Their findings indicate that social contact, especially long-term relationships based on trust and reputation, is used as a channel to diffuse knowledge that receivers find useful. Gabbay and Zuckerman [26] identified how social capital and organizational network structures affect expectations and actual job mobility in R&D organization. Their findings showed that individuals with many dispersed contacts both inside and outside of the organization expect to move on to a managerial position and are highly likely to be promoted to their preferred position. The role of social capital and network structures was further researched by Reagans and Zuckerman [68], who proposed that network structures, rather than diversity, explain the productivity of R&D teams and confirmed that network diversity (the structural holes point of view) and network density (the network closure point of view) both impact R&D outcomes.

The linkage between social capital and firm-level innovation was explored by Landry et al. [46], who examined the effect of social capital on the decision to innovate and the degree of innovation in manufacturing firms in Canada. Their findings indicated that the decision of the firms to innovate is highly influenced by the social capital of the firms. Yli-Renko et al. [81] used the concept of a resource-based view of the firm to explain the role of social capital in building the knowledge for technology-based new firms to achieve growth. They concluded that the firms should actively build, manage, and harness social capital in both their internal and external relationships. Edelman et al. [22] used empirical evidence from organizations in the United Kingdom to support the claim that social capital does not only have a positive impact on the firm, but it also has negative effects. They suggested that the organizations should develop a clear understanding of the bridging and bonding elements of social capital in order to gain benefits and avoid the pitfalls of over-using social capital in the firm's activities.

Several studies investigated the impact of social capital on relationships between the firm and outside entities. Westerlund and Svahn [77] examined how social capital impacts business partner relationships in software SMEs' entrepreneurial networks. Their empirical findings indicated that the aspects of social capital vary systematically by different types of relationships. Tether and Tajar [72] explored the use of specialist knowledge providers as additional sources of information in the innovation activities of firms beyond the traditional industry–university links. One of their findings showed that, among other factors, firms with a higher level of social capital are more likely to engage with and get benefit from specialist knowledge providers. Arranz and Fdez. de Arroyabe [5] used social capital theory and transaction costs theory to explain the governance structure of partnerships in R&D networks. They argued that both theories are complementary in explaining forms of governance through the degree of administrative and social factor. Inkpen and Tsang [39] examined how the social capital dimensions of a network affect the transfer of knowledge between network members. They proposed a set of conditions that facilitates knowledge transfer through the structural, relational, and cognitive dimensions of social capital. Tomlinson [74] surveyed 381 manufacturing firms in the UK and found that the propensity of firms participating in collective activities rises where "shared interests" emerge. Xia et al. [78] explored how firms benefit from participating in a consortium in terms of process benefits and social capital benefits. They found that firms anticipate more process benefits if they are more technically capable, value the forthcoming standards higher, and participate in a better-managed consortium.

There are also a number of studies that have focused on social capital and technology management at the regional, national, and international levels. For example, Kaasa [42] examined the effect of different dimensions of social capital on innovative activity at the regional level using survey data from several European countries for analysis. The findings provide strong support for the argument that social capital influences innovation activity. On the national level, Akçomak and ter Weel [3] identified how social capital improves national economic outcomes by investigating the relationship between social capital, innovation, and per-capita income growth. They provided a statistical model and identified innovation as an important mechanism that transforms social capital into higher income levels. As for the international aspect of social capital, Hitt et al. [35] identified the importance of social capital and its cultural implications in different perspectives among Asian and Western firms. They concluded that in the global markets, the development and management of social capital is critical for the firm's competitive advantage. Feldman [23] found that social capital, venture capital, and entrepreneurial support services, as well as actively engaged research universities, enable the successful establishment of an entrepreneurial culture. Al-Laham et al. [4] investigated biotechnology firms and found that while the effect of scientists' recruitment and alliances as two sources of knowledge flow decay overtime, high degrees of human and social capital stock reduce the speed of erosion of new assets.

Social capital has also been investigated within the R&D management setting. McFadyen and Cannella Jr. [50] analyzed the relationship between individual social capital and knowledge creation and found that the strength of relationships had a higher marginal effect on knowledge creation than the number of relationships. Reagans and Mcevily [67] suggested that teams should not be designed and managed by demographic criteria but by their members' social networks. Fischer and Pollock [25] identified the effects of management teams' social network on initial-public-offering success. Oh et al. [60] examined the role of informal socializing ties in the concept of "group social capital" and group effectiveness. Hoegl et al. [36] used a sample of 430 team leaders in a software development project to show that team perceptions alter individual networks and performance. Ahuja et al. [2] and Leenders et al. [41] used virtual R&D groups to show that network centrality was a determinant of individual performance. Bresnen et al. [12] argued the importance of social processes, patterns, and practices in project knowledge management. Huang and Newell [37] suggested that social capital plays a key role in shaping the level of coordination for knowledge integration in cross-functional projects. Cummings [20] indicated the importance of heterogeneity of team networks in promoting knowledge sharing. Athanassiou and Nigh [6] identified the importance of the top management team's social networks in determining the internationalization of a company. Mehra et al. [52] used a sample of 116 member hi-tech firms to demonstrate that self-monitoring personalities and centrality in social networks were related to both individual and group performance. Mead [51] used social network analysis to model and analyze a project team structure. Sparrowe et al. [70] used a sample of 190 employees in 38 workgroups to show that social networks were related to individual and group performance. Hansen [34] argued that weak network ties help with locating sources of information in new product development projects but strong ties are more important for transferring complex knowledge. Tidd [73] argued that open organizational networks are more effective than closed for radical innovation. A recent study by Karlsson and Wigren [43] surveyed a sample of 7,260 university employees to investigate how legitimacy and social and human capital influence employees' start-up propensity.

The studies above demonstrate that there has been a tremendous growth in R&D management research that builds on the concept of social capital. This research investigates and explains phenomena as different as the creativity, job mobility, and performance of R&D employees; the diffusion patterns of technology; the innovativeness of companies; and the governance of R&D alliances, to name just a few. Many of the findings provide valuable contributions to existing theory, but research results are scattered and are currently not integrated into a systematic understanding of the role of social capital in R&D management.

Moreover, the extension of research domains goes hand in hand with a broadening and weakening of definitions for social capital: in a review of social capital research in the management literature, Alder and Kwon [1] identified no fewer than 28 different definitions of social capital. A similar development was observed by Portes [62], who reviewed the origins and the applications of social capital in modern sociology. Portes pointed out that, even in the root discipline of social capital, the concept is increasingly defined broadly as "the ability of actors to secure benefits by virtue of membership in social networks or other social structures" (p. 8). This broad definition has acquired popularity because of its elasticity and adaptability, which allows researchers to relate their previous works with the concept. However, it has also reduced the rigor of the original concept.

Meaningful research on the role of social capital in R&D management that integrates the different findings requires sound definitions and a deeper understanding of where and how social capital impacts knowledge transfer.

13.3 Development of a Research Framework for Social Capital in R&D Management

R&D covers three activities—basic research, applied research, and experimental development [59]—that lead to new knowledge. In each stage, knowledge is transferred from prior stages, integrated with other knowledge, and transformed into new knowledge. Knowledge transfer thus binds all R&D activities together. Social capital determines how and between which entities knowledge transfer occurs [14, 39]. We therefore propose a general framework that links different dimensions of social capital to different stages in the knowledge transfer process. In the following section, we briefly outline both elements and then integrate them into a framework for social capital in R&D management.

13.3.1 Dimensions of Social Capital

We are adopting the definition of *social capital* as given by Nahapiet and Ghoshal [56]: social capital is the sum of resources embedded within, available through, and derived from the network of relationships possessed by an individual or organization. The different facets of social capital can be grouped into three dimensions: the structural dimension, the relational dimension, and the cognitive dimension of social capital [56].

13.3.1.1 Structural Dimension

The structural dimension of social capital is derived from the concept of structural embeddedness by Granovetter [32] and refers to the overall pattern of connection between actors. It is further reflected in Burt's theory on structural holes, which explains "who you reach and how you reach them" [14]. According to Inkpen and Tsang [39], important facets of the structural dimension of social capital that affect the knowledge transfer process are network ties, network configuration, and network stability. *Network ties* explains the specific ways that the actors in the networks are related to each other [39]. The ties in the network are the facilitating condition for creating opportunities for social capital transactions [1] because they provide the access to either give or receive valuable resources, such as knowledge. *Network configuration* determines the pattern of linkages between all members of the network. The properties of the network structure include network density, network connectivity, and network hierarchy, all of which have impact on the accessibility among the actors in the network [39]. *Network stability* indicates the rate of change in membership of the network. In an unstable network, the opportunities to create and sustain social capital are diminished because network ties disappear when actors leave the network [39].

13.3.1.2 Relational Dimension

The relational dimension of social capital is derived from the concept of relational embeddedness, which was first described by Granovetter [32]. It focuses on the quality of personal relationships or the bond between actors that develops through a history of interactions [39]. The quality of a relational tie can be described in terms of trust [39] and norms [56]. *Trust* is based on social judgments of the actors in the network and the assessment of costs or risk associated with the interactions. It is one of the key factors that facilitate knowledge sharing process [39]. *Norms* pertain to the degree of consensus among the actors in the network that indirectly controls their actions [56].

13.3.1.3 Cognitive Dimension

The cognitive dimension of social capital refers to the resources that provide shared meaning and understanding among actors, namely shared language and codes [56] and shared goals [39]. *Shared language and codes* represent the common ways for the actors in the network to communicate and understand each other [56]. *Shared goals* refers to the degree of common understanding and approach to the achievement of the tasks shared by all of the actors in the network [39].

13.3.2 A Knowledge Transfer Model

The knowledge transfer model depicted in Fig. 13.1 was developed by Gilbert and Cordey-Hayes [29] as a framework for exploring technological and organizational change processes. Their model identifies five stages that are necessary for knowledge transfer within an organization and that lead to development of the new core routines that mark the successful outcome of a knowledge transfer process. The five stages are (1) acquisition, (2) communication, (3) application, (4) acceptance, and (5) assimilation.

Acquisition: Knowledge has to be acquired before it can be transferred. The sources of knowledge for the organization include the experiences from lessons learned from the past, the knowledge from learning by doing, the intrinsic knowledge that comes with individuals who join the organization, and the knowledge from the continuous process of searching and scanning.

Communication: Once the knowledge is acquired, it needs to be communicated and distributed in the organization.

Application: For newly acquired and communicated knowledge to be retained in organizations, it needs to be applied.

Acceptance: The knowledge must be acceptable to the individuals in the organization so that it can be assimilated.

Assimilation: The assimilation of the knowledge results in the transformation of the knowledge into the core routines of the organization; this is the stage where the true learning process occurs.

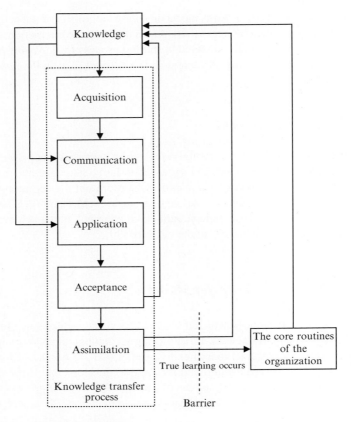

Fig. 13.1 Knowledge transfer model

13.3.3 An Integrated Framework

Social capital can function as an enabling factor or an inhibiting factor to the process of knowledge transfer. To understand the role of social capital in all knowledge transfer stages, the different dimensions of social capital have to be investigated separately. Figure 13.2 introduces a framework that serves as the basis of the following discussion.

13.3.3.1 Structural Dimension

A number of studies have linked the structural dimension of social capital to the different processes of knowledge transfer. Yli-Renko et al. [80] explored the effect of social capital and knowledge acquisition in entrepreneurial technology-based firms and found that the social interaction and network ties between the firms and

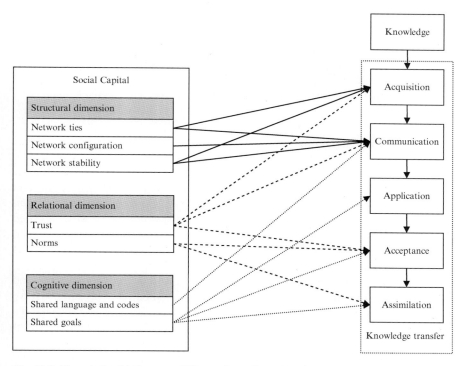

Fig. 13.2 The relationship between different dimensions of social capital and different stages of knowledge transfer

their customers were associated with greater knowledge acquisition. Ghoshal et al. [28] investigated the networking mechanism between different units of multinational corporations and found that the ties within the network had a positive effect on the frequency of communication within the corporation both on the inter-subsidiary level and the subsidiary-headquarter level. These studies both show that network ties serve as a channel for communication and thus facilitate knowledge acquisition and internal communication of newly acquired knowledge.

Inkpen and Dinur [38] examined the knowledge transfer process used by international joint venture firms and identified four key processes that lead to the connection of knowledge between the firms: technology sharing, alliance–parent interaction, personnel transfer, and strategic integration. Reagans and McEvily [66] studied the effect of network structure and knowledge transfer and proposed that social cohesion and range of the network affected the willingness of individuals to invest their time in sharing and conveying complex knowledge with others. It can thus be seen that the configuration of the network or the level of network connectivity affects the communication stage of knowledge transfer.

Carley [17] explored the impact of personnel turnover on the ability of an organization to learn and on the ultimate performance of the organization.

The study showed that organizational learning depends on institutionalized memories, which are embodied in the memories of the individuals and their learning abilities. The higher rate of personnel turnover represented the instability of the network inside the organization. The effect of an unstable network on knowledge transfer is twofold: first, it reduces the chance to acquire new knowledge from others in the network and second, it leads to the disappearance of communication channels.

13.3.3.2 Relational Dimension

Levin and Cross [48] examined the particular role of trust in knowledge transfer processes. Their results showed that trust facilitates knowledge acquisition and acceptance both from strong ties (close relationships) and from weak ties (distant relationships) in dyadic (two-party) knowledge transfer processes. Misztal stated that "trust, by keeping our mind open to all evidence, secures communication and dialogue" ([55], p. 10). High levels of trust thus enable knowledge acquisition as well as the communication and the acceptance of newly acquired knowledge.

However, Nahapiet and Ghoshal [56] pointed out that the strong norms and mutual identification that are associated with social capital do not only have positive impacts. Though they might improve group performance, they can also decrease the group's openness to new knowledge and information and foster groupthink [40] or the *not invented here* syndrome [44]. Simply stated, new knowledge might be introduced to and applied in the organization, but eventually it might not be accepted and assimilated because of the strong norms that resist any kind of change.

13.3.3.3 Cognitive Dimension

Boland and Tenkasi [9] studied the process of knowledge sharing in the communities of knowledge-intensive firms and found that language and cognitive systems contributed to the shared perspectives of the communities. Similarly, Nonaka and Takeuchi [58] studied knowledge creation in companies and pointed out that knowledge advances through new concepts and narrative forms, which are represented by a common coding system that is understood only within the organization. Shared language and codes thus have an effect on the communication stage of knowledge transfer.

Inkpen and Tsang [39] used the idea of shared vision proposed by Tsai and Ghoshal [75] to explain the shared goals of the actors in the network. A shared vision embodies the collective goals and aspirations of the members of the networks, which in turn encourages the actors to use every possible means to achieve the goals. These include the application and the acceptance of the acquired knowledge if it helps the actors to achieve their shared goals. Moreover, a theory in the absorptive capability of the firm proposed by Cohen and Levinthal [18] also suggests that the goal and aspiration level of the organization contributes to the ability of the organization to assimilate knowledge. Shared goals thus have an effect on the application stage, the acceptance stage, and the assimilation stage of the knowledge transfer process.

The discussion above shows that social capital strongly impacts all stages of knowledge transfer, but each stage is affected by different aspects of social capital. Structural social capital provides connections to knowledge owners and pathways for communication and is relevant for the early stages of knowledge transfer, namely for knowledge acquisition and communication. Trust between exchange partners improves acquisition, communication, and acceptance, while norms impact the acceptance and assimilation of knowledge. If the norms are too rigid and self-referencing, they can lead to not-invented-here attitudes. The relational dimension of social capital thus has complex impacts on early and late stages of the knowledge transfer process. The third and final dimension of social capital, the cognitive dimension, affects all but the very first stage of knowledge transfer.

13.4 Putting the Framework to Work: A Case Study in the High-Tech Industry

Case study research is suitable for exploratory, descriptive, and theory-building research designs [76, 79] when the phenomenon under investigation is complex, needs to be understood holistically within its context, and can best be studied in its natural setting [76, 79]. With the exception of theory-building case studies that follow a grounded theory design [71, 79], all case studies require a preliminary theory that integrates and synthesizes the state of the art and guides data collection and analysis [79]. The framework above provides such a preliminary theory.

In the following section, this framework is applied to collect and analyze the data derived from a descriptive case study. Descriptive case studies aim to obtain information about a particular aspect of an issue—in our case social capital in the context of R&D—and report on it. These studies answer "what" and "how" questions without moving far away from the data and without attempting to or requiring any but the most basic interpretation [27, 69]. They can serve as a starting point for other types of inquiry, but they provide value in themselves; many highly referenced and influential case studies are descriptive in nature [27, 69, 79].

The case study setting is an R&D team at a lab in a major high-tech cooperation. The team was formed in early 2000 to develop new interconnect technology, with included physical components as well as design protocols for microprocessors that enable ecosystem partners to implement the new technology. Because of the cross-cutting nature of interconnect technology, the team had to heavily engage with and transfer knowledge from and to outside partners. Case study data were collected in multiple, open-ended interviews with the R&D program manager and by analyzing internal documents that were generated by the project team to track its progress and concerns. Two researchers attended the interviews and took notes. Additionally, the interviews were recorded. The case study report was shared and discussed with the R&D team lead for validation.

13.4.1 Case Background

The computer industry has long operated under the particular paradigm to improve computing power by packing more and smaller electronic elements into smaller circuit boards [54]. Starting in the mid-2000s, high-speed digital interconnection, especially in the microwave frequency range (300 MHz [0.3 GHz] up to 300 GHz), started to replace conventional interconnect circuitry. As a result, digital designers who lay out circuit boards had to become accustomed to more sophisticated design models than they were used to and they had to learn new design languages.

This technological transition has not occurred overnight: in the early 2000s, microprocessor manufacturers invested in R&D to create next-generation interconnect technology. R&D efforts included physical components as well as design protocols for microprocessors to enable ecosystem partners to implement the new technology. The R&D team researched in the case study was tasked with these objectives. It was situated within a corporate research lab, which considered the team's project a high-priority project. The team members of the project consisted of two program managers, five engineers, and one technician. All team members were working on the project full-time. The program manager's main duty included the control of the project schedule and budget as well as interfacing with internal and external customers. The team of engineers, which consisted of both experienced members and recent Ph.D. graduates, focused on the design concept, testing software development as well as the design testing supported by the lab technician.

13.4.2 Case History

13.4.2.1 Discovery of Knowledge Needs

At the onset of the R&D project, the program manager realized that the R&D team would have difficulties solving a particular problem on high-speed interconnect and that an internal solution, if at all achievable, would take too many resources in the form of time, money, and manpower. Thus, the R&D program manager decided to leverage academic research by using the company's grant mechanism for sponsoring university research. Under this program, universities can apply for grant funding, as long as their proposed project has a corporate sponsor who is interested in the results of the research and will interact with university researchers. The funding is provided through the corporate R&D function and thus provides additional resources for company R&D teams.

The program manager started to look into candidate universities, which he identified based on their academic publications and based on recommendations from his team members, especially newly graduated engineers who still had close connection to academic researchers. As a result, the program manager ended up with a shortlist of professors whose area of research matched the need of the R&D team.

The program manager picked the best candidates for the R&D collaboration from the shortlist by reviewing the professors' educational backgrounds and academic activities, including conference papers and academic journal publications, which are the typical indicators of successful research. The program manager deemed the selected professor to be the best in the field. Moreover, the university where the selected professor worked was included in a list of universities that the company had approved as recipients of research grants because of their reputations and past collaborations. Without any prior personal connection, the program manager contacted this potential partner and explained the research interest of the team and opportunity of research grant from the company. The potential partner agreed to prepare the grant proposal to submit to the company for reviewing and approval by the company's research council, which oversees research activities between the company and academic programs. The members of the research council are the company's senior fellows who are considered top experts in the field. After the proposal was submitted, the R&D program manager acted as a promoter for his potential partner by using his personal connection with the members of research council to explain the advantage of this particular research collaboration and the benefit that the company could gain from this grant. Eventually the grant to the university partner was awarded under the condition of shared rights for the intellectual properties between the company and the university. The grant was awarded for a 3 year project with annual progress reviews. The grant amount was $40,000 per year (a total of $120,000 for 3 years).

13.4.2.2 Knowledge Source

According to the grant, the project team at the university consisted of one professor as the main investigator, one associate professor as the co-investigator, and one Ph.D. student working on the research. The team was expected to provide reliable simulation testing software as well as to publish academic conference papers and journal articles as a result of the grant. The grant was awarded from September 2000 to August 2003.

In order to prepare the partner team for this project, the program manager asked the professor to send the prospective Ph.D. students who would work for this project to come to the company for an interview. The professor sent two of his students to the interview and the program manager selected one as a summer intern. During the internship period, which preceded the actual start of the project, the student had a chance to familiarize himself with the problem as well as the working culture of the company. It was also an opportunity for the student to form a personal connection with the research team at the company lab. The program manager signaled to the student that excellent performance would not only lead to an extension of the grant after the first progress review but could also yield personal benefits because the student would have a chance to come back as an intern in a subsequent year and possibly also get a job offer after graduation. Through the internship and the interactions it generated, the lab and the university established a relationship and gained clarity about the research problem before the grant was officially awarded. The program manager expressed his intention to use this process to make sure that the partner team from the university was fully familiar with the problem and that they could start doing the research as soon as the grant was awarded to maximize the efficiency of the grant.

13.4.2.3 Knowledge Maintenance

For the grant to continue into its second year, the grant document required a progress report to the company's research council and a positive review at the end of the first year. Even though only one report was required, the program manager and the research team at the lab kept in close contact with the university. The research team went to visit the university campus every 3 months to see the progress of the research. During the visit, team members from the lab and the university had a chance to exchange ideas and clarify any problems that each side had. This gave the team an opportunity to develop a bond and trust through both official social activity (e.g., a meeting) and unofficial social activity (e.g., going out after work). On occasion, the research lab at the company provided additional support for the research beyond the grant, such as the donation of newer and more powerful computers. At the middle of the first year, the professors submitted the continuation proposal for the grant that stated the progress and expected result of the grant for the official review by research council. The grant was successfully awarded for the second and third years.

In subsequent years, the process that the program manager used to manage the grant was similar to the first year with some minor modification. As the program managers saw the progress of the research done by the Ph.D. student who came as an intern during the summer before the first year of the grant, he requested that the same student come back as an intern during the summer of the second year. Moreover, as the student was expected to graduate from the university during this year, the program manager made a job offer to the student and also requested that the professor send another prospective student who was expected to continue the research to be an additional intern. This would enable the former student to formally coach and "hand over the torch" to the new student as well as let the new student become familiar with the problem and the research team at the lab. During the second year, the program manager also invited the professor to officially visit the company and be a part of a guest lecture for the company-wide workshop organized by the lab. The objective of the workshop was to increase the awareness and visibility of the new technology inside the company; it was also a part of the company internal knowledge transfer process.

13.4.2.4 Knowledge Transfer

The research grant resulted in a test model and better simulation tools for circuit design as well as a number of academic conference presentations and journal publications that were co-authored by the university and the lab and that demonstrated

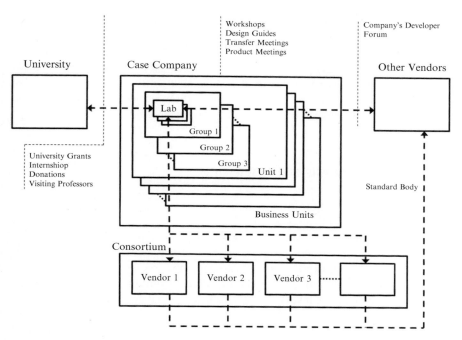

Fig. 13.3 Knowledge and technology transfer linkages between the lab, internal partners, and external partners

the project's contribution to the current state of knowledge. In addition, practical tools resulted from the collaboration, such as new design guides, books, and design tools. The grant was subsequently renewed beyond the initial 3 years: currently, the project is in its fourth renewal cycle. The knowledge transfer between the lab and the university is depicted in the linkage between both parties in Fig. 13.3, as a part of external inflow (outside-in) knowledge transfer process from the point of view of the company.

Coupled with the successful knowledge transfer from this external partner, the lab rolled out a series of workshops, design guides, books, and tools on high-speed interconnect in the form of the design concept for the first-generation (GEN 1) product with other labs in the same group of the company via the weekly transfer meetings. The aim of this single product was the proof of concept that would eventually lead to the assimilation of the new technology by the external vendors and customers of the company. Upon the successful review of the GEN 1 product, the lab came up with the design kit for the technology in the product meetings with other labs in the company and distributed the kit to the other business units of the company for the development of second-generation (GEN 2) products, which became the standard for a number of new products of the company. The technology was introduced to external partners of the company who were members of an electronics industry consortium called PCI-SIG (Peripheral Component Interconnect Special Interest Group). The members of the board of directors of PCI-SIG included representatives from several high-tech companies. PCI-SIG formally set the standard for this new technology, which would eventually be followed by the other vendors and the end users. The technology was also transferred to other vendors through the Developer Forum, which is the company's annual technology showcase that includes keynotes, insights, and technical sessions (lectures, interactive panel, hands-on labs, and hot-topic Q&As). All the linkages of the outflow (inside-out) knowledge and technology transfer between the lab and external partners are shown in Fig. 13.3.

13.4.3 Case Analysis and Discussion

A case dynamic matrix [53] can be used to trace events and their consequences to provide preliminary explanations of the case study data. Table 13.1 shows the events that led to knowledge transfer process between the company, the university, and external partners. The events are listed in chronological order from the inflow of knowledge from the university to the company, the internal knowledge transfer inside the company, and the outflow of knowledge from the company to external partners. The main actors involved in the knowledge transfer process are identified for all events along with the stages of the knowledge transfer and the dimensions of social capital involved in the knowledge transfer process during the occurrence of the events.

From Table 13.1, it can be seen that the structural dimension of social capital, especially network ties that explain the relationship between actors, is one of the facilitating conditions for knowledge acquisition. Trust, as a part of the relational dimension of social capital, also plays an important role in facilitating knowledge acquisition. This is clearly shown in the case study: the university that was chosen as a partner was on the list of preferred university partners for grant funding through the company's research council because the university and the company already had a relationship and the company had developed trust in the university. As the acquisition stage of knowledge transfer is the gate between outside knowledge and the company, it can be inferred that the presence of the structural dimension (or lack thereof) of social capital is an enabling (or inhibiting) factor for knowledge transfer to occur. However, even though the structural dimension is necessary, it is not a sufficient condition for knowledge acquisition because it should exist along with trust, which is a part of the relational dimension of social capital. The condition could be assured from the outflow of knowledge from the company to external partners as the acquisition of knowledge was facilitated by network ties and trust in the form of the industry consortium (for example, the product and technology transfer meetings between the company and PCI-SIG).

The communication of knowledge, which is the second stage of knowledge transfer process, was facilitated by both the structural dimension and relational dimension of social capital similar to the knowledge acquisition. However, as the knowledge has to transfer from one actor to the others during this stage, it also requires the medium or the means for the transfer. Shared language and shared

Table 13.1 Case dynamic matrix of social capital in the knowledge transfer process

| Events | Main actors involved | Stages of knowledge transfer | Social capital involved |||
			Structural	Relational	Cognitive
External (outside-in) flow of knowledge					
The program manager looked for candidates for R&D partnership and came up with a short list of candidates, based on academic publications	Program managers, engineers	Acquisition	Network ties		
The professor was selected for his expertise and his university affiliation. The university was in the company's pre-existing list of partner universities	Company, university	Acquisition, communication	Network stability	Trust	
With some lobbying effort by the program manager, the grant was awarded by the research council	Programs managers, research council	Acquisition, communication	Network ties, network configuration	Trust	Shared goals
One of the professor's suggested candidates for a summer internship was hired by the company and worked in the lab over the summer	Ph.D. student, Research team	Communication, application, acceptance	Network ties, network stability	Norms	Shared language and codes, Shared goals
The research team visited the campus every 3 months for formal and informal interaction	Research team, partner team	Communication, application, acceptance	Network ties, network stability	Trust, norms	Shared language and codes, Shared goals
The company donated essential tools to the university for more effective research	Company, university	Communication, application		Trust	Shared goals
The professor officially visited the lab and participated in a workshop	Professor, research team	Communication, assimilation			Shared language and codes, Shared goals
The professor sent continuation proposal to the research council to review annually	Professor, research council	Application, acceptance		Trust, norms	Shared goals
The Ph.D. student got a job offer at the lab after he graduated	Ph.D. student, Program manager	Assimilation		Trust	Shared goals

(continued)

Table 13.1 (continued)

Events	Main actors involved	Stages of knowledge transfer	Social capital involved		
			Structural	Relational	Cognitive
Internal flow of knowledge					
The lab prepared workshops, design guides, books, and tools for new technology	Research team, company	Application, acceptance, assimilation		Norms	Shared language and codes, Share goals
The program manager attended weekly knowledge transfer and product meetings	Program manager, company	Communication, application, acceptance, assimilation	Network configuration	Norms	Shared language and codes, Shared goals
The company released GEN 1 product	Research team, company	Application, acceptance, assimilation		Norms	Shared goals
External (inside-out) flow of knowledge					
The program manager attended the product meetings between the company and other partners in PCI-SIG	Company, PCI-SIG	Acquisition, communication	Network ties, network stability	Trust	Shared language and codes
The company released GEN 2 product	Company, PCI-SIG, other vendors	Application, acceptance, assimilation		Norms	Shared goals
PCI-SIG set the standard for the new technology	PCI-SIG, other vendors	Acceptance, assimilation		Norms	
The company hosted a developer forum	Company, other vendors	Communication, application, acceptance		Trust	Shared language and codes, Shared goals

codes of conduct (which is a part of the cognitive dimension of social capital) between actors are among the most important means of knowledge transfer. That is why it is necessary for actors to have the structural dimension, relational dimension, and cognitive dimension of social capital for knowledge communication to occur. In the case of the university knowledge transfer to the company, the interaction between the professor, the Ph.D. student, and the research team at the lab was facilitated by their network ties and stability (structural dimension), trust (relational dimension), and their shared language and codes as the means of communication (cognitive dimension). Similar conditions are also true for the knowledge transfer from the company to external partners as their interaction was also facilitated by the structural dimension, relational dimension, and cognitive dimension of social capital that exist in the form of the product and technology transfer meetings in the industry consortium as well as the introduction of the new technology via the company developer forum to the other vendors.

The later stages of knowledge transfer, i.e., application, acceptance, and assimilation, are focused in the internal flow of knowledge in the organization. These stages are mainly facilitated by the shared goals (the cognitive dimension), which represents the common understanding toward the achievement of all actors involved. This cognitive dimension enables the application of knowledge inside the organization that eventually leads to the acceptance and assimilation of knowledge, respectively. In the acceptance stage of knowledge transfer, trust and norms (the degree of consensus among the actors in the network) are also among the enabling factors besides shared goals. Lastly, the assimilation of knowledge occurs with shared goals and norms as an enabling factor. In our case of the outside-in knowledge transfer from the university to the internal knowledge transfer in the company, the workshops, design guides, books, and tools for new technology as well as the release of the first-generation product based on the new technology reflected these stages of knowledge transfer and the involvement of the relational and cognitive dimensions of social capital. We can see a similar effect of the relational and cognitive dimensions on the later stages of knowledge transfer in the case of inside-out knowledge transfer from the company to external partners and other vendors as shown in the release of the second- generation products as well as the setting of standards for the new technology by the industry consortium.

13.5 Discussion and Conclusions

This study has summarized and synthesized current research on social capital in R&D management in a framework that shows the effects of social capital on the knowledge transfer process. The framework differentiates three dimensions of social capital: structural, relational, and cognitive dimensions, and it links each facet of each dimension with different stages of knowledge transfer process. The framework shows that social capital is important to the entire process of knowledge transfer, but that different dimensions of social capital affect different transfer stages.

The framework thus goes beyond the current state of the art that has mainly researched social capital as a broad and somewhat fuzzily defined concept.

The framework was used to analyze a case in a corporate R&D team in a high-tech industry and traces how different aspects of social capital play out at different points in the R&D process. The framework proves itself to be a useful preliminary theory to guide case study inquiries, though naturally a single case does not allow for far-reaching generalizations. Future research, however, can use the framework to do multiple case studies, based on theoretical sampling, and subsequent cross-case comparisons in order to develop a theory on the impact of social capital on different aspects of R&D. That theory can subsequently be tested empirically.

This paper demonstrates that social capital is an important concept in R&D research, as evidenced by the large number of poorly integrated publications on social capital on R&D management and the case findings that show how strongly social capital impacts the R&D process in real-world settings. A more fully developed and empirically tested theory is very much needed. The proposed framework can contribute to filling this research need.

References

1. Adler PS, Kwon S-W (2002) Social capital: prospects for a new concept. Acad Manage Rev 27:17–40
2. Ahuja MK, Galletta DF, Carley KM (2003) Individual centrality and performance in virtual R&D groups: an empirical study. Manage Sci 49(1):21–38
3. Akçomak IS, ter Weel B (2009) Social capital, innovation and growth: evidence from Europe. Eur Econ Rev 53:544–567
4. Al-Laham A, Tzabbar D, Amburgey TL (2011) The dynamics of knowledge stocks and knowledge flows: innovation consequences of recruitment and collaboration in biotech. Ind Corp Change 20(2):555–583
5. Arranz N, Fdez. de Arroyabe JC (2007) Governance structures in R&D networks: an analysis in the European context. Technol Forecast Soc Change 74:645–662
6. Athanassiou N, Nigh D (2002) The impact of the top management team's international business experience on the firm's internationalization: social networks at work. Manage Int Rev MIR 42(2):157–181
7. Barney J (1991) Firm resources and sustained competitive advantage. J Manage 17:99–120
8. Baron S, Field J, Schuller T (eds) (2000) Social capital: critical perspectives. Oxford University Press, New York
9. Boland RJ, Tenkasi RV (1995) Perspective making and perspective taking in communities of knowing. Organ Sci 6:350–372
10. Bourdieu P (1986) The forms of capital. In: Richardson JG (ed) Handbook of theory and research for the sociology of education. Greenwood Press, New York, pp 241–258
11. Bourdieu P, Wacquant LJD (1992) An invitation to reflexive sociology. University of Chicago Press, Chicago, IL
12. Bresnen M, Edelman L, Newell S, Scarbrough H, Swan J (2003) Social practices and the management of knowledge in project environments. Int J Project Manage 21(3):157–166
13. Brookes NJ, Morton SC, Grossman S, Joesbury P, Varnes D (2007) Analyzing social capital to improve product development team performance: action-research investigations in the aerospace industry with TRW and GKN. IEEE Trans Eng Manage 54(4):814–830

14. Burt RS (1992) Structural holes: the social structure of competition. Harvard University Press, Cambridge, MA
15. Burt RS (2001) Structural holes versus network closure as social capital. In: Lin N, Cook KS, Burt RS (eds) Social capital theory and research. Aldine de Gruyter, New York, pp 31–56
16. Burt RS (2004) Structural holes and good ideas. Am J Sociol 110:349–399
17. Carley K (1992) Organizational learning and personnel turnover. Organ Sci 3:20–46
18. Cohen WM, Levinthal DA (1990) Absorptive capacity: a new perspective on learning and innovation. Adm Sci Q 35:128–152
19. Coleman JS (1988) Social capital in the creation of human capital. Am J Sociol 94:S95–S120
20. Cummings JN (2004) Work groups, structural diversity, and knowledge sharing in a global organization. Manage Sci 50(3):352–364
21. Dahl MS, Pedersen CØR (2005) Social networks in the R&D process: the case of the wireless communication industry around Aalborg, Denmark. J Eng Technol Manage 22:75–92
22. Edelman LF, Bresnen M, Newell S, Scarbrough H, Swan J (2004) The benefits and pitfalls of social capital: empirical evidence from two organizations in the United Kingdom. Brit J Manage 15:59–S69
23. Feldman MP (2001) The entrepreneurial event revisited: firm formation in a regional context. Ind Corp Change 10(4):861–891
24. Field J (2003) Social capital. Routledge, London
25. Fischer HM, Pollock TG (2004) Effects of social capital and power on surviving transformational change: the case of initial public offerings. Acad Manage J 47(4):463–481
26. Gabbay SM, Zuckerman EW (1998) Social capital and opportunity in corporate R&D: the contingent effect of contact density on mobility expectations. Soc Sci Res 27:189–217
27. Gerring J (2004) What is a case study and what is it good for? Am Polit Sci Rev 98:341–354
28. Ghoshal S, Korine H, Szulanski G (1994) Interunit communication in multinational corporations. Manage Sci 40:96–110
29. Gilbert M, Cordey-Hayes M (1996) Understanding the process of knowledge transfer to achieve successful technological innovation. Technovation 16:301–312
30. Granovetter M (1973) The strength of weak ties. Am J Sociol 78:1360–1380
31. Granovetter M (1983) The strength of weak ties: a network theory revisited. Sociol Theory 1:201–233
32. Granovetter M (1992) Problems of explanation in economic sociology. In: Nohria N, Eccles RG (eds) Networks and organizations: structure, form, and action. Harvard Business School Press, Boston, MA, pp 25–56
33. Halpern D (2004) Social capital. Polity Press, Cambridge
34. Hansen MT (1999) The search-transfer problem: the role of weak ties in sharing knowledge across organization subunits. Adm Sci Q 44(1):82–111
35. Hitt MA, Lee H-U, Yucel E (2002) The importance of social capital to the management of multinational enterprises: relational networks among Asian and western firms. Asia Pac J Manage 19:353–372
36. Hoegl M, Parboteeah KP, Munson CL (2003) Team-level antecedents of individuals' knowledge networks. Decis Sci 34(4):741–770
37. Huang JC, Newell S (2003) Knowledge integration processes and dynamics within the context of cross-functional projects. Int J Project Manage 21(3):167–176
38. Inkpen AC, Dinur A (1998) Knowledge management processes and international joint ventures. Organ Sci 9:454–468
39. Inkpen AC, Tsang EWK (2005) Social capital, networks, and knowledge transfer. Acad Manage Rev 30:146–165
40. Janis IL (1982) Groupthink. Houghton Mifflin, Boston, MA
41. Leenders RTAJ, Van Engelen JML, Kratzer J (2003) Virtuality, communication, and new product team creativity: a social network perspective. J Eng Technol Manage 20(1–2):69–92
42. Kaasa A (2009) Effects of different dimensions of social capital on innovative activity: evidence from Europe at the regional level. Technovation 29:218–233

43. Karlsson T, Wigren C (2012) Start-ups among university employees: the influence of legitimacy, human capital and social capital. J Technol Trans 37:297–312
44. Katz R, Allen TJ (1982) Investigating the not invented here (NIH) syndrome: A look at the performance, tenure, and communication patterns of 50 R&D project groups. R&D Manage 12:7–20
45. Krackhardt D (1992) The strength of strong ties: The importance of philos in organizations. In: Nohria N, Eccles RG (eds) Networks and organizations: structure, form, and action. Harvard Business School Press, Boston, MA
46. Landry R, Amara N, Lamari M (2002) Does social capital determine innovation? To what extent? Technol Forecast Soc Change 69:681–701
47. Lee S-H, Wong P-K, Chong C-L (2005) Human and social capital explanations for R&D outcomes. IEEE Trans Eng Manage 52:59–68
48. Levin DZ, Cross R (2004) The strength of weak ties you can trust: the mediating role of trust in effective knowledge transfer. Manage Sci 50:1477–1490
49. McDonough EF (2000) Investigation of factors contributing to the success of cross-functional teams. J Prod Innovat Manage 17(3):221–235
50. McFadyen MA, Cannella AA Jr (2004) Social capital and knowledge creation: diminishing returns of the number and strength of exchange relationships. Acad Manage J 47(5):735–746
51. Mead SP (2001) Using social network analysis to visualize project teams. Project Manage J 32(4):32–38
52. Mehra A, Kilduff M, Brass DJ (2001) The social networks of high and low self-monitors: implications for workplace performance. Adm Sci Q 46(1):121–146
53. Miles MB, Huberman AM (1994) Qualitative data analysis: an expanded sourcebook, 2nd edn. Sage Publications, Thousand Oaks, FL
54. Miller D (2004) Designing high-speed interconnect circuits: an introduction for signal integrity engineers. Intel Press, Santa Clara, CA
55. Misztal BA (1996) Trust in modern societies. Polity Press, Cambridge
56. Nahapiet J, Ghoshal S (1998) Social capital, intellectual capital, and the organizational advantage. Acad Manage Rev 23:242–266
57. Nelson RE (1989) The strength of strong ties: social networks and intergroup conflict in organizations. Acad Manage J 32:377–401
58. Nonaka I, Takeuchi H (1995) The knowledge-creating company. Oxford University Press USA, New York
59. OECD (2002) Frascati manual – proposed standard practice for surveys on research and experimental development. OECD Publishing, Paris
60. Oh H, Chung M-H, Labianca G (2004) Group social capital and group effectiveness: the role of informal socializing ties. Acad Manage J 47(6):860–875
61. Ostrom E (1995) Self-organization and social capital. Ind Corp Change 4(1):131–159
62. Portes A (1998) Social capital: its origins and applications in modern sociology. Ann Rev Sociol 24:1–24
63. Putnam R (2000) Bowling alone: the collapse and revival of american community. Simon & Schuster, New York
64. Putnam RD (1993) Making democracy work: civic traditions in modern Italy. Princeton University Press, Princeton NJ
65. Putnam RD (1995) Bowling alone: America's declining social capital. J Democr 6:65–65
66. Reagans R, McEvily B (2003) Network structure and knowledge transfer: the effects of cohesion and range. Adm Sci Q 48:240–267
67. Reagans R, Mcevily B (2011) How to make the team: social networks vs. as criteria demography for designing effective teams. Demography 49(1):101–133
68. Reagans R, Zuckerman EW (2001) Networks, diversity, and productivity: the social capital of corporate R&D teams. Organ Sci 12:502–517
69. Sandelowski M (2000) Whatever happened to qualitative description? Res Nurs Health 23:334–340

70. Sparrowe RT, Liden RC, Wayne SJ, Kraimer ML (2001) Social networks and the performance of individuals and groups. Acad Manage J 44(2):316–325
71. Suddaby R (2006) From the editors: what grounded theory is not. Acad Manage J 49:633–642
72. Tether BS, Tajar A (2008) Beyond industry-university links: sourcing knowledge for innovation from consultants, private research organisations and the public science-base. Res Policy 37:1079–1095
73. Tidd J (1995) Development of novel products through intraorganizational and interorganizational networks. J Prod Innovat Manage 12(4):307–322
74. Tomlinson PR (2012) Industry institutions, social capital, and firm participation in industrial development. Ind Corp Change 21(1):1–29
75. Tsai W, Ghoshal S (1998) Social capital and value creation: the role of intrafirm networks. Acad Manage J 41:464–476
76. Voss C, Tsikriktsis N, Frohlich M (2002) Case research in operations management. Int J Oper Prod Manage 22:195–219
77. Westerlund M, Svahn S (2008) A relationship value perspective of social capital in networks of software SMEs. Industr Market Manage 37:492–501
78. Xia M, Zhao K, Mahoney JT (2012) Enhancing value via cooperation: firms' process benefits from participation in a standard consortium. Ind Corp Change 21(3):699–729
79. Yin RK (2002) Case study research: design and methods, 3rd edn. Sage Publications, Thousand Oaks, CA
80. Yli-Renko H, Autio E, Sapienza HJ (2001) Social capital, knowledge acquisition, and knowledge exploitation in young technology-based firms. Strategic Manage J 22:587–613
81. Yli-Renko H, Autio E, Tontti V (2002) Social capital, knowledge, and the international growth of technology-based new firms. Int Bus Rev 11:279–304

Chapter 14
Researching Innovative Capacity of Local Subsidiaries in Selected CEE Countries

Tugrul U. Daim, Zoran Aralica, Marina Dabić, Dilek Özdemir, and A. Elvan Bayraktaroglu

Abstract The aim of the paper is to research the innovative capacities of local subsidiaries in selected CEE countries. We define innovative capacity as an ability of conducting innovation activities with innovation output variables i.e. innovation products and/or processes as the visible results of innovation inputs i.e. innovation investments. We found that the determinants of innovation input differ from the determinants of innovation output. The Innovation outputs variables are affected by productivity variables. On the other hand, *local subsidiaries as a knowledge source for other unit of MNEs group* as well as *SMEs as a type of the ownership* affect the innovation input determinants. However, similarities between innovation input and innovation output exist between business functions i.e. process engineering appear in both cases as determinants.The innovation performance measured by productivity are strongly reliant on local subsidiaries performance—*changes in value in earning before interests and taxes*, where investments into resources related to technologies are crucial i.e. *differences in number of R&D employees between 2005 and 2002* and *difference in the annual expenditure on R&D and innovation as a percentage of total sales* positively influence local subsidiaries performance.

T.U. Daim (✉)
Engineering and Technology Management Department,
Portland State University, Portland, OR, USA
e-mail: tugrul@etm.pdx.edu

Z. Aralica
Institute of Economics, Zagreb, Croatia
e-mail: zaralica@eizg.hr

M. Dabić
University of Zagreb, Zagreb, Croatia
e-mail: mdabic@efzg.hr

D. Özdemir • A.E. Bayraktaroglu
Istanbul Technical University, Istanbul, Turkey
e-mail: ozdemirdi@itu.edu.tr; bayraktaroglu@itu.edu.tr

14.1 Introduction

Researching innovative capacity is focusing on the innovation process at the firm level, it is the analysis of the manner in which innovation inputs turns into innovation outputs. The innovative capacity depends on innovation activities of firms (R&D activities, acquisition of technologies). Therefore, there is an implied connection between R&D and innovation investments on the one hand and the firm's capability to assimilate and exploit existing information within the firm [1] on the other. This ability is primarily a result of the relationship between innovation inputs and innovation outputs (i.e. internal knowledge flow) within firms, closely connected with impacts on firm performance.

Traditionally, product and process innovations (i.e. innovation output, key element of innovation capacity) have been a critical source of MNE competitive advantage [2]. As a result of internationalization, the advantages of MNEs have shifted to the role of the firm as a coordinator of a number of separate value-added activities, increasing their technological opportunities and participation in various international markets. Therefore, production of innovative products and/or processes became a source of creating and sustaining competitive advantage of local subsidiaries. Interests of local subsidiaries are primarily oriented towards enhancing their innovative capacities,[1] closely linked to resource agglomeration within subsidiaries, and in parallel with improving their significance within the MNEs network. At the same time, growth of knowledge through the creation of innovative products and/or process within the local subsidiaries could present an avenue for enhancing their autonomy with regard to MNEs.

High risks, costs and lack of available knowledge within the firms induce them to seek external sources of knowledge which stimulate formal[2] and informal[3] co-operation with other organisations and/or institutions. In that way the availability of external knowledge reduces the need for all firms to develop all stages of the innovation process within their own boundaries. In case of international economics literature, foreign sources appear as an influential element of productivity growth in developing countries [3–5] such as Central and Eastern European (CEE)

---

[1] Kamman [53] defines capacity in two ways. First, as the maximum volume of entities that: (a) can pass through a facility in a given time of period; (b) a node can produce in a given time period; (c) a node can absorb in a given time period; (d) a node can put through from one facility into another facility in a given time period; (e) can pass through the network between nodes, making use of as many facilities as is required, in a given time period; (f) does not upset the coordinating mechanism, leading to entropy, chaos or a loss in power vis-à-vis other network/nodes. Second, capacity refers to the maximum of any usually physically variable it can endure, resist, contain, or absorb, without losing its prime important task it was designed for.

[2] Thus creation of various type of innovation cooperation with other firms and/or organisations is a normal sequence enabling these activities.

[3] The firms are a source of the innovation.

countries.[4] Their innovation activities therefore become tightly connected with the availability of the technology transfer mechanisms. In this regard, Perugini et al. [6], Dabić and Pejic-Bach [7], Damijan et al. [8] argue that industrial integration via FDI led to considerable increase in productivity, technology and quality in Central Eastern European (CEE) countries especially in the period prior to the current economic crisis.[5]

Data about local subsidiaries within the manufacturing sector is applied in the selected CEE countries i.e. Eastern Germany, Romania, Slovenia, Croatia and Poland. Our empirical analysis is based on the postal survey of foreign investment enterprises in manufacturing. All the surveys took place in the period between 2006 and April and May 2007. The paper analyses the innovative capacity within local subsidiaries. Section 14.2 provides a theoretical background of the concept of innovative capacity and presents a hypothesis related to the relationship between firm innovation output and other variables i.e. innovation inputs, sources of innovation and firm's productivity. In the next section methodology and data are presented. Section 14.4 describes the model results. Concluding remarks are presented in the last section.

14.2 Background Theory: Researching Innovative Capacity Within Local Subsidiaries

Innovative capacity is the ability of conducting innovation activities aimed at gaining and sustaining the firm's competitive advantage. Improving the innovative capacity of the firm dependson various factors, most crucially the continuous supply of innovation resources and the accumulation of innovation knowledge. As an approach, innovation capacity is in line with the resource based view, a theoretical approach which acknowledges that internal capacities are a key element of the firm's technological development [9], also based on other theories such as the contingency theory where survival and success depends on the unit's responses to diverse environments [10]. Therefore, the nature of innovation performance is relative, primarily depending on internal resources and/or external opportunities (market opportunities as well as linkage to the MNE) to achieve the business entity goals, so we may

---

[4] According to UNCTAD [54], developing and transition economies, for the first time, attracted more than half of global FDI in 2010. Within the group, Eastern Asia countries considerably differ from Latin America and Central and Eastern European (CEE) countries. On the global level China belongs to countries that make up the bulk of the world's surplus, whereas Latin America countries and CEE countries belong to the deficit countries in terms of International trade. Therefore, proportion and characteristics of the FDI and innovation activities a reconnected with characteristics of the national economies, where an export oriented economy such as China presents a more fruitful area for enhancing innovation activities in comparison to the national economies which belong to the deficit economies (e.g. CEE countries).

[5] It is well established in the literature describing CEE countries and their transition that the entry of multinational corporations (MNCs) facilitated enterprise restructuring [55], export competitiveness [56] and productivity growth [57] as the most important factors influencing the integration of CEECs within the global markets.

assume that technological innovation consists of a package of interrelated assets including human capital, tangible and intangible assets [11].

Innovation performance is a result of the firm's innovation strategy. Various sources of innovation activities, both external and internal, produce different impacts and are observed at the firm level as various innovation strategies, the introduction of new products or processes within enterprises.[6] Thus, research about innovative capacity needs to include sources of innovation, innovation input variables (e.g. innovation expenditure, innovation output variables (i.e. innovation product, innovation processes) as well as measures of firm's productivity (like sales/employees) as a result of the firm's participation on the domestic and/or international markets. Moreover, local subsidiaries enhance their innovative capacities as well increase the competitive advantage of the MNC by identifying and appropriating resources, capabilities, and competencies from the local environment and finally integrating these into their MNC network [12]. Therefore, the innovative capacities within the local subsidiaries are complementary with their absorptive capacities to appropriately scan resources from their environemnt and use them internally within own firms or providing them to other firms within the network. In the context of innovative capacity, innovation output is a key variable and the relation between innovation output and other aforementioned variables are crucial. Since innovation output i.e. innovation activities could be achieved by the use of internal knowledge (R&D activities) and/or use of the external knowledge (e.g. machinery equipment acquisition) different types of relations could appear [13, 14]. That is in line with Hobday and Rush [15] finding that 'all firms are not the same' in their strategies and practices towards technology.As a result, their autonomy functions differ among the subsidiaries and it depends on their absorptive capacity and time required for obtaining it. Above mentioned relations are an indispensable part of FDI activities and the internalization of business activities [16]. Moreover, differences appear in the context of performance where innovative capacity emphasizes economic performance, with two group of indicators as potential indicators of financial performance [17, 18] and other group of indicators such as qualitative returns to the stakeholders, employee and customer satisfaction [19]. In that context, researching subsidiaries in Argentina, Marin and Bell [20] showed that more innovative subsidiaries are better involved in the national economy and global economy, but this represents a small proportion of the total number of subsidiaries. In other words, majority of the subsidiaries were disconnected from both their global corporation and the local economy, i.e. using only the public utilities (e.g. electricity and gas) from the local economies. Marin and Sasidharan [21] found that only subsidiaries oriented towards technologically creative activities have significantly positive effects on the Indian Economy in contrast to the subsidiaries mostly involved in technologically exploitative activities which generate negative effects in some circumstances.

In addition, the innovative capacity is tightly connected with the absorptive capacity,[7] a set of organizational routines and processes, by which firms acquire,

---

[6] It depends on technology acquisition, innovation strategy of their owner, level of competitiveness (cf. Aghion et al. [48]).

[7] There is another concept similar to technological capabilities (Richardson [58]) defined as appropriate knowledge, experience and skills needed by firms and organisations to introduce new products and forms of organisations.

assimilate, transform, and exploit knowledge to produce a dynamic organizational capability proficient in conducting innovative activities aimed at gaining and sustaining competitive advantage [22]. However there are differences among them. Innovative capacity as a concept relies on internal resources focusing on innovation output (e.g. innovation product and/or innovation processes) where innovation output depends on firm productivity. On the other hand, absorptive capacity points out innovation inputs as key variables within the business entities and as a crucial capability use the value of external knowledge. In case of the local subsidiaries, innovation activities depend on the linkage with MNEs [23], organizational learning capacity (cf. [24]), innovation strategy of the MNEs [25] which includes the use of various knowledge sources [26]. Both approaches emphasise the role of the learning process, stimulating an enhancement of the firm's innovative capability to resource agglomeration tightly connected with knowledge use within enterprise. Therefore, absorptive capacity and innovative capacity are complementary concepts with similar elements, where increase of absorptive capacity facilitates an increase of innovative capacities and vice versa.

H1: Determinants of innovation input differ from determinants of innovation output within local subsidiaries in CEE countries

14.2.1 Internationalization as a Determinant of Enhancing Innovative Capacity

Internationalization is defined as a process entailing coordinated activities undertaken by an enterprise increasing involvement in international operations [27] via mechanisms of international trade and/or international production where transfer of technology and skills are parallel with the transfer of capital. Within the international production theory, part of FDI theory,[8] issue of technology and technology transfers are crucial. MNEs facilitate (1) directly local subsidiaries; and (2) indirectly through spillover from other firms. MNCs operate through network of subsidiaries, and benefit from market imperfections for example by exploiting sources of low-cost labor [28], or by switching production between plants in different countries [29]. Traditionally, only parent companies had been observed as a source of the capabilities

---

[8] International production theory, market imperfections theory and Internalization theory are approaches within the theory of the FDI (Morgan and Katsikeas[16]: 70). International production theory argues the propensity of a firm to initiate foreign production will depend on the specific attractions of its home country compared with resource implications advantages of locating in another country [59]; The firm's decision to invest overseas is explained as a strategy to capitalize on certain capabilities and not shared with foreign competitors is a basis of market imperfection theory; Extension of the direct operations of the firm and bringing under common ownership and control the activities conducted by intermediate markets that link the firm to customers is a basis of internationalization theory (cf. [60]).

within the MNC network [30, 31]. Lately, appearance of the argumentation based on the transaction cost theory [32] emphasizes the role of various firms as capability sources [33]. The importance formal and informal type of co operations increased over time to be influenced by the markets-as-networks perspective [12] where the role of external partners (in majority international) had been recognised in terms of capability development in subsidiaries [34]. As a result, significance of the various types of stakeholders as sources of formal and informal mostly international innovation co-operation has increased parallel with the increase of importance of intangible resources within the network.

Regarding to above mentioned arguments, Knell and Rojec ([35]: 2) cited the following channels of technology transfer: competition, interactions with suppliers and customers, cooperation with universities, research laboratories, relevant government institutions and the international movement of capital and goods. So, the quality of technology transfer mechanisms depends on MNC and their operations as well absorptive capacities [22] and the capabilities[9] of the indigenous firms. As result the technology transfer mechanisms influence the firm productivity, the knowledge creation within the firms as well mechanism of ways in which the indigenous firms cooperate with their environment. That is in line with De la Fuenta [36] finding, arguing that technology transfers produce the reallocation of the productive factors across regions and sectors.

Extensive empirical research has found numerous possible relationships between international expansion and performance, including negative, U-shaped, S-shaped and linearly positive relationships [37–39]. Many scholars have focused on the differences in the environments in which MNEs are active, and the implications thereof for the transfer, deployment and exploitation of extant subsidiaries for specific advantages [40, 41]. MNEs active in multiple environments need to adapt to a range of settings, which can in turn lead to innovation and capabilities [42, 43]; see the firm as a social community, which is an efficient mechanism for creating and transferring 'knowledge into economically rewarding products', Kogut and Zander [44]. In context of Eastern Europe, it was shown that competition influences performance [45, 46], and this effect appears to be much more important than the effect of ownership. In particular, Carlin et al. [47] show that competition affects firm innovation and growth, where some rivalry (1–3 competitors) affects innovation positively while too much rivalry and no rivalry can both be detrimental. Contrary to that, Aghion et al. [48] found that pressure raises innovation for both new and old firms competitive, where old firms innovate to survive, while new firms innovate to escape competition. Mainly the results of MNCs in the local market depend on the role of a subsidiary [37]. The empirical research confirmed great heterogeneity in the firms' performance, with differences appearing especially in terms of knowledge capital, i.e. innovation output measured as the percentage of innovation sales to total sales.

---

[9] We understand capabilities as the fim's specific knowledge used to utilize the resources within the firms (Amit and Shoemaker [61], Makadok [62]). That is in line with Teece et al. [63] explanation fo the concept the dynamic capabilities which describe how the firms effectively use the resources within their strategic context.

Additionally, heterogeneity appears in comparing the countries on international level as differences in productivity among the countries,[10] where heterogeneity among the local subsidiaries could be explained by their different roles within the MNE network. This is tightly connected with the principles and routines which the firms accept and implement in their business practice.

Moreover, the internationalisation is tightly connected with the firm's inclination towards use of external knowledge. This is a influential element of stimulating innovation performance (cf. [50]). The external sourcing or knowledge is recognised as mechanism for innovation upgrading, influencing organizational learning [51]. In this context, the learning process is a complex activity depending on the complexity of technology, interconnectideness between product and process as well as path dependency in knowledge searching for business entities within the clusters [52]. In terms of activities of local subsidiaries with regard to nature of the relationships with other firms and/or institution (defined as embeddedeness) ([19]: 1016) is a foundation for informal cooperation (i.e. information exchange) and/or formal cooperation.

> H2: Reliance on the external knowledge explains the subsidiaries innovative performance results neglecting the role of innovation inputs

14.3 Research Design and Method

Our empirical analysis is based on the postal survey of foreign investment enterprises in the manufacturing sectors of selected countries, namely Croatia, former East Germany,[11] Poland, Romania and Slovenia. The complied dataset from these countries includes 734 business entities. On average, foreign owned SMEs in Slovenia (74.1 %), Croatia (65.2 %) and Romania (63.2 %) within a population of foreign owned firms have a favorable position (higher share of export oriented local subsidiaries in comparison to their counterparts in Poland (33.6 %) and Foreign Eastern Germany (35.4 %).On the other hand, Foreign Eastern Germany (24.8 %) and Romania (20.2 %) are leading among the analysed countries in the category of annual expenditures on R&D and innovation in percent of total sales in 2005. Moreover, on average the largest local subsidiaries exist in Romania (635) measured by number of employees, as well as averagely Croatia's local subsidiaries are the largest in criterion number of R&D employees (25.3) among the analysed countries.[12] All the surveys, apart from Croatia[13] took place during 2006. In all the selected

---

[10] Explanatory factors for the differences in the prices of the final products include the differences in sectoral structures of a national economy, and on the firm level functional structure (Steffen and Stephan [64]).

[11] Country selection is a result of participation in the U-KNOW project, partially financed by the European Commission (EC) Framework Programme 6 (contract nr CIT5-028519).

[12] Appendix 1 consists of the list of selected variables.

[13] In Croatia the survey took place in April and May 2007. Therefore the analysed years are different. In analysed countries the survey took place in 2002 and 2005 whereas in case of Croatia, the survey was conducted in 2003 and 2006.

countries the surveys were implemented by a questionnaire, consisting of three parts: basic information about the firm, the relationship between the foreign investor(s) and the firm, and R&D and innovation activities.

For the purpose of the research, three multiple regression models were used, including different types of variables: technological knowledge, innovation input, innovation output, the firms' productivity, the firms' characteristics (type of ownership, source of innovation) as well as the firms' performance variables (internationalization, learning process, competition) (Appendix 2—consists of detailed list of the variables).[14] Our framework allows us to analyse determinants of the three different stages of the innovation process, i.e. innovation inputs, innovation output and the firms' performance in the analyzed Central and Eastern European countries.

In the first model, the innovation output variables depends on innovation input, sources of innovation, productivity and technological knowledge variables. The innovation output variable includes *product innovation intensity, process innovation intensity, organizational innovation intensity and marketing innovation intensity, difference in the share of new or significantly improved products in your firm's total sales between 2005 and 2002,* and *difference in the annual expenditures on R&D and Innovation as a percentage of share of total sales between 2005 and 2002 in Euro.*

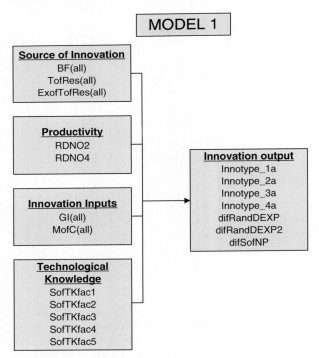

---

[14] The variables within the models appear in various forms: nominal variables, categorical variables, percentage variables and binominal variables, where we try to analyze the static dimension of the variables. Calculating the percentage difference between categorical variables allows for the inclusion of the dynamic characteristics of the variables in the analysed period.

In the second model, the innovation inputs variables depends on innovation source, the learning process, internationalization, competition, technological knowledge, business functions and ownership variables. The innovation inputs consists of *difference in number of employees between 2005 and 2002, difference in number of R&D employees between 2005 and 2002, difference in value of total sales between 2005 and 2002, difference in share of intermediate inputs/supplies as percentage of total sale between 2005 and 2002, difference in the annual expenditures on R&D and innovation as a percentage of share of total sales between 2005 and 2002 in local currency, difference in the annual expenditures on R&D and innovation as a percentage of share of total sales in the period between 2005 and 2002 in Euro as well as the share of new or significantly improved products in the firm's total sales between 2005 and 2002.*

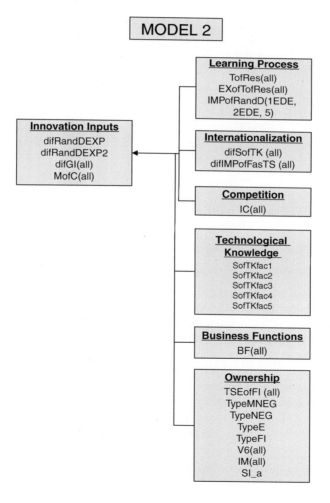

Finally, the third model assumes that the performance of *Local subsidiaries* depends on *Innovation inputs* and *Technological sources* variables. The dependant variables in our model are *Difference in productivity (value of total sales/total number of employees) between 2005 and 2002* in local currency and *Difference in innovation productivity (the share of new or significantly improved products in your firm's total sales divided by number of R&D personnel) between 2005 and 2002*.

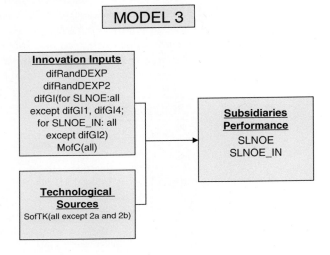

14.4 Results and Discussion

The hypotheses were tested using the models presented in the earlier section.

H1: Determinants of innovation output differ from the determinants of innovation output

This hypothesis was explored through the analysis of the determinants of innovation outputs and inputs. The innovation output variable is determined by a knowledge intensive function of process engineering and the innovation input productivity variables (R&D expenditures[15] divided by number of employees) appear more frequently as the explanation variables, compared to variable group named general information about the firms as well as magnitude of the changes.[16] More precisely, *process engineering* as a business function affects *product innovation intensity*, *organizational innovation intensity* as well as on the *share of new or significantly improved products in the firm's total sales*. The innovation input productivity variable (R&D expenditures divided by the number of employees in 2002) affects positively

---

[15] Researching the business function division between Multinational national enterprises (MNE) and local subsidiaries Aralica et al. [65] found that knowledge intensive functions, such as strategic management and process engineering are under control of the MNE whereas production of innovative products are controlled by local subsidiaries.

[16] General information data and Business function data could be found in the Appendix 2, Table 14.3.

organizational innovation intensity, marketing innovation intensity and *difference in the annual expenditures on R&D and innovation as a percentage of share of total sales in Euro between 2002 and 2005.*

In case of innovation input determinants (model two), the differences in process engineering negatively affect the *difference in number of R&D employees between 2005 and 2002*, as well as *magnitude of change in share of exports in total sales*, while positively influencing the *magnitude of change in category of market share on your most relevant market*. Although, *the difference in market research and marketing* as the business function positively influences the *magnitude of change in share of exports in total sales* and negatively the *magnitude of change in category market share on your most relevant market*. The *local subsidiaries as a knowledge source for other unit of the MNEs group* positively affects the *difference in annual expenditure on innovation and R&D expenditure, difference in number of R&D employee, difference in value of the total sales in 2005 and 2002*, as well as *magnitude of changes earnings before interest and rates*. SMEs as a type of the ownership positively affects the *difference in number of R&D employees, magnitude of changes in earnings before interests and taxes,* and negatively the *difference in values of share of intermediate inputs/supplies (as % of total sales) between 2005 and 2002*. There are, therefore differences between the determinants of innovation outputs (with a strong emphasis on the business function) and innovation inputs (with an emphasis on the local subsidiaries as a knowledge source for other unit of MNEs group as well as on SMEs as a type of the ownership). Thus the innovation input determinants are more dependent on the characteristics of business entities, whereas innovation output variables could be explained by the foreign investor enterprises' knowledge applied within the local subsidiaries. However, similarities between innovation outputs and inputs do arguably exist, since the business function appears as the determinant in both cases.

H2: Reliance on the external knowledge explains the subsidiaries innovative performance results neglecting the role of innovation inputs

This hypothesis was explored through the analysis of innovation performance determinants, explained by the dependent variable *Difference in productivity* (value of total sales/Total number of employees in the year 2005 subtracted by value of total sales/Total number of employees in the year 2002), in local currency, and the *Difference in innovation productivity* (the share of new or significantly improved products in your firm's total sales divided by Number of R&D personnel 2005 and the same values in 2002). The former dependent variable is positively affected by the difference in *total assets between 2005 and 2002, difference in number of R&D employees between 2005 and 2002*, and *changes in value in earning before interests and taxes, difference in the annual expenditures on R&D and innovation as a percentage of share of total sales in Euro between 2005 and 2002* as well as negatively affected by *changes in magnitude in value added per employees*. The latter depended variable is positively affected by the variable named *competition within foreign investor network*. It seems that innovation performance strongly depends on the resources of local subsidiaries (R&D personnel and the total assets) and the results (total revenues), where competition among the local subsidiaries stimulates innovation productivity. Here, the reliance on the external knowledge could not be confirmed in the case of local subsidiaries within the analysed Central and Eastern European countries.

14.5 Conclusions

This paper makes several contributions. The significant contributions are listed below:

- An innovation process was developed through research models explored in this paper. This provides critical insight into the innovation process within the Central and Eastern European countries, thus providing an opportunity for policy makers for focus areas, due to the fact that main characteristics of innovation process within the analysed countries were found.
- More precisely, we found that the innovation input determinants are more dependent on the characteristics of business entities. However innovation output variables could be explained by the foreign investor enterprises' knowledge effectively applied within the local subsidiaries. Thus contribution of the local subsidiaries as a knowledge source for the other unit of multinational enterprises presents critical area for the policy makers in the analysed countries.
- We also found that innovation input determinants differ from innovation output determinants. This presents an important finding which highlights the role of the institutional environment as well as the MNE knowledge which needs to be conducive for local subsidiaries as growth is measured by increase in total revenues and number of employees.

Appendix 1

Table 14.1 Descriptive analysis of the selected variables

	Poland	Romania	Croatia	Slovenia	Foreign Eastern Germany
Share of the local subsidiaries within the analysed countries	14.9 %	29.9 %	19.6 %	5.4 %	30.2 %
Share of MNE group in total number of foreign owned enterprises	52.7 %	38.6 %	38.1 %	45.1 %	54.5 %
Share of the export oriented local subsidiaries (more than 50 % of the total sales) in total number of foreign owned enterprises	33.6 %	63.2 %	65.2 %	74.1 %	35.4 %
Average number of employees in the local subsidiaries per country	349.1	672	635	415	310
Average number of R&D employees in the local subsidiaries per country	5.2	4.5	25.3	10.3	8.5
The annual expenditures on R&D and innovation in % of total sales 2005 per country	19.8 %	20.2 %	15.3 %	9.7 %	24.8 %

Appendix 2: List of the Variables in the Models

Table 14.2 Dependent variables in the models[a]

Codename	Name of variable	Type of variables	Measures	Models
Innotype_1a	Product Innovation—Intensity	Innovation output	Very low—1, below average—2, industry average—3, above average—4, very high—5, no answer—0	Model one
Innotype_2a	Process Innovation—Intensity	Innovation output	Very low—1, below average—2, industry average—3, above average—4, very high—5, no answer—0	Model one
Innotype_3a	Organizational Innovation—Intensity	Innovation output	very low—1, below average—2, industry average—3, above average—4, very high—5, no answer—0	Model one
Innotype_4a	Marketing Innovation—Intensity	Innovation output	very low—1, below average—2, industry average—3, above average—4, very high—5, no answer—0	Model one
difSofNP	Difference in the share of new or significantly improved products in your firm's total sales between 2005 and 2002 in local currency	Innovation output	Percentage points	Model one
difRandDEXP2	Difference in the annual expenditures on R&D and innovation as a percentage of share of total sales between 2005 and 2002 in Euro	Innovation output/ innovation input	Percentage points	Model one
difRandDEXP3	Difference in the annual expenditures on R&D and innovation as a percentage of share of total sales between 2005 and 2002 in local currency	Innovation input	Percentage points	Model two
difRandDEXP4	Difference in the annual expenditures on R&D and innovation between 2005 and 2002 in Euro	Innovation input	Percentage points	Model two

(continued)

Table 14.2 (continued)

Codename	Name of variable	Type of variables	Measures	Models
DifGI1	Difference in number of employees between 2005 and 2002	Innovation input	Nominal variable	Model two
DifGI4	Difference in value of total sales between 2005 and 2002	Innovation input	Nominal variable	Model two
DifGI5	Difference in share of intermediate inputs/supplies as percentage of total sale between 2005 and 2002	Innovation input	Nominal variable	Model two
SLNOE	Difference in productivity (value of total sales/total number of employees) between 2005 and 2002 in local currency	Productivity	Nominal variable	Model three
SLNOE_IN	Difference in innovation productivity (the share of new or significantly improved products in your firm's total sales) divided by (difference in number of R&D personnel 2005 and 2002)	Productivity	Percentage points	Model three

[a]In Croatia case, 2003 and 2006 were the years of the values' measurement

Table 14.3 Dependent and independent variables in the models

DifGI2	Difference in number of R&D employees between 2005 and 2002	Innovation input	Difference in categorical variable	Dependent variable in model two and independent in model three
DifGI3	Difference in value of total assets between 2005 and 2002	Innovation input	Difference in categorical variable	Dependent variable in model two and independent in model three
MofC_1	The magnitude of the changes of value earnings before interest and taxes between 2005 and 2002	Innovation input	Difference in categorical variable	Dependent variable in model two and independent in model three
MofC_3	The magnitude of the changes of value added per employee between 2005 and 2002	Innovation input	Difference in categorical variable	Dependent variable in model two and independent in model one and model three
MofC_5	The magnitude of the changes of value competition within foreign investor network between 2002 and 2005	Innovation input	Difference in categorical variable	Dependent variable in model two and independent in model one and model three

Table 14.4 Independent variables in the models

Code name	Name of variable	Type of variables	Measures	Models
GI_1a	Total number of employees 2002	Innovation input	Nominal variable	Model one
GI_2b	Number of R&D employees 2005	Innovation input	Nominal variable	Model one
GI_4a	Value of total sales (in local currency) 2002	Innovation input	Nominal variable	Model one
GI_5b	Share of intermediate inputs/supplies (as % of total sales) 2005	Innovation input	Nominal variable	Model one
BF_1	Production and operational management	Source of innovation	Categorical variables: only your firm—1, mainly your firm—2, mainly foreign investor network—3, only foreign network—4, no answer—0	Model one and model two
BF_2	Market research and marketing	Source of innovation	Categorical variables: only your firm—1, mainly your firm—2, mainly foreign investor network—3, only foreign network—4, no answer—0	Model one and model two
BF_4	Product development	Source of innovation	Categorical variables: only your firm—1, mainly your firm—2, mainly foreign investor network—3, only foreign network—4, no answer—0	Model one and model two
BF_5	Process engineering	Source of innovation	Categorical variables: only your firm—1, mainly your firm—2, mainly foreign investor network—3, only foreign network—4, no answer—0	Model one and model two
EXofToFRes_2	Expected degree of transfer of new responsibilities from the headquarters and/or other units of your foreign investor network to your firm in the field of new products	Source of innovation	Categorical variables: only your firm—1, mainly your firm—2, mainly foreign investor network—3, only foreign network—4, no answer—0	Model one

(continued)

Table 14.4 (continued)

Code name	Name of variable	Type of variables	Measures	Models
EXofTofRes_3	Expected degree of transfer of new responsibilities from the headquarters and/or other units of your foreign investor network to your firm in the field of new business function	Source of innovation	Categorical variables: only your firm—1, mainly your firm—2, mainly foreign investor network—3, only foreign network—4, no answer—0	Model one
MofC_4	The magnitude of the changes in category 'Market share on your most relevant market' in the last 3 years	Innovation input	Magnitude in categorical variables considerable reduction—1, reduction—2, no change—3; increase—4, considerable increase—5, does not apply—6	Model one
RDNO_2	R&D expenditures/number of employees in 2002 (EUR)	Productivity	Nominal variable	Model one
SofTK 2a 2b	Own R&D (at entry) divided by own R&D (today)	Technological knowledge	Divided categorical variable	Model one
SofTK 3a 3b 4a 4b	R&D carried out at the headquarters of your foreign investor network (at entry)/(today)/R&D carried out by another unit of foreign investor network (at entry)/(today)	Technological knowledge	Divided categorical variables	Model one
SofTK 9a 9b 10a 10b 11a	R&D carried out in collaboration with competitors (strategic alliance) (at entry)/(today)/R&D carried out in collaboration with scientific institutions abroad (at entry)/today	Technological knowledge	Divided categorical variables	Model one
BF_6	Strategic management and planning	Source of innovation	Categorical variable only your firm—1, mainly your firm—2, mainly foreign investor network—3, only foreign network—4	Model two
BF_7	Investment projects and finance	Source of innovation	Categorical variable only your firm—1, mainly your firm—2, mainly foreign investor network—3, only foreign network—4	Model two
SofTKfac1	Source of knowledge—R&D carried out in collaboration with suppliers abroad, suppliers local, customer abroad, customer local	Technological knowledge	Binominal variables	Model two

SofTKfac2	Source of knowledge—R&D carried out at the headquarters of your foreign investor network/another unit of foreign investor network	Technological knowledge	Binominal variables	Model two
SofTKfac3	Source of knowledge—R&D carried out in collaboration with competitors/with scientific institutions abroad/with scientific institutions local	Technological knowledge	Binominal variables	Model two
SofTKfac4	Source of knowledge—existing technology of your MNE group	Technological knowledge	Binominal variables	Model two
SofTKfac5	R&D carried out on your own (at entry)	Technological knowledge	Binominal variables	Model two
TofRes_1	New geographical markets—transfer of responsibilities from the HQ and/or other units of your foreign investor network to your firm since entry of the foreign investor	Learning process	Categorical variables—no transfer—1, limited transfer—2, considerable transfer—3, full transfer—4, no answer—9	Model two
TofRes_2	New products—transfer of responsibilities from the HQ and/or other units of your foreign investor network to your firm since entry of the foreign investor	Learning process	Categorical variables—no transfer, limited transfer, considerable transfer, full transfer, no answer	Model two
TSEofFI_1	Total share in equity held by foreign investor at the first	Ownership	Percent	Model two
TSEofFI_3	Total share in equity held by foreign investor today	Ownership	Percent	Model two
TypeFI	Type foreign investor—foreign individual or family	Ownership	Percent	Model two
TypeMNEG	Type foreign investor—MNE	Ownership	Percent	Model two
TypeNEG	Type investor—national enterprise group	Ownership	Percent	Model two
difIMPofFasTS2	Difference in the importance of your own firm as a source of technological knowledge for R&D or innovation activities of others to other units or subsidiaries of your MNE group today and at the time of entry	Internationalization	Difference between categorical variables	Model two
difIMPofFasTS3	Difference in the importance of your own firm as a source of technological knowledge for R&D or innovation activities to your supplier abroad today and at the time of entry	Internationalization	Difference between categorical variables	Model two
difIMPofFasTS4	Difference in the importance of your own firm as a source of technological knowledge for R&D or innovation activities to your local suppliers today and at the time of entry	Internationalization	Difference between categorical variables	Model two
difIMPofFasTS7	Difference in the importance of your own firm as a source of technological knowledge for R&D or innovation activities to your competitors abroad today and at the time of entry	Internationalization	Difference between categorical variables	Model two

(continued)

Table 14.4 (continued)

Code name	Name of variable	Type of variables	Measures	Models
difIMPofFasTS8	Difference in the importance of your own firm as a source of technological knowledge for R&D or innovation activities to your local competitors today and at the time of entry	Internationalization	Difference between categorical variables	Model two
difSofTK1	Difference in the importance of the existing technology of your MNE as a source of technological knowledge for R&D or innovation activities of your firm today and at the time of entry	Internationalization	Difference between categorical variables	Model two
difSofTK3	Difference in the importance of the R&D carried out at the headquarters of your foreign investor network as a source of technological knowledge for R&D or innovation activities of your firm today and at the time of entry	Internationalization	Difference between categorical variables	Model two
difSofTK5	Difference in the importance of the R&D carried out in collaboration with suppliers abroad as a source of technological knowledge for R&D or innovation activities of your firm today and at the time of entry	Internationalization	Difference between categorical variables	Model two
difSofTK7	Difference in the importance of the R&D carried out in collaboration with customers abroad as a source of technological knowledge for R&D or innovation activities of your firm today and at the time of entry	Internationalization	Difference between categorical variables	Model two
difSofTK9	Difference in the importance of the R&D carried out in collaboration with competitors (strategic alliance) as a source of technological knowledge for R&D or innovation activities of your firm today and at the time of entry	Internationalization	Difference between categorical variables	Model two
difSofTK11	Difference in the importance of the R&D carried out in collaboration with local scientific institutions as a source of technological knowledge for R&D or innovation activities of your firm today and at the time of entry	Internationalization	Difference between categorical variables	Model two
IC_2	Intensity of internal competition within your foreign investor network/multinational group–Particular or new business lines	Competition	Categorical variable no competition—1, weak intensity—2, strong intensity—3, very strong intensity—4	Model two

Appendix 3: Models Results

INDEPENDENT VARIABLES	Innotype_1a B	Innotype_1a Significance	Innotype_2a B	Innotype_2a Significance	Innotype_3a B	Innotype_3a Significance	Innotype_4a B	Innotype_4a Significance	difRandDEXP B	difRandDEXP Significance	difRandDEXP2 B	difRandDEXP2 Significance	difSofNP B	difSofNP Significance
R square	0,504		0,433		0,615		0,621		0,259		0,897		0,302	
Signicance of Reg	0,000		0,000		0,015		0,000		0,004		0,000		0,001	
Constant	0,882	0,177	1,754	0,000	1,802	0,000	3,274	0,005	1,654	0,120	557127,328	0,012	-9,017	0,234
GI_2b	0,026	0,002	-	-	-	-	-	-	-	-	-	-	-	-
BF_1	-	-	-	-	-	-	1,720	0,003	-	-	144958,950	0,013	-	-
BF_2	-	-	-	-	-	-	-	-	-	-	-97794,208	0,031	-	-
BF_4	-	-	-	-	-	-	-	-	1,804	0,001	-	-	-	-
BF_5	0,534	0,003	-	-	-	-	2,596	0,000	1,252	0,032	-	-	-	-
EXofTofRes_2	-	-	0,664	0,000	-	-	-	-	-	-	153487,353	0,000	-	-
EXofTofRes_3	-	-	-	-	-	-	-	-	-	-	-435,697	0,000	-	-
GI_1a	-	-	-	-	0,001	0,001	-	-	-	-	0,005	0,000	-	-
GI_4a	-	-	-	-	-	-	-	-	-	-	-	-	-	-
GI_5b	-	-	-	-	-	-	0,360	0,012	-	-	-	-	-	-
MofC_3	-	-	-	-	-	-	-	-	-	-	-	-	4,622	0,021
MofC_4	0,375	0,006	-	-	0,242	0,007	-	-	-	-	104677,475	0,008	-	-
MofC_5	-	-	-	-	0,000	0,015	0,000	0,003	-	-	0,275	0,000	-	-
RDNO_2	-	-	-	-	-	-	1,222	0,014	-	-	-	-	-	-
SofTK 2a 2b	-	-	-	-	-	-	-	-	-	-	-	-	-	-
SofTK 3a 3b 4a 4b	-0,366	0,047	-	-	-	-	-	-	-	-	-	-	6,020	0,004
SofTK 9a 9b 10a 10b 11a	-	-	-0,540	0,040	-	-	1,489	0,004	-	-	-	-	-	-

Fig. 14.1 Model one—multiple regression innovation output dependent variables

		difRandDEXP		difRandDEXP2		DifGI1		DifGI2		DifGI3	
	R square	0,043		0,129		0,157		0,226		0,163	
	Signicance of Reg	0,008		0,000		0,000		0,000		0,000	
		B	Sign	B	Sign	B	Sign	B	Sign	B	Sign
	Constant	3,437	0,000	-192416,880	0,136	-40,866	0,370	0,669	0,735	321203,628	0,989
INDEPENDENT VARIABLES	BF_1	-	-	-	-	-	-	-	-	-	-
	BF_2	-	-	-	-	63,642	0,004	-	-	-	-
	BF_4	-	-	-	-	-	-	-	-	13000000,00	0,018
	BF_5	-	-	-	-	-	-	-1,974	0,000	-	-
	BF_6	-	-	-	-	71,840	0,009	-1,950	0,000	-	-
	BF_7	-	-	-	-	-95,023	0,000	-	-	-	-
	difIMPofFasTS2	-	-	317831,683	0,000	-	-	2,762	0,000	-	-
	difIMPofFasTS3	-	-	-	-	-	-	-1,726	0,031	-	-
	difIMPofFasTS4	-	-	-	-	-	-	2,182	0,005	-	-
	difIMPofFasTS7	-	-	-	-	-	-	-	-	-	-
	difIMPofFasTS8	-	-	-	-	-	-	-0,940	0,078	-	-
	difSofTK1	-	-	-247904,864	0,001	-	-	-	-	-	-
	difSofTK11	-	-	-289863,563	0,045	120,209	0,001	-	-	-	-
	difSofTK3	-	-	-	-	-	-	-	-	-	-
	difSofTK5	-	-	-	-	-	-	-	-	-	-
	difSofTK7	-	-	-	-	-	-	-	-	-	-
	difSofTK9	-	-	-	-	-	-	-4,141	0,002	-	-
	EXofTofRes_1	-	-	-	-	-	-	1,177	0,008	-	-
	EXofTofRes_2	-	-	-	-	-	-	-	-	-	-
	ForeignF	-	-	-	-	-	-	2,234	0,028	-	-
	ForeignFF	-	-	-	-	-	-	-	-	-	-
	ForeignMNE	-	-	-	-	-	-	-	-	-	-
	IC_2	-0,566	0,035	182675,222	0,009	-	-	-	-	-	-
	IM_1	-	-	-	-	-	-	-0,443	0,003	-4564480,763	0,009
	IM_3	-0,187	0,024	-	-	-	-	-	-	-	-
	IM_4	-	-	-	-	-	-	-	-	-	-
	IMPofRandD_2EDE	-	-	-	-	-	-	-	-	-	-
	IMPofRandD_5	-	-	-	-	-	-	-	-	-	-
	SofTK 1a 1b	-	-	-	-	-	-	-	-	-	-
	SofTK 3a 3b 4a 4b	-	-	-	-	-	-	-	-	-	-
	TofRes_1	-	-	-	-	-	-	-	-	-1,61E+07	0,016
	TofRes_2	-	-	-	-	-	-	-	-	2,26E+07	0,001
	TSEofFI_1	-	-	-	-	-	-	-	-	-	-
	TSEofFI_3	-	-	-	-	-	-	-	-	-	-
	TypeFI	-	-	-	-	-	-	-	-	-	-
	TypeMNEG	-	-	-	-	65,847	0,043	-	-	-	-
	TypeNEG	-	-	-	-	-	-	-	-	-	-

Fig. 14.2 Model two—multiple regression innovation input dependent variables

14 Researching Innovative Capacity of Local Subsidiaries in Selected CEE Countries

DifGI4		DifGI5		MofC_1		MofC_2		MofC_3		MofC_4		MofC_5	
0,042		0,409		0,118		0,149		0,088		0,156		0,160	
0,010		0,000		0,000		0,000		0,000		0,000		0,000	
B	Sign	B	Sign	B	Sign	B	Sign	B	Sign	B	Sign	B	Sign
-1083275,292	0,897	9,163	0,028	2,649	0,000	2,890	0,000	3,102	0,000	3,672	0,000	3,808	0,000
-	-	-	-	-	-	-0,25	0,002	-	-	-	-	-	-
-	-	-	-	-	-	0,352	0	-	-	-0,266	0	-	-
-	-	-	-	-	-	-	-	-	-	-	-	-	-
-	-	-	-	-	-	-0,17	0,023	-	-	0,26	0	-	-
-	-	-	-	-	-	-	-	-	-	-	-	-	-
-	-	-	-	-	-	-	-	-	-	-	-	-	-
27400000,000	0,010	-	-	0,303	0,000	-	-	-	-	-	-	-	-
-	-	-	-	-	-	-	-	-	-	-	-	-	-
-	-	-	-	-	-	-	-	-	-	0,189	0,01	-	-
-	-	-	-	-0,101	0,011	-	-	-	-	-	-	-	-
-	-	-	-	-	-	-	-	-	-	-	-	-	-
-	-	-	-	-	-	-	-	-	-	-	-	-	-
-	-	2,221	0,035	-	-	-	-	-	-	-	-	-	-
-	-	-	-	-	-	-	-	0,282	0,002	-	-	-	-
-	-	-	-	-	-	-	-	0,188	0,022	-	-	-	-
-	-	-4,198	0,009	-	-	-	-	-	-	-	-	-	-
-	-	-	-	-	-	-	-	-	-	-	-	-	-
-	-	-	-	0,16	0,003	-	-	-	-	-	-	-0,409	0
-	-	-5,914	0,001	0,260	0,035	-	-	-	-	-	-	-	-
-	-	-	-	-	-	-	-	-	-	0,717	0,1	-	-
-	-	-	-	-	-	-	-	-	-	-	-	0,297	0,043
-	-	-2,674	0,003	-	-	-	-	-	-	-	-	-	-
-	-	-	-	-	-	-	-	-	-	-	-	-	-
-	-	-	-	-	-	-	-	-	-	-	-	-0,075	0,003
-	-	0,459	0,027	-	-	-	-	-	-	-	-	-	-
-	-	-	-	0,123	0,026	-	-	-	-	-	-	-	-
-	-	1,593	0,005	-	-	-	-	-	-	-	-	-	-
-	-	-	-	-	-	-	-	-*	-	0,132	0,02	-	-
-	-	3,053	0,001	-	-	-	-	-	-	-	-	-	-
-	-	-	-	-	-	0,215	0	0,131	0,005	-	-	-	-
-	-	-	-	-	-	-	-	-	-	-	-	0,268	0,004
-	-	0,153	0,003	-	-	-	-	-	-	-	-	-	-
-	-	-0,233	0	-	-	-	-	-	-	-	-	-	-
-	-	-	-	-	-	-	-	-	-	-	-	0,808	0,001
-	-	-	-	-	-	-	-	0,24	0,011	-	-	-	-
-	-	-	-	-	-	-	-	-	-	-	-	0,615	0,008

Fig. 14.2 (continued)

	SLNOE		SLNOE_IN	
R square	0,648		0,186	
Signicance of Reg	0,000		0,006	
	B	Significance	B	Significance
Constant	−8785154,556	0,502	−2,503	0,085
difRandDExpr2	−35,461	0,000	-	-
DifGI2	1441428,146	0,002	-	-
DifGI3	0,233	0,016	-	-
MofC_1	1,028E+07	0,002	-	-
MofC_3	−8295643,097	0,033	-	-
MofC_5			1,128	0,006

Fig. 14.3 Model three—multiple regression Innovation performance dependent variable

References

1. Lane PJ, Lubatkin M (1998) Relative absorptive capacity and interorganizational. Learn Strategic Manage J 19:461–477
2. Dunning JH (1993) Multinational enterprises and the global economy. Addison Wesley, Wokingham
3. Eaton J, Kortum S (1999) International technology diffusion. Int Econ Rev 40(3):537–570
4. Keller W (2002) Geographic localization of international technology diffusion. Am Econ Rev Am Econ Assoc 92(1):120–142
5. Keller W (2004) International technology diffusion. J Econ Lit Am Econ Assoc 42(3):752–782
6. Perugini C, Pompei F, Signorelli M (2008) FDI, R&D and human capital in Central and Eastern European countries. Post-Comm Econ 20(3):317–345
7. Dabić M, Pejic-Bach M (2008) Understanding the foreign direct investment environments in EU 27+ candidate country Croatia: the current determinants and patterns. Int J Entrep Innovat Manag 8(3):254–271
8. Damijan J, Knell M, Rojec M, Majcen B (2003) Technology transfer through FDI in top-10 transition countries: how important are direct effects, horizontal and vertical spillovers? William Davidson Institute at the University of Michigan, working paper no. 549. http://wdi.umich.edu/files/publications/workingpapers/wp549.pdf
9. Vega-Jurado J, Gutierrez-Gracia A, Fernandez-de-Lucio I (2008) Analyzing the determinants of firm's absorptive capacity: beyond R&D. R&D Manage 38:392
10. Scott WR (1992) Organizations: rational, natural, and open systems. Prentice-Hall, Englewood Cliffs, NJ
11. Cantwell J (1989) Technological innovation and multinational corporations. Basil Blackwell, Oxford
12. Schmid S, Schurig A (2003) The development of critical capabilitie in foreign subsidiaries: disentangling the role of the subsidiary's business network. Int Bus Rev 12:755–782
13. Freel M (2003) Sectoral patterns of small firm innovation, networking and proximity. Res Policy 32(5):751–770
14. Oerlemans L, Meeus M, Boekema F (1998) Do networks matter for innovation? The usefulness of the economic network approach in analysing innovation. Tijdschr Econ Soc Geogr 89:298–309

15. Hobday M, Rush H (2007) Upgrading the technological capabilities of foreign transnational subsidiaries in developing countries: the case of electronics in Thailand. Res Policy 36:1335–1356
16. Morgan RE, Katsikeas CS (1997) Theories of international trade, foreign direct investment and firm internationalization: a critique. Manage Dec 35(1):68–78
17. McMahon RGP (2001) Deriving an empirical development taxonomy for manufacturing SMEs using data from Australia's business longitudinal survey. Small Bus Econ 17(3):197–212
18. Račić D, Aralica Z, Redžepagić D (2008) Export strategies as a factor of SME growth in Croatia. Eur J Entrep Innovat Manage 8(3):286–304
19. Andersson U, Forgsen M, Pedersen T (2001) Subsidiary performance in multinational corporations: the importance of technology embeddedness. Res Policy Int Bus Rev 10:3–23
20. Marin A, Bell M (2010) The local/global integration of MNC subsidiaries and their technological behaviour: Argentina in the late 1990s. Res Policy 39(7):919–931
21. Marin A, Sasidharan S (2010) Heterogeneous MNC subsidiaries and technological spillovers: explaining positive and negative effects in India. Res Policy 39(9):1227–1241
22. Cohen WM, Levinthen DA (1990) Absorptive capacity: a new perspective on learning and innovation. Adm Sci Q 35(1):128–152
23. Scott-Kennel J, Enderwick P (2005) Foreign direct investment and inter-firm linkages: exploring the black box of the investment development path. Transnat Corporations 14(1):105–137
24. Ruigrok W, Wagner H (2003) Internationalization and firm performance: meta-analytic review and future research directions. Eur J Dev Res 18(4):642–661
25. Meyer-Krahmer F, Reger G (1999) New perspectives on the innovation strategies of multinational enterprises: lessons for technology policy in Europe. Res Policy 28:751–776
26. Frenz M, Ieto-Gilles G (2009) The impact on innovation performance of different sources of knowledge: evidence from the UK Community Innovation Survey. Res Policy 38:1125–1135
27. Welch L, Luostarinen R (1988) Internationalization: evolution of a concept. Thomson Bus 14(2):34–55
28. Vernon R (1966) International investment and international trade in the product cycle. Quart J Econ 80:190–207
29. Kogut B (1985) Designing global strategies: profiting from operating flexibility. Sloan Manage Rev 27(1):27–38
30. Birkinshaw J, Hood N (1998) Multinational subsidiary evolution: capability and charter change in foreign-owned subsidiary companies. Acad Manage Rev 23(4):773–796
31. Lipparini A, Fratocchi L (1999) The capabilities of the transnational firm: accessing knowledge and leveraging interfirm relationships. Eur Manage J 17(6):655–666
32. Coase RH (1937) The nature of the firm. Economica 4(16):386–405
33. Rugman AM (1985) Internalization is still a general theory of foreign direct investment. Weltwirtsch Arch 121(3):570–575
34. Lindstrand A (2003) The usefulness of suppliers' knowledge in international markets. In: Sharma D, Blomstermo A (eds) Learning in the internationalisation process of firms. Edward Elgar Cheltenham, Northampton, pp 105–122
35. Knell M, Rojec M (2007) The economics of knowledge and knowledge accumulation: a literature survey, internal report from the project - Understanding the Relationship between Knowledge and Competitiveness in the Enlarging European Union Framework Programme 6, Project number CIT5-CT-2005-028519
36. De la Fuenta A (2003) Human capital in a global and knowledge-based economy, part II: assessment at the EU country level. European Commission, DG for Employment and Social Affairs, Brussels
37. Andersson U (2003) Managing the transfer of capabilities within multinational corporations: the dual role of the subsidiary. Scand J Manage 19(4):425–442
38. Contractor FJ, Kundu SK, Hsu C-C (2003) A three-stage theory of international expansion: the link between multinationality and performance in the service sector. J Int Bus Stud 34:5–18
39. Gurkov I (2004) Business innovation in Russian industry. Post-Comm Econ 16(4):423–438
40. Birkinshaw J, Morrison AJ (1995) Configurations of strategy and structure in multinational subsidiaries. J Int Bus Stud 26(4):729–794

41. Peteraf M (1993) The cornerstones of competitive advantage: a resource-based view. Strategic Manage J 14:179–191
42. Barkema HG, Vermeulen F (1998) International expansion through start-up or acquisition: a learning perspective. Acad Manage J 41(1):7–26
43. Kogut B, Zander U (1992) Knowledge of the firm, combinative capabilities, and the replication of technology. Organ Sci 3(3):383–397
44. Kogut B, Zander U (1993) Knowledge of the firm and the evolutionary theory of the multinational corporation. J Int Bus Stud 24(4):625–645
45. Brzozowski M (2008) Determinants of investment and innovation expenditure in Polish manufacturing industries. Post-Commun Econ 20(2):219–230
46. Carlin W, Fries S, Schaffer M, Seabright P (2001) Competition and enterprise performance in transition economies: evidence from a cross-country survey. William Davidson Institute working paper 376, 49
47. Carlin W, Schaffer M, Seabright P (2004) A minimum of rivalry: evidence from transition economies on the importance of competition for innovation and growth. William Davidson Institute working paper 670
48. Aghion P, Carlin W, Schaffer M (2002) Competition, innovation and growth in transition: exploring the interaction between policies. William Davidson Institute working paper no. 501
49. Loof H, Heshmati A (2002) Knowledge capital and performance heterogeneity: a firm-level innovation study. Int J Prod Eco 76:61–85
50. Caloghirou Y, Kastelli I, Tsakanikas A (2004) Internal capabilities and external knowledge sources: complements or substitutes for innovative performance? Technovation 24:29–39
51. Grant RM (1996) Prospering in dynamically-competitive environments: organizational capability as knowledge integration. Organ Sci 7:375–387
52. Guo B, Guo J-J (2010) Patterns of technological learning within the knowledge systems of industrial clusters in emerging economies: evidence from China. Technovation 31(2–3):87–104
53. Kamman DJF (1993) Bottlenecks, barriers, and networks of actors. In: Ratti R, Reichman S (eds) Theory and practice of transborder cooperation. Helbing and Lichtenhahn Verlag, Basel, pp 65–102
54. UNCTAD – United Nations Conference on Trade and Development (2011) Global investments trend monitor no. 5. http://www.unctad.org/en/docs//webdiaeia20111_en.pdf
55. Djankov S, Murrell P (2002) Enterprise restructuring in transition: a quantitative survey. J Econ Lit 4:739–792
56. Rugraff E (2006) Export-oriented multinationals and the quality of international specialisation in the Central European countries. Eur J Dev Res 18(4):642–661
57. Schadler S, Mody A, Abiad A, Leigh D (2006) Growth in the Central and Eastern European Countries of the European Union, ocassional paper 252. International Monetary Fond, Washington, DC, http://www.imf.org/external/pubs/nft/op/252/op252.pdf
58. Richardson GB (1972) The organisation of industry. Eco J 82(327):883–896
59. Dunning JH (1980) Toward an eclectic theory of international production: some empirical tests. J Int Bus Stud 11(1):9–31
60. Buckley P (1988) The limits of explanation: testing the internationalization theory of the multinational enterprise. J Int Bus Stud XIX(2):181–193
61. Amit R, Schoemaker PJH (1993) Strategic assets and organizational rent. Strategic Manage J 14(1):33–46
62. Makadok R (2001) Towards a synthesis of the resource-based and dynamic-capability views of rent creation. Strategic Manage J 22(5):387–401
63. Teece DJ, Pisano G, Shuen A (1997) Dynamic capabilities and strategic management. Strategic Manage J 18(7):509–1533
64. Steffen W, Stephan JF (2008) The role of the human capital and managerial skills in explaining the productivity gaps between east and wrst. East Euro Eco 46(6):5–24
65. Aralica Z, Račić D, Redžepagić D (2009) R&D activities as a growth factor of foreign-owned SMEs in Croatia. Croat Econ Surv 11(11):73–93

Printed by Printforce, the Netherlands